1993

Mainie Jellett and the Modern Movement in Ireland

MAINIE JELLETT
and the MODERN
MOVEMENT in IRELAND

BRUCE ARNOLD

Yale University Press
New Haven & London
1991

Frontispiece: Mainie Jellett in her studio in the early 1920s.

Designed by Mary Carruthers
Set in Monophoto Perpetua by Servis Filmsetting Ltd., Manchester
Printed and bound in Vicenza, Italy through Graphicom

Library of Congress Catalog Number 91-75617
ISBN 0-300-05463-7

CONTENTS

	Acknowledgements	vi
	Prologue	vii
1	The loving union	1
2	Edwardian childhood in Dublin	7
3	Early painting years	12
4	The influence of William Orpen	17
5	Sickert: 'the first revolution'	25
6	Peace	32
7	'The second revolution': study with André Lhote	45
8	Non-representational art	56
9	'Final revolution': back to the beginning	61
10	Painting and its laws	70
11	'Sub-human art of Miss Jellett'	77
12	'L'Art d'Aujourd'hui'	84
13	'A lecture by Miss Jellett'	97
14	Moly-Sabata	105
15	'Not an ivory tower but a fortress'	113
16	Cubism 'alive and well'	125
17	Abstraction-Création	131
18	The letter to Anne Dangar	136
19	The impact of Chinese art	146
20	Mainie as teacher	154
21	'The best Miss Jellett has ever held'	163
22	Irish art and 'the Emergency'	171
23	Art as a spiritual force	179
24	The Rouault row	187
25	Her most cherished ambition fulfilled	193
26	'A wonderful picture in my mind'	198
	Notes	205
	Index	214

ACKNOWLEDGEMENTS

THIS BOOK COULD not have been written without the co-operation and goodwill of the Jellett family. I first became familiar with Mainie's work in the late 1950s, when I took violin lessons from her sister, Bay Jellett. I subsequently organised a number of exhibitions of her work in the Neptune Gallery, Dublin, with the active support of Bay, and of Eileen MacCarvill, a former pupil who had written and published the first book about the artist. Without the help and support of these two women, both now alas dead, I would not have embarked on my lifelong interest in the artist. They both gave generously of their time, producing volumes of material which constitute a rich archive. I must also make a special mention of Andrew Bonar Law, of the Neptune Gallery.

Mainie's two younger sisters, Betty Purser and Babbin Phillips, also gave great help and encouragement. One of the most pleasant tasks, during the later work on the book, was to read portions of it to the sisters, the most intense audience I could have wished for. I found my work greatly enriched by their recollections, and their criticisms were always valuable. It is a matter of deep regret that Betty did not live to see the publication of this book. Other members of the Jellett family also gave me much help and encouragement, particularly John Purser, Michael and Helen Purser, Geraldine Lloyd, Adrian and Rosamund Phillips. I owe a particular debt of gratitude to Peter Brooke, the editor during the 1980s of *Cubism*, and the moving spirit behind l'Association des Amis d'Albert Gleizes. His passionate interest in abstract Cubism, and the artists who practised – and still practise – it, has been an inspiration. His more direct involvement in my researches for this book was of enormous value and benefit. Brian Kennedy, of the Ulster Museum, made available to me the fruits of his extensive researches into twentieth-century Irish art, providing an invaluable background to the artist's life. His *Irish Art and Modernism 1880–1950*, which I saw in draft form, is the authoritative work on the period. James White knew Mainie, and was himself much in her debt. He gave valuable insights into her character and approach to art. Hélène de St Pierre, who also knew the artist towards the end of her life,

presented an interesting and challenging portrait of Mainie's character; she also provided details about her teaching of abstract principles which were of unique importance. These were helpfully corroborated by Paul Egestorff, the other pupil who was taught abstract art by Mainie. Muriel and Oliver Hone, who are currently researching a book on Evie Hone, made much information available to me, and were unfailingly helpful. I owe a particular debt to Mary Brennan-Holahan, my research assistant during the final two years of work on the book. She worked with immense care, checking details, discovering illustrations, carrying out interviews, and making suggestions.

I would also like to thank the following: Gilka Béclu, Sighle Bhreathnach-Lynch, Brian Boydell, Anne Crookshank, Norris Davidson, Barbara Dawson, Director of the Hugh Lane Municipal Gallery of Modern Art, as well as Liz Turpin, for her help with photographs, John de Vere White, Walter Firpo, Desmond Fitzgerald, Claude Gleizes, Godfrey Graham, William F. Harpur, Ted Hickey, Mary Keegan, Daniel Kelly, Raymond Keveaney, Director of the National Gallery of Ireland, as well as Brian Kennedy, Marie Bourke, also of the National Gallery of Ireland, Peter Lamb, Louis le Brocquy, Charles Lysaght, R.B. McDowell, Ciarán MacGonigal, Declan McGonigal, Director of the Irish Museum of Modern Art, as well as Gill Tipton, Dara O'Connell, and other members of the staff of the Museum, John Medlycott, Pat and Antoinette Murphy, Peter Murray of the Crawford Municipal Gallery of Art in Cork, Sean O'Criadain, Cécile Pouyaud, Daniel Robbins, Dr George Otto Simms, Andrée Sheehy-Skeffington, Mrs Skrine, Michael Solomons, Margaret Stokes, Eavan Sutton, David Webb. A number of photographers have helped in building up the substantial photographic archive on which I have drawn for this book; I would like to thank Jon and Sandy Harsch, Jacobus van Hespen, John-David Biggs, John Kellett, John Davison, R.M. Muirhead.

My family have lived their lives coloured by my enthusiasm for Mainie Jellett, and have all been involved in research of one kind or another. I would like to thank my wife, Mavis, and Hugo, Samuel and Polly for the support they have always been.

PROLOGUE

FOR OVER TWENTY years, between 1922 and her death in 1944, Mainie Jellett was the acknowledged leader of the modern art movement in Ireland. In 1923, she confronted the notoriously conservative Dublin art world with a series of stunningly beautiful, fully abstract paintings, ten years before the first abstract work of Ben Nicholson, Barbara Hepworth or Henry Moore was shown in London. She was greeted with hostility and ridicule. But the force of her personality and her courage imposed respect long before her painting was accepted. Moreover, through her teaching and her public speaking, she opened the way for freedom and experimentation to a whole generation of Irish artists.

Her own painting, however, still retains its mystery and remains a subject of controversy. She belonged to a school of painters grouped around the French Cubist master, Albert Gleizes. In fact, she was the first member of this school, together with her fellow Irishwoman, Evie Hone. She chose Albert Gleizes as her teacher before he had any ambition to form a school, obliging him to become her teacher against his will, and he has himself admitted that it was only through her insistence that he was enabled to clarify his own ideas of the early 1920s – a process that resulted in the publication of his important book, *La Peinture et ses lois* in 1924.

With Gleizes, Mainie Jellett developed a rigorous form of abstract art derived directly from the experience of Cubism. She called herself a 'Cubist'. The use of the term 'Cubist' and the very idea of 'Cubist abstraction' is itself a source of controversy and will be examined in more detail in this book. But there was no confusion in her painting. Whatever the terminology we use to explain it, her work was marked by a powerful determination and sense of direction. We will see her pass from one stage to the next, each stage following logically from the one before, yet each complete in itself, full of a radiant self-confidence. She did not change styles with the fashions of the time and she never stood still. She was always searching.

She was well respected in France. She exhibited in the Salon des Indépendants and in the important 'L'Art d'Aujourd'hui' exhibition of 1925. She was a founder member of Abstraction-Création, the spearhead of the European abstract movement in the 1930s. She could certainly have made a career for herself in Paris. Yet she chose to live and work in Ireland. She believed passionately that the principles of modern painting she had developed were as relevant to Ireland, despite the opposition she encountered, as they were to the capitals of continental Europe. Unlike so many other Irish artists and writers of the twentieth century, who deployed their commitment to Ireland outside the country, Mainie believed that her art should be integrated into the life of her native city and its people. Inevitably, she paid a price for this: her negligible reputation internationally should be compared with the powerful reputations earned by the expatriates.

Her name has always been associated with that of her friend and colleague, Evie Hone. Evie had been with her when she first went to Gleizes, and accompanied her on many of her subsequent visits to France. And yet despite their friendship and close collaboration, there were great differences between them and they deserve to be treated separately. Evie, too, was a major Irish artist of that same period. But her greatest achievement was in the field of stained-glass art in the 1930s, when she followed a different line of development to the one mapped out with Mainie and with Gleizes in the 1920s. Her intense religious conviction led Evie to enter a convent and almost to renounce painting in the mid-twenties, the time when her artistic collaboration with Mainie was closest, and the struggle for the acceptance of modern principles of painting in Ireland was at its fiercest. They were two quite distinct and independently minded individuals, inseparable as devoted friends and members of the same artistic school, but with lives and destinies of their own.

Mainie's character and her artistic inspiration were marked by an austere intellectual vigour; but also by great human warmth and enthusiasm. It is not the intention of this book to treat her as a disembodied creative intellect, an artistic problem to be unravelled. It is the author's conviction that this attitude is too prevalent in biographies of artists, and most especially of abstract artists. While aiming to understand Mainie's painting and to locate it in the general context of the art and intellectual climate of her time, I hope to give as full an account as possible of the life behind the painting in all its richness and diversity, and to convey something of the force of personality that impressed all those who met and worked with her.

She was a leading practitioner of a particularly severe form of abstract painting, and she was followed in this by relatively few other artists. But she liberated a generation, and led them with a simplicity and directness towards realisation of their own freedom and what they might do with it. She is to be judged by her works above all else. The rich profusion of oils, gouaches, watercolours, temperas and drawings she produced, has earned her the reputation of one of the most powerful and original creative spirits in Ireland in the twentieth century.

She died many years before even the most modest fulfilment or realisation of her dreams. She wanted an understanding and acceptance of abstract painting as a normal component of art generally. She strove for its liberalising force among the painters of her own generation and among her pupils, some of whom were to become the leading artists of the next and subsequent generations of Irish artists. In both this and in her own work her achievements were revolutionary. I make no secret of the fact that I regard her, not just as an interesting person, or as an interesting historical and artistic phenomenon but, quite simply, an outstanding creative figure in twentieth-century art, and a dominating influence in Irish art in her time.

THE WORKS

Mainie Jellett exhibited most of her works without giving them titles. Her catalogues list 'Tempera', 'Oil', 'Gouache', 'Painting', during the first ten years of her working life. Later, titles were included, but until the final two solo exhibitions, of 1939 and 1941, only a few works were identified in this way. Rather than use these obvious descriptions, works in this book have been titled descriptively, using 'Abstract Composition', 'Abstract Study', 'Composition', as well as 'Elements', a term she used from the mid-1920s. The artist's own titles have been used when she included them in catalogues or on picture labels. A further complication derives from the fact that titles in posthumous exhibitions, including the 1962 Retrospective Exhibition in the Municipal Gallery of Modern Art, were newly invented. This confusion has not been fully resolved.

Measurements are given in centimetres.

viii

CHAPTER ONE

The loving union

MAINIE JELLETT WAS the eldest of the four daughters of William Morgan Jellett and Janet McKensie Stokes. She was born on 20 April 1897, at 36 Fitzwilliam Square, Dublin. She was christened Mary Hariett at St Anne's Church in Dawson Street, but always called Mainie at the request of her Stokes grandfather, who had lost a much-loved sister known also as Mainie.[1]

The family regularly worshipped at St Anne's. Mainie's father liked the 10 o'clock morning service because it allowed them plenty of time to get the train out to Howth for Sunday lunch with their Stokes relations. In later years Mainie's mother attended the Magdalen Church attached to the Magdalen Asylum for children in Lower Leeson Street. The church was known by the family as 'St Stuffy's'. It had some peculiar practices. The children, most of whom were illegitimate, sat behind a heavy brown curtain, while their mothers sat in the balcony hidden away from the main body of the congregation. Throughout her life Mainie remained a practising member of the Church of Ireland, worshipping at St Bartholomew's, the High Anglican Church in Clyde Road where she attended divine service every Friday morning and on all holy days, as well as on Sundays.

Both the Jellett and Stokes families were established Protestants whose forebears had arrived in Ireland in the seventeenth century. The earlier origins of the Jelletts were Huguenot, their name either Gillett or Gillott, and they came from near Lille, arriving in England at the time of the St Bartholomew Massacre in 1572. The forefathers of Gabriel Stokes, an engineer who established the family in Ireland in about 1680, came from Wiltshire. It was supposed that the earliest grants of property dated back to the Norman Conquest.

The Irish branch of the Jellett family was established by a Captain Jellett,[2] who was married to Katherine Morgan, of Tullyard in County Down. She was a formidable woman, whose mother had successfully petitioned for land in County Down at the time of the Restoration. At her christening, Katherine was given the Morgan Tankard, a bloodstone and silver gilt vessel of about a quart capacity. In the troubled times leading up to the Battle of the Boyne she was in particular peril, in her farmlands in County Down, for her father-in-law, the Captain, was old and feeble, and her husband serving with Sir Arthur Rawdon in the armies of William III. In order to keep the tankard safe she carried it slung out of sight on a chain from her waist. And she was wearing this weighty pendant when she presented herself to the king at Hillsborough, during his march from Belfast to the Boyne. She petitioned him for two soldiers to protect herself and her property, since her main protector was fighting the king's cause. When the tankard came to the king's attention, she told him it was used as a pledging cup at family weddings. He then asked that it be filled with wine, and drank her health. At Jellett family weddings the tankard was used for the bridegroom to toast the bride, then for all those born Jellett to drink toasts and finally for a few intimate friends to do the same.

Eighteenth- and early nineteenth-century members of the family included a Dublin goldsmith, John Jellett, and a clergyman, Morgan Jellett.[3] The latter's eldest son, John Hewitt Jellett (Pl. 1),[4] who also took Holy Orders, was President of the Royal Irish Academy and a Commissioner of Irish National Education. In 1881, to the surprise and

1. John Hewitt Jellett, the artist's grandfather, with members of his family, in 1888. He was President of the Royal Irish Academy, and Provost of Trinity College, Dublin. William Jellett, the artist's father, is standing on the right.

relief of the Fellows of Trinity College, Gladstone appointed Jellett provost. With the Disestablishment of the Church of Ireland in 1870, and the need for reconstruction, Jellett became an active synodsman, relinquishing a number of university duties. He was known as 'The Clarifier', and cries of 'Jellett! Jellett!' were to be heard around Christ Church Cathedral when ticklish problems were being debated. Though of the evangelical persuasion, he was very much a reconciler of differences. He was rated a sound though not an innovative provost, but was highly regarded by his students. One of them described him as having 'pride in his port, defiance in his eye', adding that although he was 'handsome, with a fine presence and keen glance . . . the grace of humility . . . was not the Provost's'. More generally he was seen as an ally and friend of the students, always ready to give help and advice.[5] His death in 1888, led to one of Dublin's great ceremonial funerals of the late nineteenth century. All the bishops of the Church, including the Primate from Armagh, a full turnout of the judiciary, and of course staff and students of the college, went in procession from the provost's house round Library Square to the chapel, and then on to Mount Jerome cemetery.

William Morgan Jellett, Mainie's father, was born on 6 May 1857. He was the provost's eldest son, and had a distinguished academic career, being the First Classical Scholar of his year and subsequently taking a First Class Honours Degree before entering the Kings Inn. He was called to the Bar in 1882, took silk in 1899, and became a Bencher of the King's Inn in 1906. Regarded as a decisive and forcible advocate, he was a highly respected barrister and was, for many years, Father of the Irish Bar.

The marriage of William Morgan Jellett to Janet Stokes in August 1895 was a union of two families of considerable distinction, though in entirely different fields. On the Jellett side there was clear intellectual and academic attainment which Mainie undoubtedly inherited; in her own field, as theorist and practitioner, and in her comments on art generally, she could easily herself have been called 'The Clarifier'. Janet Stokes, on the other hand, was artistically gifted, somewhat unworldly, and beautiful – with finely-drawn features. Twenty-six years old at the time of her marriage, she was the second child of Henry John Stokes, himself the youngest son of the great Dublin surgeon, William Stokes. One historian of note has described the Stokes family as 'one of the great intellectual dynasties of the British Isles – producing many soldiers, lawyers, scholars, medical men, divines and servants of the Crown in India'.[6] Like the Jelletts, they came to Ireland at the end of the seventeenth century when the founder of the Irish branch, Gabriel Stokes, was responsible for proposing 'a scheme for effectually supplying every part of the city of Dublin with pipe water without any charge for water engines or any water forcers, by a close adherence to the laws of gravitation and the principles, rules and experiments of Hydrostatisticks'.[7] His sons and grandsons were all distinguished scholars in Trinity. Whitley Stokes, Janet's great-grandfather was the first to follow medicine. He was a United Irishman and friend of Wolfe Tone, though they parted company over the use of violence. Not, however, to the point where they lost either respect or friendship for each other. Whitley Stokes was an enthusiastic evangelical Protestant, who devoted himself to the study of the Irish language. He had tastes which were 'distinctly artistic', encompassing music, poetry and painting, but especially the last in which his children – he had eight – were said to have distinguished themselves. Among artists who were his friends were George Petrie and James Arthur O'Connor, who was employed to teach landscape painting to his five daughters, all of whom became competent artists. Whitley Stokes had a strong belief in the value of home education and was followed in this by Janet Stokes in the upbringing of Mainie and her sister, Bay, neither of whom ever attended school.[8]

William Stokes, his second son and Janet's grandfather, seems, however, to have been a lethargic medical student until stung into action literally by his mother's tears – she found him one day asleep over a Walter Scott novel and her warm tears falling on his face woke him up. 'Stung with remorse at having been a cause of so much sorrow, his nature appeared to undergo an immediate and salutory change, and the dreamy indolent boy suddenly became the ardent enthusiastic student.' His earliest work of note was a treatise on the stethoscope, foreshadowing his life's work, which was concerned with diseases of the chest.[9]

William Stokes pursued a style of life at his home in Ballinteer, which included theatrical and musical performances, and which set a tone and character rather different from the austere atmosphere prevailing in the Jellett household. He was a great Shakespeare enthusiast and keen on family entertainment: 'on gala nights, and at his children's festivals, he would preside at puppet shows, and act charades and throw himself heart and soul into this as into any other pursuit in life'.[10] Art was included among his more serious enthusiasms, and he once wrote to a friend, 'we are not to worship art, but to use it as a means to some great end . . . art teaches by other methods – in unwritten tongues, in varied languages; it preaches truth through beauty, and tells of the God of love . . .'.[11] It was in Stokes's house, too, that many visitors to Dublin met the city's leading figures; among others he entertained were Oscar Wilde and Thomas Carlyle, whom Stokes found a prince among bores, calling him 'hyperborean'!

In 1845, William Stokes became Regius Professor of Medicine in Trinity College. This, combined with his great interest in education, brought him into sympathetic contact with John Hewitt Jellett, Mainie's grandfather and future provost, and the two men remained lifelong friends.

William's son, Henry, Janet Stokes's father, went out to India in 1863 to join the Indian Civil Service. Janet, the second child of a family of eight, was brought up there, the family returning to Ireland some time in the 1880s. They played an active part in Dublin's musical life. Janet's father played the viola; she herself was a fine pianist, much in demand as an accompanist, while her elder sister, Elizabeth, played the violin. They gave concerts to raise money for charity, and home entertainments often included theatricals. During her time in India Janet had played 'Miss Yellowleaf' in Charles Dance's Comedy, *Bengal Tiger* at the Casino Theatre, in Simla.

William Morgan Jellett proposed to Janet Stokes at Howth in the spring of 1895, and he wrote to her often throughout their short engagement: 'I cannot go to bed without having one little word with you. I have just finished writing a lot of letters and as I have been gazing at your sweet face in the photo all the time, you can imagine that the process was not rapid.' While it was perhaps not unusual to become engaged in April and marry in July, there is a whirlwind character to his love letters, breathless dispatch of legal business, and an impatience to get on with their own affairs. 'Be sure you come here tomorrow as soon as you can and we will go out together and might go to North's about a house.' A long lease on 36 Fitzwilliam Square, a fine Georgian town house of five storeys, was bought at auction on 14 June, and by the end of the month Jellett was 'all over it with the plumbers'. They subsequently installed a bathroom with a domed glass roof, a splendid chamber with a huge Victorian cast iron bath overhung by monumental, brass taps.

The Jellett-Stokes marriage was a loving union. Though outwardly seen as gruff in manner, 'impatient of anything that was not straight' and of a 'transparent simplicity and uprightness of character', William Jellett reveals in his letters to Janet, in the spring and summer of 1895, a deep and passionate love which seems never to have wavered, and which developed into a warm family affection on which Mainie relied throughout her life. 'God bless you for all your great love for me,' he wrote to Janet at the beginning of their engagement.

> You have transformed my life and given me such happiness and peace as I never even dreamt of. You have made me a better and a nobler being. Oh Janet darling what have you not done for me! I pray for you night and morning. That dear little greenhouse at Drumleck is the most sacred spot on earth to me. There was reached the crisis of my life and there I learnt what the love of a true and noble girl can do.

William Jellett was then thirty-seven years old, well established in his profession and much under pressure. With daily appearances in court, and with the business of organising their new home, he was extremely busy. His letters to Janet at this time were often written at one and two o'clock in the morning. Yet clearly his life had indeed been transformed. A day without seeing her prompted references to 'how unutterably lonely it has been'. In mid-June he told her: 'I think I am only now beginning to realise all that you are to me when I am parted from you even for a short time . . . my whole life is bound up in you.'

In addition to the pressures of his legal work, William Jellett was busy that summer of 1895 with politics. While it had been determined Stokes family policy not to get involved in the great political movements of the time, a different attitude was taken by the Jellett family. Provost Jellett had seen politics as an extension of the educational and church interests he espoused. He belonged to the Liberal Unionist Party and was what is known as 'a steady Unionist'. He often appeared on public platforms to debate issues and, by virtue of his prominence, was a highly regarded speaker. His son William's political aspirations were more directly concerned with party matters.

These merit some explanation, since William Jellett's politics were to affect his professional life in quite a substantial way, and were of importance to his family. Lord Rosebery had succeeded Gladstone as prime minister in March 1894, but was presiding over a Liberal administration which was already crumbling, its forty-four majority dwindling perceptibly in the face of a radical reaction against having a peer as prime minister. It was a government 'ploughing the sands', in Asquith's phrase, and the inevitability of its imminent fall would have concentrated any keen Unionist politician's mind in the tense atmosphere of Irish politics at the time. They were, of course, much less tense than they had been during the previous decade. Charles Stewart Parnell's death in October 1891 had marked the end of a fairly violent phase, and with the Gladstone victory in the 1892 general election and the subsequent moving of the second Home Rule Bill a different mood prevailed. On the Conservative and Unionist side the approach was 'to kill Home Rule by Kindness', the main drift of this kindness being land reform, though educational changes were also much in the air. On the Liberal and Irish

4

2. The Wedding Party, at Rookstown, Howth, 8 August 1895.

Nationalist side at Westminster, the rift which Parnell's stormy political and personal demise had left behind was still much in need of repair. It would be some years before John Redmond could confidently present himself as the leader of an Irish parliamentary party; and even then the climate of opinion would be one reflective of his moderation, in turn a response to the events of the period.

The roots of William Jellett's Unionism would have been at best religious. He was of the Protestant Church; he had lived through Disestablishment, and saw in clear and simple terms the serial relationship between Crown, Empire and Faith. Nothing that had happened in politics during the whole Parnellite period would have done other than reinforce this basic set of beliefs, adding only greater subtlety and strength to his opinion that Home Rule would represent Rome Rule, a situation which, in terms of defence, loyalty and the general conduct of life in Ireland could only lead to trouble. This view, generally held in the wake of the Gladstone Second Home Rule Bill of 1893, had inspired Unionist political activity against it countrywide, with conventions in Belfast, Dublin and the Albert Hall in London. And it was the sense of achievement inspired by this, by the defeat of the measure in the Lords, and by Gladstone's subsequent resignation, that coloured William Jellett's political views at the time of his marriage to Janet Stokes.

Thus the marriage of William Jellett and Janet Stokes (Pl. 2), on 8 August 1895, united two of the leading Protestant families in Ireland, and brought together two rich traditions. Together, they represented a formidable tide of nineteenth-century talent and opportunity, privilege and commitment, reflecting a truer Irish aristocracy than either title or wealth could effect, based on intellectual attainment and social and scientific achievement over many generations. Their families were evenly balanced in terms of their importance and standing. Against the enormous contribution to Irish medicine made by William Stokes may be set the academic and educational impact of John Hewitt Jellett. Despite the dangers of attributing too much in the character of an individual to past generations, one can see clearly in Mainie Jellett's character a number of inherited attributes of interest, particularly in music, a love for which was passionate in both her parents. Her father was musically talented, and took an almost raffish interest in dance music, which he played entirely by ear. A richer, more considered artistic view of life derived from her mother, for whom music stood supreme among the arts. Mainie inherited also some of the public concerns and preoccupations of her better-known forebears, as well as more private family traditions which shaped her character and contributed to the definition of her artistic pursuits.

3. Mary Harriett Jellett ('Mainie') aged nine and a half months, with her mother.

4. Mainie with kitten.

CHAPTER TWO

Edwardian childhood in Dublin

THE PATTERN OF life at 36 Fitzwilliam Square after the Jelletts moved in was quickly established. William Jellett was occupied with his law practice; Janet entertained, held musical evenings and saw much of her large circle of friends. She had a fatal capacity for attracting 'lame ducks' (known collectively by the family as 'The Frumps') and then not knowing how to get rid of them. Her husband developed various ruses to force the issue, the most extreme of which was to dress up one of the dogs and send it into the drawing room, whereupon the dog's excitability often produced terror, upset music stands and occasionally savaged guests. Janet Jellett continued to offer hospitality undeterred, despite her husband's attempts to interrupt or frustrate it, until the 1920s.

Mainie's infancy, in the closing years of Queen Victoria's reign, was secure and happy. From the start it was unconventional. Brought up in the relative luxury and indolence of India, her mother did not know, for instance, that a baby needed a cot. This vagueness spread over many of her attitudes, making her reliant upon the nurses and, later, the governesses employed for the children. Mainie was photographed in infancy and early childhood by Lafayette, the leading portrait and society photographer of the day in Dublin, and her progress at everything was carefully noted (Pls. 3–7). Writing to his wife from Dublin in June 1898 while she was in Amsterdam on a visit, William Jellett reported on Mainie: 'All well here. Datooska is gradually establishing a right to walk in the Square and has twice declined to leave at request of the gardener.'

On 2 September 1901, the Jellett's second child was born. Christened Dorothea Janet, she was known throughout her life as 'Bay'. The two sisters, neither of whom married, were both to be involved throughout their lives in Dublin's artistic and musical world (Pl. 6). Mainie, then aged four, was already learning to play the piano literally at her mother's knee, and Bay quickly showed talent as a violinist. Mainie's first recorded artistic endeavour dates from 1902, when she coloured several of the illustrations in the Royal Academy annual exhibition catalogue. On 20 September 1904, at the age of 'seven and five months', on holiday in Glendalough, she completed a prodigious survey of nature in book form, mounting in a large scrapbook 123 named specimens of flowers and grasses. They received a critical reception. Seven duplicates and seventeen 'misnamed or unnamed' were listed by an unidentified judge, while Mainie's mother wrote: 'A good many of these flowers have been pressed and fastened into this book by Mainie alone – The Henbane must not count as she did not pick it.' Her first letter, to her mother, written the following spring in a copperplate hand on lined paper, records for the first time her musical efforts. 'I have learnt two verses of ''Lorraine Lorée''. I am learning a new duet, and a new exercise (Pl. 8).'

In 1907 she was taken by her father to the Irish International Exhibition, a large and memorable show of Irish art, opened by the Lord Lieutenant on 4 May and visited by King Edward VII during his state visit in July. This and other royal visits were representative of a more positive, more cohesive political atmosphere which characterised the period up to the First World War, and was in marked contrast with earlier phases of political life, the most recent in memory being the Parnell years. In 1900 Queen Victoria visited Dublin, where her son, the Duke of Connaught, was

5. Mainie, with bucket and spade, aged three.

6. Mainie with her younger sister, Bay.

7. Mainie with tennis racquet.

Commander-in-Chief. In response to the gallantry of the Irish regiments in South Africa, the Queen had ended a minor but awkward inconvenience by ordering that all Irish soldiers might wear a sprig of shamrock on St Patrick's Day. Since this 'Wearing of the Green' had been regarded as improper, the change may have contributed to the warmth of her reception. Edward VII maintained and augmented the popularity of the Monarch, and his several State visits to Ireland were popular affairs. Both he and the Prince of Wales, who had survived an assassination attempt in Belgium by a Boer sympathiser, on the very day of his grandmother's arrival in Dublin, were associated with the arts.

The question of a modern art gallery for Dublin was much discussed at the beginning of the Edwardian era. Hugh Lane, an outstanding dealer and collector at the time, had made proposals for a gallery of modern art for the city.[1] He had backed this up with offers of paintings, and, using his not inconsiderable powers of persuasion, had organised the help and support of painters and other donors. The Prince of Wales commemorated his first official visit to the city, in February 1905, by presenting to Lane four small but exquisite examples of John Constable's work for the new gallery. When in 1908, following the International Exhibition, the Municipal Gallery finally opened its doors, it represented a significant step forward for a discipline within the fine arts not regarded as characteristically Irish, then or later. In the climate of the times, somewhat artificially created by the Irish Literary Revival, Lane's efforts were welcomed; but the art form in which he dealt was seen, significantly, as a backcloth to the endeavours of writers. It is of interest that his pressure on Irish painters was for them to donate *portraits* mainly of great Irish men and women, and that *modernism* in art, meant French and other continental work. Furthermore, for anyone seriously involved at the time with Lane in his self-imposed task, the conservative, even reactionary response of the city to his enthusiastic benevolence in trying to establish a living tradition in modern art, would have sounded a tocsin of grave warning for the future. For Mainie, of course, these weighty matters were of small consequence. Yet she was growing up in a household where the arts were not only valued, but practised, and where the cultural issues of the day were much debated – by 'the Frumps', by her parents, and within the larger family circle at Howth each Sunday. Busts of the younger children by Albert Power,[2] a leading Irish sculptor at the time, were commissioned. And another notable Irish sculptor, John Hughes,[3] did a

8

May 12th:

My dear Mumps
We are
very glad you
had such a nice
crossing. I have
learnt two verses
of "Lorraine Lorée"
I am learning a
new duet, and a
new exercise.
With love from
Mainie.

8.   Mainie's first letter.

9.   'An Old Canal Boat', c.1908. Pen on paper,
9 × 11.7. Dublin, private collection. Inscribed on
reverse, 'by M.H. Jellett'.

10.   *The Flower-Seller*, c.1908. Pen on paper,
11.4 × 8.8. Dublin, private collection.

bronze portrait plaque of Mrs Jellett with Mainie at Christmas 1906.

In December 1907 the Jellett's third daughter Rosamund, who was known as Babbin, was born. Mainie was by now able to write sensible letters, and when her parents went to London for the Anglo-French Exhibition in May 1908 she reported on the affairs of the house and family with a due sense of her own importance:

> Miss Butterworth liked your letter very much and I gave her some flowers that Mr. Iseck had sent in, it is quite fine but rather cold here i hope you are haveing good weather so far, how did you enjoy the concert and that wonderful dancer. Good by i have nothing more to say as Bay says . . . we are all very lonely without you and Dad . . .

Mainie's first original works of art date from 1909 and 1910, and include *An Old Canal Boat* and various other Dublin scenes, among them the interior of a shop and two of a Dublin flower-seller (Pls. 9–11). There is one watercolour in this group, the others are pen and ink drawings. She also executed a careful and accomplished series of drawings to illustrate the nursery rhyme, 'Sing a Song of Sixpence', with three of them carefully signed in a bottom corner 'M.H.J.' They are all very domestic, the figure of the king based on her bearded grandfather, and the opening line of the nursery rhyme showing her younger sister on her mother's knee at the piano. More ambitious altogether was the work contained in two sketchbooks, one of large watercolour studies, mainly of plants, the other of domestic scenes and portraits. In line and colour the larger works are bold and assured. With vivid blues for forget-me-not and strong mauve and yellow for the crocuses. The smaller sketchbook includes some spirited little studies of Babbin playing the violin, of various family pets, and of other relations (Pl. 12).

Mainie had already taken lessons from the Yeats sisters in plant drawing, a speciality of theirs. Understandably overshadowed by their two brothers, Lily (Susan Mary) Yeats, and Lolly (Elizabeth Corbet) Yeats,[4] had absorbed much of the teaching and inspiration of William Morris during their time in England, in Bedford Park. On their return to

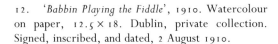

11. *Houses Seen Through an Archway*, c.1908. Watercolour on card, 11.2 × 8.8. Dublin, private collection.

12. *'Babbin Playing the Fiddle'*, 1910. Watercolour on paper, 12.5 × 18. Dublin, private collection. Signed, inscribed, and dated, 2 August 1910.

Ireland they became deeply involved in the Arts and Crafts movement. They concentrated on printing and design, and Lolly also gave lessons in brushwork with an emphasis on flower painting. Classes were held in the Jellett's home and included other children as well, among them the young Elizabeth Bowen.[5]

By 1909 Mainie was a student of May Manning,[6] a well-known Dublin art teacher, and her small sketchbook, signed and dated April 1909, also has the inscription '1st Prize painting examination'. In 1910 she wrote a number of short stories in an exercise book which has survived. 'An Adventure on the Seine' was inspired by the heavy floodings there in January which threatened the art collection at the Louvre. 'A True Ghost Story' was set in an old house in Henrietta Street, while a third was called 'A Musical Tragedy', and involved the son of an Irishman and a Russian actress. 'He was a born Musician he could play almost any instrument and compose anything he wished.' The story, unfortunately, stops there. But the other two are elaborate in plot and crammed with dramatic events.

These were secure years. The shadow of future political unrest was somewhat lessened by the sense of enlightenment and cultural optimism which had evolved at the outset of the new century. The work of Douglas Hyde and the Gaelic League,[7] the revival of theatre and literature generally, and then the development of interest in the visual arts, all contributed to an atmosphere of secure and optimistic expectation.

The period of Mainie's early growing up, from the final years of the nineteenth century and of Queen Victoria's reign, to the end of the Edwardian era, was, however, deceptively benign politically. Judicious political management of Irish affairs, combined with a period of intense cultural activity, held in check the deeper political drive towards independence, and the underlying social revolution which had really been taking place during the previous half-century. Mainie Jellett and her family belonged to a class which was under siege, and avowed a faith which had always been a minority one. It had been bolstered up, until Disestablishment in 1870, by an artificial favouring of Protestantism as a symbol of wealth and power. This was in the process of slow change. Economically, the Land Acts of the nineteenth century, and above all the decisive Land Act of 1903, were shifting wealth; so were the provisions making education more widely available. The changes in the electoral laws and in the structure of constituencies, were also changing the balance of power. None of this was imperceptible. Each issue was read and dealt with by the class most affected in the light of its immediate and long-term effects, and William Jellett was himself acutely aware of the various transitions. But the process was inexorable, and it took place on a broad front, against which there was only limited power and will. While it was hard to predict just how the relatively new European spirit of nationalism would affect Ireland, there was no denying its early strength in the cultural field, an area to which the Jelletts responded positively.

Mainie benefited from the positive atmosphere in which these changes took place. She was lucky to have experienced so much of the change during her most impressionable years. For a good deal of the subsequent, and far more bitter period of political evolution, she was to be abroad. But until the outbreak of the First World War the world she inhabited combined a traditional stability with some of the most stimulating artistic and cultural innovations Ireland has ever seen.

CHAPTER THREE

Early painting years

THE MISS BUTTERWORTH mentioned by Mainie in her letter to her mother was the governess of the time, soon to be replaced by a German, Fraulein Luise Schuster, and then by Miss Chenevix who remained with the family until after the First World War. The Jellett girls were fairly merciless to all their teachers: jumping out from behind curtains to frighten Fraulein Schuster, and forcing Miss Chenevix to change lessons whenever they got boring or difficult, was normal procedure. Elizabeth Bowen, the novelist, who lived nearby, and was a lifelong friend of Mainie's, has recalled how Dublin girls of their class walked every afternoon with their governesses and met each other in the quiet and polite purlieus of the canal-side streets and parks. Teaching was limited. Manners and behaviour were dominant.[1]

Miss Butterworth had implied at one stage that Mainie was unteachable. This surprising and somewhat harsh judgment was provoked in part by Mainie's capacity for practical jokes and teases. On one occasion she gave a particularly gluey toffee to the wife of Douglas Hyde, President of the Gaelic League and later President of Ireland, who was attending one of her mother's 'At Homes'. As a result Mrs Hyde's teeth were firmly stuck together, a joke greatly enjoyed by Mainie's father. General family discipline was fairly easy-going. William Jellett's own father, for all his authority as the head of a major university, had been indulgent towards his children, letting them play in his study in the provost's house so long as they did not quarrel.

But Miss Butterworth's frustrations with Mainie must also have derived from the fact that music and art were regarded by her parents to be equally important as the lessons which the governess was attempting to teach. Given that both pursuits required daily study and frequent visits to other teachers, there were many conflicts about the time available for Miss Butterworth.

Mainie attended the Leinster School of Music. Having been taught initially by her mother she became a pupil of Miss Länder.[2] Mainie competed regularly in the *Feis Ceoil* (Dublin's annual musical festival) and won many prizes during this period. By 1914, she was playing the solo part in a Mendelssohn piano concerto in one of the public concerts held by the school of music. She was to keep up her piano study for several more years and also taught her youngest sister, Betty, born in 1910. Throughout her life music played a central part and she remained an outstanding pianist, playing in public up to the 1930s.

The study of painting took Mainie even further afield. In 1910 she was on holiday near Boulogne, where she painted several fine watercolours. Three years later, when she was sixteen years old, she went as a pupil of Norman Garstin on a painting trip to Brittany (Pl. 13).[3] She was accompanied by her cousin, Mary Crookshank, a Miss Franks and the governess, Fraulein Schuster. They travelled from Dublin to Southampton and then by steamer to St Mâlo. Garstin, who had exhibited in the huge 1904 Guildhall Loan Exhibition of Irish art, ran his sketching classes on the continent for several months each summer in addition to his winter-time teaching in Newlyn – what he called 'tutorials' at his own self-styled Newlyn and Penzance School. He would have been a prudent choice, approved by Miss Manning, and regarded by her as a leading light in the modestly avant-

13. *House in Brittany*, 1913. Watercolour on paper mounted on card, 28 × 20. Dublin, private collection.

garde school of British Impressionism. 'Mr. Garstin is very nice but *very vague*', Mainie wrote to her mother after a journey which had proved eventful: 'I have succeeded in losing the tea basket, Miss Chambré her bag and Mary her hatbox, it was not our fault as they were put in charge of porters who kindly never took the trouble to put them in the train, we have just composed a grand letter to the 'Chef' of this Gare at St. Mâlo about them.' The hotel in which they stayed was rather fine, 'a regular château', standing in its own grounds. They had travelled by train from St Mâlo to Guémené, but then had to wait for two hours, and Mainie gave an extensive description of what she saw, including a sketch of the double flight of curved steps to the entrance of the sixteenth-century château. 'You may judge of Mr. Garstin's vagueness', she wrote. 'He managed to send all his luggage to Hamburg and then to America while coming to France one time, he was on a liner that called at the French port he was going to, when he got off no luggage; it had gone on in the steamer and he was minus any clothes except what he had on.'

Mainie thought the countryside as being 'very like Ireland only for the poplar trees and the people,' and described the room she shared with Mary as 'ripping', with one window looking out on the town, the other across the picturesque landscape towards the Noires Mountains. Guémené-sur-Scorff is a small town in central Brittany, in an area where there are many small but beautiful chapels in characteristic Breton style, dating from the fifteenth and sixteenth centuries. At that time, and indeed on into the 1920s, the women wore the traditional local peasant costume, full black skirts, 'rather like the Dutch' Mainie wrote, and small, intricate, starched bonnets.

Garstin's method of teaching on these summer 'tutorials' was relaxed. Very much a *plein airiste* himself, he allowed his mixed bag of enthusiastic pupils to set up and paint what they wanted, with modest guidance from himself, and from his daughter, Alethea, also a fine painter. Mainie thought him 'not nearly such a good teacher' as Miss Manning, but got on well with him, and certainly welcomed his praise of her work.

One of their visits was to Le Faouet, fifteen miles east of Guémené-sur-Scorff. They stayed in a hotel there for the night and were up before dawn to be at the beautiful Gothic chapel of Saint Barbera for the summer Pardon on the last Sunday in June. The chapel is set in a rocky depression on the side of a hill overlooking the River Ellé. There is an oratory as well, on a rocky spur, and a fine Renaissance stairway leading up to it. Mainie described the scene in a letter to her parents: 'it was perfectly marvellous just like Fairyland the mists were lying over the country it looked just as if the sea had come inland, then the sun rose.' They went down to the church and sketched the peasants praying outside, since it was full to overflowing. After breakfast they met the peasants coming away from the chapel 'in the most exquisite dresses some had white on pearl grey threads aprons edged with real lace and regular Elizabethan ruffs, others had the most brilliant coloured ones and their black dresses, embroidered with jet and trimmed with deep bands of black velvet.'

All their travel was by train, and, with the Pardon attracting so many people, the return journey was so crowded they had to sit on their painting stools in the guard's van. This temerity by visitors from Great Britain encouraged the French to join them and the van soon filled up. The station staff then came to put them all out, as such travel was *défendu*,

> but a gallant Frenchman stuck himself in the door and refused for us all to move out of the place, then the porter went to get someone else to turn us out but the train started off just as he arrived back and our heroic Frenchman waved his hand gaily out of door at them . . . Oh, the smell of the fish in the van and the heat what with laughing etc. we nearly burst.

She ended her painting holiday in mid-July, returning through London where she visited the Royal Academy summer exhibition. By then the whole family had gone to Scotland for the summer holidays and Mainie was to follow with her cousin, Harry

FitzGerald. The venture had been a great success. Her painting had been much admired, and she and the other girls – it seems to have been exclusively for women – had enjoyed a great deal of fun and amusement. As we have seen her letters to her mother are packed with news and vivid accounts of the daily events. She wrote frequently, asking that letters be sent on to her father in Dublin, who was finishing up his law term.

The work she brought back from France reveals a rapidly developing talent for painting from nature, something she sustained throughout her life. Watercolour studies of landscape scenes, cottages, and of grass and sand, offer convincing evidence of her technical advance during that summer.

The Jellett family holiday in Scotland that summer was, as usual, an extended affair. Weighing on William Jellett's mind was the political situation. The Conservative-Unionist Coalition, which had restructured the administration of Ireland and broken the economic power of the Irish landlords with the 1903 Land Act, had been replaced by a liberal government, allied to a revived Irish Home Rule Party. That government introduced a Home Rule Bill which was passed in the House of Commons in 1912. Feelings among Unionists were running high, and F.E. Smith – later Lord Birkenhead – claimed that 'even if this Government had the wickedness, it is wholly lacking in the nerve required to give an order which would shatter the civilisation of these islands'. Almost half a million Ulster Unionists had signed a 'Solemn Covenant' in September by which they engaged themselves to defend their position in the United Kingdom by force of arms. The Home Rule Bill was overwhelmingly defeated by the House of Lords at the end of January 1913, but, under the Parliament Act passed in 1911 to deal with just such an eventuality, the House of Lords only had power to delay implementation of the act. In the event, its implementation was prevented by the outbreak of the First World War in 1914.

William Jellett, in common with Southern Unionists generally, was in an increasingly difficult position. In that part of Ireland later to become Northern Ireland, the Unionists constituted a society in which all classes were represented. Their position was much more defensible – morally and militarily – than that of the Southern Unionists, who were a small and privileged minority. Increasingly, the option of dividing Ireland – allowing the northeast corner to remain within the United Kingdom while granting Home Rule to the rest of the country – was canvassed. With a provisional government established in Ulster, and plans in train to arm the men of the Ulster Volunteer Force, talk of civil war seemed justified. But it was strife in which no Dublin Unionists could play an effective role. Jellett regarded the Ulster Unionists as extremists whose action could only jeopardise the prospect of the whole of Ireland remaining within the Union, and the only comforting aspect of the situation in his eyes was the apparently moderate, statesmanlike stance adopted by the Nationalist leader, John Redmond.

Mainie spent Christmas of 1913 at Villars-sur-Ollon in the French Alps where she had been invited by the Greens, neighbours in Fitzwilliam Square. Green was a senior figure at the St James's Gate Brewery, in Dublin, and his wife was a woman of independent, even eccentric disposition, who frequently went big game hunting, and indeed eventually met her end in combat with a tiger! They had two daughters, Pearl and Pamela. Mainie painted a fine portrait of Pamela many years later. The holiday was a great success and Mainie supplied her mother with details: 'Mrs G. says I have exceptional good balance on skates as the 2nd day I skated I got round the mile myself and I have so far had very few falls. I love skates and so far I think it is much nicer than skiing.'

Mainie was now in her seventeenth year (Pl. 14), an accomplished pianist who could look forward to a musical career, and a promising painter whose studies under May Manning had progressed to a point where further tuition had to be considered. May Manning's advice was in favour of the Metropolitan School of Art in Dublin, which had then a high reputation. This was in part due to the teaching of William Orpen,[4] who came over from London twice each year to teach life drawing and painting. During his

14. Mainie Jellett aged sixteen.

summer visit he usually took a house at Howth, close to the Stokes' enclave. He brought his family over and then invited favoured students to join in the mixture of fun and work which seemed inseparable from his vigorous and restless nature. When at Howth he formed part of a set which included several families. While Mainie was older than any of the Orpen children, Bay was the same age as Mary Orpen, and they played together frequently. Mainie's age, and the fact that she came from a background somewhat different from that of Orpen's favoured pupils, possibly inhibited the kind of close friendship he enjoyed with the young people, especially his female students, and there is no record of her ever taking part in the student revels which Orpen so often led.

The Metropolitan School of Art was run within the Kensington Art Schools system. It placed considerable emphasis on life drawing and painting from the life, and inevitably, with Orpen's input, on portraiture. Among his protégés there were artists like Sean Keating,[5] Leo Whelan[6] and Patrick Tuohy,[7] who were to shape Irish art in the early 1920s.

CHAPTER FOUR

The influence of William Orpen

15. *Seated Female Nude*, 1915–16. Oil on canvas, 61 × 91.5. Dublin, private collection.

16. *Seated Female Nude*, 1915–16. Oil on canvas, 91.3 × 61.2. Belfast, Ulster Museum.

THE METROPOLITAN SCHOOL of Art in Dublin had figured prominently in the annual National Art Competitions for a number of years. These were held throughout the British Isles in all the disciplines, and the schools measured their competence by the number of awards they were able to achieve. It had been in these competitions that William Orpen had first distinguished himself, being showered with gold, silver and bronze medals, scholarships and book prizes, during his six years of study there in the last decade of the nineteenth century.

Since 1900, art education in Ireland had introduced a greater emphasis on industry. Gold and silver smithing, lace, stained glass, furniture design, metalwork and enamelling, as well as architectural drawing, were all stressed and this was followed by a shift towards craft-based teaching. Orpen did not approve, since he had drawn around himself a student elite whose main interest was in drawing and painting.

The distinction he had created, between 'pure art' and the craft-based studies which the headmaster favoured, was by no means the only divisive factor with which students had to contend. The art school had a large enrollment, 345 in Mainie's first year, more or less equally divided between men and women and day and evening class students. Behind this balance lay considerable prejudice: against women, against privilege and wealth, against what one student, Kathleen Fox, described as a 'thoroughly British and thoroughly Protestant atmosphere'.[1] The reality was that women, particularly the daughters of wealthy Dubliners, dominated the day-time studies, and were designated 'full-time' or 'serious' students, while men, who had to earn their living during the day, studied at night. Harry Clarke,[2] who was to become a noted stained-glass artist, gives some flavour to this in his reference to 'a favourite trick', which was to pile up the chairs at night so that the women students would have nowhere to sit the next day. He claimed, probably correctly, that 'the contemporary fashion for arts and crafts contributed to this female influx'.

Mainie's own disposition, which was to favour the relationship between fine art and craft in later years, was firmly fixed on life drawing and painting when she first went to the Metropolitan School. If one is to judge from her work of this period she responded well to the liberal impact of Orpen, painting several splendid large nudes, and a number of realist canvases which show clearly her steady development in the command of colour and technique (Pls. 15–18).

Mainie took a road that was more impressionist, more sympathetic to her subject-matter, more aware of other strands and influences. To some extent Irish art had divided between the softer, impressionist work of Nathaniel Hone, a Barbizon-trained artist, and Walter Osborne, on the one hand, and the much harder, crisper work of Orpen, with its emphasis on draughtsmanship and line. Mainie was making a conscious choice in favour of the former style. This in part may have derived from the impact of Norman Garstin's teaching. Though Walter Osborne was dead by 1903,[3] when Mainie was only six, the legacy of such a powerful painter was considerable, and it is his work which springs to mind when one considers Mainie's painting of the kneeling figure of her younger sister which dates from this period (Pl. 19).

17

17. *Reclining Nude*, 1915–16. Oil on canvas, 61 × 91.5. Dublin, private collection.

18. *Head of Girl*, 1916. Pencil on paper, 43 × 34.5. Dublin, private collection.

Orpen was active in the school for only the first year of Mainie's studies there. In 1915, the Derby Scheme and conscription led to the temporary break-up of his portrait practice in London, and he turned his attention to the role of war artist, while his studio assistant, Sean Keating, returned to Ireland, not wishing to be conscripted.

For Mainie, absorbed both in her painting and her music, the war must have seemed far off. It intruded slightly when the family went on holiday to Donegal and, due to strict military regulations, permission had to be sought for her to sketch out of doors. After correspondence between her father and the garrison commander at Buncrana, she received a 'Permit to Sketch'.[4] But beyond that the distant conflict was no more than a partial drain on student numbers and a restriction on travel. John Redmond's whole-hearted commitment of Ireland to the cause of the Allies at the outbreak of war, set the tone initially, and his view remained politically dominant, despite the postponement by the British government of the Home Rule legislation and the split within Irish nationalism which followed. There was a measure of unity between Unionists and Nationalists over recruiting, and a generally positive climate, satisfactory to those like William Jellett of Southern Unionist disposition, developed.

The situation was not even-handed, however; the formation of an Ulster Division, not keen to admit either Roman Catholics or Nationalists into its ranks, went ahead speedily while the parallel attempts to establish an Irish Division were approached with less enthusiasm. The War Office made few concessions to the nationalist feelings of Irish recruits, and the slight but effective gesture made by Queen Victoria, all those years before, over the 'wearing of the Green' by servicemen was nullified by a refusal to allow Irish recruits to carry national colours on service.

The activities of militant Sinn Féin were consistently under-estimated. The Irish Volunteers were drilled under the eyes of the police, pamphleteering went on, and the 'unthinkable' rebellion took place with army officers actually on Easter leave. The events of Easter Week 1916 had a direct impact on the school of art. Both former and present students and teachers were involved. Patrick Tuohy, who that year had

18

19. *Babbin with the Pot-Pouri*, 1916. Oil on canvas, 91.5 × 61. Dublin, private collection.

completed his two-year teachers-in-training course, and was awarded an art scholarship, was among those who fought in the General Post Office.[5] For Mainie the 1916 Rising was a betrayal. For her father it was an outrage. For Southern Unionists it was turned into a disaster beyond mitigation by the execution of almost all the 1916 leaders. One of them, Joseph Mary Plunkett,[6] married Grace Gifford[7] in his condemned cell the night before his execution.

Orpen's departure from the school – his last visit during the war period was in the summer of 1915 – left something of a vacuum. He had insisted on the traditional hierarchy of fine art, and, as we have seen, had created an elite of those who could paint and draw well. These young men and women were drawn from the more senior pupils and from those who had left the school in the formal sense to become trainee teachers or who in some cases had set up in work outside. They pursued any opportunity which would allow them to become painters, and remained closely associated with Orpen and his circle. There is no evidence of Mainie being part of the set beyond a tiny trace – in her collection of graphic works was a unique early soft ground etching by Orpen himself after Rembrandt's *Abraham Sacrificing Isaac*.[8] How it came to be in her possession is not recorded, though she was at the time venturing into etched work of her own. It is clear from occasional references in Mainie's letters that Orpen's fortunes generally, and his impact as a painter of growing reputation in London, were matters of comment, and of carefully considered judgment. But even though Mainie's canvases of this period show his influence, in the direct and honest treatment of the nude and in the full and satisfying composition of her portraits, Mainie was not satisfied.

She was already considering a move to London, to study. She wrote to her mother's friend, Gwenda Herbert, for advice and received back a helpful letter, advising her to write to Walter Sickert at Fitzroy Street,[9] and recommending him as the artist who 'would help you far the most'. She mentions Tonks,[10] but then says she thinks he has gone to France to work as a doctor. 'I would think he was rather passé!' she writes, suggesting that Mainie's letter, which has not survived, had stressed the need for a new teacher reflective of modern principles and the avant-garde. The letter mirrors a possible desperation in Mainie's appeal: 'I am quite sure your art interest will always be a delightful thing to you, don't let yourself ever be downhearted, insight comes with perseverance which I am sure you have got . . . over here you get chances of seeing more works, even if you were not over for very long.'

Mainie wrote for the Westminster School prospectus in the autumn of 1916. By the beginning of February 1917 she had begun her studies there with Sickert. He put her on still life to begin with, for two afternoons a week. And shortly afterwards she told Bay in a letter 'Mr Sickert liked my drawing last night, I am working away as usual, no violent thrills lately'. She enjoyed London, going to revues, musicals, theatres and concerts and writing full accounts of them to Bay in Dublin, enclosing the programmes with all the good tunes marked. Addressing Bay as 'Colonel O'Boo', she maintained a lively correspondence. Bay was an enthusiast for music hall, an interest shared by her father who had an extremely good ear for popular music. Mainie went to the Albert Hall for the first time. 'It is an enormous place. You feel like a flea in it, it is so huge.' She heard Moisewitch playing Rachmaninov to great applause, 'came out about four or five times and eventually played an encore, a Chopin study, beautifully'. Later, she took lessons with Moisevitch, and was clearly studying hard at her music as well as her painting.

She returned enthusiastically to London after the Easter holidays, and was soon working in the life class (Pls. 20–2), where she produced a number of early studies, including nudes. She visited many galleries, among them the New English Art Club,[11] where some of the more interesting works were from non-members such as Harold Gilman,[12] John Nash,[13] Charles Ginner,[14] Paul Pissarro[15] and William Rothenstein[16]. At that point in her development the concept of 'modernism', to the extent that it is revealed by the catalogues of exhibitions she visited, and by her letters, did not go

20. *Seated Nude, Back View*, 1917. Pencil on paper, 31.5 × 25.5. Dublin, private collection.

21. *Head of Man*, 1917. Pencil on paper, 14 × 11.5. Dublin, private collection.

22. *Study for Life Class*, 1917. Pencil on paper, 32 × 25. Dublin, private collection.

23. (*facing page*) *Girl with Ribbons*, 1917. Watercolour on paper, 37 × 28. Dublin, private collection.

24. *Life Class*, 1917. Watercolour on paper, 27 × 37. Dublin, private collection.

25. *Standing Female Nude*, 1917. Oil on canvas, 40.5 × 25.5. London, private collection.

26. *The Red-Collared Coat*, 1917. Oil on canvas, 40.5 × 53. Dublin, private collection.

27. *Standing Female Nude*, 1917. Oil on canvas, 58.5 × 41. Dublin, private collection.

beyond the Impressionism which Sickert had developed. This seemed to her more evocative of French painting, and may have obscured the more local expressions of modernism. It is ironic that her period with Sickert, coincided with the revolutionary, avant-garde work from artists such as David Bomberg[17] and Wyndham Lewis[18], which she does not seem to have known, and that by the time she actively sought to advance beyond Sickert's principles, that wave in English art had dissipated. Sickert remained the main force. His impact is strongly evident in the dated watercolours and oils of 1917 which show how rapidly and completely his teaching influenced and changed Mainie's style (Pls. 23–7).

Mainie was moving at a pace not inconsistent with developments in art generally, though there were also setbacks. The whiff of 'modernism' which, in the British Isles was exemplified by events such as the two Roger Fry Post-Impressionist exhibitions of 1911 and 1912,[19] the launching of the Camden Town Group,[20] the setting up of the Omega Workshops[21] and then the publication of *Blast* in the summer of 1914,[22] had, like more ambitious artistic manifestations elsewhere in Europe, suffered the reversal in fortune occasioned by the First World War. Artists joined up or were enlisted, and their works disappeared from exhibitions. Some were killed and the whole vital force

unleashed by Cézanne and accelerated by the Cubists became for a time fragmentary and uncertain.

The handicaps under which Mainie approached international art from a Dublin standpoint – distance, background and sex – had been swept away by the move to London. Women were taken seriously, and had been in art schools since the turn of the century, when Orpen had arrived at the Slade to study with Ursula Tyrrwhitt[23] and Ida Nettleship[24]. London offered an entirely different, 'centre-of-the-world' perspective. It was not surprising that Mainie should have felt a sense of release and renewed enthusiasm for the next stage in her artistic education, and that in choosing a teacher who espoused one of the greatest of French art traditions of all time, she had moved decisively into a new phase in her life.

CHAPTER FIVE

Sickert: 'the first revolution'

29. *Seated Woman*, 1918. Watercolour on paper, 29 × 23.5. Dublin, private collection.

28. (*facing page*) *Portrait of a Young Girl*, 1918. Watercolour, 24 × 19. Dublin, private collection.

30. *Woman in Striped Blouse*, 1918. Oil on canvas, 51 × 40.5. London, private collection.

IT WAS AS if her adult life had just begun. Years later she was to write

> I studied in Ireland till I was 18 then went to London and studied under Walter Sickert (1st revolution) when for the first time, drawing and composition came alive to me and I began to understand the work of the Old Masters. Sickert being in the direct line of French Impressionist painting was an excellent stepping stone . . .[1]

The drawings and paintings tell the story more convincingly than words: it was as if the Westminster Art School released within her a pent up tide of ability and inspiration. Sufficient work, dated from 1917 and 1918, and done in pencil, pen, watercolour and pastel, as well as on canvases of an almost serene brilliance, indicate a sudden, rich fulfilment (Pls. 28–37). It was only the first of such epiphanies; yet in the true sense it was sudden and revelatory, the essential nature and meaning of what she sought to do with her life being disclosed by an artist and an environment into which she threw herself wholeheartedly.

The drawings breathe with the life of the school, and with the spirit of Sickert; the influence of the master is apparent in every line. There is a luscious, relaxed voluptuousness about some of the early nudes which gave way subsequently to a much more rigorous and penetrating analysis of the human figure. In keeping with Sickert's realism, the students drew and painted exactly what they saw, including each other and their physical surroundings, so that the distinctive curved arches in the life-class room and the sombre grey painted brick walls aid the cataloguing of these works which cover a wide variety of subject matter.

The early drawings are particularly fine, and the sense of release is revealed through the soft tones and the detailed and subtle realisation of form and character. The models, as one might expect in any school run by Sickert, were varied: old men, negroes and girls with cropped hair, often dressed in flamboyant and fanciful clothes. Mainie signed and dated her work carefully and sometimes wrote on her drawings the critical comments made by one or other of her teachers – 'tone on vertical planes is vertical'.

Sickert dominated everything, yet in a benign and intellectually rich and challenging way. Then in his late fifties, he was, in the British context, a giant figure who commanded the bridgehead between modernism and the academic tradition. His teachers, Alphonse Legros at the Slade,[2] then Whistler[3] and then Degas[4], gave him a powerful line of authority and a stimulating mixture of traditions. Degas inspired in him an appreciation of the importance in art of the casual gesture, the accidental expression caught and set down, the indifferent scene out of which a moment in time can be rescued and made memorable by the faculties and inspiration of the artist. In that difficult area where the strict regime of drawing, so important in British art teaching under Legros and his successors at the Slade, comes to terms with the remarkable revolution in the treatment of colour by French painters, Sickert established a firm place for himself and held it with growing reputation over a surprisingly long period. Mainie's mother's friend had been shrewd in advising her to choose him in 1916.

At that time Sickert had only recently returned to the Westminster School. He had

31. *Woman in Summer Hat*, 1918. Watercolour on paper, 30 × 25. London, private collection.

32. *Watercolour Class*, 1918. Watercolour on paper, 23 × 32.5. Dublin, private collection.

33. *The Artist's Mother*, c.1920. Watercolour on paper, 21.5 × 19.5. Dublin, private collection.

34. *Babbin and Betty*, 1918. Oil on canvas, 63 × 78 cm. Ireland, private collection. A back view of Mainie's youngest two sisters, in the nursery at 36 Fitzwilliam Square, in the evening before they went to bed. Babbin, on the right, is drinking cocoa.

35. *Walter Bayes*, 1918. Oil on canvas, 30.5 × 25.5. Dublin, private collection. Walter Bayes taught Mainie at the Westminster School of Art.

36. *The Life Class*, 1918. Oil on canvas, 40.5 × 33. Dublin, private collection.

given up his original teaching job there in 1912, and had been replaced by Spencer Gore[5]. When Gore died in the summer of 1914 Sickert was living in France, and did not return until well after the outbreak of war.

He loved teaching, and his attitude inspired other teachers at the school, among them Walter Bayes,[6] of whom Mainie did a fine portrait in oil (Pl. 35). Sickert was stimulating in other ways; he was widely read and kept open house in his Fitzroy Street studio, 'The Frith', where the Victorian painter, William Powell Frith, had been a predecessor. He attracted a large circle of friends, young and old.

Some time after her arrival in London, probably in the autumn of 1917, Mainie met Evie Hone.[7] It was arguably the most important personal encounter of her life. The two women were to become lifelong friends, and their subsequent relationship as artists changed the course of twentieth-century Irish art. On a personal level, Mainie was to be a great support to her friend, lifting her spirits when she was depressed, helping her overcome her physical handicap, and sharing all her thoughts on life and art.

When Evie first met Mainie she had no intention of returning to Ireland. Childhood polio had left her very disabled and she required treatment in London. Her main priority was to be able to walk, and she underwent many operations. She was eventually able to go to the Byam Shaw School of Art,[8] and later to study with Sickert followed by Bernard Meninsky.[9]

By the time she met Mainie, Evie's sense of betrayal common to her class throughout the British Isles caused by the events of 1916 would have been quite pronounced. Her eventual return to Ireland was motivated more by the fact that two of her three sisters were then living there, one in Galway and the other outside Dublin, than by any burning desire to identify with the country of her birth. There was a natural sympathy between the two young women, however, and a concern on Mainie's part for Evie's physical disability which remained throughout Mainie's life.

They were not particularly close to begin with, meeting only on social occasions, and there was no greater common ground for friendship than existed with Mainie's other companions at the time. Though, theoretically, Evie Hone was more experienced in London art school life, from the earliest point in their friendship it is clear that Mainie was the more dominant figure as indeed she already was among the other students at the Westminster School. Their close association really developed when they were both pupils together under André Lhote,[10] in 1921, despite becoming his students by separate routes.

Little is known of the period when Evie studied with Mainie at the Westminster School, though it did lead to them meeting Bernard Meninsky, who was later instrumental in persuading them to study in France, when the war was over. Meninsky, who had been born in the Ukraine in 1891, and brought up in Liverpool, had studied in Paris at the Académie Julian.[11] He had then worked at the Slade, and with Edward Gordon Craig[12] in his school of theatre design in Florence before joining the Central School of Arts and Crafts to teach drawing.[13] He was a member of the London Group and a friend of Sickert, whom he eventually succeeded in 1918 at the Westminster School. He was a brilliant and inspiring teacher, but when Mainie and Evie met him he was going through a difficult period. He had joined the Royal Fusiliers as a clerk, and had then become an official war artist which gave him a salary (of £300 per annum, over his service pay) but precluded him from outside work *of any kind*.

It also meant that the artists' total output was made over to the State. In Meninsky's case the works retained by the Imperial War Museum number only six and were painted in the last year of the war, recording troop arrivals at Victoria Station or the departure platform for the Front. Based in London, it seems he went on teaching during this period in 1918, contrary to the agreed terms of the scheme. He was pursued by the authorities for this, and forced to make reparation.

Walter Bayes, a member of the Sickert circle, had considerable influence on Mainie at

37. *The Blue Girl*, 1919. Oil on canvas, 15 × 14 cm.
Ireland, private collection.

this time. She also formed a good working relationship with the painter and sculptor, Mervyn Lawrence.[14]

The sudden surge forward in Mainie's art under Sickert's teaching, in the autumn of 1917, bore fruit the following year when she painted a number of splendid portraits, nudes, and genre scenes. She had developed her style through many phases which can be briefly summarised. Her earliest, childhood works show a good grasp of colour and a surprisingly assured line in drawing. She demonstrated an early aptitude for depicting the human figure in movement, evident in her illustrations of nursery rhymes, and of landscape in drawings and watercolours of the canal near her home, Georgian archways and buildings.

Her work with May Manning, had given her a grounding in basic watercolour technique, demonstrated with confidence and even brilliance in her visits to France in 1911 and 1913. Both May Manning and Norman Garstin had instilled in her sufficient respect for an impressionist approach to landscape and the painting of the human figure to protect her to a certain degree from the strict linear precision of Orpen's teaching when she went to him in 1914. Her work of this period is more relaxed than that, say, of her contemporary, Patrick Tuohy; perhaps also less dramatic. But she did drawings under Orpen which advanced her work substantially in terms of professional competence and character penetration. Her time with Sickert took her still further.

On 28 April 1918, Mainie celebrated her twenty-first birthday in London. 'You are the best daughter any man ever had', her father wrote, 'and may you have a long and happy life.' Her twenty-first birthday present from her parents was a brooch made by the noted metalworker, Mia Cranwill.[15] Her work, among the best Celtic revival craftwork of this period, was well known to Mainie who had studied her technique. Mainie's mother had been less sure about the choice for so important a gift:

> At first I was a little disappointed with Miss Cranwill's brooch, but it distinctly grows on you, and the workmanship is very nice, and it is solid and good, and the design unique – she wanted to set the stones with a solid back, so as to make the back of the brooch beautiful, as she said you admired the backs of her things almost more than the fronts.

The special affection with which Mainie's parents regarded their eldest child is evident from her mother's letters to her at this time:

> You, & Dad, and I have had 21 years of real enjoyment and the children according to their ages, and if we never had another, we will have that as a blessed thankful memory. Long life to you and every blessing for now and hereafter. We'll be drinking your health and thinking of our old Doo many times tomorrow.

It was a particularly lovely spring in Ireland that year. 'I hope you have the sunshine we have', Janet Jellett wrote to her daughter, 'it's glorious, every day the same – There are sprays of hawthorn in bloom, and I see lots of lilac and a tree yellow with laburnum.' But four years of war had taken its toll in thousands of Irish deaths. Janet Jellett wrote about their friends, the Moores: 'Their son is missing, he is the only one, so it's bad.'

The sadness in Ireland was greatly aggravated by the activities of Sinn Féin which Janet described to her daughter:

> Today is a *black disgrace* to Ireland – A day's strike ordered by the Sinn Féiners RC Church and Co. The shops all shut, the Electric light cut off, no bread, no newspapers, to our surprise a postman appeared – The streets swarming with loafers ashamed to look you in the face adorned with flags in their buttonholes with Conscription on one side and 'be D- to it' on the other side.'

The Bishop of Meath's house in Fitzwilliam Square was taken over by the military. 'We hear it is to be Lord French's headquarters – I hope he'll have bayonettes bristling out of every window and a guard in the area . . . I think no one will dare force Home Rule now – The patriots are showing their horns and tails too openly even for the English.'

But Mainie was too preoccupied to be greatly concerned by events in Dublin. Known as 'Jelly', she had become a popular figure at the Westminster School. On one occasion her brief absence provoked a letter from 'Men's Life – Westminster School of Art' signed by fourteen of her fellow-students and written out on a large sheet of drawing paper as though drawn up in imitation of a legal document.

> We the students and rising artists of the Westminster desire to know where you have put yourself. If it is between the sheets with Flue our regrets are overpowering. Oh come back to us for behold the sun no longer shines on the model. Verily Verily and indeed we mourn for thee greatly. Behold Sickert will come this morning and dissolve into tears at your absence. Oh give not thy Flue unto us lest we also depart from hence. Your loving and admiring Crew.

Mainie's contact with Sickert came at a high point in his career, at a time when his teaching was relaxed, confident and effective. He thought professionally in terms of

38. *Reclining Nude*, 1919. Oil on canvas, 45.5 × 41. Dublin, private collection.

39. *Seated Nude*, 1919. Oil on canvas, 76.2 × 50.7. Dublin, private collection.

'groups' and 'schools', as was the pattern in France, and was a founder-member of the Camden Town Group and the London Group[16]. He gave enormous stature to Impressionism and Post-Impressionism as *styles*, making much easier the careers of a younger generation of artists. In his own work he transformed the essence, the best both technically and emotionally of French painting up to Cézanne, into a peculiarly English vision, redolent of London and the English class predicament.

But in spite of his giant stature, both his style of painting and his choice of subject-matter, remained highly controversial. He was attacked by fellow artists for his treatment of such subjects as prostitution, murder and poverty which were judged to have rendered his art 'worthless', and Fred Brown, Professor of Painting at the Slade, severed his friendship with Sickert on account of the 'sordid nature' of his art.[17]

In her last year at the Westminster School Mainie produced a magnificent body of work. Her output of drawings — in pen, pencil, gouache and watercolour — was outstanding. But it was in her oils that the fuller debt to Sickert was displayed. There is an almost casual mastery in the brilliance with which she handled nudes (Pls. 38–9). More than a dozen more formal portraits derive from this period. And triumphantly she carried home to Ireland her burgeoning talent and exercised it on family subjects, producing perceptive portraits and charming domestic scenes.

Her two years in London gave her assurance and self-confidence, a distinctive sense of her own style, a greatly enhanced range of technical accomplishment, and a defining of her palette in a brilliant range of clear, graded and balanced colours which was never to to desert her. As a painter, in the sense of being equipped for a profession, she had finished her studies. But as an artist, seeking a vision, a purpose, a direction, she remained unfulfilled. Sickert had set her upon a road towards the expression of her own soul in line and colour, but had given her no spiritual challenge. She was a performer, wanting to create. She was an artist in search of a further creative revolution.

CHAPTER SIX

Peace

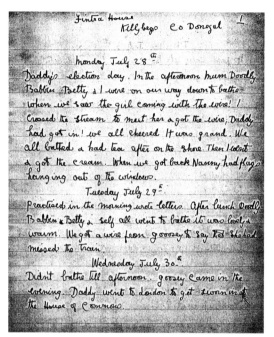

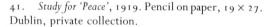

40. The first page of Bay Jellett's diary for July, 1919.

41. *Study for 'Peace'*, 1919. Pencil on paper, 19 × 27. Dublin, private collection.

IN JULY 1919 there was a general election and William Jellett successfully contested one of the Trinity College seats as a Unionist. The family had already gone on holiday to Killybegs in Co Donegal and were staying in Fintragh House waiting for the telegram which would announce the result. 'We all cheered', Bay wrote in her diary. 'It was grand. We all bathed and had tea after on the shore. Then I went and got the cream. When we got back Nanny had flags hanging out of the windows' (Pl. 40).

William Jellett went to London to be sworn in at the House of Commons, and joined his family in Donegal on 8 August, his twenty-fourth wedding anniversary. He gave Janet *Mr Punch's History of the War*. She gave him a pipe.

The Jellett family holidays in Donegal, lasting many weeks, were occasions of untrammelled pleasure, recalled with loving nostalgia by Mainie's two surviving sisters, sixty years later. Friends came to stay and Bay's diary records the days spent on the beach, swimming, fishing, and having huge picnic parties with fires and tea kettles. They played tennis, went for long walks and laid night-lines in the river at dusk.

The children loved cycling but Mainie had never learned, and she took lessons that summer on the driveway up to the house, demonstrating an infallible ability to hit the largest potholes and fall off. There was grave concern about damage to the machine she used, which happened to belong to their cousin. Mainie was very distressed, even in tears. 'Everyone talks about the bicycle. Nobody worries about me.' But Betty did. She idolised her eldest sister, so good at everything, and she remembered every detail of the day. It was the first time she had seen Mainie cry and it left a lasting impression.

Mainie spent most of her days sketching. She had conceived of an idea for a major canvas, *Peace* (Pl. 43), and the studies for it occupied most of her holiday (Pls. 41–2). Among them was a sketch of Babbin in a yellow dress which she gave to her mother as a birthday present. On another occasion, while Bay read to them, Mainie did a superb small sketch of Betty in a wide-brimmed hat, which then became an oil (Pls. 44–5), and subsequently featured as the central focus in the final canvas. She also did a portrait drawing of Bay. But quite frequently Mainie went off sketching with another artist and friend, Judith Weir, who lived with her mother near-by. Mrs Weir was allegedly gifted with second sight. She was able to tell the two girls where they had been, what they had been sketching and when they had stopped to have their picnic lunch. During the war she was reputed to have given quite accurate information on the whereabouts of German U Boats.

By now Mainie was free from formal study. She had stayed at the Westminster Art School from early 1917 to the summer of 1919. Her last year was likewise Sickert's and his impending departure may well have decided her not to enrol for a further year although she maintained contact with some of the students and with her friend, the painter Mervyn Lawrence who taught at the school. He also knew Donegal well and shared Mainie's love of its countryside. One of his principal works, in oil, was *A Donegal Tinker*.

On her return from holiday to Dublin she wrote to Lawrence to ask him about priming her canvases. At that time she was using a comparatively close-weave material,

42. *Study for 'Peace'*, 1919. Pencil on paper, 38 × 56. Donegal, The Glebe Gallery.

43. *Peace*, 1919. Oil on canvas, 61.5 × 81.5. Dublin, private collection. This painting was the work with which Mainie Jellett won the Taylor Prize in 1920. It was begun at Fintragh House, Donegal, in the summer of 1919, and finished that autumn or winter. It is also known by the title, *The Beach Pool*.

44. *Betty on the Rocks*, 1919. Oil on canvas, 51 × 41. Dublin, private collection.

45. *Study for 'Betty on the Rocks'*, 1919. Pencil on paper, 24 × 17.5. Dublin, private collection.

47. (*facing page*) *Geraldine Fitzgerald*, 1920. Oil on canvas, 89 × 71. Dublin, private collection.

46. *The Artist's Father*, 1919. Pencil on paper, 23 × 23. Dublin, private collection.

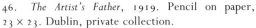
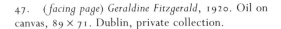

Winsor and Newton and George Rowney 'B Quality' both being employed in paintings from the Sickert period. Later she was to turn to much coarser weave. Lawrence advised her on an equal mixture of parchment size and whitening.

Warm or dissolve size in a good saucepan – add whitening in powder form <u>stirring all the time</u> – to prevent burning – do not allow it to cake on saucepan. A mixture of half and half weight is good. Try it on back of canvas first – It ought not to be too thick – You can put it on warm. It thickens with cooling. The amount of size depends on whether you want an absorbent surface or not. The more size the less absorbent it is. If too thick I add a little boiling water, keep it on the thin side. You can give it a second coat when thoroughly dry if necessary. Please write if there is anything more you want to know about it. You may give your priming a thick coat of size if too absorbent when done.

Lawrence mentioned a commercial priming then available from Roberson's, a geiss powder, but said that its convenience was outweighed by the fact that it was expensive.

48. *Judith*, 1920. Pencil on paper, 29 × 23. Dublin, private collection.

49. *Study for Theatre Scene*, 1919. Watercolour on paper, 18 × 15. Dublin, private collection.

'The first recipe is more workmanlike and goes a long way.' The technical details were immensely important to her, then and later. Always a perfectionist, and already an outstanding colourist, she maintained a deep interest throughout her life in artists' techniques, read widely, and kept careful notes about all aspects of the process of painting.

The Westminster School was returning to some kind of normality after the war. It is quite clear from almost all of Mainie's drawings of the life class that during her time there was, understandably, a preponderence of females. 'We are getting on well,' Lawrence wrote, after she had left. 'Life class here on Wednesday mornings now. School getting full and also more men are coming, though they are scarce commodities still.'

Mainie could have stayed at this point in her development. Both her technical and imaginative abilities had been richly realised in drawings, watercolours and paintings of outstanding impact (Pls. 46–9). From the simplest life-class studies to the complex and statuesque canvases in which she explores this most difficult form of art she reveals a sureness of composition, a sensitivity towards flesh tones and a marvellous grasp on anatomy which results in quite masterly works. She has Sickert's naturalism, but without that hint of sordid drama which he seemed to need in so much of his painting. There is a purity in her vision which derives from a totally objective honesty with the

50. *Seated Nude*, 1920. Oil on board, 30 × 24. London, private collection.

body as object. At the same time there is a moving sense of eroticism and a powerful understanding of human character conveyed through the portraiture, an essential element in the effective painting of the nude (Pl. 50).

In this combination she was a better painter of the nude than Sickert. She was, however, less good in genre scenes for she lacked his interest in the dramatic. Indeed, she was later to come to the conclusion that drama and anecdote, in painting, were essentially a confusion of the proper use of the art of painting, and many of her later lectures equate the anecdotal in art with materialism and a certain false sophistication which it was the purpose of abstract art to challenge, purifying the basic work of the artist in the process. For example, in 1927, after suffering much adverse criticism at the hands of George Russell, she retaliated, in a lecture to the Dublin Literary Society, where she produced the example of a characteristic 'literary' type who expected every picture to tell a story. Instead, she sought to equate painting more closely with music, both art forms being, in her view, *essentially* abstract.

55. *Portrait of a Young Man*, 1920. Oil on canvas, 46 × 30.5. Dublin, private collection.
56. *Portrait of a Young Boy*, 1920. Oil on canvas, 40.5 × 31. Dublin, private collection.

facing page
51. *Babbin*, 1920. Oil on canvas, 51 × 43. Dublin, private collection. This was exhibited in 1920 at the annual Oireachtas Exhibition (Number 55) as *Bobbin*, a further example of the mispellings which seemed to dog the Jellett family. Mainie wrote to Bay: 'What a pity Miss Williams did not put your name in Irish in the catalogue as a title for your picture, I am sure you are disappointed she didn't!' Many of the painters and painting titles were given in the Irish language.
52. *Portrait of Bay Jellett*, 1921. Oil on canvas, 41.5 × 30.5. Dublin, private collection.
53. *Babbin in the Nursery at Fitzwilliam Square*, 1920. Oil on canvas, 51 × 41. Dublin, private collection.
54. *Bay Jellett Sitting in the Gardens in Fitzwilliam Square*, 1920. Oil on board, 25.5 × 20.5 Dublin, private collection.

She spent the winter of 1919 in Dublin. To this period belongs a notable group of canvases of family groups and domestic scenes. She painted a portrait of Babbin, dressed in pink (see Pl. 51). She completed a head and shoulders of Bay, who was then eighteen years old (Pl. 52), and she did several portraits of her mother, playing the piano, reading and sewing, and of other members of the family, and family friends (Pls. 53–7). But her major project was the beach scene, *Peace*, (see Pl. 43). The painting was to be her entry in the Taylor Prize competition for the following spring.[1] She had returned to Dublin wanting to practise her art more freely, and prepare canvases for submission to exhibitions and competitions from which she had been excluded by her period of study in England. She intended to re-enter the world of Irish art in a professional capacity; and though she realised that this would inevitably involve teaching, she was determined to acquire a position in the realm of professional painting as well.

In the previous year Dermod O'Brien,[2] and Sarah Purser,[3] had been two of the Taylor Prize judges. It had been their view that the work in the painting class had not merited the award of the scholarship prize at all, and the judges' report was generally gloomy about the response of the country's art students to the generous terms of the bequest. It was an open invitation to talent: Mainie was determined to respond.

The judges were the same in 1920. In each class a specific subject or title was designated, with the most significant awards – two £50 scholarships – offered in Classes 1

and 2, together with £10 prizes, for painting and modelling respectively. Painters had a choice between figure and landscape subjects. The experience of the ending of the war and the immense sense of relief felt among her class, had inspired in her the idea of expressing peace in terms of the family's first real holiday in five years.

Mainie won the Taylor Prize in Class 1, and the £50 scholarship with her entry. That same year she exhibited again at the Royal Hibernian Academy and also in the Oireachtas exhibition, where she showed four works including the fine portrait of Babbin. She was a medal winner at the *feis ceoil*, in the Instrumental Trio. Other prizes were won by the previous year's entrants, women students from the Metropolitan School of Art and the School of Art in Belfast. A new entrant who took a £10 prize in Class 4 was Mary Crookshank, who had been with Mainie on her holiday in Brittany.

Judith Weir wrote to Mainie that winter from Donegal. She described the arrival of a destroyer at Killybegs which she went out to visit, and talked about making chocolates and fudge for Christmas presents. Subsequent letters were more serious, and she told Mainie about a boyfriend who had been killed on the Somme in 1916.

> When he was dying he said he'd 'thanked God every minute since he first saw me; and I'd turned Hell into Heaven'. But then we lost our hearts at the very first time we looked at each other! – at a hospital dance; he was 6'4" and I the tallest girl there, as it happened, our eyes sort of met over the 100 or so there, and he came straight over – I'm afraid we danced and sat out most of the evening! But I was much nicer looking – I was only a child.

She apologised to Mainie for 'unburdening my heart'. Her story was even sadder subsequently. She became fond of an army officer called Jock, posted to India, who had been wounded at Loos in 1916, where he had lost a hand. Without money or prospects, marriage was out of the question. Yet he managed to send her a tin box filled with mountain fox fur from India. He had ridden 42 miles from Srinigar, in Kashmir, to buy them. 'In a way aren't I a lucky, lucky girl!'

William Jellett decided that a summer holiday in Ireland in 1920, was not possible, and the family returned to the house in Argyllshire where at least some of them had spent summer holidays from 1911 until the outbreak of the war. It is perhaps surprising that this decision had not also been made in 1919, though apart from the disruption of the rail services by strikes, that summer had been relatively peaceful, at least for them. In reality a steady decline in the safe and comfortable circumstances enjoyed by their class, and by those of William Jellett's political views, had been taking place since well before the end of the war. Eamon de Valera's[4] return from prison to victory in the East Clare by-election in July 1917 had signalled a shift in power and a hardening of attitudes. Sinn Féin and the Republican parties were united in a mood of confrontation; this was fiercely reinforced by the British Cabinet's decision that conscription would be applied throughout Ireland. Total opposition prevented its enforcement, but the counter-action to this was the appointment of Lord French as Viceroy and the effective creation of a military administration to rule Ireland. Prominent Sinn Féin and Republican leaders were arrested, the various elements in the organisation were 'proclaimed', and in the general election of 1918 Sinn Féin returned 73 Members out of a total of 106 Irish constituencies.

At this time William Jellett was increasingly active on the political front. His position became an extreme one, motivated increasingly by the sense of isolation which Southern Unionists felt. He and John E. Walsh, also a Dublin barrister, led a group mainly of country gentlemen in the more southerly counties of Ireland. On 20 February 1918, they formed the Southern Unionist Committee of which Walsh was honorary secretary. They issued a 'Call to Unionists' in March which was a restatement of extreme unionism and a protest against developments in the Irish Convention, which was recommending an Irish Parliament. Southern Unionists, despite the fact that the Home Rule Act was on the statute book, did not believe the situation was irreversible. Strange as it may seem now, their view in 1918–19 was that the 1914 Act could be disregarded, indeed *should* be disregarded, and that they should continue to fight for the Union. Their motivation in this derived from the very success of Sinn Féin. By the end of the First World War the parliamentary party was clearly a spent force, and any future Irish Parliament would be dominated by Sinn Féin. Southern Unionists were dismayed at this prospect, not just because of Sinn Féin's pro-German attitude during the recent war – about which feelings still ran extremely high – but also because of the implicit threat to their land and property. Pamphlets, letters to *The Irish Times* and other papers, and innumerable meetings, took place on the subject of Home Rule. One of these meetings, held at 10 Leinster Street, Dublin, on 1 April 1920, for the Annual General Meeting of the City of Dublin Unionists, was attended by Mainie and her mother. William Jellett was away in London 'in opposition to the Home Rule Bill', and the newspaper, reporting on the adoption of the report, quoted the chairman:

> They owed a deep debt of gratitude to their Vice-Chairman, Mr. Jellett, who was over in London doing admirable work. Mr. Jellett had his back against the wall and he would fight for all he was worth to the bitter end. In his (the Chairman's) opinion that was the position every one of them should take up, and then, if they went down it would be with the flag flying.

The Southern Unionists were certainly in a delicate – some would have said a doomed – situation. At an earlier meeting William Jellett had analysed the situation facing the Southern Unionists at the forthcoming Irish Unionist Association's meeting to consider the report of the Irish Convention, and he expressed with some subtlety their position when he outlined their problem as being best resolved if they could win *without* the Ulster members, 'we would have attained our object . . . but he [would] rather win *with* them than *lose* without them.'

The unfortunate reality for Southern Unionists was that the British government took the views of Lord Midleton,[5] who was anxious to achieve a broad settlement under Home Rule, with safeguards for the Unionist and Protestant minority in the twenty-six counties, and not those of the more hard-line Southern Unionists led by Walsh and Jellett. This led to open confrontation; Jellett was one of a group of Unionists to move a vote of censure on the government on 31 October 1921, during the seemingly interminable Treaty negotiations with Sinn Féin. This did rouse some sympathy for the plight of the southern minority, but had no deeper impact. It provoked from Jellett a forthright speech contradicting the Prime Minister, Lloyd George,[6] but at that stage substantial numbers among the Unionist ranks, while appreciating the fact that Southern Unionists appeared to be unprotected and at risk, had already settled for the division of Ireland.

Mainie became directly involved in Unionist politics when she produced designs for the cover of a Southern Unionist pamphlet, intended to be published by the Irish Unionist Alliance in December 1920, and called *Notes from Ireland*. It was to be quarterly and to cost threepence. The illustration on the cover was of three women, one in the centre holding a flowing cloak above the shoulders of the other two – presumably representative of North and South – and with the title beneath the drawing, *Quis Separabit*. Another illustration on the cover shows a design of rose, thistle and shamrock, introducing the idea of England, Scotland and Ireland. The fact that one of the women holds a ship in her arms could refer equally to Belfast or the River Clyde, both at the time substantial centres of world shipbuilding.

To William Jellett, the growing insurrection represented the crumbling of his world, already isolated as a result of the breach between Unionists north and south. The violence was by no means immediately recognised for what it was, and its escalation during these critical years was accompanied by the sometimes bizarre conjunction of horror and normal life. Family letters and the diary which Bay Jellett kept on holiday during the summers of 1919 and 1920 reflect irritation with strikes and disturbances. By contrast, the anniversary of the outbreak of the war and the sinking of the *Leinster* are duly noted in terms which reflect the heroic and sad circumstances surrounding these events. The steady deterioration of the political situation went on through the autumn of 1919, after the family had returned from Donegal. It worsened considerably with the misguided decision of the British government in the spring of 1920, to suppress republicanism by force.[7]

But all of this was far from the minds of the Jellett family as they enjoyed their Scottish holiday with their usual enthusiasm. William Jellett arrived in time to celebrate his Silver Wedding, and to join in the programme of holiday outings which included expeditions to a number of Highland Games. At Ardkinglas Games they all competed in the egg-and-spoon race. There were sports in the village, and a busy round of visits when cricket, rounders and tennis were played. In the evenings they played Hide-and-Seek, Sardines, General Post, and a game called 'Grunts'.

On holiday in Scotland, as in Donegal, Mainie sketched a good deal, and her companion on some of the expeditions was Ralph Cusack,[8] a cousin who was to become a follower of hers in Dublin during the 1920s and 1930s. He was not then a painter in any committed way, though he became so from the mid-1930s. But he enjoyed his cousin's company.

As has been said, Mainie was endeavouring to establish a career for herself out of teaching, design work and the exhibition and sale of paintings. Like other students before her she may have returned to the Metropolitan School of Art for a time; the dates of her travel to and from Scotland suggest this. She was now working on her entry for the 1921 Taylor Prize. The subject set for Class 1, in the figurative paintings section, was the *Metamorphosis of the Children of Lir*. This legend concerns the jealousy of Lir's second wife, who turns her three step-children into swans condemned to remain for nine hundred years on lakes in the centre of Ireland. When they awake they are old, but Christianity has come, and they are reunited and blessed before they die.

Mainie attacked the difficulties head-on, with the kneeling figure of the mother in the centre of the canvas and the main scene of transformation taking place in an arc on the right of the picture. Studies in pencil and watercolour, show no real departure from, or development of, the basic concept. There is a stylistic departure: no longer do we have the soft and rounded textures of Sickert's influence, with his emphasis on chiaroscuro. A faint hint of Art Deco is present, a search for deliberate stylisation of her fairly surreal subject matter is there in the final canvas, the main merit of which lies in her glowing, luminous blue.

Since her return to Dublin the previous autumn, Mainie's belief that she was ready to embark on a professional career as a painter and teacher in the city had faltered. She was increasingly attracted by the sense she had that an explosion of avant-garde styles and attitudes was taking place in post-war Paris, and that more modern painting techniques were being pursued there. She wanted to explore these, rather than settle for the limited achievements that seemed possible within the conventional art scene in Dublin.

The influence at this stage in her career is hard to determine, but seems to derive in part from Jack Yeats[9] by way of his great admirer, Lilian Lucy Davidson[10]. She was a friend of Mainie's, and the two women decided to hold an exhibition of their work.[11] In what must have been one of the gloomiest autumns Ireland had ever experienced, the tone of *The Irish Times* critic's review was very welcome: 'There is a joyful note in Miss Jellett's pictures that appeal to the eye. The artist revels in the seashore and conveys her impressions in lucid style.' *Judith*, a painting of a girl asleep beside a rock, was a portrait of Mainie's friend, Judith Weir (see Pl. 48). There were other portraits, and views in and around Fintra. But the main work was her Taylor Prize picture, *Peace*, which received much praise. 'It is gratifying', the review concludes, 'to find art joyously disporting itself in Dublin in these troublous times, and a visit to this exhibition is a tonic which can be safely recommended to worried citizens.'

Dublin was under constant curfew. Attacks and reprisals were countrywide. Then, in November, came the climactic killing of eleven unarmed officers in the city, on suspicion that they were engaged in intelligence work. Several of them were billeted in Upper Pembroke Street in a house only a couple of doors down from the Jelletts. They heard the shooting, saw the gunmen from the windows of the house and witnessed the police activity which followed. Later that day 'Black and Tans' fired indiscriminately into a football crowd, causing a stampede resulting in twelve deaths. There could be no doubt in anyone's mind that this was war against England.

In the autumn of 1920, independently of Mainie, Evie Hone had gone to Paris and enrolled at the atelier where André Lhote taught. It was already attracting a growing number of students. Mainie was familiar with Lhote's work, having seen some of it in London. She spent the Christmas of 1920 at home and, early in the New Year, she, too, departed for Paris.

CHAPTER SEVEN

'The second revolution': study with André Lhote

WHEN MAINIE WENT to Paris, she entered an artistic environment quite different from anything she had known in Ireland or in England. Since the mid-nineteenth century, France had been the centre of artistic innovation in Europe. French painting had passed through the Realism of Courbet; the Impressionism of Monet and Pissarro; the Neo-Impressionism of Seurat and Signac; the Fauvism of Matisse and Derain. Since Impressionism, however, the tendency in France had been to explore all the possibilities offered by colour to the extent that colour had begun to be used as an element in its own right and no longer as a means of conveying the realistic appearance of the outside world. The Neo-Impressionists had developed a system based on the scientific understanding of the properties of colour. The Nabis, of whom the best known representatives were Pierre Bonnard and Edouard Vuillard, had followed Gauguin in heightening the tones of the colours seen in the natural world. The Fauves had gone further in the same direction, hence their nickname, the 'wild animals'. But at the beginning of the twentieth century all these innovations had been challenged by a much more radical innovation, so radical that nearly a century later it can still be said to mark the division between 'traditional' art which, however outrageous it may have seemed at the time, has achieved general acceptance, and 'modern art'.

Cubism was born from the long, lonely researches of Paul Cézanne who had been closely associated with the Impressionists, especially with Camille Pissarro. He was dissatisfied with the loss of form in Impressionist painting and sought a solid formal construction in his painting that would have the solidity he found in the masters of the past – especially Nicholas Poussin. 'Poussin' he said 'is closer to me than the postman who brings me my letters.' One of his best known sayings was that the painter should learn to see in nature elementary geometrical forms – the cone, the sphere, the cylinder – and use these as the basis for his pictorial composition.

Cézanne's paintings and his ideas had an enormous impact among French painters at the beginning of the century, especially among the Fauves. The small points of colour with which the Neo-Impressionist, or *Pointillistes* had made up their pictures, began to be replaced by cubes, more formal and more related, with their straight lines, to the overall rectangular shape of the picture. Derain, Dufy and Matisse, all prominent among the Fauves, began to experiment with the new style, though Matisse was soon to turn violently against it. But the most radical experiments were carried out by Georges Braque, a young painter who had already completed distinguished work as a Neo-Impressionist. In 1908, his first Cubist paintings were rejected by the jury of the Salon d'Automne, which, together with the freer and more experimental Salon des Indépendants, was the great annual showcase for innovation in painting at the time. One of the members of the Salon d'Automne was Henri Matisse, who opposed Braque. (Another member was the Irish painter, Roderic O'Connor.[1])

As a result, Braque withdrew from any contact with the 'official' avant-garde of the salons and signed a contract with a private gallery owner, Daniel-Henry Kahnweiler,[2] who acquired rights over his entire output and took on the sole responsibility for showing and selling them. Kahnweiler had a similar contract with the Spanish painter,

58. André Lhote, *Buste de Femme*, (1919). Oil on canvas. Musée d'Art Moderne de la Ville de Paris.

59. André Lhote, *Homage to Watteau*, 1919. Oil on canvas, 116 × 89. Musée Petit Palais, Geneva.

Pablo Picasso, whose whole formation and approach to painting was radically different from that of the French innovators. A partnership began between them which is usually seen as marking the beginning of Cubism as a school of painting. However, a number of other painters, including Albert Gleizes,[3] with whom Mainie was soon to be closely associated, were working independently in a similar direction. The whole question of what Cubism is, and who influenced whom, is still highly controversial.[4] What is certain is that the impact of Cézanne launched a new period of radical innovation and exploration of form rather than of colour, whereby the external resemblance of whatever subject was being represented was quickly lost in a maze of shapes which looked to the uninitiated like little more than exercises in geometry. A break was made between the pictorial research of the painters, and the old idea that a painting should look like something other than itself. As we shall soon see, even many of the most radical painters still believed the picture should have a 'subject' drawn from the reality outside itself, but they had abandoned the idea that the form of the painting should correspond to that of the subject.

The succession of new ideas, new developments, new schools, new associations among artists, had created a ferment of change, much of it closely followed by art critics and commentators. And while the First World War had disrupted much of the artistic activity, forcing some painters to enlist, and others to leave France, the immediate aftermath saw a vital and energetic period of revival. It was this atmosphere which drew Mainie to Paris.

At the beginning of February 1921, she went to study with André Lhote. Lhote is often dismissed as a minor follower of the Cubists who reduced Cubism to a system that could easily be taught. This implies that the task of the artist – especially of the twentieth century artist – is to innovate. If we do not see something in the work of art that we have never seen before – something that is original in the artist – then it cannot be very interesting. This view had been decisively and consciously rejected by Lhote after the war. Lhote had a profound love for the history of painting. He saw painting as a craft, to be mastered through long and patient study. Since 1910 he had, so to speak, accompanied the innovators of Cubism by studying them. He wanted to understand and master what he considered permanent in their achievement.

But his first loyalty was to Cézanne and after the war he rejected much of what had been discovered by the Cubists to devote himself to the problems posed by Cézanne – the problem of adapting an essentially representational subject to the demands of the picture plane – the problem of reconciling the 'plastic' properties of nature to the plastic means available to the painter.

The very 'conservatism' that has damaged his reputation among the historians of modern art was one of his strengths as a teacher. The tension between the demands of the subject – the appearance of the external world – and the demands of the painting – paint applied to a flat surface – runs through the whole history of art. But it had been posed with particular acuity by Cézanne and by the early Cubists. For many painters it was resolved by simply abandoning the appearances of the external world. For the painter who loves nature, who loves looking at the world, this was not a step that could or should be taken easily. The tension between nature and pictorial construction that is at the heart of the painting of Cézanne is fully present in the paintings of André Lhote and was the basis of his teaching (Pls. 58–60). It was an excellent standpoint from which to view the achievements of the past. Lhote taught his pupils to see this tension in the whole history of representational painting – in the work of Giotto and Signorelli, and in Rubens, as surely as in the work of his more immediate masters, Gauguin, Cézanne and the Cubists.

His influence is almost immeasurable, but it is hidden by the tendency of art historians to concentrate on the work of the great innovators and to ignore the host of painters, scattered about the world, whose reputation was merely local but who struggled in the inter-war years to affirm principles of pictorial construction derived from Cubism in

61. *Male Torso*, 1921. Oil on canvas, 66 × 49.5. Dublin, private collection.

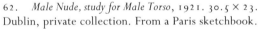

60. André Lhote, *The Fourteenth of July at Avignon*, 1923. Oil on canvas, 148 × 178. Musée des Beaux-Arts, Pau.

62. *Male Nude, study for Male Torso*, 1921. 30.5 × 23. Dublin, private collection. From a Paris sketchbook.

opposition to painting in which the appearances of the external world were predominant. From the standpoint of the period after the Second World War, when innovation became easy and even obligatory, this work seems conservative. In the context of the time and of the countries in which it took place, it was radical and courageous. But, more importantly, it was serious. It posed the problems of construction and rhythmic movement in painting which Mainie Jellett and Evie Hone were to pursue further with Albert Gleizes. These problems remain important even if many artists have abandoned them. Lhote's writings – the *Traité sur le paysage, Traité sur le figure, Les Invariants plastique, Parlons peinture*, remain among the most valuable books on painting written this century.

By 1921, when Mainie arrived in Paris to join Evie Hone, the studio where André Lhote taught had attracted a large number of Scandinavian students and they were the dominant influence. There were Russians and Americans, very few French, and one English girl. It was, in Mainie's view, the most advanced public academy of the time, and 'far the best', and she described Lhote himself as 'one of the outstanding influences in the art world of Paris'.[5]

He had a powerful influence on the development of her style, and was responsible for the second of the three 'major revolutions' in her work. 'He opened our minds to the vast realm of research and riches in the Old Masters and showed us clearly how his teaching and ideals followed logically the living tradition based on permanent truths which are the heritage of all great art, but which seek re-expression in each new cycle of art movements.'

As it had been with Sickert, the encounter with André Lhote provoked a rich response. In a period of tuition lasting less than ten months she filled one sketchbook after another with drawings from the life, studies of Old Masters, landscapes, portrait drawings, and exercises in compositional analysis which represent an electrifying leap forward (Pls. 61–70). Her grounding in anatomy, and the quality of her life drawing and management of colour and composition in larger oil paintings stood her now in good stead for the total reapplication of her talent to the Cubist teaching of Lhote.

63. (*facing page*) *Portrait of a Young Woman*, 1921. Oil on canvas, 51 × 40.5. Dublin, private collection.

64. *Girl in Blue*, 1922. Oil on canvas, 45.5 × 61. Dublin, private collection.

65. *Study for Portrait of Young Woman*, 1921. Pencil on paper, 30.5 × 23. Dublin, private collection. From a Paris sketchbook, dated February 1921.

66. *Study for Girl in Blue*, 1921. Pencil on paper, 25.5 × 29. Dublin, private collection. From a Paris sketchbook.

69. (*facing page, far right*) *Seated Female Nude*, 1921. Oil on canvas, 56.3 × 46.2. Belfast, Ulster Museum.

67. *The Three Graces*, 1921. Oil on board, 40.5 × 28. Dublin, private collection.

68. *Standing Female Nude*, 1922. Oil on canvas, 61.5 × 38.5. Dublin, private collection.

70. *Study for Seated Female Nude*, 1922. Pencil on paper, 31 × 23. Dublin, private collection. From a Paris sketchbook, dated March 1922.

Lhote's teaching programme was straightforward enough. His students worked directly from the model for three hours on Monday morning, making sketches towards a composition which was squared up and enlarged onto canvas the following day. The painting was then worked on until Friday when Lhote carried out a 'correction' of students' work. He did this collectively, so each learned from the others' mistakes. Mainie's work immediately reflected his teaching and the emphasis – though natural and realistic – on simplification of the human figure into cubes, cylinders and cones.

For Mainie, Lhote was of greater interest as teacher and writer than as an artist. 'He is a fine draughtsman,' she told her audience in a lecture given at the Contemporary Picture Galleries in Dublin, in November 1940, 'but his colour sense, to my mind, is not nearly so pronounced as his sense of form, except perhaps in watercolours, where his colour seems much more harmonious and sensitive.'

The austere simplicity of these 1921–2 sketchbook drawings (Pls. 71–9), seems at

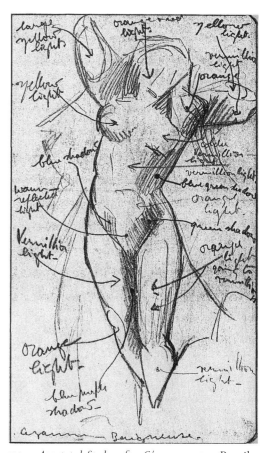

74. *Annotated Study, after Cézanne*, 1921. Pencil on paper, 20.3 × 12. Dublin, private collection. From the first of the artist's Lhote period sketchbooks. Inscribed 'Cezanne Baigneuse'.

76. *Standing Female Nude*, 1921. Pencil on paper, 30.5 × 23. Dublin, private collection. From a Lhote period sketchbook.

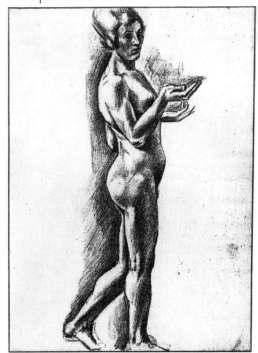

71. (*top left*) *Studies after Signorelli and El Greco*, 1921. Pencil on paper, 27 × 19. Dublin, private collection. From a Lhote period sketchbook.

72. (*above*) *Studies after Signorelli*, 1921. Pencil on paper, 30 × 10. Dublin, private collection. From a Lhote period sketchbook.

73. (*above left*) *Study after El Greco*, 1921. Pencil on paper, 27 × 19. Dublin, private collection. From a Lhote period sketchbook.

75. (*left*) *Study after Renoir*, 1921. Pencil on paper, 23 × 31. Dublin, private collection. From a Lhote period sketchbook. Inscribed 'Renoir Baigneuse'.

77. *Reclining Nude*, 1921. Pencil on paper, 16.8 × 22.7. Dublin, private collection. From a Lhote period sketchbook.

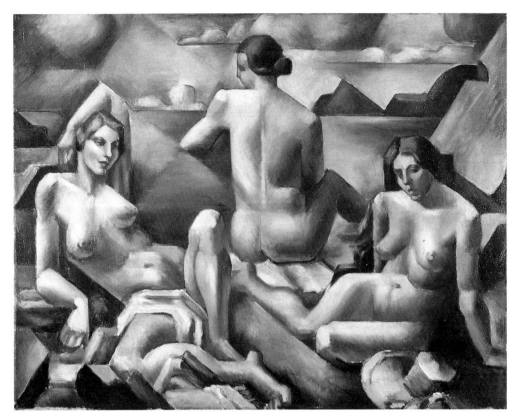

78. *Figures in a Landscape*, 1921. Oil on canvas, (?). Dublin, private collection.

79. *Nude Figures in a Landscape*, 1921. Pencil on paper, 22.8 × 30.5. Dublin, private collection. From a Lhote period sketchbook.

first almost retrograde. One is witnessing a rigorous pursuit of theory in which the inherent, traditional appeal of the subject seems deliberately to have been suppressed. Yet one is also observing a stern rigour of pictorial construction and the development of thought processes which are directly related to the model, to human movement, and to the physical action of the human figure. Through the angularity of the compositional approach adopted there emerges a form of Cubist realism which is fully alive.

That first sketchbook, which represents her baptism into basic Cubist theory, begins with a series of rapid outline drawings from a nude male model, as if the atelier master had organised rapid changes of pose in order to exercise the minds and pencils of his students in a creative 'work-out'. The drawings soon become more deliberate, and there are compositional studies, the first of which is for two seated nudes. This clearly met with a measure of approval. Several sketches were completed of the individual figures, and a canvas survives of this subject.

A series of female nude studies, made harsh and angular by the vigorous cross-hatching, but with a fine sense of volume and movement to them, fill the centre of the sketchbook, and among them are at least three more detailed drawings of the female nude which became oil paintings. At the end of the sketchbook appear several studies for her delicate *Portrait of a Girl*, and a further preparatory composition, a drawing for *The Three Graces*.

The other sketchbooks develop different themes and ideas, and include a number of landscape studies as well as Old Master copies or Cubist developments of these, consistent with Lhote's practice of sending his pupils off to the Louvre to study how great painters in the past solved problems which had not in essence changed over the centuries. Some of the austerity of the classical French approach to teaching, even in a modernist establishment like Lhote's studio, is apparent in this ancient tradition of dismembering great works in order to 'see how the background and figures were combined and developed on mainly geometrical lines and basic forces in the composition'.[6] His interpretation of such works was a revelation, and it emerges in

80. *Garve, Scotland*, 1921. Pencil on paper, 30 × 25. Dublin, private collection. From a Lhote period sketchbook.

81. *Haycocks*, 1921. Watercolour on paper, (?). Dublin private collection. Painted in Scotland, in the summer of 1921.

several of the overall compositional studies where the lines of stress and impact are sketched in, explaining the bold and powerful presence of the relatively few final oil studies and paintings which have survived from this period.

The second sketchbook, dated March 1921, is very much a working document, with few studies which can be directly related to canvases, and a vast number of preliminary and mainly female nude studies. At the end of March, in the third sketchbook, there appear a number of studies, after Poussin, Signorelli and El Greco, dealt with in pursuit of the same rhythmic and geometric end. There are also landscape studies, including some of Garve, in the Scottish Highlands, and a series at the end of the sketchbook, in black wash. These are of a single, reclining female nude, later the subject of one of the artist's rare etchings, and of a version of Susannah and the Elders. But the most interesting study, quite slight, is of a seated girl, a composition which became one of the artist's most important oils of this period (see Pls. 64, 66).

The fourth sketchbook has portrait studies of an elderly woman, followed by a long series of preparatory drawings of a seated female nude holding a pitcher. A number of further portrait studies follow, and other nudes, some of which became oils.

In the only dated sketchbook from the following year (1922) are a number of circus and horse studies, as well as studies for the seated nude. Anatomy, landscape, and colour, are explored further in a smaller sketchbook; and then, in what seems to be the final sketchbook, there are a number of studies which suggest that it had a special status for the artist. Into it she has accumulated a number of visual ideas which are contained in less refined forms in the larger books. It repeats Susannah and the Elders, in a different version, the reclining nude which became an etching, further Old Master studies after Perugino and Signorelli, a number of studies of a male nude violinist, the expression of certain compositional ideas, such as 'parallelism', 'convergence' and 'divergence', and a substantial series of female nude drawings, several of which became finished oils. They are all essentially her working sketchbooks, beside her in the Academy life room, for preliminary studies during the three-hour sessions with the life model, as aids to the main drawing on which she was working. They are also her diary, a close and intimate record of her thoughts and ideas, her tentative proposals about the direction she intends to take, together with bold and impressive intellectual and creative assaults on the physical matter which we see in its final form in the canvases from those years. By 1922, she had already moved on to her first lessons with Albert Gleizes.

The André Lhote period included intense periods of study. But neither Mainie nor Evie were obsessive about this to the exclusion of entertainment and friendships. The cosmopolitan atmosphere in Paris was a harmonious one for the two young Irish painters. Mainie kept up her music, attended concerts and theatre, and read French literature avidly. Works by Maurice Maeterlinck, Guillaume Apollinaire and Jean Jaurès, in the small Librairie Stock 'yellowback' editions, survive in her library from that time, as do numerous art books, among them the first tentative examinations of the modern trends in which she was so intensely involved.

In the summer of 1921 Mainie went on holiday with her family again to Scotland, but this time much further north, to the village of Plockton, in Rossshire. There she painted mainly in watercolour, producing a number of landscapes in the Lhote manner, the angular, incipient Cubism giving great impact to the soft Scottish summer light on haycocks and blue mountains, on harvest scenes and the sweep of lake water (Pls. 80–1). It was a holiday they all loved; but it was overshadowed by political events. In the spring elections, in the six Northern Ireland counties, the Unionists secured forty of the fifty-two seats and the future 'State' went ahead with its inauguration; the Viceroy opened the Northern Ireland Parliament at Stormont on 7 June, and on 22 June King George V and Queen Mary visited Belfast. The Monarch urged harmony and goodwill on all Irish men and women, and in the south a truce was signed which at last brought all hostilities between Republican forces and the British Army to an end.

Though the relief in the south was intense, the Jellett's Scottish holiday began under the shadow of de Valera's rejection of Lloyd George's offer of dominion status within the British Empire. For Southern Unionists the isolation, which they had long seen as inevitable, had become manifest. It so happened that Lloyd George was in Scotland that summer, on holiday, and staying not far from the Jelletts. Mainie's father went to see him, and put forcefully the case for the minority. He came back dejected from the encounter. It was clear to him that Lloyd George had already set in train a process which would lead to an independence in which those of Jellett's persuasion would have to fend for themselves, in an increasingly unprotected environment.

The Treaty negotiations went on through the summer and autumn of 1921 by which time Mainie had returned to Paris. In a galaxy of critical dates, which punctuate Irish memory and stir Irish patriotism, one stands out as especially significant: 6 December, when the parties to the Treaty actually put their names to the final document. To Mainie the day was of historic importance for a quite different reason: on that Tuesday she had her first lesson with Albert Gleizes. It cost her 30 francs. She recorded in the back of her address book the payment to him of 240 francs for eight lessons, on Tuesdays and Fridays, to the end of that month. She was to spend her second Christmas away from home. She was about to enter into the third and final 'revolution' in her art.

WHY MAINIE JELLETT should have chosen Gleizes as her teacher remains something of a mystery. She herself has said that she wanted to go further in the direction of 'extreme Cubism', a term which would have had a very precise meaning in the Paris of 1922: it would have referred to the painters grouped at the time round Léonce Rosenberg's Galerie de l'Effort Moderne.[1]

The Galerie de l'Effort Moderne showed paintings by a number of artists whose reputation had been established before the war, including Juan Gris, Fernand Léger, Gino Severini, Jean Metzinger and Albert Gleizes. The Dutch painter, Piet Mondrian, who had returned to Paris in 1919, and the 'Purists', Amédée Ozenfant and Charles-Edouard Jeanneret, soon to be better known as the architect Le Corbusier, also joined. In 1918, Ozenfant and Jeanneret had published a book called *Après le Cubisme* which attacked what they saw as the intellectual and emotional confusion of the early Cubists and called for a development into an austere, simple, rational painting, in line with the principles Le Corbusier was to develop for architecture. Gris, Metzinger and Severini meanwhile had been developing in a similar direction. While there were important differences between them, all these painters were emphasising the virtues of balance and harmony and, perhaps most importantly, all were insisting on the essential flatness of the picture plane – painting was to be true to its nature as an essentially two-dimensional art. It is this that most immediately distinguishes them from the Cubism of Lhote – and of Mainie while she was working with Lhote – who was still insisting on the careful study of nature in its three dimensions, on volume as an essential characteristic in painting.

Rosenberg was an idealist, enthusiastically committed to the new, rational, classical painting that had replaced the dynamism and excitement of the pre-war period. But, despite his support for Mondrian, this new painting was not generally abstract. Ozenfant and Jeanneret in particular insisted on maintaining a representational base, albeit the emotionally neutral one of the still life. Gris had developed the opposite view, that the starting point for the painting should be a pure, non-representational, geometrically based harmony, but it would still arrive at a recognisable subject. The general mood in Paris was opposed to purely non-representational painting. Léger had been painting dynamic, violent, near-abstract canvases after his return from the war but in the actual context of the time, these had a *passéiste* character – they looked back to the pre-war mood. Rosenberg told Léger that he had taken him on, not because he liked his current work, but because he thought it showed promise for the future, and about 1921 Léger also began to settle into the new classicism. Picasso, who was attached to Rosenberg's brother, Paul, had for some time been intrigued by the possibilities of a straightforward representational style. Like Severini, he was painting fully illusionist paintings alongside his more Cubist work, which, in line with the current trend, had become flat and rational even if embellished with Picasso-style jokes. Mondrian's painting, despite Rosenberg's support, made little impact until a major De Stijl exhibition held at the Galerie de l'Effort Moderne in 1923 but, even then, abstract art was felt to be mainly useful as an element in architecture. Without a subject, even if the subject was of no importance in itself, painting risked being merely 'ornamental', as Ozenfant and

82. Albert Gleizes, *Portrait of Mrs Walter Fleisher*, 1921. Lithograph, 41 × 30.5.

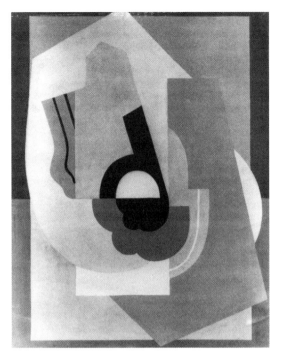

83. Albert Gleizes, *Composition*, 1921. Tempera on panel, 90 × 71, The Tate Gallery, London.

84. Albert Gleizes, *Landscape with Houses*, 1923. Oil on canvas, 21 × 26. Dublin, National Gallery of Ireland.

Jeanneret put it. The 'abstract expressionism' of Kandinsky was unthinkable in the Paris of the early 1920s; the experiments of the Russians were virtually unknown and the Dutch De Stijl was seen as purely decorative. Among French painters only Auguste Herbin, Georges Valmier, Albert Gleizes and perhaps Jacques Villon could be called 'abstract' painters.

Albert Gleizes was well known as one of the pioneers of Cubism. The paintings of Gleizes, Metzinger, Le Fauconnier, Delaunay and Léger had created a sensation at the Salon des Indépendants in 1911, comparable to the sensation created by Stravinsky's *Rite of Spring* performed in Paris two years later. This was before the general public became aware of Picasso and Braque, whose work was known only to a small circle of private collectors. Although he is often dismissed as a minor follower of Picasso and Braque, Gleizes claimed that it was only in the autumn of 1911, after his own reputation as a Cubist was securely established, that he first saw their work.[2] He always maintained a rather distrustful attitude towards them. The term 'Epic Cubism' has been used to distinguish Gleizes' ambitious painting, with its intense social and philosophical implications, from the more intimate and personal Cubism of Picasso and Braque.[3]

Together with Jean Metzinger – who was influenced by the earlier paintings of Picasso and Braque – Gleizes published the first major explanation and defence of Cubism – *Du Cubisme* – in 1912.[4] He spent most of the war period in New York where he was closely associated with Marcel Duchamp and Francis Picabia. The studio at Puteaux where he worked with Mainie Jellett and Evie Hone had been lent to him on his return to Paris by Raymond Duchamp-Villon, brother of Jacques and of Marcel Duchamp. Before he left for New York he had painted his first fully non-representational painting, the *Composition* of 1915. It was derived from his very radical portrait of the composer Florent Schmitt, with whom he shared a *caserne* at Toul at the time. He did not immediately follow the line of research it had opened up. It was in New York, two years later, that he discovered the belief in God that was to play such an important part in his subsequent thinking, though it was not until 1942 that he finally became a practising Roman Catholic. Despite his initial enthusiasm for New York, which resulted in a marvellous series of Cubist impressions of the city,[5] he became disillusioned and began to question the virtues of city life and industrialisation – a questioning which adds to the difficulties of situating him in the broad stream of modernism.

Gleizes returned to Paris in 1919 and in 1920 he attempted a synthesis of the Cubist experience up to that point in his *Du Cubisme et les moyens de le comprendre*.[6] If Mainie had been attracted by his ideas prior to meeting him it is probably here that she found them; that she attached importance to the book is suggested by the fact that a summary was found among papers of her pupil, Hélène de St Pierre.[7]

In many respects, *Du Cubisme et les moyens de le comprendre* seems typical of the mood in Paris at the time. Gleizes was deeply impressed by what had been achieved during his absence. He said later that his own principles of 'translation' and 'rotation', which were to be the basis of his work with Jellett and Hone, had been pioneered in the wartime paintings of Metzinger and Gris.[8] His treatment of form and colour was drastically simplified soon after his return to Paris (Pls. 82–4). *Du Cubisme et les moyens de le comprendre* welcomes the alliance between painting and architecture, and the search for solid, permanent principles in painting; it looks to the development of an 'impersonal' art in which the names of individual painters would cease to matter; and it argues that with the simplification of colours and forms it would be possible to copy paintings in large numbers, which would reduce the price and undermine the hegemony of the individual, 'bourgeois' collectors. Although this last idea seems to be a very reasonable extension of the contemporary fashion for the mass-produced object, it greatly alarmed the gallery owner, Rosenberg, who refused to allow Léger to participate in Gleizes' schemes.[9]

However, *Du Cubisme et les moyens de le comprendre* is also a criticism of contemporary

85. Albert Gleizes, *Painting*, 1923. Oil on canvas, 105 × 75. Dublin, National Gallery of Ireland.

86. Albert Gleizes, *Octagonal Composition*, c. 1922. Oil on canvas, 89.3 × 69.5. Whereabouts Unknown.

trends in painting, and expresses a profound dissatisfaction with what had been achieved by the Cubists. Gleizes insists that there were two currents in Cubism, one represented by Picasso and Braque, the other by the painters who had shown at the 1911 Salon des Indépendants – himself, Léger, Le Fauconnier, Delaunay and Metzinger. This latter group were soon to be joined by Gris, Marcoussis, Villon, Duchamp, Picabia, Survage, Ferat and Herbin (though Gleizes was soon to break dramatically with Picabia and oppose the Dada movement). Lhote he mentions together with Derain and de La Fresnaye as a lesser, more undecided contributor. He is highly critical of the contribution of Braque and Picasso. He recognises that they had broken up the old laws of the representational image; but they had merely broken them up – they had not challenged them fundamentally. They still used traditional chiaroscuro light effects and deprived themselves of all the means offered by colour. They rearranged the canvas according to their arbitrary taste, not according to new principles of construction (this is perhaps more true of Picasso than of Braque): 'the internal life' of the painting 'was not changed and the agitation was still only a surface appearance'. He had made similar criticisms shortly after he first saw Picasso and Braque's work in 1911.

The other school had been motivated by a desire to recover permanent principles for the construction of the painting and, in the first instance, had looked to classicism and the reassertion of volume, hence the emphasis on the cube. This had not satisfied them for very long and soon they had flattened the cubes out. The forms interpenetrated each other on the flat surface. But they did not know how to handle the new means they were discovering and fell into the same arbitrariness and confusion as Picasso and Braque. Insistence on individualism and a refusal to submit to laws were still preventing them from developing what was necessary: 'a close, hierarchically based collaboration in the building up of the impersonal work of art following laws that are well-defined and nonetheless very simple'.[10]

The use of simple forms such as squares and cylinders was not enough. This was just a matter of changing the subject. Nor was it enough to portray dynamic or 'modern' subjects: 'A picture is a manifestation that is silent and unmoving. The movement to which it gives rise exists only in the mind of the spectator, but not the slightest change can occur on the flat surface'.[11]

Nonetheless, Gleizes is insisting on movement and life: 'Painting is the art of bringing a flat surface to life'(Pls. 85–6).[12] This movement is sharply distinguished from the superficial 'agitation' he criticises in Picasso's early work, or the 'dynamism' of Léger and the pre-war Italian Futurists. But it also distinguishes him from the 'Purists' (Ozenfant and Jeanneret) whose work was essentially static, based on harmony and balance. Harmony and balance are necessary but not sufficient. The tendency of the Effort Moderne painters, and also of Picasso, was to look back to Classicism, evoking the names of Poussin, Chardin, Ingres and David. For Gleizes, the 'classical' period of Cubism had occurred in 1910 and was already over. He too was looking back, but not to Greece and Rome. He looks back to the ninth century. The popular, impersonal art he aimed for was an early medieval ideal, not a classical one.

The Effort Moderne painters were fond of comparing a painting to a well-conceived machine. Gleizes compares it to a flower. Like a flower it appeals immediately to the eye. It is attractive. But, after this initial attraction, the mind or spirit ('*l'esprit*') becomes engrossed in its structure. It is in the spirit, the consciousness of the spectator, that the painting acquires its life and movement. It becomes, to use Gleizes' later term, a 'support for contemplation'. At the time of *Du Cubisme et les moyens de le comprendre*, Gleizes was arguing that simple laws had to be found for the organisation of this movement. But he was as yet unable to formulate them beyond the assertion that there must be a centre, that the painting must move round an axis. He was to begin to formulate these laws more clearly in his work with Mainie Jellett and Evie Hone (Pls. 87–8).

58

87. Albert Gleizes, *Composition, Serrières*, 1923. Oil on canvas. 200 × 125. (Sale: Parke Bernet 9 April 1969.)

88. Albert Gleizes, *Composition*, 1923. Sériegraphe, 42.5 × 35.5. Dublin, private collection.

Did Mainie and Evie go to Gleizes thinking that he would simply initiate them into the secrets of the 'extreme Cubists' at the Galerie de l'Effort Moderne? If so, they could have been disappointed since Gleizes was far from being a typical Effort Moderne painter; indeed, there was no such being, and the *effort* itself became dissipated. Certainly, there is no evidence of disappointment in the ten years the two Irish women spent closely engaged in researches with Gleizes. Rosenberg's 'extreme Cubists' were nearly all dispersed by the middle of the decade. Gris was dead, Jeanneret was almost wholly engrossed in architecture, Ozenfant changed his style completely, Severini's Cubist side finally gave way to his figurative side, and Léger and Metzinger both developed further in the direction of a fully representational style, albeit strongly disciplined by their Cubist experience. Of the French painters prominent in the early 1920s only Herbin, Georges Valmier and Gleizes continued their researches into the possibilities of non-representational painting. Surrealism had replaced Purism as the centre of avant-garde fashion. Rosenberg, whose relations with Gleizes had been stormy

89. Albert Gleizes, at the time of meeting Mainie and Evie.

in the early 1920s, was to write to him in 1934 to say that although Gleizes had seemed to start more slowly than the other painters, he had been able to follow his line of development more consistently, and that, while Braque, Picasso, Léger, Metzinger were collapsing into 'Cubisto-Surrealism', Gleizes' painting was becoming 'ever more complete and radiant.'[13]

If Mainie chose Gleizes by chance (perhaps because he was the 'extreme Cubist' closest to Lhote) it was a happy chance since it enabled her to embark on a long voyage of discovery which would not have been possible with any other painter.[14] It seems much more likely that she recognised in *Du Cubisme et les moyens de le comprendre* qualities that she did not find in any of the other painters – a rigour that refused all notions of 'self-expression' and was prepared to go the full lengths of abandoning the subject altogether; but also a tenderness, an insistence that the painting should correspond to the reality of human nature, not to the perfection of the machine. Perhaps, too, the reference to the ninth century struck a chord, given her admiration for early Christian Irish art. This is confirmed by Anne Dangar,[15] a later pupil of Gleizes and friend of Mainie's, who says that Mainie and Evie had seen Gleizes' most recent paintings prior to meeting him, and that 'they had a construction which reminded them of the Irish books of the seventh century in the University of Dublin'.[16] Mainie already knew of a non-representational art much more advanced than anything the twentieth century had yet produced. And though Gleizes' non-representational paintings of 1921–2 are, by his own admission, crude and primitive,[17] it was nevertheless with him that Mainie was able to develop a painting comparable in its intellectual complexity and human, spiritual, depth to the masterpieces of Celtic art.

CHAPTER NINE

'Final revolution': back to the beginning

IT WAS A strange encounter. Two girls, in their twenties, standing on the doorstep of Gleizes' apartment on the Boulevard Lannes, close to the Bois de Boulogne, insisting that he teach them his method; and Albert Gleizes, then an established Cubist painter, just forty, wondering, did he have a method, was it teachable? He refused. They insisted. Their argument was simple: 'It is with you we should like to work now. What you are doing corresponds exactly to what we are striving after.'[1]

Years later he described their gentle tones and their tenacity and said that it terrified him. He didn't teach; he didn't know how to go about it, or what to tell them. He was in confusion. He said to them: 'I already have all the problems in the world trying to sort myself out personally, how do you want me to help you?'[2] He made every excuse possible. When they told him they were pupils of André Lhote he made a last desperate effort to invoke his friendship with the other painter as a barrier to taking his pupils from him. But they replied: 'We are quite free to choose any master we like.'[3]

To call what followed 'lessons', in any sense comparable to what they had gone through before, would be misleading. Mainie herself put it simply enough: 'I went right back to the beginning with him, and was put to the severest type of exercise in pure form and colour, evolved on a certain system of composition. I now felt I had come to essentials . . .'[4] Gleizes, for all his experience as a major figure among the Cubists painting ten years earlier was also at a starting point. What had been achieved over that period he now regarded as slight. The works which had so shocked Paris when shown 'on the line' at the Salons des Indépendants during those years immediately before the war, he now described as *timides*. They had 'conformed perfectly to tradition',[5] in his view (which perhaps seems to us eccentric, in the light of what he actually achieved). More than anything else, he felt, the earliest work had served as a recall to order, bringing before people's eyes the essential principles of *classical* art based on volume and structure, in opposition to the Impressionists and Fauves who had underplayed structure for the sake of the sensual pleasure of colour.

But even the Cubist research into structure was undertaken in an uncertain and unresolved fashion. There had been the valuable re-examination of the concept of 'unity of perspective'. Upon this was focused much of the derision and controversy they provoked. Yet Gleizes was sceptical about how far this had gone and how deeply it had been understood. The scandals surrounding the various manifestations of Cubism in its first ten years had derived mainly from the fact that the *means* were noted without any grasp of the purpose, a usual handicap for the artist determined to break new ground and one which promotes excessive critical emphasis upon appearances and upon the more obvious visual characteristics of style. *La pluralité des points perspectifs* became an easy focus for argument and controversy, obscuring the fact that it was a very preliminary stage of a longer research – the research after mobility in painting, a mobility which he saw as essential to life. 'In reality, this apparent retrogression (to a classical concern with volume) was merely the most simple and most direct means of upsetting an immutability of figurative representation which had become intolerable.'

But in 1921 he was addressing a far chillier option for the painter: that of pure

90. Photograph of M. and Mme Gleizes.

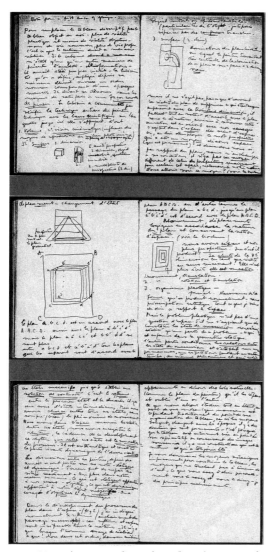

91. Mainie's notes from her first lesson with Gleizes.

abstraction. And he was addressing it from within the framework of Cubism's logic as he understood it. For almost two years Gleizes had been working more or less exclusively on abstract theory and practice, and though in his mind there was a clear conviction that the elimination of the subject from his paintings would lead to pictorial expansion, the technical means for this, the structure of laws that would have to be observed, eluded him. 'The technical resources at my disposal, even though they appeared to me indisputable, were of the slenderest. What I had gained in certitude had brought a not less certain impoverishment due to the voluntary renunciation of all aesthetic tricks.' Gleizes' processes appeared logical to him, yet he found it quite impossible to define them. Not surprisingly, he was extremely reluctant to take on pupils, or to give lessons. Who would teach whom? And what would they teach? 'How was I going to do it? What was I going to tell them, and, above all, what help was I going to give them?'[6]

The intensity of Mainie and Evie's expectation had a disturbing effect on Gleizes. There was a totality in their demand upon him to put logic and laws upon non-representational art. They already accepted the justification for 'painting-without-subject'; they wanted to know how, and on what foundation to build.

Mainie's notes on her first lesson with Gleizes have survived (Pl. 91), together with sketches which illustrate the basic concepts of movement within the two-dimensional frame of the canvas. She carried with her at that time her anatomy notebook from Westminster School days, its first quarter filled with closely written details of the human form which was now to be abandoned. In it she wrote:

Replace the descriptive painting with the painting as an object in itself . . . more objective reality – less life attached to reminiscence, more of its own life. That is what Cubism as I understand it must achieve. If Cubism was merely a means of presenting anecdotes – information – it would have been more or less pointless. Cubism as it has been defined, explained since its birth, must open the way for a new order, correspond to the needs of a new age.

Their first lesson, on that historic day consisted of a general statement, or restatement by Gleizes, of the continuing relevance of Cubism, followed by a practical demonstration which began with two tiny drawings. He then told them, if one can accurately reconstruct the sequence of the lesson from Mainie's notes, written in rapid script and in her far from perfect French, to suspend for a moment what had been achieved and consider an idea that was new to them all: that of the object and spectator put into movement in the context of a two dimensional surface. The three dimensional scene presented by the perspective mechanism was essentially static. Not only did it show a moment frozen in time but it had to be constructed around the fixed centre provided by the vanishing point. Of course all the great masters were able to guide the eye round their paintings from one form or colour to the next. But this movement round the painting was in essential conflict with the immobile nature of the subjects represented and with the contrary movement into the painting provided by the perspective. With the new principles the movement round the surface of the painting was to be liberated. It was not a successive movement in time such as we see in the cinema, or in the 'kinetic' art that can be dated back to this period and to the experiments of Marcel Duchamp and Naum Gabo. Through the principles of translation and rotation it was to be the internal life of the spectator that was to be engaged, through his ability to see the logical progression of colours and forms within the painting. 'Objet immobile, spectateur immobile' was to become 'objet mobile, spectateur mobile'.

Gleizes then went on to demonstrate the *élimination* of perspective by constructing a further pair of drawings, one showing the diminution of scale within the laws of classical perspective and the other employing the same idea of planes, one behind the other, on the canvas, but *without* that perspective. Depth was denied. The logical derivation then became a series of planes which were theoretically common with the surface of the

62

canvas and could be moved about by the artist as the objective material for his work of art. The problem then confronting him was a logic for that movement. According to what laws would the simple series of shapes, themselves, basically an echo of the shape of the canvas itself, become living, organic, rhythmic components?

There were two ways in which this problem could be answered: 'translation' was the first, involving the horizontal and vertical movement of variously sized rectangles parallel to the shape of the canvas. The movement allowed by these planes was very limited. Their role was rather to affirm the basic stability of the painting, its proportion and equilibrium. In the second stage, 'rotation', the rectangles were tilted to the right or to the left: the eye begins to experience the possibility of an essentially circular movement. It is through the juxtaposition of the translation and rotation that the painting begins to realise its rhythm which replaces the vanishing point of the perspective mechanism as the source of its unity. Whether Gleizes used the practical demonstration or not, Mainie certainly did later. Hélène de St Pierre records that she took a simple office spike and put on it a series of rectangles which were then turned on the axis of the spike to show movement in composition.[7] Gleizes had effectively brought the compositional requirements in abstract painting – which he generally referred to as *peintures sans sujet* – to two basic concepts of movement. The movement from large to small, from outside to inside, from side to side – translation; and the circular movement around an axis – rotation.

The real lessons then began with the presentation of three approaches to painting: first the study of volume; then, what Gleizes called *vision cinématique*; and finally *surface*.

Vision cinématique refers to movement as it is perceived in the succession of events, one thing after the other, the field in which representational painting was being challenged by the 'moving picture'. Gleizes was later to say:

> I remember our painters' agony when we compared our frozen images, the course of whose life was stopped, with the bustling and lively images which followed one another on the cinema screen. That was one of the factors that determined this re-evaluation of the current classical notion of form, since it is certainly in those terms that we must define that work that is still unfinished in the present day and which marked my generation so profoundly.[8]

The crude first reaction of some of the Cubists and, much more so, the Italian Futurists to the challenge of capturing the reality of movement had been to show successive stages of the movement of a figure simultaneously on the canvas. The well-known Cubist device of walking round the subject to portray it from different angles is based on a similar idea. In this case, the subject is broken up into component parts seen from different angles and rearranged in the picture. But in Gleizes' view, this did little more than pose the problem of mobility. Its strength lay not in the *vision cinématique* but in the freedom the painters were claiming to rearrange the subject according to needs that they did not initially fully understand. Those needs were imposed by the very surface with which they were working and with which the new form they were creating had to comply. Thus, a research which had begun with asserting the importance of volume (hence the derisive term 'Cubism') was to end by eliminating it altogether.

There is almost an atmosphere of disdain in the tiny cube with which Mainie Jellett shows the first approach to painting – the assertion of volume, that corresponds to the stage of the development of Cubism that was still being taught by André Lhote. Accompanying it is the comment – 'Perspective unity, 3 dimensions, immobile object, immobile spectator.' It is followed by a drawing of that same set of frames or facets, but fragmented in the manner of what Gleizes saw as the second phase of Cubism – when the artist, weary of the immobility of the subject seen from one fixed point of view, claimed the right to see it from different angles, and walked round it. This is the *vision cinématique*, an attempt to imitate the mobility of the camera. Accompanying it is the

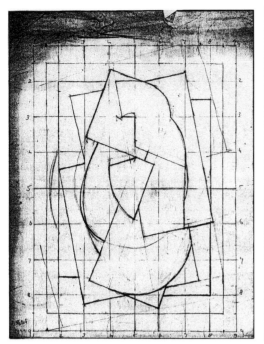
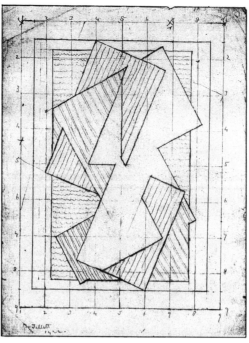
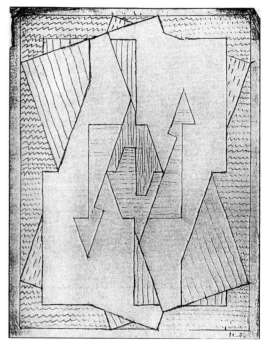

All the above works are on sheets 26.5 × 20 cm

remark: 'multiple perspective (3 dimensions), object in movement or spectator in movement'. We pass then to the third stage – *surface* – in which the third dimension, all trace of perspective whether single or multiple, has been suppressed. The painter no longer attempts to imitate the mobility of the cinema either by trying to show his own mobility in walking round the subject and seeing it from different angles, or in trying to show a subject that is itself moving. He accepts the two dimensional and essentially static nature of the picture plane, but he creates a different kind of movement, the movement of the eye from one thing to the other, established by the most elementary means available to the painter, the interaction of plane surfaces, line and colour.

These three 'stages' of Cubism (much simpler, clearer and more comprehensive than the system of 'analytical' and 'synthetic' Cubism which is so often used by historians) is

64

92.   *Study for Abstract Composition*, 1922. Pencil on paper, 22.9 × 16.5. Dublin, private collection.

93.   *Study for Abstract Composition*, 1922. Pencil on paper, 22.8 × 16.4. Dublin, private collection.

94.   *Study for Abstract Composition*, 1922. Pencil on paper, 25.6 × 19.2. Dublin, private collection.

95.   *Study for Abstract Composition*, June 1922. Pencil on paper, 20.5 × 15.2. Dublin, private collection.

96.   *Study for Abstract Composition*, August 1922. Pencil on paper, 22.2 × 17.8. Dublin, private collection.

97.   *Study for Abstract Composition*, August 1922. Pencil on paper, 22.3 × 17.9. Dublin, private collection.

the basis of Gleizes' book, *Kubismus*.[9] The three stages are clearly shown in a wide selection of illustrations from the work of himself, Metzinger, Picasso, Braque, Léger, Gris, Valmier, Herbin and many others, including Jellett and Hone, and two other pupils of Gleizes who were to join them shortly, Robert Pouyaud,[10] and a Polish painter, Yanaga Posnansky.[11] Jellett, Hone, Pouyaud and Posnansky are included as representatives of this 'third stage' Cubism, with paintings that are all entirely abstract, but paintings by Léger, Picasso and Marcelle Cahn, which have a clearly stated representational subject, are also included as 'third stage' Cubist paintings. The dividing line is not abstraction as such but faithfulness to the flat surface. The question of abstraction will be looked at in more detail in the next chapter but it is important to note here that Gleizes never made a fetish of abstraction. He saw it as a means to an end, not as an end in itself.

And so on 6 December 1921, in the early afternoon, Mainie Jellett and Evie Hone came for their first lesson, and sat down to watch Gleizes working with large sheets of paper on stretchers and drawing with charcoal, as he put order upon his riotous thoughts. Twice a week they would struggle with the theoretical problem of filling space with life and movement according to unwritten laws. As they went along they would write the laws. These were oracular encounters. From them derived vision and understanding. 'Usually we did not leave the studio', Gleizes recalled, 'until about seven o'clock. We would all be tired out and though my pupils were gracious about it the first sittings did not give me confidence in myself. Their attention was so keen that I felt my responsibility all the more.'[12]

They would assure him that they understood. He would know that they could not because he did not understand himself. He was moving towards a way of dividing the surface of the painting and putting it into movement without organically changing its nature, without creating the illusion of a third dimension. For this to be possible, a system of deriving the forms and colours of the painting from the inherent qualities of the surface itself had to be devised. To begin with, the only shape that was *inherent* was that of the canvas itself, the rectangle. But by moving the rectangle to the left or right, or up and down, and perhaps more importantly by oscillating it around its own axis, two distinct and basic concepts emerged – *translation* and *rotation*. 'I had deduced,' Gleizes says, 'the theory from the practice instead of doing the contrary as has been imagined by so many critics.'[13]

He remained grateful for the rest of his life to his two Irish pupils who had exacted from him the most powerful lesson any teacher gives, which is self-knowledge. 'One has first of all to know oneself, it was this knowledge which I had just acquired', he said, and he admitted that this may not have been possible without their calm yet relentless insistence.[14]

We have from this period a wealth of detail in the form of drawings which simply explore the theory of movement within the framework of a two-dimensional surface (Pls. 92–7). The three of them did not confine their efforts to the rectangle. As a theoretical inevitability prescribed by academic painting over the centuries, they accepted that their theories would have to work for the oval, the round, the triangular canvas and for other even odder shapes which seem at times to push them towards complex geometric exploration for its own sake. But the effort has a deeper purpose than mathematical resolution. And though these more eccentric tests were vital in stretching their evolving theories to the fullest extent, they recognised the central inescapability of the rectangle, and devoted their major attention to it.

Mainie and Evie remained in Paris, both working at André Lhote's *and* with Gleizes, through the winter and into the spring of the following year. They lived at Rue Vavin, at the Hotel de Blois, which Evie called 'beloved' in comparison with other lodgings to which she moved in the summer of 1922. In March 1921 Sarah Purser wrote a long letter to Mainie, full of news about art events in Dublin, and particularly the Taylor Prize and

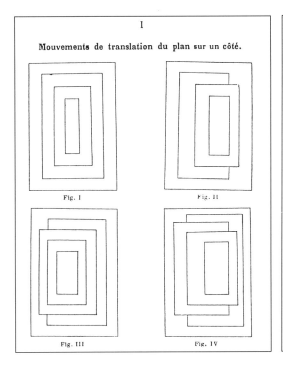

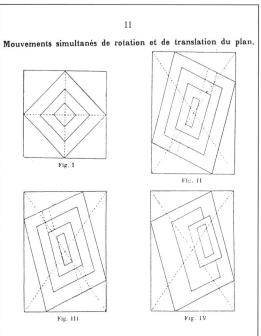

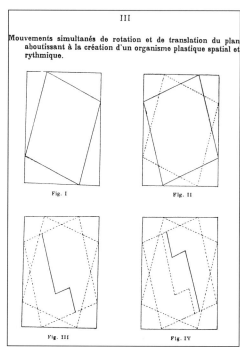

I

Mouvements de translation du plan sur un côté.

Fig. I   Fig. II

Fig. III   Fig. IV

II

Mouvements simultanés de rotation et de translation du plan.

Fig. I   Fig. II

Fig. III   Fig. IV

III

Mouvements simultanés de rotation et de translation du plan aboutissant à la création d'un organisme plastique spatial et rythmique.

Fig. I   Fig. II

Fig. III   Fig. IV

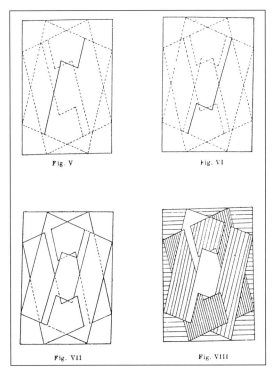

Fig. V   Fig. VI

Fig. VII   Fig. VIII

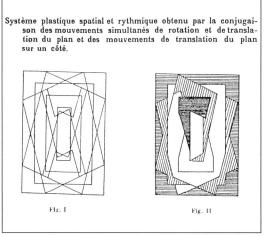

Système plastique spatial et rythmique obtenu par la conjugaison des mouvements simultanés de rotation et de translation du plan et des mouvements de translation du plan sur un côté.

Fig. I   Fig. II

98. Diagrams for translation and rotation from *La Peinture et ses lois*.

difficulties among the judges. Langton Douglas 'as usual disappointed at the last moment'.[15] Sarah Purser had been asked to join the panel, but because she had seen Mainie's entries – 'Yours were the only ones had the least modernness about them' – she declined. Thomas Bodkin,[16] who was to play a modest but important part in the controversies which would affect art in Ireland through the next two decades, was chosen instead. Bodkin was then thirty-five. He had already run foul of Sarah Purser through what was perhaps excessive praise of her stained-glass rival, Harry Clarke. (He later remarked that 'Miss Purser and her pals were already referring to him as Clarke's ''press agent'''.)[17]

In March 1922, Mainie returned to Dublin, while Evie went to London. Albert

66

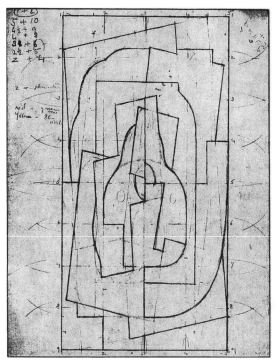

99. *Study for Abstract Composition*, 1922. Pencil on paper, 25.3 × 12.6. Dublin, private collection.

100. *Study for Abstract Composition*, 1922. Pencil on paper, 19.5 × 13.9. Dublin, private collection.

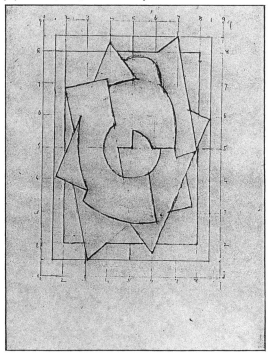

Gleizes immediately began working on *La Peinture et ses lois*. It was during those months of intense collaboration, spending many hours together each week and exhausting themselves on that simple but essential problem of abstract art – 'How can a flat surface come alive?' – that Gleizes, Mainie Jellett and Evie Hone worked out the basis for their future working methods, and gave to Gleizes the main motivation for his book, which though much developed in his later thinking, was to be the basis of all his subsequent work. He wrote in August 1948: 'I owe it to Mainie Jellett and Evie Hone, and I am not likely, even now, to forget my gratitude to them.'[18] The results of their studies became the diagrams used for *La Peinture et ses lois* (Pl. 98). The drawings which were recorded by Mainie after her first lesson were developed, and many survive (Pls. 99–101), together with the paintings developed from them (Pl. 102). And in June, when Evie returned to Paris on her own she was able to report: 'I went out to Gleizes yesterday getting there at 1 I never arrived back till after 7 o'c he was most excited over his book he began writing it just after we left and he says he cant sleep at all at night it is so enthralling.'[19] Evie was not as enthusiastic, and found some difficulty in understanding the flood of ideas he poured out to her. On her return she found there was another pupil, Colette Allendy.[20] Colette Allendy's work did not meet with Gleizes' approval at all. 'Colette hadnt done it right and he was as tactless as usual but she got it alright in the end.'[21] Her mistakes may have resulted from the fact that Gleizes, who previously had worked with them through every stage was far too excited about his writing. 'He retired behind a barrier of pictures and wrote his marvellous book and forgot all about us. When he eventually appeared he quite approved of what I had done.'[22]

Evie claimed that virtually all that Gleizes said to them had been said before

> except that now if people ask 'what are the laws that the cubists work on' that one could answer Rhythm and Spacing – space taking the place of the perspective that you see in pictures by Raphael etc – and obtained by placing one object over another – he said this idea of space was rather like Einsteins theory do you know it? – I dont – he said the picture of the future the next generation would tend to more and more to be circular and revolve inside itself not like as in Giotto or in those things we have done go in planes but like this [illustration]! I dont expect you can make anything out he was so thrilled by his own ideas for this book it was difficult to follow him. He produced the L. Vinci book you have and said he was going to quote from it to show how necessary if you did perspective at all to do it very exactly – but he said L. was full of contradictions and so complicated that it wd give you a dégout for painting for ever to have to follow all those rules whereas the work he is arriving at is all based on Rhythm and repetition and is simple in itself – I am afraid I cant put it any clearer now – I do hope you are alright. Miss you awfully – Yr loving Evie.[23]

At the time both women were friendly with Eileen Gray,[24] the artist and designer whose rugs and furniture, particularly her lacquer screens, were already celebrated. Her great friend, Kate Weatherby,[25] was planning a six-week trip to the south of France with Eileen, and offered Evie the use of her flat in Paris. Mainie and Evie were clearly somewhat in awe of Eileen Gray. While Kate Weatherby is 'K' or 'Kate', references to her friend are to 'Miss Gray'. Evie saw Kate later, and was asked for her copies of Ozenfant's paper *L'Esprit Nouveau* 'for the beloved Miss Gray who had to have them at once! But I would not, I am sure I was very disagreeable but it is rather nonsense, and I am sure Kate would never get them replaced so I was firm and horrid over it.'

Gray was a crucial figure in the development and adaptation of many abstract principles to the discipline of craft and design, and in time this was to have much greater relevance to both Mainie and Evie. Just then, however, the purer ether of abstract principle obsessed them, and may have accounted for Evie's slightly tart view of Kate Weatherby cadging magazines for Eileen Gray to pore over. Certainly the main burden of Evie's letters concerns Gleizes' teaching.

101. *Gouache Study for Abstract Composition*, 1922. Gouache on paper mounted on card, 19.5 × 13.9. Dublin, private collection.

102. *Abstract Composition*, 1922. Oil on canvas, 89 × 45.5. Dublin, private collection.

Mainie had sent a group of pencil drawings and gouaches to be shown to the 'Master' and Evie reports on these in a letter dated 25 June:

> He said to tell you he was very pleased and that you had worked very well he liked the colour ones very much. He said you could get gradually less violent contrasts now keeping the principal the same, he wants you to do bigger designs work out the designs to the outside lines as he says these are too cramped and one ought to make the design always appear bigger than its size whereas these designs are too concentrated round the centre and give the appearance of drawing the design in — I marked the designs I hope you dont mind at the top to explain what he meant.[26]

Though both Mainie and Evie were working hard to earn Gleizes' approbation, clearly Colette Allendy was not. 'Colette was in great woe yesterday he wont let her do any curves he says she is too impressionist She is nice to me and I like her but she is queer not to do more I think she never works on her own in between.'[27]

These letters are an invaluable insight into the working methods of the three artists, Evie's dependence on Mainie is evident. So is the way in which she reflects Gleizes' admiration for Mainie. There is even a hint of censure about Gleizes himself. The crucial problem facing them was clearly the issue of curves, and their introduction into the process of translation. There was an order in the working out of their abstract designs: first, the disposition of planes; second, the introduction of curves.

> I do think the curves are horribly difficult I did one he liked yesterday and told me to send it to you and say he liked it — I think I am arriving at it a little the idea seems to be to carry each curve round some how and if you want to emphasise it put a smaller curve the same shape inside — he said each line must be belonging to another *une père et mère et des enfants* rather a good description I think.

Gleizes wanted the curves never to be too apparent, 'not shout', but to manifest themselves always as inevitable and therefore natural. Evie tried so hard and was flummoxed when Gleizes seemed not to follow his own teaching: 'I really dont think one can keep the exact measurements 1 1/2 or 1 4th etc all through in working out the design. I do to start with, and for the very long lines, but not afterwards when I put in the curves, and I know he does not at all himself — as he took a design I brought and worked it out and showed it to me afterwards and he had not done it a bit.'[28]

Gleizes at the time was having trouble with his father-in-law, formerly a powerful figure in the French Government, and a farcical situation developed in the studio as a result of M. Roche's threat to visit the painter.

> He is rather distraught apparently having a row with his beau père yesterday he kept jumping up and hiding behind the other door when ever he heard a sound on the stairs outside and eventually the beau pères chauffeur appeared for him and Colette had to go and say he was not there! but he was thoroughly agitated he says the beau père is too old and always getting stupid ideas in his head, he used to be a rather big person in France Minister of something — and Gleize (sic) says he has all the Elysée people by the ears and he cant bear politicians himself but he really was too funny bolting out of the room at every sound — and it rather upset the work I think he is awfully nice and patient and just the same always.[29]

Evie was planning to return to England in early July with a friend called Ella. She had her nurse, Brady, with her, and was able to be independent in her own cottage in Lower Swell, near her sister, Leland, who lived at Stow-on-the-Wold. There was no question of going to Ireland. Indeed the thought just then was of concern for Mainie's safety in the civil war which was causing so much distress. 'I dont mention Ireland as I know you have enough of it as it seems rather callous not to. I do sympathise with you so much it must be awful for everyone there.'[30]

CHAPTER TEN

Painting and its laws

GLEIZES WORKED AT his ideas on abstract art during the winter of 1922–3 with Mainie and Evie, and also on the text of *La Peinture et ses lois*. To an extent which, though substantial, is hard to define, the two Irish women acted as his testing ground for ideas and their transformation into actual works. Of the two, Mainie bore the larger burden of this collaboration, as is clear from the letters and from other inferences drawn from friends and contemporaries. It is clear, too, from the abundance of her exploratory work. In addition to many studies, she produced, late in 1922 or early in 1923, a 'Fugue Theory' for art, applying the principles of the musical fugue to abstract composition (Pls. 103–7). And her sketches and diagrams, in pencil and monochrome wash, led to gouaches, and finished oils (Pls. 108–17). Mainie was aggressively determined to meet Gleizes' every demand, and to match him in the confrontation of what were entirely original, and therefore difficult, conceptual ideas.

The actual account of 'the new mechanism' of translation and rotation only takes up part of this remarkable book. Most of it is devoted to a historical essay in which Gleizes argues that the new painting is at least in part a return to earlier principles of painting – principles that were widespread before the introduction of the perspective mechanism and which achieved one of their highest realisations in the painting, sculpture and architecture of the Romanesque period. This view of the history of painting – greatly developed and refined in his later writings – distinguishes Gleizes sharply from other non-representational painters such as Malevich or Mondrian, both of whom saw the history of painting and of mankind in general as a continuous, linear progress leading to the present day when the development into abstract art, even if it derived logically from the past, was in itself entirely new. Gleizes' view of history was, by contrast, cyclical. He argued that Europe had passed through a cycle when its spiritual life was based on religious principles – the relation between man and God – but that since the thirteenth century a new, materialist, cycle had begun when all our attention and highest endeavours were turned towards the appearances of the external world about us. Painting began to create the illusion of external space; 'science', understood in terms of the observation and analysis of matter, became increasingly important. The new needs felt by the Cubists, Gleizes argued, indicated that man was beginning to return to a religious cycle. The Romanesque period, whose importance Gleizes had already stressed in his essay, *Le Cubisme et la tradition*,[1] published in 1913, was to become very fashionable among French non-representational painters of the 1930s and 1940s, though the paintings of Alfred Manessier, Maurice Estève and Jean Bazaine are still very different from those of Gleizes.

Although Gleizes was the only one of the original French Cubist group who committed himself fully to non-representational painting in the 1920s, the idea of abstract art had been very much in the air since before the war. In their book *Du Cubisme* Gleizes and Metzinger mention it as a possibility and a logical development from Cubism: 'Let the picture imitate nothing, and let it show nakedly the reason for its existence! We would be ungrateful were we to deplore the absence of everything – flowers, countryside or a face – of which it can be no more than a reflection.'[2] But they

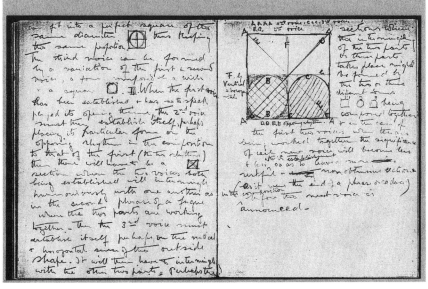

103. (left) Mainie's *Notes on Composition: Fugue Theory*.

104. (below) *Fugue Theory: Drawing I*, 1922. Pencil and ink on paper, 20 × 19.7. Dublin, private collection.

Below from left to right

105. *Fugue Theory: Drawing II*, 1922. Pencil and ink on paper, 20 × 19.7. Dublin, private collection.

106. *Fugue Theory: Drawing III*, 1922. Pencil and ink on paper, 20 × 19.7. Dublin, private collection.

107. *Fugue Theory: Drawing IV*, 1922. Pencil and ink on paper, 20 × 19.7. Dublin, private collection.

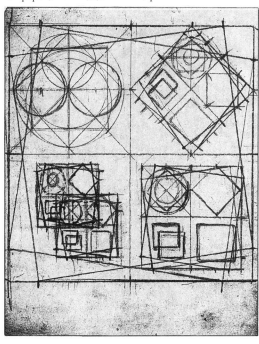

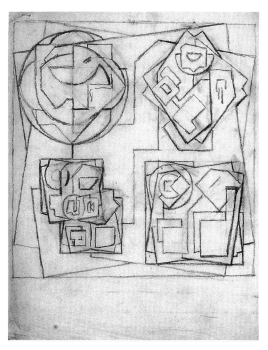

108. (*above left*) *Abstract Composition*, 1922. Oil on canvas, 89 × 45.5. Dublin, private collection.

109. (*above*) *Abstract Study*, 1922. Tempera on board, 114.5 × 57.5. Dublin, private collection.

110. *Study for Abstract Composition*, 1922. Gouache on paper, 26 × 19.2. Dublin, private collection.

111. (*right*) *Abstract Study*, 1922. Pen and ink with brown wash on paper mounted on card, 12.5 × 16. Dublin, private collection.
112–15 (*below*) *Drawings for Abstract Study*, 1922. Pencil on paper, each 11.5 × 15.3. Dublin, private collection.

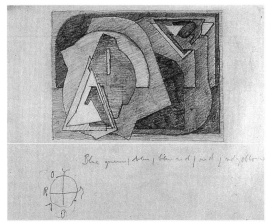

go on to say: 'Nonetheless, we must admit that the reminiscence of natural forms cannot be entirely abolished, at least at the present time. One cannot lift an art all at once up to the level of a pure effusion.'[3] This caution is typical of Gleizes. Each stage had to be fully explored before passing on to the next one. One of his pupils, Walter Firpo,[4] reports that Gleizes told him that the painters, himself included, had been in too much of a hurry to pass into non-representational painting and that there was still much that could have been done with the 'multiple perspective' of early Cubism.

Gleizes and Metzinger were far from being alone at the time in envisaging the possibility of 'pure painting' as it was called at the time. The Czech painter, Frantisek Kupka,[5] was living not far from the Villon studio where Gleizes and his associates met, and he sometimes participated in their discussions. His own painting was quite independent of the Cubists but he has some claim to be regarded as the first purely non-representational painter. Closer to the Cubists, Robert Delaunay[6] had developed his studies of the Eiffel Tower seen through a window to a stage of near abstraction in his great 'Windows' series. In 1912–13 he began a series of 'Suns', 'Moons' and 'Discs', which bear a superficial resemblance to Kupka (his 'Discs of Newton', for example) though his approach is much more 'painterly' and less philosophical. These can fairly be regarded as fully abstract paintings, though his wife, Sonia Delaunay,[7] tells us that they were based on studying the colours and circles that we see when we look at the sun or moon directly.

Gleizes was later to regard these paintings as the furthest point achieved by Cubism at this time, and they had considerable influence on his own later work. But Delaunay himself broke with the Cubists and refused to exhibit with them at the Section d'Or exhibition of 1912. Gleizes was to say that the Cubists themselves, himself included, had not understood Delaunay, were suspicious of his radiant colour, and thought he wanted to lead them back to the formless mists of Impressionism. Delaunay was, however, greatly appreciated by the German painters of the Blaue Reiter group and was closely associated with Wassily Kandinsky, Paul Klee and Franz Marc.

He was also championed by the poet, Guillaume Apollinaire, who saw his work as the centre of a new school, more lyrical and colourful than Cubism which he called 'Orphism'. Apollinaire considered the German painters to be Orphists too, and, among French painters, saw Léger and Picabia as developing in the same direction. Both, but Picabia especially, were to paint more or less fully non-representational paintings before the war.

So much was the idea of 'pure painting' in the air that we may well ask why the Cubists, so keen to experiment, were so hesitant about it. We must remember that their entire formation as painters had been based on the study of subjects. The idea of painting without a subject seemed as absurd and inconceivable as the idea of poetry without a subject. Even Kupka, Delaunay and Léger had reached their abstract painting on the basis of the continual analysis of a subject. Picasso set himself resolutely against the abandonment of the subject. His gallery owner, Daniel-Henry Kahnweiler, whose book *Das Weg Zum Kubismus* is the basis of much of what had been subsequently written on the subject of Cubism,[8] argued that the person looking at a picture will always look for a subject and that the painter, however radical he may be, had better put one in, in order to prevent the spectator from going off on a false track. He maintained that the painter's job was to help the spectator to look at reality – i.e. the appearance of the world outside painting – differently.

The prestige of Kahnweiler, and of the painters associated with him – above all Picasso and Braque – is such that the very idea of 'abstract Cubism' appears to many to be a contradiction in terms. This is certainly the case if the paintings of Picasso and Braque are to be taken as the standard of 'true Cubism'. But the term 'Cubism' was first popularised as a derisive description of the paintings of Le Fauconnier, Metzinger, Léger, Gleizes and Delaunay, three of whom – Delaunay, Léger and Gleizes – had come close to abstraction prior to the war.

Gleizes continued all his life to insist that his work was a development of the first Cubist experiments and the collection of essays demonstrating his thinking of the 1930s was entitled *Puissances du Cubisme*.[9] The term 'Cubist abstract' is therefore fully appropriate when applied to him and to the painters most closely associated with him, including Jellett – provided we accept a wider definition of the word 'Cubism' than that given by Kahnweiler and championed by Douglas Cooper in *The Essential Cubism*.[10]

Outside Paris, very important developments in the history of non-representational painting took place during and after the war, especially in Russia and in the Netherlands, among painters who had been profoundly influenced by Cubism. This is not the place in which to discuss these painters and the very lively disputes which occurred among them but some general remarks may be made to distinguish Gleizes from the other European abstract artists who had passed through Cubism.

The Russians (Malevich, Tatlin, Rodchenko and the enormous and impressive range of painters and sculptors associated with them), and the Dutch De Stijl group were all 'modernists' in the simple sense that they believed that what they were doing was unprecedented whereas Gleizes, as we have seen, believed that he was uncovering permanent principles that had been practised in all the great religious epochs of human history. They all believed in the power of the simplest geometrical shapes – usually the square or rectangle, but also the circle or trapezoid – presented nakedly, as elements in their own right. Gleizes' rectangles, on the other hand, were no more than a scaffolding, a first stage in the mapping out of the painting, destined to disappear, or at least to recede into the background, as the painting progressed. And they all made a moral principle of the rejection of naturalistic imagery: they proclaimed that the elimination of what they called the 'object' (Gleizes called it the 'subject') was an end in itself, inaugurating a new age of the spirit in conformity with the 'conquest of nature' by the machine. The question is complicated by Malevich's return to figurative imagery at the end of his life but in the early 1920s there was no doubt that for him, as for Mondrian, the rejection of the appearances of the external world was a moral gesture with profound metaphysical

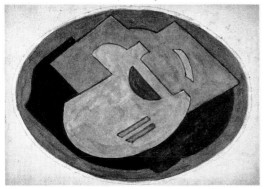

116. *Abstract Study*, 1922. Brown wash on paper laid on card, oval 16 × 23. Dublin, private collection.

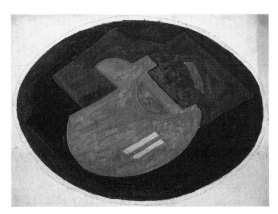

117. *Abstract Study*, 1922. Gouache on paper laid on card, oval 16 × 23. Dublin, private collection.

implications. It could almost be said that the 'non-objective world' had become the subject of their painting. They were representing it as an idea. For Gleizes, by contrast, the rejection of the figurative image was merely a means. This image had its own laws which conflicted with those of the picture plane and provided a focus of attention which obstructed the movement of the eye. It may be this difference in principle that has led some commentators to attribute a figurative content even to the paintings of the early 1920s, and thus to deny that Gleizes was a 'pure abstract' painter.

Although all these painters professed an interest in movement and 'dynamism', Gleizes would have seen their paintings as essentially static, or at least considered that the movement did not go anywhere. The only possible movement in a painting, Gleizes argued, was the spiral – *within* the clearly defined limits of the picture frame. He was to say later that the problem with many abstract painters was that they used the elementary geometrical shapes as 'figures' – elements essentially static in themselves and arranged on the canvas as a representational painter might arrange the subjects he wished to represent. They did not derive logically from – in many cases they actually struggled against – the overall frame of the painting. As such, Gleizes saw this work as a retrograde step in relation to early Cubism which broke up the integrity of the (still representational) figure to put it into a dynamic formal relationship with the painting as a whole.

We may also point to a difference in what may be called their 'religious' preoccupations. Metaphysical, philosophical and religious concerns have played an enormous role in the history of twentieth century painting which has still not been fully examined or understood. Kupka and Mondrian were both strongly marked by the theosophy of Mme Blavatsky and her followers, Kandinsky by the 'anthroposophy' of Rudolf Steiner, while Malevich worked out a bleak and essentially sceptical metaphysical system of his own. Gleizes, and almost all his close associates (Mainie Jellett, Evie Hone, Robert Pouyaud, Anne Dangar) were Christians. Unlike Jellett, Hone and Dangar, Gleizes arrived at Christianity from an atheistic standpoint.

What impressed him was the depth and richness of civilisations founded on religious principles. He was interested in the role of religion in forming whole societies, rather than in a personal metaphysical research. As such, he envisaged a marriage between the highest theological speculation and a popular art capable of touching the hearts and minds of ordinary people. He believed that this had been achieved by the Roman Catholic church in the past, but at the time he began his work with Jellett and Hone, he did not believe that the Church was adequate to the task. At that precise moment he was placing his hopes in the Russian Revolution and he was perhaps more in touch with Russian developments than most of his French contemporaries.

In an essay written at this time, the period of his first collaboration with Mainie Jellett, Gleizes complained that his own work was still too theoretical, too geometrical.[11] Painting, he said, was 'a song for the eye which touches the heart and captures the mind'; but at this early stage in the development of a new art,

> the struggle is taking place on the slippery slopes of reason and argument. The most recent paintings and sculptures are in an intermediate stage between the new order in the process of formation but still broken down into its constituent parts; and aspirations which have no sense of direction or co-ordination at all. The best of them, those which come closest to the laws which are in the process of being discovered, are still too intellectual really to appeal to people who can only respond to paintings by means of their feelings, their tenderness.[12]

There is no contempt in this reference to 'feelings' and 'tenderness' as there might have been had the passage been written by Malevich or Mondrian. Gleizes wishes to appeal to such feelings but for the moment basic principles take up all the artist's attention and therefore take on an importance in the external appearance of the work, going beyond the essential but *internal* role which they must play in the final achievement.

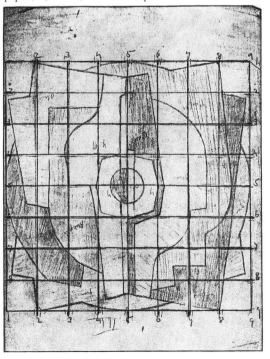

CHAPTER ELEVEN

'Sub-human art of Miss Jellett'

119. *Abstract Composition*, 1922. Oil on canvas, 60.5 × 49. Dublin, private collection.

118. (*facing page*) *Abstract Composition*, 1922. Oil on canvas, 89 × 89. Dublin, private collection.

120. *Study for Abstract Composition*, 1922. Pencil on paper, 19.2 × 19.2. Dublin, private collection.

MAINIE JOINED EVIE in Paris in the autumn of 1922 and they spent Christmas there together. Her father sent her a brief letter which hints at an almost masculine solidarity between himself and his eldest daughter, whom he clearly misses. 'The female population here is in the usual dotty condition. I give them a wide berth as they are sometimes quite dangerous.' He sent her a Christmas gift of money, adding: 'No present that I could give you would convey what I feel. The unspoken word is sometimes more elegant than volumes of talk. You are the very best.' He says also in his letter, 'It is grand about your exhibition.'

Four of Mainie's abstract oils had been accepted for the Salon des Indépendents for showing in the early part of 1923 (Pl. 119).[1] These works were the severest of abstract canvases, and among the most austere and powerful works she ever produced. They are representative of the first, 'single-voice' phase in the development of her Cubist abstract work, and the public exhibition of these paintings was itself an endorsement of their collective work over the previous year, and represented an important breakthrough. The works stand as an expression of an individual and independent spirit. It is difficult to perceive any direct trace of Gleizes in any of them, and they relate to his own paintings of the period only in the theoretical sense of being based on similar ideas of disposition of form and relationships of colour. In vision and conception they stand more clearly apart than was to be the case later in the 1920s, when continued collaboration on quite detailed theories of composition produced works which are more closely parallel between the two painters.

In this first bold exploration of the learning process, and its transformation into what was really her heart's desire – the creation of living and lasting works of pure abstract art – she had a stately and elegant capacity for expressing her inner soul. She believed later that this work which dated from the very beginning of her abstract art was too severe, and still at an experimental stage. It was only slowly that she 'gained a wider and more emotional power of expression'. Yet the dramatic impact and simplicity of these early abstracts have a strong penetrative power. It is in part *because* she does not yet have the abundance of means which she was later to develop, but there is a strength in these paintings which – relatively static as they still are – gives them a monumental quality comparable to the best work of the early Cubists. It should be pointed out that these pictures and the first 'multi-voice' abstracts which followed them, were painted before the ideas presented in *La Peinture et ses lois* had been fully worked out. Even the terms 'translation' and 'rotation' did not exist at first, only the barest idea of shapes interlocking on the flat surface. Gleizes was being quite truthful when he said he had little to offer his pupils at this stage. The strength of these paintings is largely intuitive and very much Mainie's own.

If anything, it is in the next phase of her work, from the mid-1920s on, that she develops along lines which are often highly cerebral. And looking still further forward, into the 1930s, the forces which resolve this intensely intellectual middle period of her life's work are two-fold: the introduction of religious themes, and the exploration of colour in brilliant and vivid ways. But all of that lay in the future. For the present we

121. *Abstract Composition*, 1922. Oil on canvas, 114.5 × 38.5. Dublin, private collection.

facing page

122. *Abstract Composition*, 1922. Tempera on board, 63.5 × 91.5. Dublin, private collection.

123. *Abstract Composition*, 1922. Tempera on board, 44.5 × 89. Dublin, private collection.

must consider her both at an early stage in the investigation of Cubist abstract art, while also being capable of producing a first group of austere, non-representational paintings which, to this day, stand among her finest achievements (Pls. 118, 120).

Mainie remained in Paris well into the spring of 1923. Her mother joined her for a fortnight at the end of March, by which time the exhibition at the Salon des Indépendents was over. They returned to Ireland together, Mainie to work for a group show in Dublin. She wanted to bring to Dublin some of the spiritual force of her work with Gleizes and to exhibit abstract paintings to a public which previously regarded her as an artist who painted in the style of Sickert, and she worked on further single-voice abstract works to this end (Pls. 121–3). It was a brave decision, inspired by the energy and excitement of a period of immense discovery and tremendous output. But she was clearly attracted to the idea of working in a country which was emerging from a long period of revolution, and to be back once more with her loving and supportive family.

William Jellett's Christmas letter to his daughter betrays nothing of the mood of disappointment and of disillusionment which must have faced him. With the coming of independence, the state briefs which had provided him with a lucrative practice at the bar slackened off as some of the work was placed elsewhere. The family had no inherited wealth to speak of and were dependent on his income. And for the two elder daughters, whose education was now nearing completion, the need to contribute to the family's resources was essential. The changed situation was reflected, modestly enough it must be said, in the fact that holidays on the continent and in Scotland ceased. 'Funds were low in 1923', Bay Jellett recalled,[2] and the family went to Howth that summer.

Mainie returned to Dublin full of confidence and conviction. She immediately became involved with the Society of Dublin Painters,[3] and prepared work for exhibition in their autumn show. Those who exhibited, in 1923, in addition to Mainie Jellett and Evie Hone, included Letitia Hamilton,[4] her sister, Eva,[5] Grace Henry,[6] Harriet Kirkwood,[7] Paul Henry,[8] Harry Clarke, Charles Lamb,[9] William Conor[10] and – though temporarily absent in 1923 – Edward O'Rourke Dickey.[11] By 1923, Mary Swanzy,[12] though remaining a member, had left Dublin. Jack Yeats[13] had ceased to be a member, but remained sympathetic to the group. It was in response to the advent of abstract Cubism with the return to Dublin of Mainie Jellett and Evie Hone in 1923, that he delivered his *bon mot*: 'Who the blazes Gleizes?' The two-syllable pronunciation was preferred in Dublin as a device to mock; it is still employed by the American associate of Gleizes, Walter Firpo. It should not be inferred from Jack Yeat's witticism that he did not respect the new movement which these two women represented. He was a modernist himself, and was supportive of his former fellow-members; he just did not wish for continued formal involvement in the group.

The catholic nature of the group embraced the Post-Impressionist style of Paul and Grace Henry, the Expressionism of Letitia Hamilton and Harriet Kirkwood, the urban and rural realism of William Conor and Charles Lamb respectively, and the quaint and detailed vision of Harry Clarke. The Dublin public had been prepared for their styles of painting by a succession of modernist exhibitions dating back to the January 1911 Post-Impressionist show at the United Arts Club.[14] This was followed by a series of such shows, interrupted by the First World War, but then renewed in 1922 with Dublin Arts Week,[15] organised in part by Paul Henry. He arranged a show, 'Some Modern Pictures', in the Mills Hall,[16] which included Vlaminck, Modigliani, Marchand, Maillot, as well as a number of avant-garde English artists: Gilman, Gore, Vanessa Bell, Bevan, Ginner and Nash. But the Dublin public had in no sense been prepared for abstract art.

The *Irish Times* reviewer wrote:

Miss Maimie Jellett [she was dogged throughout her life by this misspelling of her Christian name] is showing two paintings and two drawings. I fear that I did not in the least understand her two paintings. They are in squares, cubes, odd shapes and

TWO FREAK PICTURES.

ART—

One of the two Futurist Pictures by Miss Maimie Jellett at the Exhibition at No. 7 St. Stephen's Green. Our Art Critic on Saturday declared that "to me they presented an insoluble puzzle." Perhaps our readers can provide a solution.

—AND NATURE.

Not a Natural History Study, but a Picture of an Onion!

124. 'Two Freak Pictures', 1923. From *The Irish Times* of 23 October 1923.

125. *Decoration*, 1923. Tempera on board, 89 × 53. Dublin, National Gallery of Ireland. This is the first abstract painting to be exhibited in Dublin, at the Society of Dublin Painters, in October 1923.

clashing colours. They may, to the man who understands the most up-to-date, modern art, mean something; but to me they presented an insoluble puzzle.[17]

The Irish Times pursued this theme early the following week by publishing, under the heading 'TWO FREAK PICTURES', one of Mainie Jellett's abstracts and a photograph of an onion which resembled a bird sitting on a nest. Readers were invited to 'provide a solution' (Pl. 124).[18]

The crucial work was *Decoration* (Pl. 125). A five-sided work, with more than a hint of religion in its shape, but no religious imagery at all in its composition, the painting belonged to Evie Hone until her death, when it was bequeathed to the National Gallery of Ireland. If one wanted a single work of art from which the start of modernism in Ireland can be dated, then this austere, abstract panel is that example.

The most severe onslaught upon it, and upon its creator, came from a fellow painter. George Russell was editor of the *Irish Statesman*, a well-produced fortnightly paper on current affairs which gave considerable space to the arts. He wrote a good deal of it himself, including the art criticism which he signed with the initials 'Y.O.' In the review of 'The Dublin Painters' he wrote eloquently about Harry Clarke's works, describing them as 'harmonies of sinister colour' and his imagination as one of 'malignant beauty and dark intensity no other Irish artist has reached, except, perhaps, Jack Yeats . . .' He then went on:

We turn from Clarke's pictures and find Miss Jellett a late victim to Cubism in some sub-section of this artistic malaria. She seems as heartily as any of the cubists to have adopted as motto Fuseli's famous outburst, 'Damn nature. She always puts me out.' The real defect in this form of art is that the convention is so simple that nothing can be said in it. It is as impossible to be subtle in this convention as it would be to write poetry if the poet was limited to use fifty words, the same words, no matter how many poems he wrote or what moods he wanted to express. In fact, what Miss Jellett says in one of her decorations she says in the other, and that is nothing . . . the sorcery of Harry Clarke and Miss Jellett's incautious exposure of herself have occupied all the space a stern editor will allot to a reverie over art . . . The exhibition is well worth seeing, and we hope the visitors will not be led away, as we were, by the super humanities of Harry Clarke or the sub-human art of Miss Jellett.[19]

This savage onslaught sparked off a controversy about modernism which was to last for the rest of Mainie's life. Whether she felt wounded or distressed by George Russells's review is not recorded. That she immediately took action to counter the attack is clear and it is equally clear that the Society of Dublin Painters saw it as an attack on all of them.

Maude Ball,[20] champion of the group, wrote to *The Irish Times*.[21] She took up the parallels between music and art, pointing out that there was a ready acceptance of 'abstract harmony' in music, indeed a preference for it over such music as attempted to be 'descriptive'. She dealt with the question of the various 'languages' used by interpreters and artists;

when an artist chooses to follow the path of abstract harmony by means of colours and forms, and the spectator approaches the work looking for the realistic, confusion is bound to occur. The only rational way to consider his pictures is whether he has succeeded in getting this harmony. The interpreter has chosen, perhaps, a language which we do not yet understand.

Since the artists felt that Maude Ball had addressed the central problem, she was encouraged to compose another letter to the editor of the *Irish Statesman*. She sent a draft to Mainie for approval:

I've done my best, nearly burst in the effort, and this is the result. It is in the exact form in which I propose to send it in if you all approve. Rameau nearly did for me! . . .

Let me know as soon as you can after you have all considered it. I should like, if I could, to send it in tomorrow . . . Don't be downhearted to please anybody, it's wonderful what most of us get through and survive.[22]

Russell published the letter in the the *Irish Statesman*.[23] It was a serious attempt to relate painting and music in terms of colour, form, harmony and rhythm, and it quoted Rameau and Goulinat, as well as Sir Charles Stanford on Mozart: 'he is before all things the great economist'. Russell was not impressed. He appended a note which began 'We are not enlightened by our correspondent's references to violins and pianos.' He used a good number of words in discussing the idea of 'vibrations' and concluded: 'In art, as in literature, there is such a thing as being simple even to imbecility. There is a super-subtlety which arrives at the same psychological goal. The cubists reach it in art: their apologists come perilously near to it in literature.' Russell had already set his face firmly against modernism in art, and was to maintain his opposition for some years, doing so with an eloquence enforced by the curious position he had of being his own arbiter. Fair to begin with, he became perverse and deceitful later.

The October 1923 controversy by no means stopped there. Very soon both Thomas McGreevy,[24] (on the side of the Moderns) and Thomas Bodkin (against them) were drawn in. McGreevy published an essay that autumn in a Dublin quarterly called *The Klaxon*,[25] entitled 'Picasso, Maimie (sic) Jellett and Dublin Criticism'. 'Miss Jellett is the first resident artist to exhibit a cubist picture in Dublin, and our critics are as hopelessly at sea in front of her work as her benighted predecessors were about Picasso and Othon Frieze (sic) and Matisse in 1912.' Comparing her with Picasso, MacGreevy says:

> Miss Jellett does not need to go back to Paris. She, too, has learned all that France can teach her, and her future depends upon herself . . . her words and phrases, her colours and her relating of them to each other that is to say, produced, it seemed to me, a pleasing harmonic effect. That the freedom from subject, from painted psychology, from symbolism, has heightened the aesthetic value of her work is not, I think, to be doubted by anyone who has seen the pictures she has exhibited in Dublin during the past four or five years.

Nothing better could have happened to Mainie Jellett on the occasion of her showing her first abstract works in Ireland, than this very public conflict involving men who were already, or were to become, significant figures in artistic affairs for the next twenty years. She had been noticed, she had been attacked, she had been defended. She was suddenly the focus of modernism in all its controversial ramifications. In addition to her own art, she had a mission affecting the art of others: to teach and to convert, through education and understanding. She never, in fact, taught abstract art as such unless specifically requested. And this happened with only two or three painters. But she espoused it as a cause, just as she espoused all expressions of modern painting.

Mainie was the only painter who consistently produced and exhibited pure abstract works during the 1920s in the British Isles. She was around ten years ahead of Ben Nicholson in this, a pioneering figure in the front lines of modernism. In the exchanges between herself and Maude Ball over their response to Russell's criticism, the two women considered many quotations as apt (but did not, in fact, use them). To the end of her life Mainie kept together these scraps of paper. One of them contained an extract from Plato's *Philebus*, which had already been used for the purpose of defending modern art by Ozenfant, in his journal, *L'Elan*, in 1916. In it, Socrates expands on the innate beauty of abstract form:

> *Socrates*: I do not mean by beauty of form such beauty as that of animals or pictures . . . but, understand me to mean straight lines and circles, and the plane or solid figures which are formed out of them by turning-lathes and rulers and measurers of angles; for

these I affirm to be not only relatively beautiful, like other things, but they are eternally and absolutely beautiful . . . And there are colours which are of the same character, and have similar pleasures; now do you understand my meaning?

Protarchus: I am trying to understand, Socrates, and I hope you will try to make your meaning clearer.

Socrates: When sounds are smooth and clear, and have a single pure tone, then I mean to say they are not relatively but absolutely beautiful, and have natural pleasures associated with them.[26]

Mainie had aspired to a purity of understanding and a clarity of purpose which emulated Socrates and which, in the company of Gleizes and her friend Evie, had echoes of the Socratic dialogue. From it a new art had sprung with new laws and new inspiration. She had brought it back to a new country and presented it in an uncompromising and direct fashion – the public arena of the exhibition. No Protarchus had stepped forward to say: I am trying to understand, I hope *you* will make your meaning clearer. Yet to her friends, especially the admirable and brave Maude Ball, the message was clear. It was as if she held within herself a secret to a part of artistic life that was precious and indestructible. And it was a secret she wanted desperately to impart. The task of doing so would now fill her days for the rest of her life.

CHAPTER TWELVE

'L'Art d'Aujourd'hui'

126. John Butler Yeats, *George Russell*, 1903. Oil on canvas, 112 × 87. Dublin, National Gallery of Ireland.

MAINIE HAD RETURNED to Ireland to teach. In practical terms this was how she intended to earn her living and make a modest contribution to the household. She was given as a studio a long and lofty room on the first floor at the back of the Fitzwilliam Square house, with a single large window facing west and overlooking the garden. The room was joined by double doors to the family drawing room. She outlined her conditions for teaching: pencil drawing, painting in oil and watercolour and 'sketching classes out of doors in the summer months' and listed her fees: drawing and painting without a model was at the hourly rate of three shillings; private lessons and lessons with a life model were four shillings an hour; on Saturday mornings she held classes for children. 'Life, still life and composition studies' would seem to imply that something approaching modernist techniques were included in the programme of work offered, but it did not extend to abstract theory and practice. More likely, it was a version of the kind of teaching which she had received from André Lhote. Certainly through the 1920s and into the 1930s Lhote remained a significant name among Dublin artists and was a clear influence on a number of them, while Gleizes and his style remained far more obscure and rarified.

The modern art controversy, which raged everywhere during the 1920s, had found a focus in Dublin in Mainie Jellett. And in classic Dublin fashion positions were adopted and attitudes taken up, from which neither side could easily withdraw. In March 1924, at a time when two more of Mainie's abstract paintings were being shown in Paris, at the Indépendants, the New Irish Salon exhibition in Dublin gave the critics another opportunity to 'debate' modernism, and they took to it with relish. The Salon exhibition – the first of six held in consecutive years up to 1928 – was a large one, containing almost 300 works and including paintings by Gleizes and Lhote as well as Mainie and Evie and Cecil French Salkeld (Pls. 127–8).[1] The bewilderment of the *Irish Times* critic, whose article was unsigned, centred on the issue of whether or not these abstract paintings were anything more than 'design'. Did they have anything to 'say' beyond that? In the case of Gleizes his 'designs' had 'something less than the interest of Celtic scroll work. The *tempera* of Maimie [sic] H. Jellett has a certain flow of design, but not more . . . than a child will often show when asked to fill a space with colour. Pictorial art may have become worn out, but in work such as that of Gleizes, Lhote, Cecil F. Salkeld, E.S. Hone and Maimie Jellett, it may be said to have advanced to second childishness.' Other members of the Society of Dublin Painters, including O'Rourke Dickey, Grace Henry and Letitia Hamilton, exhibited their work in the show, and the strong emphasis on what the critic saw as no more than design or the childish decoration of space is indicative of a public expectation that the question of modernism was to be addressed and answers given.[2]

In his notice in the *Irish Statesman* George Russell (Pl. 126) met this expectation by reverting to the disease imagery with which he had dismissed Mainie the previous autumn.[3] It was not malaria now, but a deeper and more virulent form of corruption made up of 'inflammations, ulcers and blotches'. An 'aesthetic bacteria' had been at work in art since the beginning of the century, and Russell is prepared to give it some credit for making the age recognise how completely bored it had become with 'careful,

127. *Four Elements*, 1924. Oil on canvas, 63.5 × 86.5. Dublin, private collection.

128. *Study for Four Elements*, 1924. Pencil on paper, mounted on card, 17 × 26. Dublin, private collection.

uninspired academic art'. The only merit he is prepared to concede to 'the Gleizes, the Lhotes, the Salkelds and the Jelletts' is colour sense. Sometimes they have it, sometimes not: 'We regret to say that some of them had no more beauty of colour than is usual in a pattern on oilcloth.' Russell saw the 'moderns' as helping in the process of 'burying academic art into the tomb'; but he adds: 'where they themselves will soon be buried'. He concluded that the most potent charm of Cubism was its capacity to provoke controversy: 'the storm lasted long after midnight, and you went to bed feeling you had got something for your money'. It is ironic that George Russell, who was undoubtedly part of that broad movement in the arts which challenged academic authority and sought to overthrow the old order in favour of new principles and a new concept of life in art, should have been so virulent in his opposition to that challenge coming from another quarter, and so reluctant to find out anything that might have altered his firm conviction that it all 'said' nothing. As a painter who was also a critic, and, moreover, the editor of a magazine uniquely placed to co-ordinate and give a platform to the views being expressed by painters who clearly challenged what he challenged, he could have done much. Instead, he delivered tirade after tirade against what he clearly never tried to understand.

Mainie and Evie prepared for their joint exhibition at the Dublin Painters' Gallery, planned for June 1924. It was to be a statement and a firm counter attack on their critics. But it needed to achieve much more than simply to assert the continued vigour and determination of the tiny group of painters and supporters who were committed to the extreme cause of abstract art. It had become clear, through Maude Ball's letters and through the evident uncertainty in Thomas MacGreevy's vigorous and supportive prose, that the ragged recruits to the army of revolutionary modernism were in urgent need of training themselves. The intense labours with Gleizes had inspired his two Irish associates. They knew what they were doing, and where his teaching would lead them. There is some evidence that Cecil French Salkeld had also grasped the purpose of their work. But others were a long way from it, and needed leadership and further explanation. That was not all; the bewilderment and hostility had also created a need to justify in terms of some kind of pedigree the artistic legitimacy of what they were doing. And it seems to have been this which caused the two women to place on the back of their catalogue quotations from Sir Joshua Reynolds and Eugène Delacroix designed to contradict the idea of art as an imitation of nature. 'Man has innate feelings within his soul which realistic objects will never satisfy', Delacroix had written, 'the imagination of the painter and the poet gives to these feelings form and life. The first of the arts, music, what does it imitate?'[4] From Reynolds' Eighteenth Discourse they took three quite specific rejections of the idea of nature's imitation being relevant in art.[5] Even more was done at the opening of the exhibition itself, where 'a sympathiser' (not identified, but probably Maude Ball) handed round a copy of notes which attempted to explain the two artists' aims:

> The essential qualities in cubism are rhythm, the preservation of the character of the flat surface of the canvas, and the creation of form on the space of the canvas in such a way as to keep it throughout in direct and harmonious relation to the outside dimensions of the canvas itself. To secure the second of these qualities it is obviously necessary to dispense with linear perspective, space is merely suggested by the reciprocal influence of a succession of flat forms.

The substance of the joint exhibition was carefully thought out. It was the only one they ever held together as, apart from group exhibitions, their ways largely diverged from the second half of the 1920s. A total of fifty-nine works were put on show, Mainie being responsible for the larger share. She had seven works in oil, eight in tempera, seven gouaches and eleven drawings. She also had a screen, and this, with two of the drawings, was not for sale. Prices ranged from fourteen to two guineas. She took the trouble to have the works photographed, and these prints, some with the exhibition numbers still visible, go some way towards identifying the character of what was then shown, including work done in 1922, as well as 1923 (Pl. 129). But a major problem of identification is raised by the titling, which simply refers to medium, giving no indication of size or subject. The main works, in fact, were of single and multi-voice abstract composition, showing a considerable advance in complexity over the paintings exhibited in Paris and in the Dublin Painters' Group show the previous autumn, but with some loss of clarity and power.

Early in 1924 Evie and Mainie joined up in Paris to renew their work with Gleizes. To judge from the difference in Mainie's work between the abstracts shown in October 1923, at the Dublin Painters, and the substantial body of more complex, more sophisticated abstract art exhibited the following June with Evie, enormous strides were made technically. The most obvious development was into 'multi-voice' abstractions, in which two or more 'elements' — constructions that are in themselves organically self-sufficient — are presented simultaneously in the picture, the overall movement passing from one to the other like the eddies and whirlpools of a stream, or, in a more formal artistic sense, like the repeated fugue theme for which we have seen Mainie had already

129.   Part of a wall in the Dublin Painters' Gallery, showing three Jellett works in the joint Jellett-Hone Exhibition of June 1924. The two horizontal paintings, on the right, date from 1922. They are tempera on panel.

worked out a system. Later, the division between the elements (Gleizes' term) or 'voices' (Mainie's term) was to be very clearly marked, the canvas arranged in a simple, balanced geometrical pattern – usually one large element flanked by evenly distributed smaller ones. But at this stage – which is better represented in the work of Jellett than in that of Gleizes – the division is arbitrary. There is also a conscious effort to vary the texture of the different interacting shapes used in the painting which in the earlier work had been distinguished by strong, simple colours (Pls. 130–1).

Now lines, straight and waved, dots, dashes, spots and cross-hatchings became dominant, modifying the direct impact of colour. And there is a muted, restrained palette behind several of the major works of this period. In form, there is a rugged sense of experiment; there is a rawness of finish, a powerful, blunt approach in her composition. The main body of work did not sell. Among the large canvases there were one-, two-, three- and four-voice compositions, bold in their construction, somewhat more united in colour and introducing a number of those new characteristics, such as heavy cross-hatchings, blobs and spots, wavy and zig-zag lines, and a multiplicity of forms interlocked in concentrated structures which at times seem to squeeze out colour. She has subordinated her palette to the designs, producing a less powerful impact than in many of the single-voice abstract compositions in the first phase of her work, from 1922 to the early part of 1923.

The eleven drawings were exhibited in Dublin, in part anyway, to counter the foolish idea that abstract art was the result of painters who could not tackle realism. And these drawings are exemplary works of clear, compelling draughtsmanship. From her days in the Dublin Metropolitan School Mainie had always drawn well. Since 1921 she had developed a remarkable economy of line and applied it to still life and portraiture with telling effect. The drawings, which date from 1922, are among her finest.

It probably came as no surprise to the two artists when the critics seized on the verbal

130. *Abstract Composition*, 1924. Oil on canvas, 91.5 × 71. Dublin, private collection.

131. *Abstract Composition*, 1924. Gouache on paper, 86.5 × 63.5. Dublin, private collection.

aids to understanding, and used them as cudgels with which to belabour their heads. Larry Morrow, writing in *The Freeman's Journal*, dismissed the Reynolds' wisdom: the great man had lent himself, no doubt, 'in a few hastily-penned apothegms to an anarchy which may well seem, nowadays, to threaten the whole outlook of art and the artist'.[6] Morrow had been a declared opponent. He had referred the previous autumn to Mainie's 'pretty patterns' which he claimed were causing her to lose 'her really fine talents as a painter'.[7] And he reiterated his original animosity towards her work: 'It is not so very long ago since I expressed my dislike for Miss Jellett's work.' But then he went on: 'Since then her vision has improved, if I may say so, immeasurably; so much so, in fact, that I now believe that she really has something to say. She has probably had something to say all along, while it is only now that her technique has assumed adequate proportions.'

Morrow's was by far the biggest notice of their exhibition, and the most carefully reasoned. He recommended patience; 'A little introspection before condemning these pictures or dismissing them as inconsequential things will go a long way to a finer understanding of them, and incidentally of one's self.' Morrow preferred Evie Hone, calling her 'the purer artist' and praising her 'escape at times from the tyranny of colour into the realms of the purely abstract'.

A more considerable figure in art and letters, Seamus O'Sullivan, editor of *The Dublin Magazine*, challenged this vague and speculative criticism, confronting the newspaper reviewers with the charge that they were doing no more than making the observation, 'who knows but there may be something in it?'[8] Remarkably for the time, Seamus O'Sullivan went to the trouble of reading *La Peinture et ses lois*, which had only just been published. Even in France the book was not widely read, nor understood, and certainly no other critic or commentator in Ireland, then or later, reveals any appreciation of the theory of abstract Cubist painting set down by Gleizes, nor its roots in the art of the Middle Ages.

Seamus O'Sullivan devoted only a short essay to the theories enunciated by Gleizes, but in one paragraph (worth quoting in full) he compressed more essential understanding of the problems which Mainie Jellett and Evie Hone were trying to resolve in their art than all the other Irish art critics were able to do in the next ten years.

The claim of the Cubists is that, so far from denying the past, they lean upon the past in order that they may make a more exact conquest of the order of nature; only to-day one must do what formerly one only spoke of. Thus in the Cubist philosophy of art, painting has always proposed as an end the animation of a plane surface, which means rhythmising space. The plane surface is the first objective reality, the brute matter which is to come to life under the subjective impulse of the painter. In the Middle Ages the fresco was a subjective divine manifestation, rhythm dominating and animating the inert affabulation of Space-Matter, across which God should be revealed. The material discontinuous realised itself continuous in the spiritual. With the Renaissance, Matter, by imitation of the atmospheric milieu, and the forms which render it spatial, sought to realise itself objectively. To-day, with the recognition of the plane surface as the first objective reality, matter is to be recognised outside of appearance, on the one hand, and of the doctrine of the Middle Ages on the other.[9]

He went on to assert that

with the Cubists, *or wherever Cubism is to lead* [my italics], the quality of the artist is to enter into the objective milieu without other help than that of the law which rules natural creations – nature avowing itself of the same general law. We shall then perceive the value of the individual psyche easily as it demonstrates itself physiologically, in its particular optic, without aid of anecdote, association, etc.[10]

O'Sullivan pointed out that a theory, no matter how convincing or ingenious, does not produce great art. He was expressing an understanding and acceptance of pure abstraction at a time when it was little understood, and when there was a strong reaction against it internationally. His brief analysis was a bench-mark for Mainie and must have strengthened her resolve, encouraging her in the belief that a process of teaching and explanation would have to go side by side with her painting. In this she was establishing a set of tasks parallel to those which Gleizes was to impose upon himself during the second half of the 1920s.

1924 was the year of the Paris Olympic Games, and an international exhibition was held in the city to celebrate sport in art. Jack Yeats exhibited *The Liffey Swim*, and was awarded a silver medal. Ireland had its own national 'Tailteann' Games in the summer, and a large exhibition of paintings was organised in the Engineers' Hall at Ballsbridge. It ranged broadly across all styles of work, with Sean Keating winning the Tailteann Trophy for his large canvas 'Homage to Hugh Lane',[11] a work derived rather clumsily, in both its emotional inspiration and its composition from Orpen's 'Homage to Manet'.[12] It was a suitably patriotic gesture to honour both it and Orpen, but had little to do with artistic quality. Mainie had work in the show: 'Miss Jellett is the only representative of the futurist school . . . that much-discussed style'.[13]

Despite her teaching programme in Dublin, which included the summer sketching classes, Mainie remained firmly committed to exhibitions abroad and to her working visits to Gleizes. She had two paintings in the Salon des Indépendants, which ran from 27

132. *Abstract Composition*, 1925. Oil on canvas, 92 × 73. Dublin, private collection. This painting was used by Albert Gleizes as an illustration in his book, *Kubismus*, published as Volume 13 in the Bahausbucher series, in 1928. It was used as part of the substantial body of work to demonstrate the Third Stage of Cubism ('Epic Cubism').

133. *Abstract Composition*, 1924. Oil on canvas, 63 × 49.5. Dublin, National Gallery of Ireland.

January to 3 March in 1925. And she submitted a work to the London Group exhibition, an abstract gouache – the only one in the show – which prompted *The Sunday Times* art critic, Frank Rutter, to write: 'it is sufficiently promising and pleasant in colour to tempt me to murmur approvingly, ''continuez mon enfant. Ça arrivera.'' '[14] She was in the company of John Banting – described as 'more academic in character', as well as Roger Fry, Duncan Grant, William Roberts, John Nash, Robert Bevan and Mark Gertler.

But the main event for Mainie Jellett in 1925 was 'L'Art d'Aujourd'hui', a major modernist exhibition, international in character and held in Paris, which attracted enormous critical attention. 'L'Art d'Aujourd'hui' was a personal initiative on the part of Gleizes' pupil, Posnansky, who financed it himself principally with a view to championing the cause of non-representational art as an international movement. (The original title had been 'L'Art Abstrait'.)[15] Mainie's works were hung together with those of Delaunay, Gleizes and Léger, and she came in for frequent critical attention, references being made to her 'researches' and to the fact that she was a pupil of Gleizes. Evie and May Guinness also had works in the exhibition. One paper attributed May Guinness, Evie and Mainie – along with an artist called Buchanan – to Canada!

Paris Midi, in a short diary piece about the opening, recalled an encounter with Picasso, who was widely regarded as the lion of the show. Despite this, one of his paintings had been hung in a neglected corner. The journalist deploring this fact got the answer from the artist: 'Where I am, *that* is the place of honour.'[16] *The Paris Times* claimed that

134. *Cotswold Landscape*, 1924. Oil on canvas, 85 × 70. London, private collection.

Bohemia and Hobohemia attended in force to stare at the sort of radical painting and sculpture at which they've stared for more than a decade. And modern, even more than modern, music was executed, so to speak, by several young persons who were not entirely unacquainted with the works of Strawinsky (sic), Satie and other modern composers. And during the breathing spells only the most modern conversation, studded with the most modern opinions made it appear that a most modern evening was had by all. Ask Dad; he knows.[17]

But this tone, in Paris, was a minority one. Waldemar George, writing his regular critical piece, 'Chronique', took up the declared objective of the exhibition, which was to carry out an assessment of art '*non imitatif*'.[18] He was unsympathetic; his long introductory essay, in which he invoked the great art of the past to belittle the search for lyricism which he saw as an inadequate objective for 'L'Art d'Aujourd'hui', ended with the comment: 'L'objet éliminé, le problème reste entier.' But he did give serious attention to the essential purpose of the exhibition, and he saw clearly its roots in Cubism, and was prepared to debate the abstract direction the majority of artists were taking.

The first solo exhibition of Mainie's career was held from 8 to 21 June 1925 at the Dublin Painters' Gallery in St Stephen's Green. The *Irish Statesman* had yet another reviewer, James Winder Good, who praised her sincerity while declaring himself able to see 'little or nothing' in her 'Futurist' works (Pls. 132–3).[19] He gave warm praise to her portrait drawings and landscape studies, which included five views near Avila, and her paintings of Gloucestershire (Pl. 134). Shortly before the show she had been staying with Evie in her cottage near Stow-on-the-Wold. These works were also praised in the short, unsigned notice in the *Irish Independent*, which expressed admiration for her Cubist work as well: 'She shows a remarkable command of technique, together with a fine sense of colour and the courage to put her own theories of art into practice. The result is work of considerable power, with splendid harmony of colour.'[20] Slightly more constrained praise was offered by the *Irish Times* review, her abstract work being seen as 'an expression of the times we live in'.[21]

Mainie got herself a puppy that autumn. – 'He eats paint brushes and everything!!' she wrote in an affectionate letter to Gleizes, shortly before Christmas.[22] From its tone it is clear she had not been in touch for some time; she asks if she can visit him after Christmas for lessons, and bring some work to be criticised. At the Rue de la Ville-l'Evêque there was another modernist exhibition in December. Both she and Evie were included, but not May Guinness. 'I'm sorry Miss Guinness's pictures were not accepted but I suppose they were too realistic. She was very pleased with the letter you wrote her, as I think she was rather hurt in her feelings, she counts such a lot on exhibitions.' May Guinness, who was in Paris at the time, had reported favourably in a letter to Mainie, on Gleizes' own works in the show, particularly 'one with a look of green in it', but had said her own and Evie's works looked 'low in tone which I expect they do'.

In November 1925, Evie Hone, who had been considering the religious life for some time, entered an Anglican convent known as 'The Community of the Epiphany'. It is still in existence, in Truro. Her departure was a severe blow to Mainie who felt she had lost her closest colleague, privy to the inner secrets of Cubism which they had learned from Gleizes. Evie's decision also troubled Mainie in the sense that it questioned the only vocation she knew, one which she had thought was Evie's as well. Her initial response was to ignore what had happened and get on with a busy programme of exhibitions, meetings, lectures and lessons, both her own and those she planned to attend in France with Gleizes. It was to be a busy and productive year, and it began with Mainie's participation in the 'Seven and Five' show at the Beaux Art Galleries in London.[23]

Though Evie was later to exhibit more than once with the 'Seven and Five' Group, Mainie was not satisfied that it fulfilled her own needs. A real battle had been running with 'L'Art d'Aujourd'hui' in Paris the previous year, where the elimination of object was understood and taken on as a serious objective by a substantial body of painters. Mainie felt that the concept of pure abstract painting, as a concept, was only being treated superficially among English artists, and this was a compromise. It was not greatly to her taste nor the logical cast of her mind.

The clear rigour of her understanding of Cubism, and its presentation to the public, was now put to the test in her first public lecture on 'Cubism and Subsequent Movements in Painting' given to the Dublin Literary Society.[24] The moment was well-timed. On Friday 22 January, the Minister for External Affairs, Desmond FitzGerald,[25] opened a major exhibition of Modern French and Irish art, the largest since the days of Hugh Lane's activities before the First World War. It was held in Daniel Egan's Salon,[26] in St Stephen's Green, and his expressed purpose was 'to give Irish art-lovers an opportunity of seeing and studying the Continental art and comparing it with what is being done at home'. FitzGerald echoed these sentiments. 'Ireland had done a great deal for Continental culture, and it was very fitting that they should get something back which might help in the development of Modern Irish art'.[27] It was Paul Henry, in his reply and vote of thanks, who suggested a series of popular public lectures on art, and he and Daniel Egan offered themselves as organisers.

Mainie gave her lecture on 3 February. It was broad in its construction, covering Impressionism, Cézanne, his roots in classical art and his role in the early evolution of Cubism. She went on to develop the idea of Cubism's responsibility for abstract painting and the need to see it, not as an end in itself but as a stage on the way, 'an indication of what was to come, an effort to develop, with the spirit of the age, while preserving the universal laws of creation'. This represented the public declaration of where the modernist artists saw themselves. At a more private level – though of course public in the sense of being addressed at the not inconsiderable first audience she had – it was a statement of belief of some importance.

Mainie began with the essential argument about Impressionists and Cézanne: for all their greatness, recognised by Cézanne among the rest, 'their ideas and their attempts to record effects and impressions of the moment, contained the seeds of the fatal idea that *imitation is the aim and end of all art*.[28] What Cézanne had sought was an order and construction in composition which Impressionism had set aside in favour of the emphasis on colour and light. He had to look elsewhere for it, and she listed his chosen influences: Ingres, Rubens, Poussin, El Greco, the great Renaissance masters, the Primitives, Egyptian and Negro art. She stressed that he was *against* lawlessness and anarchy in art; rather, he sought to rediscover what Mainie characterised as 'the universal laws of art which have been lost and neglected owing to imitation since the Renaissance . . . I do not wish to imply that it is wrong to work from nature or to be inspired by her, but when imitation is the chief aim of art the *creative power* dies.

Mainie told her audience that the movement she espoused covered all the arts and was aimed at the 'purification' of art, and she related this to mankind's wider instinct to create, or recreate, a better order for itself. The state of upheaval and unrest following the First World War, needed attention in the arts as in life generally. She felt that the movement of self-purification, through modernist principles, was weakest among artists in the British Isles.

She said that the first Cubist painters (and sculptors) had 'started with nature as their foundation but simplified and purposely distorted the natural forms so as to reduce them as nearly as possible to the cubic and cylindrical forms of geometry and to make them comply with the interior geometrical composition.' She described their work as 'entirely research work' and experimental, and then went on to explain the transition from three-dimensional to two-dimensional, and away from subject and anecdote. 'A picture was no longer supposed to illustrate some particular story or scene in life, the literary aspect was completely ignored and left to the poets and writers whose business it was, an artist created a picture carefully and thoughtfully in his Studio according to laws parallel to those of a musician who starts composing a piece of music.'

She turned then to the dislocation of realism apparent in Renaissance painting before the tyranny of perspective: Cimabue, Duccio, Giotto, Fra Angelico are cited as having in the main idea of their work that of the harmonious and rhythmic filling of two-dimensional space: 'The subject of the picture was subordinate to the interior organisation.' Given the immense authority of the Church, the main patron for such painters, and the restraints of belief and dogma, it is an interesting aspect of Mainie's lecture that she emphasises so strongly this point about form and composition. Yet it is crucial to her thesis in this and later lectures; the fullness of her examination, covering as it does all periods, and doing so in the context of the most modern works of art imaginable at that time, was particularly important to her audience in Ireland, culturally very much on the European fringes.

She was at pains to enunciate a central thesis of what she believed to be the true avant-garde of the early 1920s: that Cubism had achieved the important point of recognition that art had to work in more direct response to the two-dimensional flatness of the picture-plane, but had not gone beyond this into the realms of non-representation now being explored by Gleizes, Evie and herself.

Indeed, as we have seen, many of the early Cubists were now arguing that the great contribution of Cubism had been to rediscover the importance of precise mathematical measurement in establishing principles of proportion and harmony, and were using these principles to return to a full representational classicism in imitation of the early Renaissance. This development was given its fullest theoretical exposition by the former

Italian Futurist, Gino Severini, in his *Du Cubisme au classicisme (esthetique du compas et du nombre)* published in 1921, but the tendency had been present for some time before then. Gleizes' former colleague, Jean Metzinger, had followed the same direction, as had Picasso in his own way (he had little patience with mathematical precision or geometrical formulae).

The focal point of Mainie's lecture, arguably the most important statement of her life, was the issue discussed at such length with Gleizes; could modern abstract painting, far from renouncing nature, give it new birth and new understanding. Perspective and realism had, in her view, belittled and distorted what they sought to represent. 'Gleizes and his followers' – meaning herself, Evie and Robert Pouyaud who had joined them in 1924 – endeavoured

> to penetrate beneath the exterior forms of nature, and to discover her natural laws and to construct accordingly. A picture should be a miniature universe, with all its forms interdependent, as the organisation of the universe itself. It should have a centre and unlimiting point of interest like the sun in the solar system . . . A picture should be as complete as the human body so that the removal of any of its members would upset the equilibrium of the whole. . . .[28]

She then quoted Gleizes' rejection of the third dimension. She was deeply concerned about the inner properties of things. Architecture – and she cited the Parthenon, the Pyramids, a great Gothic cathedral – did not copy nature; such buildings recreated a concept of the human mind governed by laws which sprang from the properties of the materials themselves – wood, glass, marble, stone. Painting had to do the same. And the essential starting point was the canvas. Those who looked at paintings needed to give up the idea that a painting was a kind of souvenir, like something out of a photograph album.

> You will not find blue sea and white clouds and waves, which make you feel you want to bathe and remind you of hot summer days; but instead, if you can look at these pictures with an open mind and without prejudice, they will give you a sensation of their own, resulting from the abstract qualities of the good or bad harmony of form and colour, balance and movement. They will affect you through your eyes and thence to your brain, the same way as music affects you through your ear and thence to your brain.

She considered art to be in an infinitely more difficult position than music when it came to persuading people to sidestep reality and accept the convention of abstraction. 'Art is, and must always be, a convention; every artist, directly he is faced with nature, has to start compromising . . . when faced with nature, at once, from the very start, it is a problem of selection and rejection for the artist, and increased by the limitations due to the medium he uses.'

She returned at the end of her lecture, to the theme she had touched on when she started: that the modernist movement was only an indication of what was to come; in no sense was her work an end in itself 'but an effort to develop with the spirit of the age while preserving the universal law of creation'.

Mainie spent March of that year working and studying with Gleizes and on her way through London she visited the exhibition of Belgian and Flemish Art.[29] Both she and Gleizes were deeply affected by the absence of Evie from their lives. In a letter to Mainie, now lost, but referred to in one of her replies, Gleizes had already expressed his doubts about the wisdom of testing out a second vocation on top of one as powerful as his own and Mainie's clearly were, within the realms of art. Mainie felt the same herself. All three of them were deeply religious, their faith a living part of their working lives. Sacrifice, persecution and ridicule about what they stood for, proselytising and teaching the rudiments of a set of beliefs, preaching a gospel, were all terms that closely described their work, and were echoed in their Christianity in far less strident or aggressive terms than they were in art. Undoubtedly Evie did not share the positive determination which guided Mainie and Gleizes. It is clear from her earliest letters that she placed a heavy dependence on her friend both in terms of the theory and the practice of their art. There was never any doubt about Mainie's leadership. And after the joint show in 1924 there was a divergence strongly reinforced by the two-year absence from the fray occasioned by Evie's investigation of her second vocation. But they wanted her back. She was needed for the fight.

Mainie again exhibited with the London Group in the summer of 1926, and again the familiar prejudice against abstract art was voiced, well before any English painters were even exhibiting pure abstract works. P.G. Konody, in *The Observer*, seemed to echo some of the Dublin prejudice when he plucked out certain artists, with relief, who 'do not allow their vision to be warped by their admiration for Cézanne'.[30] He linked together John Banting and Mainie Jellett as the two most modernist artists who 'belong to the category of decorative, two-dimensional cubism, if I may use this apparently contradictory term. The former has at least the appeal of a pretty colour pattern; the other might be a ground plan of a building plot or a gold mine.' Like George Russell, Konody seemed to view Cézanne with circumspection, though he detected in William Roberts 'a wholesome discipline' which was derived from 'Cubist experiments'. As Mainie said in a letter to Gleizes after the show, Konody, one of the best art critics writing for one of the best English papers, was 'not as advanced as Clive Bell,[31] Wyndham Lewis and Roger Fry'.[32] And when in due course it came to judging them, she was less than impressed by their prejudices and limitations, particularly Fry's and Bell's dependence on 'significant form' as a portmanteau term to deal with pictures which in her view they only partially understood.

Gleizes was involved at this time in a project for an international art magazine dealing with the theory and practice of abstract painting, and he wrote to Mainie at the end of August, asking for her help with potential contributors from England.[33] What he wanted was someone to 'direct' the English section. She put forward Wyndham Lewis's name, 'he is certainly one of the most advanced of the English artists'. Next to him came Clive Bell, and then Roger Fry.

Dublin was too isolated for Mainie to offer help.

One reason alone would have made it almost impossible for me to do it – the fact of living in Ireland – one would be out of touch with the chief British Exhibitions which are held in London and the modern English painters are mostly centred in London; so that it would be essential to have someone to do the job who lives in London . . .

She mentioned the *Sunday Times* art critic, Frank Rutter, in the letter of 8 September, referring to his 'quite good criticism of one of my pictures that I exhibited at the "London Group" about a year ago'.[34] Rutter had just published his book on modern art, and Mainie undertook to get a copy of it for Gleizes. 'I think his interpretation of your pictures quite mad!' she wrote, underscoring the sentence.

Her real feelings about what was happening in English painting at this time were at best sceptical. As she wrote to Gleizes:

I think the English people are slowly waking up to the fact that there is a new movement in painting, but they are still only half awake – The Tate Gallery, the gallery that is equivalent to the Luxembourg in Paris, has now started to buy modern French pictures – they have got some five Cézannes, Van Gogh, Matisse, Bracque (sic) etc. which is a beginning, as before the Gallery was the haven of the worst forms of early Victorian art!

In a long passage in her letter devoted to the relationship between theology, science and philosophy, of deep interest at that time to Gleizes, and always a dominant intellectual issue with Mainie, she writes:

The fact of Evie going to a convent and giving up her life to an idea, does not help me one way or [the] other to believe more fully in Christianity or not — I think she is a person who has a passion for self-sacrifice and that she may put up with a lot from that point of view that she would not otherwise. I will certainly send her your letter to me as I am sure she will be very interested to see it. Also of course you can write to her and I think it would be a very good thing if you did.

Gleizes greatly admired the early Christian monastic movement but in his *Vie et mort de l'occident chrétien*,[35] which he was writing at this time, he argued that Christianity no longer lived up to its spiritual calling. In a letter to Mainie that is now lost, he seems to have expressed this view with regard to Evie's convent: 'I also think what you say about Evie is true,' Mainie wrote, 'but I don't think the convents are entirely without "Esprit".'

At the end of her letter Mainie expressed her pleasure that Gleizes and his wife were 'having a good rest at Cavalaire', the house they owned on the coast near St Tropez. However, their holiday was rudely interrupted by a car accident on the way back from Toulon. The chauffeur and Madame Gleizes were unhurt, but Gleizes was thrown from the vehicle, breaking both ankles. He spent two weeks in the clinic at Toulon. As well as giving her news about the accident, Gleizes responded to her comments about the English critics with some severe words about them, naming Roger Fry as the worst — 'Fry surtout est fantastique.' They deal, he said, with 'subjects about which they know nothing'. The new review, he went on, would be designed to allow the artists to write for each other, exchanging points of view, in order to discover similarities of technique and ideas. With her own experience of critics in Dublin up to that time Mainie could only agree wholeheartedly with Gleizes' view.

CHAPTER THIRTEEN

'A lecture by Miss Jellett'

IN 1926 THE Jellett family holiday was spent with friends in Glandore, a pretty little fishing village in west Cork. Daniel Corkery, author of *The Hidden Ireland*,[1] described the promontory between Glandore and Castle Haven as 'one of the most secret places in Ireland, without traffic, almost without pulse of life'. A pulse of summer excitement, however, was brought to the Marine Hotel in Glandore by the large party from Dublin who went there to dances, and enjoyed picnics and swimming with enthusiasm. 'I bathe every day', Mainie wrote to Gleizes, 'but I expect the water is far colder than the Mediterranean.' She told him that she had many students, was planning another solo exhibition in January, and wanted to go to him after that for a period of work and study. She was also working at abstract compositions, 'a bit every day, and think we certainly have advanced a lot with the new way of planning the colours in simple masses'.

Evie's religious life was still a cause for concern: 'I am afraid I like the idea of what she is doing <u>less</u> and <u>less</u>', Mainie wrote. At the end of September she visited Evie in the convent in Truro. She took with her letters and books, including those she had received from Gleizes, and they talked about art. But the nuns, sympathetic though they were to Evie's past vocation, were of the view that it was a distraction. By December they had decided that she was 'not to be let do her painting now till she becomes a "sister" if she does become one!' In a letter to Gleizes just two days before Christmas, Mainie wrote: 'Evie is just the same and is still in the Convent, sometimes one thinks she is quite settled there, and then she says something that reveals the chaotic condition of her mind which makes one anxious again'.

Mainie's 1927 exhibition opened on 7 January and was reviewed in both *The Irish Times* and the *Irish Independent*. Neither of the two notices was signed. A mixture of bafflement and admiration brought the *Irish Times* critic rather abruptly to his conclusions, with references to the 'average' man's difficulties offset by 'many artistic folk in the city' getting satisfaction for their modern tastes.[2] The writer in the *Irish Independent* was altogether more positive, detecting 'rapid' development and an increased influence of pre-Renaissance painting. 'Her work is arresting and intellectually stimulating. Miss Jellett's colour sense is so well developed that the beauty of her work is at once obvious and undeniable.' The writer found the pursuit of pure abstraction had the merit of 'high courage'.[3]

George Russell, reviewing the show in the *Irish Statesman*,[4] chose to repeat at very considerable length his original and basic objection to Mainie's work: that it was flawed because it relied on 'the deliberately limited vocabulary of the cubists'. Her exhibition included two landscapes, four drawings and two still-life studies, as well as Cubist works ranging from one- to six-element compositions. Russell analysed a landscape in order to admire her cleverness as a painter, revealing as he does so his own somewhat conventional approach to artistic emotion: 'That house with its gloomy woods behind it might hold some romantic story though not a figure stands in its shadowy sunshine to suggest a poetic sentiment.' And of course from such a standpoint of critical expectation no work of pure abstraction could possibly influence him. This was decidedly the case of course in a critic who had not encountered, discussed or apparently studied Cubist

137. *Abstract Composition*, 1925. Oil on canvas, 79 × 65. Scotland, private collection.

135. *Abstract Composition*, 1925. Oil on canvas, 51 × 66. Dublin, private collection.

136. *Abstract Composition*, 1925. Oil on canvas, 71 × 95.1. London, private collection.

theory. 'I feel, somehow,' Russell wrote, 'that the cubist movement is wrong-headed, and that it springs from the reason rather than the imagination.'

The merit of 'high courage'; a flawed and limited vocabulary: are these critical constraints consistent with the advances apparent in Mainie's works from 1925 to 1927, in which so many of the problems evident in the years 1922–4 are resolved? Her *Abstract Composition* (Pl. 135) reveals an open and adventurous use of space in the composition, together with a great sense of harmony. *Abstract Composition* (Pl. 136) represents a new departure, with the horizontal division of the two 'voices' mid-way in the canvas creating great cohesion and tension between the warm and cool colours. In contrast with this work, *Abstract Composition* (Pl. 137) achieves a quite different resolution, basically in terms of colour, with a close relationship rather than a contrast between the two 'voices'.

Russell had come close, in his review, to a statement of his own, somewhat ambivalent position. As we have seen, he was decidedly against the academic tradition and wanted to see it overturned by some new and inspired movement in visual art. But his poetic sensibilities, combined with his theosophical beliefs, simply could not accommodate the idea that this new movement in art might derive from 'modernism' as he saw it. This is clear from a central passage in his review of Mainie's show which almost certainly became a bone of contention between them. It is worth quoting at length:

Many artists, tired of realistic painting, dreamed of an art which would be like music which does not rely on any mimicry of the sound of nature but moves us by echoes of our bodiless and soundless moods. Some may have thought it possible for the painter deserting all mimicry of natural forms to move us by artful arrangements of abstract colour and form. Of course in so far as the colour sense or the decorative sense is real, there is a pleasure in looking at such compositions. But what I feel is that they are compositions, not imaginations, and because they are intellectual in their begetting they are limited no less than by the narrow range of forms. I can imagine an art corresponding to music which would ignore the representation of natural forms and which would only concern itself with whatever images were born in the imagination, but I do not feel that these cubist forms are the forms imagination takes. They belong to a school and are almost common property in that school, and if they appear before the inner eye of any artist it is because he has seen them with his open eyes in the compositions of Picasso, Gleizes, Juan Gris, Fernand Leger and others of the same school.

Russell sought fundamental change in art, but refused to recognise that it might come as a result of Cubist painting, particularly where this was abstract. And his criticisms of Mainie's work founder on this basic lack of judgment. He is additionally confused about the roles played in the development of modern art up to 1927, by his named painters. He was not a regular visitor to Paris and its art galleries, and in no sense as familiar with events there as the artist whose work he was criticising.

Mainie responded, after considerable thought. First, in a lecture given to the Dublin Literary Society,[5] in which she dealt with the precise point raised by Russell on the analogy between music and abstract art. Her own work, she explained, 'was an attempt to create in the abstract right from the beginning, as musicians do'. She put before her audience certain 'characteristic types of people who look at pictures'. Among these she listed 'the literary type, who expect every picture to tell a story.' Whether deliberately or not, the reference embraced Russell's own work, which was frequently anecdotal.

In addition, she prepared an article on abstract Cubism, and sent it in to the editor of the *Irish Statesman*. Russell ran away from the prospect of a debate which could have had enormous impact on the artistic life of the city at that time, and of course on the group of painters who saw Mainie as their leader. 'Dear Miss Jellett, I would have been very glad to have printed your article but I am not at present accepting new MSS for the *Irish*

138. *Abstract Composition*, *c*.1926. Oil on canvas, 89 × 71. London, private collection.

139. *Abstract Composition*, *c*.1925. Gouache on paper, 16 × 20. Dublin, private collection.

Statesman whose copy-boxes are filled to overflowing. Yours sincerely, George Russell.'[6]

It was an unsatisfactory evasion of an issue which he had provoked at length in his own review. Mainie did not try again. Her own public lecture had worked to her advantage. *The Irish Times* described her as 'the only serious exponent in this country of the ultra-modernist school of painting',[7] and the lecture itself was a substantial and comprehensive view of art as seen by the artist rather than the critic.

Mainie saw in her own form of modernist painting a return to simple basic rules of composition as they had emerged from Cézanne's redefinition of his own early Impressionist roots. This catechism, classical in its simplicity even then, brought her audience right at the beginning of her lecture to the dramatic confrontation between Impressionism and Post-Impressionism, between light as a chief characteristic and pure form as a central objective for the painter. All of this was reflected in the kind of work being done by painters and sculptors on the Continent, as well as by Mainie herself. It was not otherwise present in Britain and Ireland, whose record in the visual arts was too rooted in the past, in the academic tradition. It was literary rather than visual, in both countries.

Mainie chose carefully the ground on which to open her lecture to the Dublin Literary Society: that of England's and Ireland's position within the overall framework of visual art internationally.

England though it has some fine artists has never been a country of painters; but has taken its place in the forefront of literature. Perhaps England's richest artistic era was the Middle Ages, when she was fully immersed in the great Gothic and Christian revival of art. We have her magnificent cathedrals and churches, some of them still

140. *Abstract Composition*, 1926. Oil on canvas, 152.5 × 71. London, private collection.

showing vestiges of a great school of fresco painters, as a living witness to the genuine artistic spirit of that time . . .

In Ireland very much the same thing occurs, though Ireland with the Celtic blood still running in her veins has an artistic background that ought to be more productive of artistic effort than it is . . . Ireland again like England is living in her literature, which is far in advance of her painting . . .

The saving grace for all the arts, she maintained, outside the academic tradition which was stationary, was the current emphasis on research and experiment in painting, with its associated upheaval. This, she felt, was leading towards a struggle to rise out of the present 'decadent torpor', thereby creating 'the foundation of a new curve upwards'.

Of most interest to herself, and probably to her audience in the light of the controversy about abstract art which was still going on in Dublin after four years, was the question of Cubism. What has particular point to us today, with particular reference to her own position, is her definition of the groups within Cubism, and their aims, at that time.

Braque, Picasso, Metzinger, Léger and Gris, she claimed, were the main artists taking realistic form as their inspiration; Gleizes, Valmier, Herbin, Van Doesburgh and Kandinsky, with 'Picasso in certain pictures', belonged to the non-realistic Cubist tradition. Among the latter group she said: 'the painter's aim was then to make that flat surface live and not to destroy its initial truth by boring holes in it, the result of Renaissance perspective.' (This charming image, of the effects of perspective, together with substantial passages of practical theory about Cubism, were cut from the published version of the lecture.)

What Mainie Jellett said at this time was reflected directly in the work she was exhibiting – her lecture was given within a month of her solo show in January 1927 – so that the words have a certain practical intensity (Pls. 138–40). And central to what she was saying, both in the immediate practical sense of the formal structure of her composition, and in the traditional and historical sources to which she referred, was the idea of mobility.

> The surface whether wall or canvas was considered as a space to be filled harmoniously with forms and colours related to the particular exterior shape of that surface. The picture becomes a living organism in itself, a complete whole, like any natural living organism. If a human body loses a limb there is at once a lack of equilibrium, likewise if a picture is incomplete there is lack of equilibrium. A picture to the Cubist artist ought to be complete in every part, its movement organised like the movement of a small universe, in fact an organisation of living colour and form expressed through the medium of paint on a flat surface; the third dimension depth, being the special property of the sculptor. One of the great differences between the cubist theories and the post renaissance theories is in their idea of form. Form through the ages has ever moved between two extremes, one mobile, the other immobile. One non-materialistic the other materialistic. The Cubists and Futurists have chosen the mobile non-materialistic ideal of the Middle Ages in France and Italy and the Celtic and Eastern ideals in contrast to the immobile materialistic ideal of the late Renaissance in Europe.

The principle of movement, related to rhythm, was associated by Mainie with the solar system and the sense that if it had shape at all it was circular and revolving: 'the form of a living object is not an aspect of that object or an instantaneous impression, but is the completed movement of that object in space'. This was in direct contrast with the Renaissance idea of a painting being a scene observed through the window of the picture's frame, distanced and formalised, even made mechanical, by the inevitable imposition of perspective. What Impressionism achieved was to bring this 'immobile, materialistic ideal' to an extreme point. 'It was sufficient for those artists to express the instantaneous registration of a camera, which gives one the representation of an arrested movement in the cycle of movements which make a complete form.' What Cézanne had agonised over, as a painter, was the conflict between what his mind told him and what his eye told him: two different, quite formal ideals of interpretation confronted each other in his mind and in his creative vision as an artist. Mainie, like Gleizes, like her earlier teacher, André Lhote, saw him as a crucial figure, but in danger of being recognised and admired without being understood. In a further extensive section of her lecture (again, deleted from the published version), she gave a lengthy, but highly important analysis and examination of Cézanne, drawn directly from Gleizes:

Cézanne worked from nature. Having arranged on a table all the elements of his picture, (in this case a Still Life group) a fruit dish, apples, a table napkin, he then looked at his canvas and then from it to the realistic subject he was ready to draw. At this juncture the drama began. What he had arranged on the table, what he had felt with his hands and appreciated, what his eyes had grasped ceased to exist when he receded from the table. An untruthful description had substituted itself for reality. The fruit dish with the beautiful circle of its bowl, related to the plane of the table, and being in the same order, became flattened into an oval without formal significance; the noble harmony of the objects in relation to one another was lost . . . It was necessary for him to make a great intellectual effort to re-establish in their reality these losses, and to rediscover their real plastic values. On a flat surface such as the surface of a canvas on which is evolved the fact of painting, which is plastic, measurable, and controllable in its nature, Cézanne saw clearly the participation of the circle . . . this circle justified itself by exalting the rectangular plane, it was part of it, and of the same family . . . Cézanne, impregnated by the habits which his intellectual formation had given him, was all his life persuaded of the necessity of description as the starting point of a work of art . . . He tried to associate in an impossible unity two contradictions, the painted work which recounts something and the *plastic act* which *realises* something; the image of the fruit dish on [the] one hand, and on the other the plastic circle, the first considering the plane of the canvas as a picture theoretically explaining the exterior world of three dimensions, the second born of the nature of the surface or plane and considered first and last as a plastic reality . . . The Impressionists exhausted their own formulas, but in Cézanne the intensity of his research is such that it does not stop with his death . . . his pictures are insufficient solutions of the problem which he wished to solve . . . He worked always in a manner which tended towards recreating formally the descriptive anti-plastic image. He talked of cylinders, cubes, and spheres, thinking that their purity could unify all. The result did not satisfy him, he tried to free himself from the fetters of description . . . His eyes tired by the exterior vision looked to the interior vision where he found a plastic participation with what he was striving for – the cylinder, the cube, the sphere, (thinking three-dimensionally) would become, (two-dimensionally) the right angle, the plane, the circle, because the picture is a plane or surface; modelling or gradation would be the contrast. He died at the moment when the explication was in his grasp.[8]

With Cézanne she linked three other Post-Impressionists: Van Gogh, Seurat and Gauguin. She dealt also with the Fauves, characterising Henri Matisse as 'France's greatest colourist of the present time,' and with Futurism and Surrealism. The lecture was a prodigious achievement. As will have been noted it dealt with ideas put forward in her lecture the previous year, but was far more extensive and profound. It combined the best of socratic and didactic purposes. She was both declaring her faith and offering a unique measure of carefully reasoned teaching.

She dealt too with academic painting, particularly portraiture:

141. *Babbin*, 1925. Pencil on paper, 27 × 21. Dublin, private collection.

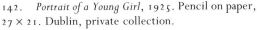

142. *Portrait of a Young Girl*, 1925. Pencil on paper, 27 × 21. Dublin, private collection.

the public like to feel they can pick the ribbons off a woman's dress, or caress the shimmering satin of its material and touch with their fingers the soft modelled flesh of her arm, all sensations which they welcome in what to them is a successful academy picture . . . Academic painting will always remain hostile to new movements, till the new movement in its turn has become academic and moribund. Then its members will be exalted to the Olympian heights of academicians.'

Her own abilities in portraiture were at that time confined to drawings; but she demonstrated, in a number of portrait sketches of her sister, Babbin, and of an unknown young girl, her talent for economy and directness (Pls. 141–2).

Lecturing sometimes led to the sale of her works. On one occasion she lectured to a group in the parish hall at Sutton, near Howth. Kathleen Fox, a painter and sculptor, and Norris Davidson, were among the audience, and Davidson recalls being 'asked, ordered to, implored to or something like that, to go to a lecture by Miss Jellett. Kathleen and I realised that everyone else present thought they were wasting their time over nonsense. They kept trying to see things . . . a fish, a tea-pot or a bicycle in the abstracts.'[9] The Davidsons and the Jelletts knew each other, and Norris had the distinct impression that his mother did everything possible to avoid going to the lecture herself, sending him to represent the family. He was greatly taken by Mainie's abstract paintings and his mother later visited Mainie in her studio in order to buy the gouache which he had particularly liked, but Mainie was unable to find it and, instead, Mrs Davidson bought her son the big oil painting done from the smaller work. It cost her £20, no mean sum in 1927.

All her work at this time – painting, lecturing, writing and teaching – has a closely woven texture to it. Gleizes and his ideas were central to it all, as is apparent from her letters to him.

> I have also been lending your books to various people who have come to me – and they have all been very interested in them. I have been painting big pictures from the gouaches I did with you and teaching and trying to write the article you wanted me to write on the way I practice your methods of painting. I have nearly done the letter press but still have ten diagrams to draw out I expect you will think it very stupid but in any event I feel the writing of it has helped me to clarify my ideas a bit.

These exchanges were reinforced by a visit to him at Serrières in March.[10]

Ireland was in the throes of a general election that June, the first of two in 1927. W.T. Cosgrave had governed for five years since the first Free State election of 1923, and was now seeking a fresh mandate. Mainie wrote in a letter to Gleizes: 'We are in the middle of a General Election here, but there is no excitement or interest. I think the Irish are getting tired of politics at last.' This was not of course the case since it was a crucial time, politically. The main opposition party Fianna Fáil had up until then remained outside constitutional politics, refusing to take their seats in the Dáil on account of the oath of allegiance. This changed, and the change was fundamental.[11]

James Winder Good, who replaced 'Y.O.' as art critic for the *Irish Statesman* offered light-hearted political analogies in his review of the June exhibition of the Society of Dublin Painters. 'I can recommend it to the politicians, to most of whom it will probably come as a surprise to hear that artists can teach them something about the essentials of their own trade.' He recommended William Conor's 'humorous sympathy' as an example of reconciliation between candidates and voters, and Grace Henry's landscapes as a better guide to the Gaeltacht than the statistical tables which had been debated during the campaign. 'Miss Mainie Jellett's abstraction in one, three and five elements might fitly symbolise the mental bewilderment of the ordinary man who tried to puzzle out the intricacies of cross-voting under P.R. in a Saorstát constituency.'[12]

By the early summer it was beginning to seem that Evie would not remain with the 'Community of the Epiphany'. Her letters to Mainie indicated growing doubt about a religious vocation and Mainie passed the information on to Gleizes. 'I shall be very surprised', she wrote on 9 June,

> if she stays on in the Convent and takes her final vows . . . I do wish she could definitely make up her mind what to do, but on the other hand if she comes out without giving herself every chance she will start regretting she had not stayed her full novitiate – she is such a complex character – it is very difficult to form an opinion as to what she may do. I really do think it would be a very good thing if you did write to her and let her see that if she does come out of the Convent people have not forgotten about her and that there is her painting.

It seems that Gleizes did not write. He was not the best of correspondents, as Mainie was quick to point out in the same letter: 'This will be the third letter I have written into space so I think you ought to begin to have a guilty conscience!!' She also asks whether his new book is out, which may have prompted Gleizes to send her a copy. This was *Tradition et Cubisme*.[13] It was an exercise in retrenchment and a historical summary of all that had been achieved, and similar to Mainie's assessment in her lecture as noted above. It was an approach reinforced by the decision made in the late summer by Evie that she had no religious vocation. One vocation – that of her art – was enough.

On 3 October Evie wrote to Gleizes to tell him that she had decided to leave the community. 'I do not feel I have a vocation', she told him. 'It has been very difficult to see but I feel quite at peace now about it and as certain as one can be of anything.' She wrote from London, where she had been staying for six weeks in one of the branch houses of the 'Community of the Epiphany'. 'They have been most awfully considerate and kind especially when I know they thought I was mistaken which made it all very difficult for every one. However I expect I was meant to test it and I am very grateful for being shown so clearly that I have no real vocation'. Mainie made a detour to see Evie in London on her way to Scotland to join the rest of her family, bringing with her a copy of *Tradition et Cubisme* together with a number of her own most recent drawings, gouaches and paintings.

Thus, suddenly, at the end of a long period of enforced separation during which one of them had struggled with her soul and conscience, while the other had pursued a solitary road , the two women were again together and planning an early trip to France to join Gleizes once more in further exploration of abstract Cubism. In a letter at the end of November 1927, containing plans for another visit that year to the 'community' at Serrières,[14] Mainie wrote: 'Evie is working hard, I give her lessons and try to help her whenever I see her.' By then Evie had moved back to Ireland and was living with her sister near Lucan, outside Dublin. 'I see her as much as possible and I think she is getting back again into her painting very quickly, and already doing very good work.'

143. *Design for Carpet*, c.1928. Gouache on paper mounted on card, 19 × 16.3. Dublin, private collection.

144. *Outline Design for Carpet*, c.1928. Pencil on paper, 13.4 × 11.7. Dublin, private collection. Inscribed on back 'This side for A'(merica). Another carpet design of the same period carries the inscription: 'Other Side America'.

IT IS HARD to date accurately the point when Mainie began to develop the relationship between abstract Cubism and the decorative arts, but in her solo exhibition in the summer of 1928 she showed carpet designs for the first time. They were to become a regular feature of her work from then on (Pls. 143–6). The development was noted with approval.[1]

There were obvious dangers. After the difficult, painful and isolated years of study, exploration and neglect there was suddenly the prospect of admiration and the profitable application of a style. The Arts and Crafts movement had been, and still was, strong in Ireland and set a precedent for Mainie. The Jellett family were friends and supporters of the Yeats sisters and of Cuala Industries,[2] and the whole family tradition, going back to William Stokes and his views on education, was sympathetic to the idea of art's application to people's lives at as many levels as possible.

Moreover, it was never the intention of Gleizes and his group to appeal only to refined or eccentric sensibilities. From the earliest days Gleizes regretted that art had become such a rarefied activity and, in his writing on the Middle Ages, he emphasises – as surely as any of the founders of the Arts and Crafts movement – the coherence of artistic activity, from the most ambitious architectural enterprises to the humblest domestic bowl. The Dutch De Stijl group, the Russian Constructivists and the German Bauhaus were all anxious to apply the non-representational principles they had developed in painting to articles of everyday use. Although Gleizes was in touch with these developments, he rejected their enthusiasm for industrial production. Closer in spirit to the English Arts and Crafts movement, he attached great importance to individual craftsmanship as opposed to the application of design to industrial products.

Gleizes was also involved with Mainie in the carpet enterprise. They had both submitted sketches, drawings and finished gouache designs to Myrbor, a Paris manufacturer. Gleizes was also working on costume and stage sets for a ballet, as did Mainie later on. But he seems disparaging about this particular application of the art they practised although he would hardly have undertaken such complex design commitments without attaching some value to the work. Gleizes, after all, was married to a relatively wealthy woman and did not need to do such work for a living. But he had moved on from the period of intense exploration of pure theory, undertaken with Mainie and Evie between 1921 and 1923, to a period of *practice* of pure abstract Cubism, and this had brought about further evolutions in his art and in its application. All his life Gleizes saw art as a creative function which could improve the world and make it a more just and equitable place to live.

Nor was he a stranger to the collective approach of artists to the problems of making their lives and work applicable to each other and to the world of everyday production of which they had a duty to form part. Indeed it is probable that at least one of the persuasive forces which led Mainie and Evie in the direction of Gleizes in the first place was the fame of l'Abbaye de Créteil, the artists' collective founded in 1906.[3] The Créteil experience had had a profound effect on Gleizes' art, moving him forward from an Impressionist dependence on light to a powerful, Post-Impressionist grappling with volume, mass and colour. He was deeply influenced emotionally and intellectually as

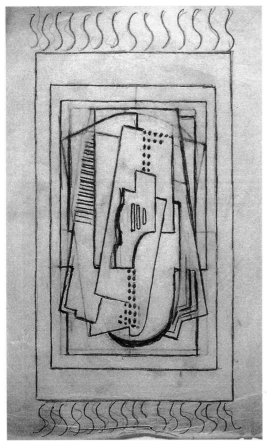

145. *Design for Carpet*, c.1928. Pencil on Paper, 19.8 × 10.5. Dublin, private collection.

146. *Design for Carpet*, c.1928. Pencil and red crayon on paper, 19.8 × 10.5. Dublin, private collection.

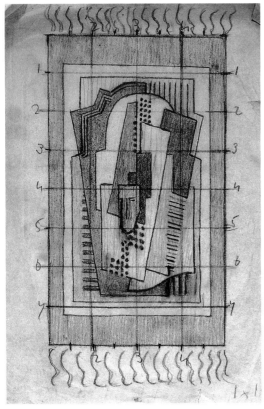

well, and yet almost twenty years were to pass before he could undertake a similar artistic experiment, this time involving Mainie and Evie and Robert Pouyaud.

Pouyaud first met Mainie and Evie at Gleizes' studio in the Rue Gally, at Neuilly, in November 1924. Anne Dangar gives an amusing account of their relationship:

> Mainie, who was the most intelligent and most logical woman I have ever met in my life, had greatly helped Mr Gleizes to develop this method of translation and rotation. She had written about it in English and illustrated it with superb drawings. When Pouyaud (two years later) asked for lessons from Mr Gleizes, he was a little disappointed when Mr Gleizes passed him on to Mainie – the French do not have a great deal of confidence in the teaching of women. Pouyaud took three days before he could bring himself to submit to this indignity. But after his first lesson, the proud Robert Pouyaud was filled with respect and even awe for this Irish woman.[4]

Pouyaud explains how the researches into abstract art led inevitably towards the community which was eventually set up on the banks of the Rhône, south of Lyons.

> Our method of work was tirelessly to execute a series of tracings on the basis of a common structure, so as to derive from it a eurhythmic, plastic organism. The operation of the painting-object was born out of our collective work and it was marvellous to see the expansion of four very distinct individuals willingly disciplined through contact with the angular austerity of the planes put into movement according to the laws of the universe.
>
> As a result of our long conversations, our discoveries, our advances, our mistakes, the doctrine of Albert Gleizes was clarified. The implications for the social field are well known: decentralisation, return to the land, a healthy life far from the towns, rediscovery of the rhythm of nature, rediscovery of man's role as microcosm. At that time, our ideas struck no chord in the world about us and we understood that we would have to live on the margins of this society so virulently condemned by Albert Gleizes.[5]

Pouyaud continued to dream about the possibilities of a community of artists, but it was not until the summer of 1927 that he made the tentative decision to leave Paris with his wife and endeavour to put Gleizes' ideas into practice.

In keeping with the innate caution with which we have seen Gleizes make the important decisions in his life, the ideas put forward by Pouyaud were considered with great care and answered in painstaking detail. Pouyaud was proposing that he and his wife would leave Paris and move to the country, somewhere near Gleizes, so that they could pursue their artistic interests together. Gleizes was concerned about how the young couple would survive, and what they would live on. He suggested instead that Pouyaud should consider their own property at Serrières. It consisted of three houses, one of which was empty; the gardens were large and well cultivated, and could be relied on for fruit and vegetables throughout the year. There were hens to provide eggs and meat and a goat to ensure a supply of milk and cheese. Once established there, Gleizes pointed out, Pouyaud would find other local resources. He would explain all of this when they met and he proposed a visit in late September. 'We will sort out all the details of how it can be organised and you can be sure, dear friend, that we will do everything we can to help you to achieve your freedom.'[6]

The visit took place in October. Pouyaud decided against taking the empty house at Serrières and was preparing to rent another small house for a year when he was stopped by Gleizes. Something much more exciting had been found. Across the broad expanse of the Rhône, in the small village of Sablons, stood an ancient staging post for river barges, known as 'Moly-Sabata'. Gleizes identified it as late eighteenth century. It stood directly on the river bank, with quay and moorings and balconies giving a view up and down the river. Its main rooms, about twelve in number, were on the upper floor with a staircase up to them from the sizeable walled garden. In Gleizes' opinion it would be very suitable, both as a home for his pupil, and as an artistic centre: 'A slap of whitewash over the too old and ugly paper, and you'll have a very nice place to live in.'[7]

Gleizes had already invited Mainie and Evie to stay in December, and they would be followed, he told Pouyaud, by a Romanian poet, Dobo. The parish priest had offered his full support for the project, and the local architect was enthusiastic. But Gleizes expressed a note of caution: 'Ne brulez pas vos vaisseaux derrière vous.' He counselled that they should retain access to employment in Paris, and an interest in their apartment there in case the experiment came to nothing.

Moly-Sabata made a fairly grim impression on Pouyaud and his wife, and this was seriously aggravated, first by a bitterly cold winter, and then by floods. On 12 February the Rhône burst its banks, and by the following day the house itself was cut off, surrounded by more than a metre of water. Mainie and Evie had wisely stayed with Gleizes, in Serrières, and were able to signal across the river while watching the waves beating against the walls of the old house, where the three intrepid inhabitants were somewhat fearful. Dobo was all for attempting to swim across the river but was dissuaded and eventually the flood subsided.

The four painters – Gleizes, Mainie, Evie and Pouyaud – worked together in the studios, both at Serrières and at Moly-Sabata, and, with the exception of Evie, whose disability prevented her from joining them, continued their discussions during long walks in the surrounding countryside. Madame Pouyaud recalls that even the walk from Serrières to Moly, a distance of perhaps two kilometres, was too much for Evie. It was, according to Pouyaud, 'une période extrêmement féconde'. In the evenings they held parties at Moly-Sabata, sometimes inviting in the village neighbours. Dobo would dress up in a smoking jacket and dance with the village girls to the music from the radio. He remained, for the brief period he spent at Moly-Sabata, a droll and provocative member of the community.[8] They kept bees and rabbits, spent much time on the upkeep of the old house – Pouyaud often climbing onto the roof to replace tiles and seal up leakages – and struggled to get vegetables and fruit going in the gardens. Their income was also augmented by the sale of *pochoirs*, which various collectors sought at the time and which were also sold in Paris. These were mainly of Gleizes' paintings, but also included works by the others.

The development of the community at Moly-Sabata presented difficulties from its inception in the winter of 1927, until Pouyaud and his wife left, exactly three years to the day after their arrival. The work involved in making a modest living was arduous, and impinged on Pouyaud's painting, and the winter of 1928, though not as bad as the previous year, was lonely and difficult and made worse by the death of their child. Eventually he asked Gleizes to find someone to help him share the burden of the house and in September 1929 Francis Manevy and his wife agreed to the terms of membership and moved in.

Manevy was responsible for the Lyon section of the *Fêtes du Peuple*,[10] and had opened a gallery in Nice. While there, he became friendly with the painter, Walter Firpo, and introduced him to Gleizes. However, according to Mme Gleizes, Manevy had no business sense, and the gallery soon failed. Its last exhibition was of paintings by Gleizes, Hone, Jellett, Firpo and Ben Nicholson. When the gallery closed, Manevy asked if he and his wife could live at Moly-Sabata, though, as Mme Gleizes says, he was far from being touched by 'la mystique agricole'.

The expansion of the community led to the writing of a set of regulations for the men, women and children who might take part, an extensive and detailed document which reflects Pouyaud's longing for a monastic discipline.[11] To his despair, it was never really put into practice. By the spring of 1930 serious disagreements had developed. Pouyaud wrote of the dream being turned into a nightmare and of himself and his wife facing 'la plus grande désillusion de notre vie.'

It was at this time that Anne Dangar, who was to become the most important person at Moly-Sabata, arrived from Sydney. For eighteen years, nine as a student and nine as a colleague, Anne Dangar had worked with an Australian *plein air* painter, Julia Ashton. In the 1920s, passing through Paris on her way to London, she had been converted to Cubist and abstract art, and had studied under Lhote with her friend, Grace Crowley. In 1927 or 1928, shortly before she returned to Australia, she had seen some paintings by Gleizes, and had been profoundly impressed by them. She tried at the time, unsuccessfully, to make contact with him. On her return to Australia she resumed her teaching, setting up her own school which was very successful. But she found having to teach naturalistic painting increasingly intolerable. Mme Gleizes says that two of her pupils came to Paris and worked with Gleizes in the summer of 1929. It is possible that one of them was in, fact, her friend, Grace Crowley. When they heard about Moly-Sabata, they said that it would be perfect for Anne Dangar. Gleizes wrote to her and she replied immediately with a telegram saying she would come in February, if the position was certain. She arrived at the beginning of March.

It is a remarkable story. She had, without hesitation, abandoned a promising career for an uncertain future. In some ways her background shows a surprising similarity to that of both Mainie and Evie. Like them she had a solid formation in academic painting, from which she turned, first to Lhote, then to Gleizes. The Dangar family is still a considerable power in New South Wales, though she came from a less powerful branch of it. She has the same, semi-aristocratic self-confidence which one associates with Mainie, and something of the humility and desire to be of service which one associates more with Evie. Her grandfather on her mother's side was a Protestant minister who, according to Mme Gleizes, had been obliged to leave Ireland because he was 'too much involved in struggles with the Catholics'. She always stressed the Irish side of her family rather than the powerful land-owning side. She lived in Moly-Sabata for over twenty years until her death in 1951 and left behind an affectionate memory that is still very much alive in the region.[12]

Pouyaud introduced her to local potters called Nicholas, at St-Désirat, and she embarked on the craft which was to occupy and sustain herself and Moly-Sabata for the rest of her life. He also taught her the technique of making *pochoirs*. He wrote of: 'her ardent Irish nature, her self-assurance, her radiant energy, her Australian bluntness, her idealism based on her belief in the Anglican religion, made of her an incomparable companion'.

At about this time there was a serious breach between Manevy and Pouyaud, essentially a clash of personality and of authority. Gleizes seems to have sided with the Manevys, despite an explanation from Anne Dangar that placed them firmly in the wrong. Pouyaud's emotional and moral dependence on Mainie is evident in his long letter of 19 June 1930, as is his deep sense of hurt and his sense of betrayal by Gleizes. 'Moly-Sabata has gone in a direction which is no longer mine – this direction has delivered Moly-Sabata up to chance and obliged it to open its doors to individuals who have no intellectual value and are only interested by the untroubled and easy material life they can have in it.'

The Pouyauds left in November and the Manevys some time after, leaving Anne Dangar alone. She was, however, to be joined by the musician César Geoffray.[13] The Geoffrays brought with them their maid, Lucie Deveyle, who fell in love with the house and its way of life and went on to become a weaver, second only in importance to Anne Dangar in maintaining the life of Moly-Sabata where she lived until her death in 1956.[14] The Geoffrays were based in Moly-Sabata from 1930 to 1940, and their lively, light-hearted approach was sometimes to cause problems for Anne Dangar, with her more religious and often apparently austere commitment.

At the end of July Mainie wrote to Gleizes commenting on Pouyaud's decision to leave Moly-Sabata.

I wish Pouyaud would have settled to stay at Moly-Sabata, though I don't think he ever would, and I don't expect you would want him to either. I know he is greatly to blame, but all the same he has a very great respect for you and I think feels it all very much – as you do too, I am sure. Evie heard from him the other day but I have not seen the letter as she does not come back till Tuesday – He has sent us an article he has written on colour – I wish he was more humane and less of a fanatic.

Mainie's view of the Moly-Sabata experiment was sympathetic at first, mainly on account of the earlier collaboration in Paris with Pouyaud, of whom she had become fond, but also of course because Gleizes was enthusiastic. She had written in November 1927 when it all began, 'You can explain to us your other plans and ideas about the "Community" where M. Pouyaud and his wife are – It sounds a most interesting idea, we shall be very interested to hear all about it when we come.' But Mainie was also cautious about getting directly involved. Both her own and Evie's relationship with Gleizes was of a different kind, and she needed to maintain it at a level where only pure ideas about abstract painting would be discussed, uninterrupted by petty rows and jealousies. Pouyaud depended very much on her. In a letter which Gleizes wrote to Mainie in October 1928 he referred to Pouyaud 'counting the days' until she would come again and they could resume their long discussions about painting and their practical studio work together. He kept her informed about the evolution of events at Moly-Sabata, sending her examples of the *pochoirs* on which he was working and long documents about the techniques they followed in their painting.

The period during which Pouyaud had been at Moly-Sabata had drawn all four of them much closer together. The letters which Mainie wrote, particularly during 1930, were among her longest and richest in terms of the diversity of issues, and both in 1929 and 1930 she and Evie travelled twice to the south of France, in February and again in September. In 1929 they joined Gleizes and his wife at Cavalaire, and the following year stayed with them at Les Méjades.

Discussion continued about colour and about its relationship to sensuality. Gleizes expressed his belief to Mainie that brilliant colours – he was himself working with a much more aggressively colourful palette at the time – resulted in more sensual painting. She replied in a letter:

I don't at all agree that to work in brilliant colour schemes should necessarily result in a picture being more sensual than if it was painted in greys or sombre colours. To me the big blue picture which you have just finished is the best or one of the best pictures you have ever done – it is the fact of the living organisation of colour and form in it that to my mind lifts it far above your other work. The colour is considered as a living force and whether the general scheme of colouring was in brilliant colours or in greys and subdued colours the principle is exactly the same – to me whether a picture is sensual or not has nothing to do with the colour scheme but has to do with the psychology of the artist – I think you are perfectly right to tell Pouyaud and to tell us as you do, that we are to find our own way and not to follow you blindly as you are older than we are and at another stage of development. But I do not feel that your return to brighter, purer, work is a sign of weakness, I think when I look back at my own work (non-realistic) I certainly for a time lost a great deal of the vitality and strength of colour which I had in my realistic work and which I would now like to bring back . . . I feel that one should have such control over colour as to be able to use it like a beautiful instrument and produce a range of sounds or tones ranging from the greatest delicacy to the greatest brilliancy or strength. I do not want to bother you with this tirade only I feel I must defend the blue picture.

Mainie had been exchanging ideas with Pouyaud on colour, and she pointed out that he

147. *Abstract Composition*, 1927. Oil on canvas, 111.7 × 56. Dublin, private collection.

148. *Abstract Composition*, 1929. Gouache on paper mounted on card, 16 × 23.5. London, private collection.

149. *Abstract Composition*, c.1929. Gouache on paper mounted on card, 47 × 28.5. Dublin, private collection.

'has a totally different temperament from any of us and I am sure he is quite right to work in subdued tones.'

In February 1930 Mainie was invited by Norris Davidson to address the members of the James Shirley Society at Cambridge University[15] and she drove there with her cousin, Dorothy FitzGerald. Mainie was enchanted by the city on this, her first visit, much preferring it to Oxford. 'You feel transported back to the Middle Ages'. The lecture was given in one of the student's rooms where Mainie was delighted to see her oil painting bought for Norris Davidson by his mother (Pl. 147). The room was packed, and people were sitting on the floor. She was amused that a nearby bridge foursome had been deprived of their chairs, and left standing round their card-table! She illustrated her talk with *pochoirs* and gouaches by herself and Evie as well as Pouyaud. Tom Henn, the Yeats scholar and poet from Paradise, in County Clare, was in the audience.[16] 'He asked a good many questions', she wrote in an account of the evening to Gleizes.

and seemed to want me to give him a set formula by which one could judge a picture – He was a friend of Roger Fry and Clive Bell and started using their pet phrase about 'significant form'. I never quite know what it is! He had a very rationalistic outlook and was the sort of person who would want everything proved to the utmost degree before he would accept it. He thank goodness turned his attention to my cousin Dorothy FitzGerald and left me to talk to the others who were very much nicer and she tackled him splendidly.

She was tremendously well received by the students.

Back in Dublin, Mainie resumed work. Her output is extensive at this time, her gouaches and paintings mainly pure abstract in their theme, the clear line and precise distinction of colour quite pronounced (Pls. 148–9). She also painted at this time a work thought to be based on Piero di Cosimo's *Mythological Subject*, in the National Gallery, London, though in terms of composition this is open to question, and the work may be derived from another source (Pl. 150).[17] In an attempt to confront Dublin's conservatism more than anything else, Mainie submitted two of her abstract gouaches to the annual show of the Royal Hibernian Academy ('equivalent to the Salon des Beaux Arts here'). 'They have accepted one and just hung it about 4 inches inside the door! But I suppose it is a sign they are not entirely hostile if they handle it at all – I was very amused as I am now 4 inches inside Paradise.' Moreover the President of the Academy, Dermod O'Brien invited her to a 'crazy dinner party' at the Arts Club 'on the evening of the *vernissage* – I am becoming quite academic now!'[18]

Both she and Evie were included in the big exhibition of Irish art at the Palais des Beaux-Arts in Brussels,[19] Evie by 'one of the best things she has done', a big tempera panel from one of her gouaches, entitled in the catalogue 'Etude pour décoration murale', and Mainie by two paintings and a gouache. It was a major showing of Irish art. The President of the Executive Council (effectively the Prime Minister of the Irish Free State) was president of the Committee of Honour. Thomas Bodkin, by then Director of the National Gallery of Ireland, was the moving spirit behind the exhibition, revealing an enthusiastic nationalism in his foreword to the catalogue. At the same time he delivered himself of the classic canard, that Irish art over no less than five centuries failed to flourish because 'all the attention of the Irish people was absorbed by the political situation'![20] Literature and music, he claimed, resisted the torment of oppression, but not painting. His remarks on twentieth-century art in Ireland were strongly supportive of the academic tradition, and the exhibition itself reflected this, with the Royal Hibernian Academy providing substantial financial backing. But in addition to Mainie and Evie, a number of other members of the Society of Dublin Painters were included, among them Grace Henry, Letitia and Eva Hamilton, Mary Swanzy and Charles Lamb. Mainie was understandably pleased to be able to report her participation to Gleizes, and

150. *Death of Procris*, 1929. Oil on canvas, 70 × 120.
Dublin, private collection.

she attached importance to the fact that their works would be hung together 'so as to make a group'. Modernism may have sustained much antipathy, but it was seen as an entity and its place in the order of things was accepted.

CHAPTER FIFTEEN

'Not an ivory tower but a fortress'

MAINIE WAS NOT surprised by Robert Pouyaud's departure from the community at Moly-Sabata. Her judgment of the younger man's intense, almost fanatical nature was probably correct. At the time of his arrival when not even the building was in a state to be used, a messianic approach was required if Gleizes' ideas were to be once again realised. And, of course, the Master himself quite wisely stood back from the practicalities, realising that his followers had to find their own way. In such circumstances the pioneering spirit is often badly put out by the changes in emphasis and direction which later arrivals introduce into any community. Pouyaud himself did not alter the direction of his work after his departure from Moly-Sabata. He moved north into the Bourgogne region where his parents lived – his mother was sick, his father frail – and lived with them not far from the great Abbey of Vézelay, from which all of them, at different times, took inspiration.[1]

We have seen how Mainie's work had developed in phases through the 1920s. The first of these, ostensibly experimental and including the initial winter of detailed and intense study, lasted from 1921 to 1923 and included several outstanding abstract paintings conceived on simple but immensely powerful lines. These early paintings, which were directly related to the researches with Gleizes and to his publication of *La Peinture et ses lois* in 1923, included canvases which juxtaposed flat panels of colour and relied on the combination of a strong but open formal pattern with clear colours, in general modulated by pattern or line. Between 1923 and 1925, as the complexity of formal construction developed with the implementation of the rules associated with translation and rotation, there was some uncertainty in her work; a crudeness which was saved by vigour, but which contained elements – blobs of colour floating on panels, small circles, dots – to some extent justifying, if for the wrong reasons, the bewilderment of critics. In addition, there developed during this period the idea of multi-voiced compositions, but these were executed without a fully resolved integration of the voices. Both she and Evie painted more complex, multi-element compositions using a number of images and textures, their canvases generally very rough, and the overall treatment somewhat crude and uncertain. The elements of a simple composition seem at times to be at war with each other, and the abundance of ideas, requiring an extended range of colours, as well as shapes and designs, produces a neutralising of impact quite different from the clear, soaring achievement of the small group of abstract canvases which can be dated to 1922. Thus, from the end of 1921 to the end of 1924, there was a clear movement from an abstract style which could be related to other, more general developments in abstract art, towards a more distinctively Gleizean form of composition. This development was to become more pronounced.

In 1925 greater clarity emerges in certain works, leading to a strongly linear phase where the dominant force seems to be translation rather than rotation. It is of course impossible to have the one without the other, except in formal, elementary studies or in the simplest of compositions, but the essential character of a good deal of work from 1925–7 resulted in rectangles, either vertical or horizontal, where the straight, severe lines and angles predominate, and the arcs and curves seem no more than a softening of

151. *Abstract Composition*, 1928. Oil on canvas, 91.5 × 137. London, private collection.

the severity of compositions which are architectural. This was accompanied by a phase of sobriety in Mainie's palette – which as we have seen she stoutly defended to Gleizes in their debate on the relationship between colour and sensuality – and a painting like the one which Norris Davidson's mother bought for her son epitomises this period well. There is a tentative, respectful note in her comments about what she is doing when she writes to Gleizes. The same is to be found in Evie's letters, and both of them were guided by him in the direction of their work, in what they wrote, and in the exhibitions at which they chose to show. But behind the deference there resides an independent vigour and confidence.

There was a cohesiveness about their work. It had been entirely natural, from their very first encounter with Gleizes, to work jointly on individual compositional ideas. What Mainie did, what Evie did, what Gleizes did, indeed what Pouyaud did in the mid-twenties and later, were often of a piece, with some of the thinking shared between them all. The idea of work transcended the idea of possession. The wish of posterity to separate and assign, reinforced by market forces, would have been generally alien.

The developments at Serrières, from Pouyaud's move there late in 1927, until the early 1930s, had a considerable influence on the intense emphasis placed on theory and ideas. It is during this period that we see numerous and detailed preliminary drawings and gouaches for major paintings (Pls. 151–61). The major paintings include, as in this sequence, pure abstract subjects, but also there are examples of decisive religious

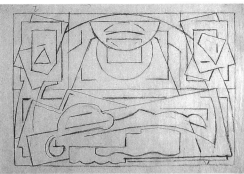

152–9. *Studies for Abstract Composition*, 1928. Pencil on paper, each 15.2 × 23. Dublin, private collection.

160. *(below left) Abstract Composition*, 1928. Gouache on paper mounted on card, 29 × 42.5. Dublin, private collection.

161. *(below right) Abstract Composition*, 1928. Gouache on paper mounted on card, 15.5 × 23.5. London, private collection.

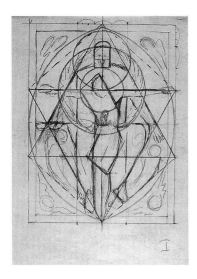

163–70. *Studies for Abstract Crucifixion*, 1928. Pencil on paper, each 20 × 15. Dublin, private collection.

imagery, as in *Abstract Crucifixion* (Pl. 162). This involved an extensive range of drawings and of gouaches of various sizes and tonal combinations (Pls. 163–77).

Each year, as we have seen, Mainie and Evie travelled to the south of France, to work with Gleizes, and when apart they sent works to each other, seeking and giving criticism, the flux of ideas serving as inspiration and pushing them always forward. At the end of 1927 Mainie shouldered the burden of bringing Evie up to date with all that had happened between herself and Gleizes while her friend was in the convent in Truro. But by the end of 1928 Evie was very much back in the swim, writing to Gleizes about her intention to submit works to exhibitions in Paris. In letters at this time Gleizes even found himself addressing them jointly – 'Chères Mainie – Evie' – and then designating sections of his letter, mainly advice, to each of them in turn.

In one of these joint letters Gleizes refers to a particular type of paint known as 'Stic B', indicating at the same time something of their working relationship when he refers to 'two large paintings <u>for which we did the studies together</u> . . . we will have to execute some things together on your next trip. We will leave the sketches and do some painting.'[2] Gleizes was presumably interested in 'Stic B' for his mural project; indeed, what attracted artists to it was its claim to emulate the qualities of ancient fresco materials by its richness of colour, its thick and immutable texture, its lacquer-like hardness muted by its matt finish. And this had added appeal for artists working in a severely two-dimensional style, where the flat, opaque character was highly desirable.

162. (*facing page*) *Abstract Crucifixion*, 1928. Oil on canvas, 107 × 84. Ireland, private collection.

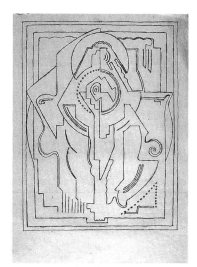   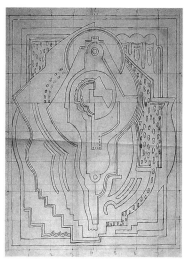

171–2.   *Studies for Abstract Crucifixion*, 1928. Pencil on paper, each 20 × 15. Dublin, private collection.

173–4.   *Studies for Abstract Crucifixion*, 1928. Pencil, with red and blue crayon, on paper, each 20 × 15. Dublin, private collection.

Plates 168–173 are numbered I to VI, in roman numerals.

Numbering at the end is interesting; the pink gouache is numbered on the back 21, the blue gouache is numbered 22, the second of the blue and red crayon drawings is 23, and the rough sketch, reverting to the crucifixion, and giving the composition design in the form of two triangles, one inverted, is number 24.

175.   *Gouache Study for Abstract Crucifixion*, 1928. Pencil and gouache on paper laid down on card, 20 × 15. Dublin, private collection.

176.   *Gouache Study for Abstract Crucifixion*, 1928. Pencil and gouache on paper laid down on card, 20 × 15. Dublin, private collection.

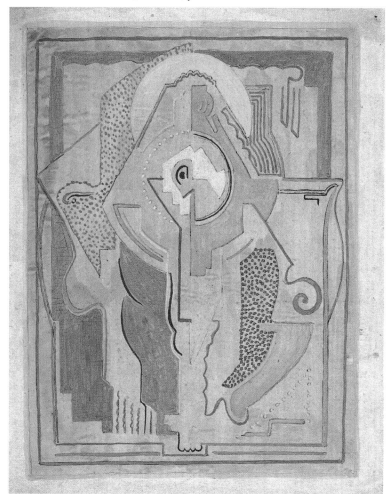 

177. *Rough Sketch for Abstract Crucifixion*, 1928. Pencil on paper, 20 × 15. Dublin, private collection.

They all experimented with the new paint. Mainie ordered an artist's palette of colours, including red and yellow ochre, cobalt blue, french blue and chrome yellow. Unfortunately, no example of her work in 'Stic B', yet identified as such, has survived.

As the 1920s drew to a close there developed a growing awareness of the 'politics' of their situation as abstract painters who, in many ways, were out of sympathy with some of the directions modern art had taken. 'Modern art' had become fashionable and, in the case of a small handful of artists, including Jean Cocteau, highly lucrative. Gleizes was always hostile to art dealers, with the possible exception of Léonce Rosenberg, and his own religious earnestness was not at all fashionable. Nor was his refusal of the representational image, to which Paris was still attached. Both Mainie and Evie, by their regular and persistent showing of works at exhibitions in Paris and elsewhere in France, were inextricably associated with him, and they constituted a 'school' not just in the loose sense of that word but in its more precise meaning of close collaboration over research and performance. Other individuals and small groups were in sympathy with them, yet they had an invaluable ten-year period of working together, and this they guarded most jealously. Their form of abstract Cubism was under attack throughout the 1920s in France as well as in Ireland. Many of Gleizes' letters refer to such attacks, and there were occasions when these had to be answered. One occurred with the publication of Guillaume Janneau's *L'Art Cubiste*.[3] Mainie bought the book in Paris, on her way home from France that summer. She understandably thought Janneau's standpoint was sympathetic, since he had quoted extensively from Gleizes' own writings. Furthermore, his book was really the first serious study of Cubism, carrying forward the analysis of it into the decade of the 1920s, and recognising something which later works on the subject either neglected or deliberately avoided: that a movement as diverse and powerful as early Cubism could not simply come to an end. But once she got into it Mainie realised there was 'a decided prejudice against you, though he could not help but mention your work . . . realising your position in the Cubist movement'.

Gleizes, acutely conscious of this, was deeply upset. He sent Mainie a copy of his letter to Janneau, which he had also sent to *L'Intransigeant*, and added: 'these proceedings must be stopped'. He asked her if she could arrange for publication of the letter in an Irish newspaper. Mainie replied that there would be no point in trying to have the letter published in Dublin: 'It will probably take at least 50 years for the book itself or books of this kind to be reviewed or noticed in our newspapers, but I will show it to anyone who is interested and likely to come in touch with the book abroad.'

In another letter Gleizes returned to the subject again, 'There is something behind this whole business. This Janneau was employed by the Bernheims. And he seems to be advertising the Zoubaloff Collection.'[4] The illustrations in Janneau's book were mainly of pictures from this collection, then on the market. Gleizes' letter to Janneau was a long and ruthlessly logical disquisition on his own work and how it had been misunderstood and misrepresented by the author. Mainie was distressed at the idea that Janneau had a hidden purpose in writing the book. 'I expect what you say about the future sale of the collection from which the illustrations in the book are taken is the pretext for the publication of the book – It is just the usual way of going on and makes me feel furious and very helpless against such a sea of dishonesty.'

More generally, the book won Mainie's guarded approval. There was so little literature on modern art available, and this study gave a coverage to Cubism as it had developed beyond 1921. Indeed, its particular emphasis on artists like Herbin and Severini was subject for further comment on Janneau, by Mainie, who saw it as quite absurd to criticise Gleizes for being 'too intellectual and mecanical (sic)' while at the same time praising the other two painters' works which she thought of as relentless in their mathematical and mechanical approaches.

Mainie Jellett's 1929 solo exhibition in Dublin contained twenty-one paintings and drawings, two designs for carpets and seven completed rugs. This time George Russell,

179. *Study for Homage to Fra Angelico*, 1928. Pencil on paper, 20 × 20. Dublin, private collection. An early, outline version, numbered 'II' by Mainie.

178. (*facing page*) *Homage to Fra Angelico*, 1928. Oil on canvas, 167.5 × 167.5. London, private collection. Robert Fermor-Hesketh.

180. *Study for Homage to Fra Angelico*, 1928. Pencil on paper, 20 × 20. Dublin, private collection. Number 'VI' in the series.

in his review for the *Irish Statesman*, adopted a more conciliatory tone.[5] An infinitely more intelligent review appeared over the initials 'D.H.V.' in *T.C.D. A College Miscellany*, at the end of November.[6]

Mainie's palette, at the end of the decade, seems to have been released from the austere, sombre phase. Rainbow-like mixtures of colour flood several of her canvases and an intense concern with colour and with the textures and properties of individual paints, as we have seen in respect of 'Stic B', concerned all of them. Combined with this there is a compositional development away from the straight lines and severe angles one associates with translation and towards arcs and curves which give a domed effect to many of the paintings.

It is easy to confuse this with a return to realism. This did come; indeed both Gleizes and Mainie refer to it, defending the apparent contradiction of allowing the 'subjective' and 'objective' voices to intermingle. And in reality it happened anyway, with the development in a specific and major canvas – Mainie's *Homage to Fra Angelico* (Pl. 178). But one is considering two distinct developments: the shift in emphasis towards a softer, more rounded formal structure to each composition (which incidentally occurred when her palette was becoming intensely more colourful), and a deliberate shift towards the two-dimensional exploration of works by the Italian primitives, painted before the time of Raphael.

Mainie worked almost exclusively in pure abstraction throughout the 1920s, at least in the main canvases, and although she 'kept up' with realism with great accomplishment in pencil drawings, gouaches and watercolour, which were regularly exhibited, it comes as something of a surprise when her largest canvas in the 1928 solo exhibition, which opened on 11 June, is *Homage to Fra Angelico*. The painting was related to a projected mural for the parish church at Serrières for which there are also numerous related studies by Gleizes and Pouyaud. The project had been enthusiastically supported by the parish priest but was vetoed, after all the preparatory work had been done, by his bishop. This figurative composition was based on The *Coronation of the Virgin* in the Uffizi (not, as is often asserted, on the work in the Louvre). There is an equivalent work by Gleizes. Both Mainie and Gleizes were familiar with the larger *Coronation* in the Louvre, and there is no record of either of them visiting Florence at any time; it must therefore be assumed that they worked from reproductions.

The two Fra Angelico paintings are different in a number of respects including the outside shape, the Uffizi's *Coronation* having the arched top to it which appears as a significant feature in Mainie's canvas. There is more fluidity and perhaps more spirituality in the smaller, Uffizi work; it has less of the architectural realism of the Louvre painting, which seems to have been adapted, intellectually, to the Renaissance mind. Vast literature exists on the subject of both works, neither of them precisely dated, and the relevance of any comparison between them to Mainie's choice and approach is of limited but not insignificant importance. The one she chose to base her own picture on has a more ethereal structure. The figures of Christ and the Virgin float above a soft platform of blue cloud, surrounded by angels and celestial trumpets all of whom constitute a group which is half the scale of the remaining figures of saints and worshippers. It is this fact which gives both perspective and a sense of spiritual elevation to the painting quite different from the substantially more realistic presentation of the figures of Christ and the Virgin in the Louvre painting; they are seated at the top of a flight of richly decorated steps and in front of an ornately decorated throne, so that the surrounding scene is much more like the court of a monarch than any heavenly setting.

Mainie's initial sketches block in the essential elements of the composition in broad panels with the exception of the figures of Christ and the Virgin, who from the beginning are treated semi-figuratively. The early drawings are somewhat akin to art-school analysis of composition: circles to left and right indicate the intermediate groups of figures; the foreground groupings, again to left and right, are divided by a triangular

181. *Study for Homage to Fra Angelico*, 1928. Pencil on paper, 20 × 20. Dublin, private collection. Unnumbered drawing, squared in red crayon for enlargement.

182. *Abstract Composition*, c.1928. Gouache on paper, 40 × 23. Dublin, private collection.

space the apex of which leads into the lower centre of the picture. By the fourth drawing Mainie has transformed the planes of the original, so that the emphasis is on five points, or areas in the overall composition. The significance of this formal re-structuring is that all sense of perspective has been eliminated and in its place there now exists the flat, two-dimensional, essentially abstract collection of forms which can now be developed according to Mainie's own needs and her vision. It is at this point that the figurative returns, with the saints in the foreground emerging in highly stylised form. Increasingly, the emphasis is on a circular movement within the composition from which its powerful sense of balance derives. The central figures are surrounded by a Cubist halo of precise lines and arcs; the outer circle of figures is in part transformed to Cubist design, and the most pure abstract treatment is given to the circles on the left and right of the composition.

The painting met with something approaching enthusiasm from the *Irish Statesman*:

> I found the large painting entitled 'Homage to Fra Angelico' most impressive. In composition, colour, form and line, it manifests the organic completeness which makes an entity. The artist has taken as subject the Master's design for the *Coronation of the Virgin*. And having dissected, analyzed and studied this work, has sought to create something which while based on and retaining the religious significance and colour beauty of the Angelico evinces the simplicity of form and absence of representationalism which are the essence of modern decorative art.[7]

The style of this unsigned review is not Russell's. The attitude adopted is frankly new. The visitor is invited to realise, firstly, that 'the mere representation of objects . . . does not constitute a work of art', secondly, that ridicule without analysis is ignorance, thirdly, that there is something 'inhuman' in the derision directed at modernism, and, finally, that the outcome of this *reductio* should be sincere attention and interest.

> There is a sense of construction which is almost architectural in all Miss Jellett's work, which is also characterised by a masterly sense of arrangement, a refined colour feeling and decorative sensibility. It reminded me of the feeling produced on entering a Gothic Cathedral. One is first aware of the still grey gloom at the base, then slowly one is lured upwards to the sudden glory of the coloured windows and the light diffused on high.

'A marked advance' was detected in the 1928 show also by the *Irish Times* critic,[8] and as well as widespread reference to the painting after Fra Angelico, there was also a good deal of praise for landscapes done in Rossshire and Rathfarnham, and for her rug and carpet designs. In her work generally, Mainie did maintain an interest in realism, and regularly painted landscapes. These were rarely major works in oil, though such paintings were not ruled out; more often, she employed gouache and watercolour, both of which are particularly suited to holiday and travel. But in addition she was a regular supporter of the Society of Irish Watercolour Painters, showing most years in the annual summer exhibition, to which many of her more realistic works were submitted.

Homage to Fra Angelico seems to prefigure her own return to figurative imagery – especially religious imagery – in the 1930s. But at this stage in her career it remains an isolated example, at least in the overt re-statement of the Fra Angelico message, since the main thrust of her work continues to be abstract. And this is emphasised by the titling of works, which continues to divulge nothing of a narrative or descriptive intent. Nevertheless, looking at the illustrations of works exhibited in the 1929 and the 1931 shows, and at other dated works of the period, there are echoes of what can loosely be defined as 'religious' imagery. Without going so far as to depict a *Pietà*, a Crucifixion, or a Virgin and Child, the very spirituality which is at the heart of Mainie's abstract painting creates the illusion of religious art. It may in specific canvases have been inspired by actual religious paintings. But it is equally likely that the simpler idea of a spiritual

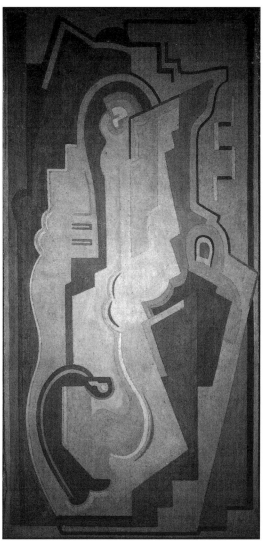

183. *Abstract Composition*, 1929. Oil on canvas, 183 × 91.5. London, private collection.

inspiration, consistent with her Cubist abstract theories of movement within the canvas, is responsible for the 'beings' which seem to emerge in her works at this time. Were it music we would not question the transcendental force emerging from the technique of notes, rhythms, harmonies, and creating within us an experience of spirituality which at times takes on religious overtones; in painting, the desire to recognise, still a demand for the vast majority of people, was even more of an imperative then. It is clear that the *Irish Statesman*'s critic was responsive to the more obvious religious message of *Homage to Fra Angelico*, but unsympathetic when that message became diffused, or simply more subtle.

Thus, we are witnessing, at this period in Mainie's development, a shift in composition which was to usher in the more directly religious works of the 1930s. These were to become stylised representations of events in the Life of Christ, and would culminate in far more overtly religious paintings, like *The Nativity* of 1940, which, compared with *Homage to Fra Angelico*, is almost crude in its obvious message. It is, of course, impossible to suggest any order in the shift towards religious painting. As early as 1923 there are pure abstract paintings which suggest the figurative idea of a Madonna, or Madonna and Child. There is the pre-Gleizes inspiration of Celtic Christian art. There is the shared enthusiasm for Romanesque art which inspired much of their study in the 1920s. There is the basic spirituality in both her life and art throughout these years. And there is the evidence in the 1929 and 1931 developments in her art of that spirituality taking on a religious form in individual canvases. Whatever the complex reasoning, by the early 1930s the stylised representation of religious events in her canvases forms at least part of her imagery.

Many of her canvases at this time are large and the texture finer than in the 1920s. She often uses a woven linen. While there is an undoubted heightening of colour in many works from the late 1920s on, there is a sense in which individual paintings are set in a key, like music, with muted, minor-key canvases quite distinct from the bold, rich colours of major-key works.

We are lucky that photographs survive not only of Mainie's November 1929 solo exhibition, showing five works clearly enough to indicate her stylistic advances, but also of Evie Hone's May 1929 solo exhibition, which is also most interesting in its revelations of style and direction. Evie was still fundamentally a painter at this stage, having made no overtures in the direction of stained-glass work. C.P. Curran, perhaps simplistically, asserted that 'she presently grew tired of the dryness of abstract art and parted from its exclusive practice'.[9] This view, which appeared in published form in the early 1940s, became accepted and repeated by other writers and painters, though its actual basis in fact is open to question. Even if true, the transition to stained glass did not take place until the 1930s.

Evie's progress as a painter during the 1920s is somewhat different from Mainie's, partly because of the two-year gap when she was in the convent, partly because of her undoubtedly less assured grasp of the principles of abstract painting. Her dependence on Mainie increased when she returned to painting again in early 1928, and is somewhat evident in her 1929 show. This preceded Mainie's by six months, and when the November catalogue for her friend's exhibition was being done, Evie contributed an introductory note. Though they did not have solo shows in 1930, the November exhibition of the Society of Dublin Painters gave over the end-wall of the gallery in St Stephen's Green to Evie and Mainie, and they were treated to joint criticism. The description of them in one Dublin newspaper as 'the apostles of impressionism' must have been slightly galling, since it was the last thing they wanted to be seen as, but the general approach was respectful, even if the level of comprehension remained as abysmal as ever.

The two women had achieved an enormous amount. They had revolutionised thinking in Dublin about art generally. They had both consistently produced and exhibited some of the most avant-garde painting in the British Isles, earlier than any other artists in the

184. *Abstract Composition*, 1928. Oil on canvas, 122 × 71. London, private collection.

field of abstract art, and had gone on doing so with great consistency and steady development throughout the decade. The actual output of work, in Mainie's case, had been extensive. Following her first showing of abstract paintings in the 1923 group show of the Society of Dublin Painters, and the joint show with Evie the following year, she had held a solo exhibition every year from 1925 to 1929.[10] And she had developed alongside this a capacity for argument, teaching and polemic which had made her the focus of all serious artistic controversy over a period of years. She had managed all of this with dignity, balance, and a measure of wit which is evident in her letters. She had won the admiration of her critics in Dublin, a hard-fought battle. She had remained a noticed member of the Gleizes 'school' in a variety of European exhibitions. At the end of her life she referred to the 'years of misunderstanding and walls of prejudice'[11] which she had anticipated on her return to Dublin. Yet by the end of the 1920s, she had created understanding, and confronted prejudice with relative success. In a contained and carefully considered way, Mainie Jellett had constructed for herself an interpretation of art which Elizabeth Bowen later decribed as 'not an ivory tower but a fortress'.[12]

CHAPTER SIXTEEN

Cubism 'alive and well'

BY THE END of 1931 and the opening of her solo show, it is evident that Mainie's style had again progressed considerably. As we have seen, she was in part responding to Gleizes' views on the use of brilliant colours, as her palette shifts decidedly towards a lighter tone, she uses more primary colours with far greater contrasts, and with a splendid rainbow effect in certain works (Pls. 185–7). The preceding years from 1927 to 1931, were enormously fruitful. In addition to the shows already mentioned, she showed regularly with the Dublin Painters, the New Irish Salon, the Watercolour Society of Ireland, the London Group, the Surindépendents and even the Royal Hibernian Academy. As we have seen she lectured regularly on art, fitting abstract Cubism into the framework of modern art more generally, and ranging widely in her subject matter. She was undoubtedly the leader of a movement within Ireland which was given many different epithets by the press: Modernism, Futurism, Cubism, even Impressionism! But she was seen, and indeed saw herself, as much more than that. She spoke and lectured on behalf of modern art with the distinct and express purpose of awakening and extending understanding as far as she possibly could. This included a growing involvement with children, both in teaching them in her own studio, and in lecturing them publicly, taking groups of them on tours of the National Gallery.

In August 1931 Mainie's younger sister, Babbin, married William Phillips and went to live in Antwerp where he worked as a chemist in the brewing industry. The wedding was at St Bartholomew's Church in Clyde Road, and was a big social occasion. Mainie had already arranged that she would take a summer holiday in Europe in September so that she could then spend time in Antwerp with the newly-married couple when they returned there after their honeymoon. An alternative plan, to go and stay with Gleizes and his wife in Cavalaire, had been scrapped.

She left for Europe at the end of August on a liner from Queenstown and sailed to Hamburg from where she travelled to Nidden, in Lithuania. Her heavily stamped passport, with special Irish Department of External Affairs validations for Latvia, Lithuania, Estonia and the 'Free City of Dantzic and Polish Corridor', records her visit to Nidden lasting from 4–27 September. She travelled with Honor Purser[1] and Christine Duff.[2]

Nidden was then a rural community, its economy based on fishing and agriculture. The countryside was flat and thickly covered with forests from which the elks emerged fearlessly, since they were not shot for food or skins. 'About as high as a llama and big antlers,' Mainie wrote to her mother. She completed several landscapes in gouaches and watercolour. She reported in detail on the Lutheran church service which they had attended. It included

> curious old chorales (one could easily see where the rhythm of Bach's chorales came from) the prayers seemed to be in the form of litanies and all the responses were sung. There was a cross on the Altar and four big candelsticks and what looked like a tabernacle and lots of crosses on the altar hangings, etc. a portrait of Luther (I think) on the wall and over the altar a disastrous picture of Christ (modern) lifting S. Peter

185. *Abstract Composition, c.*1931. Oil on canvas, 106.7 × 83.8. London, private collection.

186. *Abstract Composition, c.*1931. Oil on canvas, 104 × 81.5. Cork, Crawford Municipal Gallery of Modern Art.

187. *Abstract Composition, c.*1931. Oil on canvas, 137.5 × 92. Dublin, private collection.

out of the water when he tried to walk on the water and lost faith, just the usual style of bad religious art. It was much more like the Altar in a country R.C. Church. Apparently the Lutherans can have a cross and candles when we cant, and Luther was the founder of Protestantism! . . . The people all seem very earnest and have fine open faces. The church is in a lovely situation looking over the estuary . . . the graveyard is beside it, with all the graves in the sand covered with bright autumn flowers and the tombstones mostly wooden crosses. It is very happy looking with the flowers and wonderfully peaceful. Over the rough wood gateway is in German and Lithuanian, 'I am the resurrection and the life'.

Mainie's mother, religious and Low Church in her beliefs, would have been intensely interested in such detail, despite the indications of Mainie's own preference for High Church ritual. Both her parents had been ill, and her letters are filled with concern about them and about her beloved dogs. To her surprise one of the Cambridge students who had been at her lecture on Cubism the previous year, arrived in this remote corner of the Lithuanian coast, travelling with a German professor who insisted that Mainie and her friends should visit him on their way back through Germany to Belgium. Christine Duff had attracted an admirer at this stage, upsetting the group of three, but Mainie was able to report, half-way through the holiday, that he had 'been extinguished thank goodness'!

The party left Nidden at the end of the month and travelled to Berlin, where they stayed for two nights. They had lunch with Dr Binchy, the minister at the Irish legation, who had Irish works of art hanging in his rooms. These included two by Mainie herself, as

well as Dun Emer carpets and furniture by the Dublin cabinet-maker, James Hicks. In an interview given later to the *Evening Mail*, Mainie said how impressed she was with the way modern art was officially recognised by the German government, with special rooms being devoted to the work of prominent artists. She did some sight-seeing: 'I spent the morning in the Kaiser Friedrich Museum which is really magnificent, and came across the original carved wood statue of Christ on the Donkey 13th C. that Sir W. Orpen put into that dreadful picture with his three daughters as Angels in last years Academy – the statue is a most beautiful thing.'[3] She also visited the famous Berlin zoo. The three of them then took first-class sleepers to Cologne, arriving in the morning, visiting the Cathedral and the thirteenth-century Gothic Church of St Ursula, where the Saint 'is buried with all the martyred virgins who were killed with her'. They departed for Antwerp in mid-afternoon.

Mainie was horrifed to find what she described as 'attrocious' Belgian taste. Babbin and Will were too polite to object to the more outrageous examples with which their landlady had filled their rooms, but they were comfortable and 'Madame could not be nicer and gives them very good food and very well cooked'. Antwerp she found very ugly, except for the area around the cathedral, but she loved the art gallery and found time to visit Brussels and Bruges. Will Phillips, an accomplished pianist, had bought a fine Bechstein boudoir grand piano. 'I do think Babbin is awfully happy', Mainie wrote home. 'She is just as vague and does not change in the least bit . . . the piano is a great thing. Will is mad about it and is always playing. He would love some Beethoven duets, perhaps we could send them Grainne Stokes's edition if it were not too heavy.'

She returned home to a busy autumn. Her solo exhibition opened at the end of October, when she was also due to give a major lecture on 'Modern Art and its Relation to the Past'. Sustained interest in, and controversy about, modern art was newsworthy, and the Dublin *Daily Express* special correspondent filed a pre-emptive news story based on an interview, and printed under a succession of eye-catching headlines: 'WHAT CUBISM MEANS. ''MAKES YOU UNDERSTAND OLD MASTERS.'' EARLY IDEAL OF ART REINTERPRETED. WOMAN'S COMING EXHIBITION.'[4] The story itself was cast in similarly dynamic terms: '''Since the Free State Government came into power,'' said Miss Jellett to me today, ''art has been encouraged in Ireland, and the presence of the different members of the Diplomatic Corps here has also helped to broaden our ideas with regard to what is going on in the world of art outside. We have been, so to speak, lifted out of our isolation.''' The writer accurately assessed the continuing appeal Mainie Jellett had in terms of confrontation: 'Her first exhibition, a few years ago, when she introduced the new idea in art to the Irish public, met with a hostile reception that is still fresh in the minds of Irish artists and art critics.' And he went on to give a racy account of her career, well suited to *Daily Express* readers. 'I asked her if she thought that the Cubist movement would live. She replied that it was out of this movement that the art of the future would come.'

The exhibition was reviewed extensively, and with a backward view over her career usually associated with a retrospective. She had been exhibiting Cubist abstract works for only eight years, yet the context given to her endeavours was related back by several writers to the whole evolution of Cubism, placing her firmly in the position of one who had challenged all the voices of doom, and stood in the forefront of modernist practice. 'Those who remember Miss Jellett's first essays in Cubism will recognise that she is feeling and revealing colour sense more intensely. Of necessity she has gradually enlarged her canvases, her structure of design has become more complicated, the appeal of her tones to the eye is absolute. She has become a devout worshipper of colour in itself'.[5]

Though her lecture was entitled 'Modern Art and its Relation to the Past' it was believed by every commentator to be a lecture about Cubism. There was much debate as to whether Cubism was alive and well. 'MOVEMENT NOT DEAD' was the heading above the final paragraph of the long summary in the *Daily Express*.[6] 'Miss Jellett denied that Cubism was dead, and said that the proof of its being alive was its influence on modern music, literature, printed fabrics, furniture, carpets and architecture.' She listed a number of Dublin buildings which were inspired by Cubism. During 1931 she had made further progress in her own involvement in the application of Cubist art to carpet and linoleum design. In a letter to Gleizes earlier in the year she had referred to visits to a linoleum plant in Paris 'where they were extremely nice and seemed very interested in my designs and want me to work them out according to their technical necessities and then submit them to the firm. They had some good cubistic designs, but of course masses of awful designs too – I may get something out of it, I hope so.' She also visited a carpet manufactory at the same time, implying that the aspect of practical application of abstract art to design was much on her mind.

Nevertheless, the main direction of her thoughts in this lecture is towards the contrast and conflict between spiritual and materialist forces in painting, between the inner rhythms in art and the outward appearances, between inspired creation and perceived representation. Her principle challenge is against the idea of 'progress'. She considered the presentation of art as a process of 'refinement' and the placing of painters in hierarchies of excellence or greatness to be glib and superficial. In this her 1931 lecture echoes those given earlier, just as it picks up the essential substance of much of the writing of Gleizes.[7]

When she comes to Cubism there is a careful reassessment of who led whom. She examines the differences between the 'realist' – Braque, Picasso, Léger and others – who 'take the natural material and with that material recreate afresh a harmony of form and colour inspired by realism and re-organised by their own emotional and mental processes', and the abstract Cubists, like herself, led by Gleizes. To them,

> a picture is a mobile living thing with an organisation controlled by a definite rhythm (or movement) and like any natural organism, flowers, trees, human beings, complete in itself. They do not deny nature, they could not, but they wish to copy nature, not in her eternal aspects, but in her internal organisation, to create as far as their human powers will let them, as nature is created.

In a long section edited out of the published version of her lecture, Mainie examined in some detail the inter-relationship of the arts among the artists who follow modernist principles.

> Modern musicians are stretching out towards new forms of expression, at the same time looking back with a fresh eye to the storehouses of the past. As an example of this we have the renewed interest in plain song not only from a religious stand point but as a means of inspiration, and an example of simplicity of means being able to produce unparalleled richness coupled with immense rhythmic variety. This form of music being essentially rhythmic and thus appealing to the rhythmic researches of modern musicians and artists.

In even greater detail she addressed the Cubist content of, and influence upon, modern architecture. The austerity of Dublin's essentially eighteenth-century, Georgian style was, she thought, more suited to modern buildings. Through her involvement with the Gate Theatre she had come to know the architect, Michael Scott,[8] who remained a friend and owned paintings by her. His own early work was influenced by Cubism.

Mainie saw the inspiration of Cubism as offering salvation at a time when one civilisation was disintegrating and another coming into existence.

> We do sincerely believe that the only living movement in the art of our time is the movement resulting from the Cubist and other movements affiliated to it. Our light is

a very feeble one but we hope that we may pass it on to the civilisation that is coming into being, and that a future generation will bring it to fruition in a way that we can never do, who are the last of a dying civilisation and only groping towards the new.

In her discussions with Gleizes, and in her reading, much attention was given to art's role in its relationship with religion, science and industry. She was interested in the work and contribution of figures as diverse as Ernst Planck, the Prince of Broglie, Sir James Jeans, Paul Painlevé, Josiah Stamp, A.S. Eddington and Julian Huxley.[9] She and Evie had discussed Berkeley's philosophy, both among themselves and with Gleizes. They had sent Gleizes various volumes of the eighteenth-century philosopher's work and he had responded enthusiastically to Berkeleyan ideas. Their collective enthusiasm was reinforced by the fact that the Irish man of letters, Joseph Hone,[10] was also working on a book about Berkeley at this time. Gleizes was giving important lectures on art and its relationship to the community.[11] All of them, however, were faced with an even more intense and immediate challenge to their analysis of their art and its relevance, with the foundation, in 1931, of Abstraction-Création.

CHAPTER SEVENTEEN

Abstraction-Création

ABSTRACTION-CRÉATION WAS an association of artists, founded in 1931, to provide for the organisation of exhibitions, debates and conferences on the subject of non-figurative art. Gleizes was one of the eight founder members.[1] He kept Mainie informed of the plans for 1931–2, which included an exhibition, and more importantly, a manifesto which would draw together the practitioners of non-figurative art and allow them to publish individual personal statements.

In December Auguste Herbin wrote to Mainie and Evie, inviting them to send him two photographs of paintings 'and a page of text for his review'.[2] This, puzzled Evie, for she did not know how much this meant, but in any case she sent Gleizes a copy of what she had written. 'I hope you won't think it very stupid.' It was quite different from what Mainie had sent 'which makes it better'.

Evie's statement gives three objectives. The first is the satisfaction of the artist's sense of beauty through colour and form used in harmony and deriving life and rhythm from the painting itself. The second is the justification of the artist's spiritual nature through an entirely new dependence – on form, on rhythm, on colour. The third was an approach to truth which she related to Irish roots in Celtic art, the abstract motivation of which she saw as a purifying condition.

The original draft of Mainie's personal manifesto was written in December 1931 and has survived. It was written in English and translated for her by Herbin. Although it was hard work and contained many alterations it is a model of simplicity and directness:

> The surface is my starting point, my aim is to make it live.
>
> The surface on which a painter works can be either wall, panel, canvas or paper; the primary truth of that surface is its flatness.
>
> I wish to preserve that flatness and to oppose Renaissance perspective.
>
> I recognise a natural perspective of colours and forms, for example, the power of certain colours to dominate others and to come nearer the eye; and of forms by their placing in the composition having the same effect, but this I recognise as natural perspective which can be organised in the general composition, its effects nullified if desired by careful arrangement of colour and form.
>
> A picture to me is a mobile living object with an organisation controlled by a definite rhythm and like any natural organisation, flowers, trees, human beings, complete in itself.
>
> I do not deny nature. I would not; but I wish to copy nature not in her external aspects but in her internal organisation; to create as far as my human power will let me as nature is created.
>
> I wish my pictures to be as perfect organisations of form and colour as it is in my power to make them.
>
> My pictures are first conceived in my mind and then worked out according to the laws of colour, the formal composition and rhythmic movement peculiar to the surface and shape I am filling.
>
> The organisation of a picture of this kind is somewhat similar to the orchestration of a musical composition which is first conceived in the mind and then is presented to

the world through the medium of sound organised by the laws of harmony and counterpoint.

Conceived in the mind, my picture becomes a concrete fact, an interpretation of the original mental conception through the medium of form and colour, controlled by the laws of composition.

A picture should be capable of producing an emotional reaction on the spectator entirely on its merits as a colour organisation and formal composition without a realistic appeal.'[3]

The collective body of work to be found in that first issue of *Abstraction-Création* constitutes a remarkable set of miniature manifestos, all with a common theme – the personal justification of the principles of pure abstraction in art – but drawn from a wide range of sources, both in the sense of geography and of artistic disposition.

There were forty-one painters and sculptors who took part in the first publication of *Abstraction-Création*. The only British artist was Edward Wadsworth,[4] though the following year Ben Nicholson[5] and Barbara Hepworth[6] joined, together with Paule Vézelay[7]. She claimed, not without some justification, that 'I am the first *English* (my italics) abstract artist to have made an international reputation; in fact my abstract works were made some time before those of Henry Moore, Ben Nicholson, Hepworth.' Yet her reputation was no greater than that of either Mainie or Evie, who had preceded her by several years on the road of pure abstract art, and who, by 1931, had several solo exhibitions and many appearances in group shows to their credit.

It is interesting that the Australian Cubist, John Power,[8] who had experimented with Cubism in the early 1920s, was also part of the first Abstraction-Création grouping. His work, though it has definite tendencies towards perspective and hints of Léger-like distorted realism, also has an understanding of the underlying importance of movement.

Something of the strength and diversity of the first *Abstraction-Création* publication can be gauged from the presence of major twentieth-century figures such as Jean Hans Arp, Willi Baumeister, Alexander Calder, Robert and Sonia Delaunay, the brothers Naum Gabo and Antoine Pevsner, Kupka, Moholy-Nagy, one of the teachers from the Bauhaus, Mondrian and Kurt Schwitters. Yet its strength, and the sustained emphasis on the theory and practice of pure forms of abstraction, relied on a small core of committee members, including Gleizes, Jean Hélion,[9] Herbin and Georges Vantongerloo.[10] Another collaborator was Michel Seuphor,[11] who was later to spend some time at Moly-Sabata but was completely out of sympathy with its way of life and with Anne Dangar's devotion to Gleizes.

Mainie sent a draft of her *Abstraction-Création* document to Gleizes, apologising for it being 'not very good' and regretting the difficulties imposed by compressing 'all one wants to say on a page'. Gleizes himself accepted no such restrictions; his essay was twice the length of Mainie's, while Hélion, who was in editorial control of the 1932 magazine, wrote at even greater length. Vantongerloo's piece was the longest of them all, a prodigious examination in three parts of the nature of space and time, a philosophic interest whose relevance to painting was also felt by Gleizes.

There was also trouble with the layout. Mainie first sent photographs of predominantly horizontal paintings; these did not fit, and were replaced by others, less impressive in her view (Pl. 188). But generally, reception of the first publication of the Abstraction-Création movement was positive. Joe Hone told Evie that he thought '<u>our</u> group of work much the best.'[12] Mainie wrote to Gleizes saying that overall what she called 'Herbin's Review' was 'quite interesting, more so from the letterpress than the pictures which were very disappointing with a few exceptions – I thought yours stood out amongst them – the Review seems to divide itself into two sections, those who accept curves and those who don't – Personally I think Mondrian and his followers produce very dull work.'

188. *Sea*, 1931, Oil on canvas, 45 × 115. Dublin, private collection.

Something of the purpose, as well as the importance of the publication may be gauged from these remarks. All of the participants were exhibitors in a variety of different places. Mainie , by the time she sent off her own personal manifesto, had regularly shown in London, Dublin and Paris . She was to take part in an Abstraction-Création group show of ten members, including Vantongerloo (Pl. 189). What the 'review' offered was the cohesion of ideas, visual images, and the sense of there being a large, widely diffused movement with fundamentally the same objectives.

Mainie considered herself lucky to make the trip to Serrières early in 1932. She stayed for a month, returning to London in the middle of March. By June the economic situation in Ireland made the idea of further travel temporarily difficult. The run on sterling the previous September which had forced Britain off the gold standard had led to an immediate devaluation of the pound. Ireland was then part of the Sterling area, and therefore similarly affected. With her Unionist, Protestant background, Mainie had reason to take a closer interest in political developments at home. After ten years in opposition Eamon de Valera won the March general election and in April, with the support of the Labour Party, assumed power.

The essential difficulty he faced was the issue of Republicanism: Labour politicians supported his domestic policies, were in favour of a protectionism which would preserve jobs, but were opposed to any change in the Anglo-Irish Treaty. Within his own Fianna Fáil party, de Valera faced various degrees of hard-line Republicanism all demanding that the Treaty should go. Perhaps as a sop, the oath of allegiance to the British Crown was abolished within ten days of the new administration taking over.

Mainie's initial reaction to the new government in Ireland was negative. Of de Valera's management of the country she wrote to Gleizes in May:

189. Invitation to Abstraction-Création Exhibition.

BRIGNONI   JELLETT
CALDER   SCHIESS
FISCHLI   VANTONGERLOO
GLARNER   VARGAS
HUF   VULLIAMY

ABSTRACTION - CRÉATION
44, AVENUE DE WAGRAM, PARIS-8ᵉ
DE 10 h. A MIDI ET DE 15 h. A 19 h.
PREMIÈRE SÉRIE DU 19 AU 31 JANVIER
VERNISSAGE LE 19 JANVIER DE 16 h. A 19 h.

Politically we the Irish are in an awful mess – the de Valera government is going on in the most ridiculous way, putting taxes on everything, even books – we all wish Irish industries to be protected but this government is taxing every sort of thing whether it is made here or not, thinking new factories will automatically spring up, the only results so far is that the existing factories and people in control of labour are disbanding their workers as they can't pay the increased taxes on capital and goods coming into the country. We had hoped de Valera and his party were going to do the best for the country, but up to the present their legislation has been criminally conceived and stupid and trade is at a standstill.

Internationally 1932 was a remarkable year, characterised by violence and political change around the globe. India witnessed the confrontation between Gandhi's Congress

133

Party and the British administration, leading to violence, the banning of the party, and Gandhi's arrest. In the Far East Japan's aggression led to the setting up of a puppet regime in Manchuria and continued military assaults in China. The French President was assassinated. Roosevelt swept to power in the United States and inaugurated the New Deal. And in Germany, though narrowly defeated by Hindenburg for the country's presidency, Hitler achieved a huge moral and tactical advance in his inexorable rise to power.

Huge crowds arrived in Dublin that summer for the Eucharistic Congress and the heightened religious fervour amused Mainie. She hoped the whole thing would have a good effect on the characters of the participants, but was generally rather sceptical.

> When one knows they are seriously thinking of Civil War again one can't help feeling the effect of the Congress won't last long – the whole thing was built up on a system of indulgences, if you hung a Congress flag out of your window you got an indulgence. If you went to the big Mass you got an indulgence. If you bought a candle you got an indulgence – a wonderful system of money-making and the excitable, ignorant, superstitious Irish are excellent material to work it on – thank goodness the weather was fine if it had been the normal Irish weather I can't imagine what would have happened.

Meanwhile Mainie was enjoying a relaxed summer, travelling out to Howth by train to bathe, though she complained of the time it took. 'The water is lovely', she wrote to Gleizes. 'You would think it very cold but the open sea has such life that you don't mind.' In July she took a week's holiday with her sister, Bay and their three dogs: Mainie's poodle, a fox terrier and Bay's cairn terrier, a breed she favoured all her life They travelled in the big Morris car which had been left to them by their uncle, Adrian Stokes.[13]

Earlier in the spring, on her return through London from France, Mainie had visited the Royal Academy exhibition of French Art[14] which she had been anticipating with considerable enthusiasm since January. This inspired a lecture which she gave with slides in the church hall of St Bartholomew's on 21 April. It was 'an artist's view', the distinctive point of view of 'a painter of extreme modern tendencies'.

As an artist she deplored what she called 'the one irreparable mistake' made by the organisers of not having extended their coverage into the twentieth century. France, in contrast with Italy where the nineteenth-century artistic performance had been 'a deplorable fiasco ending in a riot of sentimentality and rank materialism', had produced superior work, full of 'vigour . . . sincerity of purpose and a spirit of research and adventure.'

The purpose of Mainie's lecture, from the outset, centres upon the transition from the spiritual and non-materialistic art from the thirteenth to the fifteenth centuries into the 'exuberance, glory and sensuality of the great Renaissance period and the approaching victory of the material over the spiritual'. This had to be faced as a problem rather than a triumph, and in addressing it in this way Mainie was conscious of the Irish and Celtic sympathy her views would inspire in a Dublin audience of that period; in the references she made to early Christian art, and its emphasis on pattern and design and an essentially two-dimensional view, in which she saw a 'non-materialistic spiritual ideal predominating'. No special claims were made for Celtic predominance; both Byzantine and Romanesque art, in Europe generally and in France, were linked with Celtic art in a huge Euro-Asian, Christian-inspired first movement. This gave way to an intermediate transition period represented by Maitre de Moulins, Fouquet, and other decorative works, leading to the full flowering of Renaissance exuberance with Clouet, Corneille de Lyons, the Le Nain brothers, 'The spiritual aloofness of the early pictures is gone – We leave the gold backgrounds which gave such a sense of the surface, and plunge into the wonderful three-dimensional effect . . . the beautiful human Madonnas, roundly modelled, living in rooms or landscapes related to their proportions & considered from a realistic point of view.'

Her final transition covered the art of the seventeenth, eighteenth and nineteenth centuries, with Poussin, Chardin, Watteau, Boucher and Fragonard epitomising the wit, elegance and the fantasy of their period, but giving way in turn to the strength of purpose which came with the Revolution, with David, Ingres and then Delacroix. No real challenge to 'the materialistic ideal' came until the Post-Impressionists. Mainie emphasised that her argument was not *between* two ideals, one spiritual and one materialistic, but *against* the idea of one being a progression from the other, and *against* the idea of using the same critical standpoint for two quite different inspirations. At the same time she detected progressions in a different way: the Barbizon School painters, she said, 'had got all they could from direct contact with nature, the Impressionists had done the same from another standpoint that of registering the fleeting effects of light and motion in Nature', and this had led to the even more radical advances of Post-Impressionism.

She praised the structure of the London's Royal Academy exhibition. Out of eleven rooms at Burlington House four were given to the nineteenth century, another to the transition period of the French Revolution. When the first Post-Impressionist works had been shown in 1911, she said, 'the reaction of the London public was a disgrace to the English nation, no form of abuse was bad enough for these pictures and when the same group was sent on here they met with a similar reception.' In no sense did she see the battle as over. Judgment of art still depended too much on the expectation of realism and truth to nature.

We must realise once and for all that the worst thing from an artistic point of view that came out of the nineteenth century is this passion for the photographic representation of nature in art. I have said it many times but I say it again, art is not the power of copying nature – Could a masterpiece like Hamlet be produced by having a gramophone recording machine registering word for word what was said by a band of people at a critical stage of their lives reacting to the hand of fate directed against them? No work of art whether literary or otherwise can be produced by copying – the one main function of the artist is to create – he may create with purely imaginary forms or images, he may create with natural forms, but the function of creation is what makes the work a work of art, and according to the degree of imagination, constructive power and selective power of the creator depends the life of the work of art whether in literature, music, painting, sculpture or any other art – If this was not so the artistic heritage of the ages would not count and a photograph would be of greater artistic value than any picture – Eastern art has happily kept its ideal pure from this base form of materialism but Western art is ever fluctuating between the two.

This lecture was widely and extensively noted. Its didacticism led to it being presented very much as an exploration of the phenomenon of 'modernism' and the reaction of the artist, despite the fact that the exhibition itself covered a period only to the end of the nineteenth century. Indeed, the *Irish Times* review[15] concentrated exclusively on the 'extreme modern tendency' and its view of French art of the past 500 years. Mainie described the event in a letter to Gleizes mentioning that the French minister in Dublin had attended: 'he spoke in quite an interesting way when he had finished making beautiful polite phrases to me – I thought he was very bored all the same but when he got up to speak he sounded as if he had been interested.' The Czechoslovakian Consul General and his wife, also present, were interested in Mainie's work. They knew Franz Kupka and Emil Filla,[16] and were also aware of Gleizes' writings. 'Various other people,' Mainie concluded, 'seem to be getting more interested and Evie and I are beginning to be looked upon as respectable members of the community, such as it is.'

CHAPTER EIGHTEEN

The letter to Anne Dangar

FROM THE TIME of their first encounter with Gleizes the annual visits which Mainie and Evie made to France to work with him had generally taken place in the early part of the year. There were often additional summer and early autumn visits, more relaxed, less exclusively concentrated on work and discussion about the theory of their painting, and a friendship and affection developed between them all which, though it revolved principally around Gleizes, included Mme Gleizes. She took a keen interest in the philosophic discussions as well as the politics of modern art. She was also a painter, and a writer, and published articles alongside her husband in a number of journals.

The remoteness of Moly-Sabata was important for their intellectual exchanges. Gleizes increasingly chose to be there, 'far from the restlessness of art circles in the capital' and was conscious of the threatening shadows of political developments. He wrote of 'the disintegration of our world' and the need to bring about a new one in which the craftsman would play a leading role. But if the need for a new world became greater with political and social developments in the 1930s, so too did the difficulties and restrictions. Both within Ireland, and internationally, the economic and political circumstances of the new decade brought changes to the pattern of all their lives, and these took on a more definite character from about 1932. Travel abroad for Mainie became more difficult due to her family's limited financial resources.

The situation in Ireland was difficult for a number of reasons as discussed in the previous chapter. The coming to power of Eamon de Valera had inevitably changed the relationship between the Irish Free State and Britain. For a time, a more narrow-minded form of nationalism evolved – anathema to people of Mainie's class and background – and this provoked an outburst in a letter to Gleizes on 9 October 1932:

> Times here are very bad, everyone on the verge of financial disaster and de Valera clothing us all with his mad nationalism and narrow-minded men – this is naturally not a wheat-growing country, it is too damp, the weather too uncertain, every farmer says the same thing – he destroys our cattle trade and butter trade and then tells the farmers to grow wheat instead which they know is useless. He is in a very difficult position – the extremists of his own party and the power behind is Bolshevist and will probably get rid of him soon – the farmers are trying to get together and protect their own interests as the Government seem to have no inclination to do anything practical for them.

Her view, which reflects some of the hysteria felt by many people in Ireland when de Valera came to power, was to change substantially. Indeed a mutual respect developed between de Valera, as well as other politicians in his party, and the modernist artists. Later in the 1930s, when Fianna Fáil had established a secure and more respected power-base, the artists were increasingly supported abroad. When they organised exhibitions, they were given commissions, and their value was recognised as a cultural dimension of importance within the State. But in the early 1930s the political line taken by de Valera was isolationist in terms of trade, the vast bulk of which was with Britain, and this had a negative effect on culture and travel. There was also a moral and spiritual dimension.

190.   Mainie, Gleizes, and Mme Gleizes on holiday at Aigues-Mortes, in the South of France, September 1929.

The last thing de Valera could afford to do was to alienate the Roman Catholic Church. Hugely powerful in the 1930s, it was in the main unsympathetic to modern trends in the arts. While its main instinct for censorship was principally directed against literature and to a lesser extent film, its general impact on the other arts was fairly depressing. Modernism had little impact on standards of church architecture and decoration; the multitudinous statuary adorning the vast and ugly churches throughout the country were frequently derived from English or continental mass-producers. Where Irish artists were commissioned to do work, the doctrinal strictures and general conservatism resulted in church art of a very limited quality. There was quite an active Academy of Christian Art,[1] with a programme of lectures involving writers and historians; but there is little evidence of a modernist dimension to its work during Mainie's lifetime.

The gloom induced by Ireland's political isolation and the poverty resulting from de Valera's policies continued the following year, with Mainie reporting to Gleizes that the Church in the west of Ireland 'forces the women to have huge families though they have not the means to feed or clothe them . . . the poverty . . . is appalling the babies having to be wrapped in newspapers.'

Alongside these changes came a distancing, not just between Mainie and Gleizes, but also between Mainie and Evie. This latter development was the inevitable result of Evie becoming a stained-glass artist, and of Mainie's growing commitments as the recognised leader of a movement in modern painting in Ireland. Evie, because of her physical disability as well as her less assertive nature, shunned the public eye and played no significant role in the leadership and education of a public trying to understand what modern art was about. This function was enthusiastically espoused by Mainie. And while Evie was loyal and supportive and their friendship remained strong, their careers must be considered separately from about 1932 on.

As far as their relationship with Gleizes was concerned – indeed the relationship of all the artists who worked in loose association with him – this evolved, developed and changed. The intense exploration of the 1920s had involved a great deal of austere theory about pure abstract painting, and had kept all of them close together stylistically, particularly in the period 1922–6. Late in the second half of the decade the first works which were Cubist versions of Old Master paintings, particularly works of the Italian primitives, emerged and led to an evolution in practice away from the collective activity which had characterised life for them all when they met, during the period up to and including the establishing of the Moly-Sabata experiment.

There was greater independence, partly as a result of this, partly because, in terms of stylistic development and their differing views on colour, Mainie and Gleizes diverged somewhat. Also, with the formation of Abstraction-Création, the broader sense of solidarity among all abstract painters had the effect of placing the followers of Gleizes in a much wider context, with Mainie making numerous judgments about the relevance, impact and depth of other styles and other artists, and feeling instinctively, that she was among the leaders of a large group, rather than being a follower in a very small group.

The 1933 number of *Abstraction-Création* disappointed her; she reported to Gleizes:

can't say I am very thrilled by it, with a few exceptions I think the work is very dead and empty – I liked Delaunay's picture one of the best – your two look very well and one feels strength behind but so many of the others are nothing more than the old taunt that is flung at our heads – carpet designs – and when it arrives at an artist showing the grains of his canvas as his pictorial achievement, or something which looks like plain canvas I think it is going too far. Our work must be looked upon as early Victorian story pictures by these people. I would be interested to know what you think of the work in this number – I hate Herbin's curves and twists, I quite like Power and Valmier, Reth, Garcin and some of the sculpture, but I do not care for all the Mondrian followers.

In 1933 Barbara Hepworth and Ben Nicholson joined Abstraction-Création, the former with two abstract sculptures in marble, the latter with a single canvas.[2] Mainie was not greatly impressed by his work. 'Ben Nicholson seems to be having a great success in London, personally I think his work very slight from a <u>form</u> standpoint, but he has great charm of colour and texture.' She thought Edward Wadsworth a more serious and more interesting painter.

She told Gleizes that there seemed to be 'a decided interest arising in London for abstract art – I wish your work could be shown there. There is a new Gallery called the Mayor Gallery mainly for abstract painting and semi-realist work.'[3] This 'decided interest arising in London' was a belated phenomenon. Apart from the Seven and Five, which had held exhibitions during the 1920s, modernism in England was still largely dominated by Roger Fry and Post-Impressionism. In their diligent hunt for 'significant form', English painters and critics were missing out on the more vital and vigorous thrust of what was happening in other European countries, including Ireland. There was no sustained abstract tradition at all. When it came – in the 1930s, with the setting up of the Mayor Gallery and the showing of works of decidedly modernist style – the main names involved were Henry Moore,[4] Barbara Hepworth and Ben Nicholson, with Herbert Read as the first art critic to make an effort at understanding abstract art, its principles, and techniques.[5]

Read was confused. While he favoured abstract painting, for a time he favoured surrealism even more, and had to be weaned from it, by Nicholson in particular. Nicholson, who was a dominant and politically astute painter, saw the potential value of Read as his spokesman. Moore had a similar view of the critic. What is of interest is the fact that ten years after Mainie had embarked on the consistent output, exhibition, and sale of abstract paintings on a regular basis, in Dublin, London only began to move towards such a situation very hesitantly in the early 1930s.

Gleizes was not by nature a dominant man. If anything he leaned towards timidity in his personal relationships. He was deferential towards his wife, who was the source of the wealth which made possible their comfortable way of life, with their three properties in the south of France and apartment and studio in Paris. However, he had no doubt about the worth of his own achievements in painting, and the group of artists around him, including Pouyaud, Anne Dangar, Firpo and Jean Chevalier,[6] referred to him as 'master'. To Evie he wrote: 'Affectionate greetings from your master who does not forget you and his wife who likes you so much. . . . I am very proud of my pupils'. He particularly liked the diversity of activity which was taking place – Anne Dangar with her pottery, Evie Hone moving into stained glass by 1932, and Pouyaud into sculpture – 'Art in Life' is how he described it.

By the 1930s, however, he was becoming increasingly aware of a marked tendency to underplay or ignore his contribution to the history of modern art and this sensitivity caused him to remonstrate with Mainie when she sent him an article she had written called 'Modern Art and the Dual Ideal of Form through the Ages'. It appeared in October and upset Gleizes because it did not mention his name,[7] although it explored his basic teaching and incorporated his essential ideas. It was a trivial matter as far as Mainie was concerned; the article had been part of the lecture given in Cambridge and had been written simply to add to the collective explanation of her abstract painting. The idea of mentioning or not mentioning Gleizes had been nowhere in her thoughts, but she was upset by his distress and hastened to make amends:

I am <u>very</u> sorry that I have hurt you in any way by not mentioning your name in the article – no one knows more than I do how much your ideas are my ideas and how I have come to these ideas through contact with you – As a matter of fact this article was part of the lecture I gave at Cambridge, where I spoke clearly about the different stages of Cubism and showed reproductions of your pictures, bringing in clearly your position as being the leader of the group of Cubists who work from their imagination and mind and not from material objects and the exterior forms of nature . . . I wished it to stand simply as <u>our</u> idea of form and it never occurred to me to put in your name as I now see I should have done . . . In the lecture I gave last year at my Exhibition I went most carefully into the whole position of the first stages of the Cubist movement and stated from extracts out of your article 'L'Epopée' in 'Le Rouge et le Noir' the whole position of your group and Picasso, etc. who came in after, I translated and quoted the press notices which you quoted in your article . . . In the lecture I gave in October to the Arts and Crafts Society of Ireland, I had your book on view and the reproduction of your picture from the <u>Cimabue</u> in the Louvre pinned on the wall behind where I stood for people to see. Everyone here knows Evie and I are your pupils in fact I am often attacked for going to work with you and we do, and Evie also, as people think we will loose [sic] our individuality by doing so, and say nonsense of that kind to us. The lecture I am giving tomorrow is in a school and mainly for children but <u>there</u>, when I come to the Cubists, I have clearly divided your group from that of Picasso – I will mention your 'Forme et Histoire' most certainly but you probably don't realise how slowly one has to go to here and that you can't go into a lot of technicalities as lots of people have never even heard of Post Impressionism yet! They are <u>frightfully</u> ignorant and very few want to learn. Evie and I tell you of our successes but they are only very intermittent as we have a prolonged struggle against prejudice the whole time, and are now after ten years beginning to get a little recognition here – you know the Battle much better than we as you have had it all of your life, but you had others doing the same thing and were not the only two in a country doing it – and no outside work being shown to let the public know what the rest of the art world was at . . . please realise how sorry I am for not having put your name in the article, I will always be more than grateful to both you and Madame Gleizes for your great goodness to me and would never wish any misunderstanding to arise between us.

The master's feelings were ameliorated by this long letter, sent in November 1932. It came towards the end of a year in which correspondence had flourished, and for two further years Mainie wrote to Gleizes more frequently than at any other time, covering a vast range of subjects, including philosophic and social issues, political events in Ireland and Europe and her own domestic affairs, which included the marriage of her youngest sister, Betty. The intensity of this correspondence is particularly interesting, given the importance of the period in Gleizes' own development leading to the revolution that took place in his painting in 1934.

They were brought together into a closer association during these years on account of their involvement in Abstraction-Création. It also brought their work into direct comparison with that of other non-realist, non-representational painters, and demonstrated the extent and diversity of activity. This was of particular importance to Mainie. It is clear from her November 1932 letter that her sense of isolation was increased by political and economic developments at home, while whatever difficulties Gleizes faced, in having his ideas and work accepted, or at least treated with intelligent interest and respect, no such framework existed for Mainie's work in Ireland. She was constructing it herself: one carefully-reasoned lecture following another, one carefully articulated painting ranged beside another in her now regular shows.

In 1933 and, particularly 1934, Gleizes was passing into a new and very important phase in his development. This was best formulated in a letter he wrote in September 1934 to Anne Dangar.[8] In it, he said that he had felt increasingly that the paintings of the 1920s had not achieved the rotation to which he had long attached such crucial importance. The tilting of the planes to right or to left which he had called rotation in the 1920s was not sufficient. The translation-rotation he now felt to be simply at the level of translation, asserting the essentially static nature of the construction. For some time he had tried to give a unifying movement to his painting through the addition of simple grey circular curves, but he was still dissatisfied: 'I tried the impossible', he wrote, 'to bring them to a conclusion, the integration of the curves, the play of light . . .I was still unsatisfied . . .The final circles were still too much outside the <u>translation</u> and <u>rotation</u>; or rather, these last, even because of the rigour of the newly arrived circles, showed themselves to be imperfect, confused, disordered, badly divided.'

And so Gleizes reconsidered the sequential nature of all their art. The starting point was the static space, the basic construction, the 'figure', which he called translation though it corresponded to what had previously been called translation-rotation. As previously, this was rigorously derived from the – rectangular – shape of the canvas. But it gave rise to the second stage – of great circular curves like the haloes in Romanesque paintings. These curves were divided according to lines of force given by the original construction and they used its colours though in a highly ordered way. Gleizes related them to the rainbow. It was these circular curves that introduced time into the painting – the ordering of time in an act of contemplation. Gleizes insisted that the nature of space and time is radically different. The translation was an exploration of space in which, as in a Renaissance painting, time is frozen. With the rotation, the eye is put in movement: it passes from one thing to the other, in time.

But there was also a third stage: a simple, grey circle which Gleizes related to eternity, light, rhythm and form. With the translation and rotation we are in a world of variety, diversity and colour, however harmoniously arranged. But the diversity of the world as we see it is given its unity and form by the action of light; and the diversity of time, Gleizes believed, finds its unity and form in eternity. It is important to recognise that Gleizes was not trying to devise symbols by which religious truths could be represented. He believed that in his creative activity man participates in the creative activity of God, and that therefore the work of man in its fullness will have the same characteristics as the work of God. It is in this sense that man is the image of God and that the work of art can address our whole nature in its three aspects of space, time and eternity.

All of Gleizes' career can be seen as a research into the nature of form. The Cubist period had shown a desire to reassert the structural form that had been lost by the Impressionists. Increasingly, Gleizes came to identify form and movement. When Aristotle says that the soul is the form of the body, is he not identifying form with life, distinguishing it from the external appearance of the body? For Gleizes this external appearance is merely a 'figure'. It has its own importance but only corresponds to one aspect of our nature. For twenty years he had worked to endow this figure with movement – not an agitated, directionless movement but a rational, purposeful movement, hence his use of the word 'rhythm'. But now he felt that the three natures – figure, movement, form or rhythm – were different and that their difference should be fully understood by the painter and worked on as three successive stages in the realisation of the painting: 'So, the figures, dominated by *straight lines*, then the periodical displacement of straight line and curves; finally the unity, the circles.' The final circles were to be grey – a simple mixture of black and white. To understand the importance of grey in this context, we need to take a short detour into the realms of colour theory.

Any colour is made up of those rays of light falling on an object that have not been absorbed by that object. A red object is an object that has absorbed all the rays of the colour spectrum apart from the red ones. A white object is one that has absorbed none of the rays of the colour spectrum, a black object is one that has absorbed all of them. When we look at a colour in isolation it is surrounded by an 'aura' consisting of its complementary – of the sum of the other colours, those that have been absorbed by the object – red for green, yellow for violet and so on. Thus, the interaction of two colours placed side by side is determined by the mutual exchange of the effect of their complementaries: a blue placed beside a violet will acquire a slightly greenish tinge owing to the projection of yellow from the violet; the violet will be reddened by the projection of orange from the blue. The advantage of grey is that – like white or black – it does not cast an aura of its own and therefore does not have the effect of modifying the colour placed next to it. At the same time, it receives the aura of that colour. If placed beside a red it will acquire a greenish tint which will further enhance the intensity and purity of the red. This is why the greatly underestimated French nineteenth-century painter, Jules Bastien Lepage, argued that grey was necessary to establish a real sensation of space, light and depth in the landscape. Without it, the multitude of colours and their interactions give a crowded, agitated impression and this is one reason why the early Cubists tended to be so restrained in their use of colour.

The early part of Gleizes' letter to Anne Dangar stresses the way in which individual colours evolve, by movement, into different colours: 'for example, a blue square, that is to say, seen by itself, put in movement becomes a <u>green</u> which, continuing the movement becomes a <u>yellow</u>, which itself becomes an orange . . . etc. and the <u>circle</u> is the light in which this regular dance takes place.' This movement from blue to green to yellow to orange is the movement round the colour circle: blue — blue + yellow — yellow — yellow + red. The eye passes easily from blue to green because of the blue that is in green, and from green to yellow because of the yellow that is in green. Thus what Gleizes calls a 'cadence' is established, and these cadences – from one colour to another without changing tone – are the means by which colour enters into time, movement, rotation. The development of an individual colour from light to dark or dark to light, Gleizes argues, corresponds to the order of translation.

Among Mainie's papers can be found a short introduction to the principles of painting as they were formulated in the 1920s. When she talks about colour, she simply indicates the need to balance opposites: the balance of light and dark, of warm and cold, of complementaries. This was still an essentially static, restrained and tasteful use of colour. Now the colour was no longer something to be added to the form. The distinction between colour and form was ended: structure and colour were engaged in a common movement culminating in the grey circle which could be called form in its structural aspect and 'light' in relation to colour (since it brought the colour to its fullness, reconstituting the fullness of the light from which it derived):

> the circular light appears as an inevitability [*fatalité*] and no longer as something just thrown into the bargain as they [the grey circles] were in the canvases you saw [he refers to the canvases completed by April 1934] which are above all interesting for their intention and their intuition, but are badly ordered. Now the light is something expected, satisfying, conclusive.

This new development had a remarkably liberating effect on Gleizes' work. Into the paintings of 1934 and later, sweeping curves and circles are introduced which intensify the movement and vitality. A second aspect of the 'liberation' was Gleizes' re-acceptance of the figurative image in painting, not in its loaded, Renaissance form, 'the heavily mechanical expression of a sight without intelligence', against which he had preached and lectured for so long, but 'mnemonic in character, which is to say psychological, which is to say delivered from the memory not from the senses.'

In the relatively short essay which constitutes this letter, Gleizes attempts to explain the final process in the evolution of the abstract painting pursued by himself and his pupils since 1921–2. He also examines the means by which they could again take up the figurative image in their work without confusion or conflict. The apparent 'problem' in Mainie Jellett's painting – how she could paint severely non-representational abstract works side by side with flat-pattern Cubist representations of classical and religious subjects – is most easily resolved by a careful reading of what Gleizes, Evie and Mainie had been discovering together in the period of closest collaborative working, from 1928

191. *Study for Virgin and Child*, 1936. Pencil and ink on tracing paper, 44.5 × 25.5. Dublin, private collection. Annotated 'White, green, pomegranate – greys – & rainbows'.

192. *Abstract Composition*, 1937. Oil on canvas, 76 × 76. London, private collection. Illustrated in photograph of Dublin Painters' Gallery (Pl. 205). This was Number One in the catalogue, titled, as was usual, *Oil Painting*, and priced £15. It was hung between *Man* and *Woman*, which were also £15.

193. *Virgin and Child*, c. 1936. Oil on canvas, 61 × 46. Dublin, private collection.

until this letter. And it seems at the very least probable, that the lengthy missive sent to Anne Dangar is a record, not just of Gleizes's own and solitary self-discovery, but of a collective outcome to which he pays less than fair tribute. Touchy about receiving credit for what he gave to Mainie, he seems curiously reluctant to give reciprocal credit to those who went with him along the road towards this discovery of a new dimension in *their* abstract cubism.

Whatever the reciprocal debts, the exposition is profoundly relevant to the development of Mainie's art from 1933 to the end of the decade. Her use of the figurative image, the icon-like religious representation of such key subjects as the Adoration of the Virgin, the Deposition, the Pietà, the Annunciation, and the Crucifixion, should be viewed in the light of Gleizes's letter of April 1934.

> Now we can understand that the rejection of the image as experienced by the senses is only a means, more or less temporary, to understand, without being constrained by an oppressive habit, what we have ignored and lost of a great tradition which we are now once again beginning to feel. The image thus had to be abandoned in its renaissance, and ultimately photographic, expression, in its expression so grossly dependent on sensation, on sight considered simply as a mechanism. Once the true process is recognised and known, what importance is there left for our terror of the figurative image? What in the end is this figurative image.

To Gleizes, the figurative image, coming down from the Renaissance, had become a heavy burden. It had achieved its ultimate perfection in the photograph which merely records whatever is in front of it however 'artistically' it might be arranged. By renouncing the dead weight of the external, essentially lifeless appearances of things, painting had the possibility of addressing the spirit whose particular property is movement, growth, life. 'Are we on the side of the atom or on that of the seed? That is the question that is facing us' was a favourite expression. Once the essential movement or rhythm of the painting had been established, the question of whether or not there were recognisable images in it became a very secondary matter. The principle thing was to get rid of illusionism – the illusion of a real but motionless space situated in front of the spectator: 'We must pitilessly reject the sense-based, exclusive Renaissance image.'

Gleizes appended to his letter three tiny but crucial drawings which expressed his new understanding of translation-rotation-rhythm. These same drawings appeared also in the much briefer letter to Mainie. This summarised the 'findings' of Gleizes's very strenuous work during the summer of 1934, but in a form of shorthand between painters who had worked together on the problem. Moreover, Mainie had seen his early essays in this direction, and had commented adversely about the grey circles being detached from the central ideas of form and colour. Gleizes accepted what she said: 'Your comments were judicious, and I realised that my grey circles were too much outside the composition.'

Mainie's response to all this was the most natural and direct. In several pure abstract paintings dating from 1934 and 1935 she introduced the grey circles, and in her 1936 *Virgin and Child* (Pl. 193) she did the same with a religious subject with remarkable success.

This exchange ended the last significant period of collaboration between Gleizes and Mainie although they continued to correspond. The most natural explanation is that their collective work, which spanned twelve years, was really at an end. As far as Evie was concerned, this change in the artistic relationship among the former pupils and associates of Gleizes took a different direction, but reinforced her no less than it did Mainie in an independence of spirit and action. In 1933 she had joined An Túr Gloine, the stained-glass workshop set up by Sarah Purser. In that same year she produced her first public work, three panels which were incorporated into a single window for Saint Naithi's Church in Dundrum, County Dublin, near her home at Marlay. This was

Church of Ireland, and indeed her early commissions, until the Blackrock College Chapel windows in 1937, were for Protestant establishments, including the King's Hospital School Chapel window of 1936. She was of the view, appropriate in the light of the Gleizes letter, and recorded by her friend, Stella Frost, that stained glass demanded 'an altogether different approach' and she summarised it in Matisse's words: 'Stained glass is coloured light, it is a luminous orchestra. There is no need of stories. If stained glass becomes again a symphony of colours it can find its place in any architecture.'[9] It was to this end, and within this artistic framework of design and architecture, that Evie was now firmly dedicated. It so happens that An Túr Gloine had its workshops in a mews about 50 yards from the Jellett's house in Fitzwilliam Square, so that Evie called often to see Mainie. But the professional divergence was more marked than it had been in the previous ten years.

Mainie does not appear to have written to Gleizes during 1935. She was in France only for a week, in June, and visited exhibitions in Paris, but does not seem to have travelled south, either to Serrières or Cavalaire. There were affectionate exchanges between Mainie and Gleizes in 1936; he had written a kind letter on her father's death, and there was some reference in an earlier letter in that year to Evie's work on stained glass and Mainie's teaching.

A richly fertile period of collaboration, covering more than twelve years, had run side by side with two independent artistic careers. To understand fully the achievement it is necessary to see the intellectual and technical side of what they did together in a different context from the painting which they did quite separately. At the very beginning the collaboration was close in every sense. In the mid-1920s this changed, as Mainie forged ahead with her own work, and with the succession of exhibitions in Dublin. From then until the 1930s, the regular meetings, for periods of between a month and six weeks, were like symposiums or conferences on the laws and the inner nature of what they were doing, but not necessarily productive of major works of art. What *are* often referred to are the gouaches brought back from France and then developed. Seen in this light, the relationship is less open to the glib criticisms which Mainie faced at the time, and to which she referred in her letters, that she was somehow an imitative offshoot of Gleizes and his form of Cubism.

The overall process was liberating, and among other things explains much of what happened in Mainie's art during the last years of her life. Gleizes expressed it thus:

> To discard the subject does not, after all, mean liberation from the laws that govern painting. They remain and become even more imperative. But where they are acknowledged and accepted an immense field of possibilities opens before the painter. We, Mainie, Evie and I, and some other painters as well, did not have to wait long to realise this. The more the plastic technique suitable to painting and derived from the eye became familiar to us the more did we become aware that figurative iconographical suggestions were possible; that these images, instead of being representations, externally perceived, and arising from angles of perspective, arose accidentally in the interlacing of the melodic line, as one might imagine them, transient in the movement of clouds, or fixed and assertive in the convoluted shapes of roots. To translate the casual into the deliberate became a problem, of interest to the painter, allowing him to invest his melodic phrase with ambiguous figures which while giving it intellectual significance do not nevertheless change its nature. In the works of Mainie Jellett one may find such accidental or deliberate allusions. But we must not be deceived; they are not the product of an arbitrary reduction of a classical drawing, but evocative signs of our pictorial repertory seized on as they happen, or skilfully blended from the different suggestions that arise in the linear organisation of a composition.[10]

CHAPTER NINETEEN

The impact of Chinese Art

SOUTHERN UPPER-CLASS Unionist families who stayed on after the granting of independence went through the baptism of fire which the Civil War represented, but then settled down to a life which changed less than they might have anticipated. The vengeful violence against them, which drove many to abandon their houses and land in rural Ireland, particularly in the west and south, and move mainly to homes in England, lasted only a short time. It was replaced by a strict rule of law with which the names of those in power – particularly William T. Cosgrave, who was Prime Minister, and Kevin O'Higgins, his Minister for Justice – became synonomous. The State settled down to making its institutions work without the direct economic and administrative support of the imperial parliament. Of course indirectly it was there. Ireland remained within the Empire. The vast majority of civil servants were Irish and they simply transferred their allegiance. Economically the involvement of British investment and the control of wealth in the country did not change. The more radical of the two sides in Ireland, was led by Eamon de Valera and his Fianna Fáil party remained a 'revolutionary' party, committed to the completion of 'unfinished business'. Basically, this meant the achievement of a thirty-two-county republic instead of the twenty-six-county 'Free State', still within the British Empire and with a Governor General appointed by the parliament at Westminster.

By the time this party approach changed, first in the second half of the 1920s, with the decision to enter the Dáil, and then more fundamentally, in 1932, when Eamon de Valera came to power, the Jelletts had all come to terms with their position in Irish society. As we have seen, Mainie was an established painter by this time, travelling freely in Europe and bringing back theories and ideas which she was able to present vigorously in an intellectual and cultural environment which was receptive and highly creative. Her father had become reconciled to the State's viability, having worked trenchantly throughout his political life against Home Rule, and having been initially pessimistic. Though his continued participation in Free State politics was canvassed, he retired from politics after 1922, and practised law exclusively from then on.

He found the climate in the 1920s, and perhaps even more so in the 1930s, less lucrative in the field of chancery law in which he had specialised, and it was said of him that his family were left not too well off because of this. The truth, as is so often the case, is more complicated. To his surprise, he found that after independence many of his briefs came from nationalist clients, and he was in fact treated generously by the very people whose politics he had so fervently opposed. There is little evidence that his outspoken Unionism militated against him professionally. Nevertheless, he was never a wealthy man.

The process of intellectual reconciliation with an independent Ireland went on through the first change of government in 1932. It was essentially a social rather than a political perception. William Jellett had lived through a period of intense bitterness and divisiveness between those who supported the link with Britain and those who sought independence, and had seen these wounds being healed. By becoming aloof from active politics in the period after 1922, he was less directly involved in the new divisiveness and bitterness which derived from the Civil War, and which was to dominate Irish politics for decades after his death.

From his standpoint the overall prospects for the country were seen as more positive under an independent Dublin sovereignty, whatever its detailed political colouring, and this view is the one remembered by members of his family as the one which prevailed at the end. It may also have been responsible, in later years, for his widow's determined support of Eamon de Valera. 'We all thought he was *awful*,' a surviving sister of Mainie's has said, describing the sense of family outrage when their mother, Janet Jellett, insisted she would 'Vote for Dev'.

Perhaps part of the reason for this change of heart can be traced to the normality of life which had been successfully established by those first ten years of stable democratic government. If there were hesitations in 1932 about how things might develop under Eamon de Valera the first auguries were at the very least that stable democracy would be maintained. Placed in a world context, the calm of Irish political life was comparatively attractive, and the dropping of the oath of allegiance, mentioned earlier, takes on only a mildly symbolic tone.

By the early 1930s two of the four Jellett daughters had married and moved away, Babbin and her husband to Belgium, Betty and Sean Purser to Glasgow where he taught at the university. Sean was the nephew of Sarah Purser, the Irish painter and founder of An Tur Gloine.[1] Within the next few years the two married daughters had young families. At this time Bay was increasingly involved in her work at Dublin's Gate Theatre, as its musical director, while Mainie, working full-time as a painter increasingly focused her attention on the artistic life of Dublin, on her regular solo exhibitions, and on the urgent task – in her eyes – of teaching modernism.

She was given the opportunity to reach a much wider audience in the summer of 1933 when she was invited to broadcast a series of talks on art, the first of which concentrated on the pictures in Dublin's Municipal Gallery, the main collection of modern works in the country. Although only her rough notes survive, they show that she began her talk in characteristically controversial style, by dealing with the essentials set out by Hugh Lane in his 'Preparatory Note' to the original catalogue of 1908.[2] Dublin then, unlike every other capital city in Europe, had no gallery of modern art. By 1933 Dublin Corporation had modified Charlemont House[3] and added rooms to the back, confidently claiming that by so doing it had discharged the conditions in the codicil to Hugh Lane's will by which he intended to bequeath to the city his important collection of Impressionist and other paintings. This development, in turn, had reactivated the demands by the Irish government for a handover by the British government of the thirty-nine Lane Bequest Pictures.

The precise attitude adopted by Mainie to the controversy, either on the occasion of her lecture or more generally, is not clear from these notes. What is clear, from her correspondence at the time, and the attitude towards Ireland and modern art generally which can be traced in many of her lectures, is that she was profoundly sceptical of its seriousness at several levels.

The State's attitude to practising painters was generally negative, as it was to all the arts. Modernism was widely interpreted in highly nationalist and romantic terms, and the kind of modernism she espoused was suspect. While Mainie's good sense, cautious balance and fairness would have prevented her from a polemical talk on radio – where her first duty was to educate and to encourage people to look at the pictures – her objective, as indicated in her notes, was first of all to address the historical perspective. Dublin's first need, recognised by Lane, was of a modern gallery. The second requirement was that it should remain modern 'by ceding to the National Gallery those pictures which, having stood the test of time, are no longer modern – [and] make room for good examples of the movements of the day.'

Her radio talk then dealt with the paintings in the collection, the main emphasis being on Impressionist and Barbizon works, though it is interesting that she covered in some detail works from the British School. The early collection was rich in such works: she lists D.Y. Cameron, Frank Brangwyn, Watts, Ricketts, Steer, Clausen, Sickert, Whistler, Rothenstein, Nash and Bernard Meninsky. Neither then nor later did the collection contain any works by artists who were her associates in Paris and elsewhere in Europe. The most modern French artist she could name was Monet.

That summer of 1933 Mainie made a trip to Amsterdam. She was accompanied by Evie Hone, though it seems that only Mainie went in a vaguely official capacity to study the art and architecture. This was of sufficient interest to merit newspaper coverage: The *Irish Independent* noted that she was going to study architecture and the Dutch Galleries.[4] The paper referred to her solo exhibition at the Dublin Painters' Gallery:

> Miss Jellett . . . is one of the finest of our modern painters and designers, and enjoys no small reputation in several Continental countries where her art finds a bigger public than here. Miss Jellett has exhibited in London, Paris, Brussels, Amsterdam and Vienna, and reproductions of her work have appeared in many French and German periodicals.[5]

Mainie found Amsterdam highly congenial. 'Holland in this period of upheaval seems to have maintained an equilibrium which cannot fail to impress an outsider on entering the country.' She subsequently wrote about the architecture and gave a broadcast talk, her second. It may be that the journey was sponsored by the diplomatic representative in Dublin for the Netherlands. Many of the diplomats, with little to do in the Irish capital, became quite keenly interested in art and there are references to several who regularly attended Mainie's lectures. If so, the Dutch Minister's reward was evident in her glowing account of the buildings and parks of Amsterdam, the careful matching of new buildings with old, the employment of modern stained-glass artists, like Roland Holst,[6] in the structure of the new town hall whose Council Chamber was decorated with Thorn Prikker's wall paintings. 'One could not help thinking how long would it be before an Irish Government would have time to consider the artistic organisation and interior decoration of public buildings.'

She turned her attention to every kind of building – banks, schools, synagogues, churches, private houses and apartment blocks – and her analysis is simple yet comprehensive, dealing with proportion, colour, materials, and the employment of craftsmen and artists. The emphasis on stained glass by the architect Jantzen and by Brochelin as well as by Holst no doubt derived from Evie's enthusiasm for her new direction as an artist. 'When new buildings are being constructed one feels a sincere effort to plan out the ground and design and construct with thought. Holland is using her architects, sculptors, painters and designers in an intelligent way. When will we in Ireland do the same?'

Her other interest during the visit, in modern painting, focused on Vincent Van Gogh, 'one of the greatest modern painters', who brought to modern art 'something . . . far removed from the logical French spirit, an amazing sense of movement and life and above all humanity, which may be his natural legacy, and which one feels so intensely in the early Dutch painters and the work of Dutch artists such as Ver Meer, Rembrandt and Riusdael.' (Mainie's own spellings.) She reported on the excellent display of his work and of more modern artists, such as Mondrian and Van Doesburgh, and there is a hint of declared, proselytising envy at the difference between Holland and Ireland, an envy which echoes her earlier Radio Eireann broadcast about Charlemont House.

Mainie was still new to broadcasting, and had to work quite hard at cutting down her words to the ten minutes allowed for her talk. She also modified her outspokenness, deleting a reference to Ireland being 'defaced with appalling buildings without design or plan . . . totally void of architectural significance'.

Early in 1934, as a result of her broadcast, Mainie was invited by the Architects'

194. *Circular Rug Design*, 1933. Black wash on paper, dia. 16.8. Dublin, private collection.

Association of Ireland to lecture on modern art. Her theme related directly to her visit to Amsterdam, not only in the emphasis she placed on Van Gogh's role as a major part of 'the fountainhead of inspiration for future generations', but also in the extent to which she linked the arts together, especially modern abstract Cubism with architecture.

> I would like to close this lecture by saying that modern painting, particularly the type of painting that has evolved from the Cubist Movement, is essentially linked with modern architecture. It is two-dimensional in its foundation, its starting point is the wall or surface it is to fill, its aim to animate that surface and make it live without destroying – as with Renaissance perspective – the natural properties of that surface. The architects have already recognised two-dimensional modern sculpture [with] Epstein and Gill in England, and in Holland, France, Germany were at once given greater significance by the organic introduction of sculpture cut direct in stone, not treated as filling on (sic) a cake as is so often the case in bad baroque architecture and the worst type of 19th C and 20th C architecture – I think the same use could be made of painting inside the great modern buildings and more especially with abstract painting as it is an art that has its foundations in the same ideals of harmony and form as modern architecture.

Like Gleizes, Mainie placed a perspective in the lecture on the historical losses which resulted from the break-up of the Guild System, and then from the industrial era, both of which isolated the painter and sculptor. There had been a transfer of tasks with mechanised processes absorbing much of the creative function and leaving the artist 'on the fringe of society as it were, with no definite status and looked on as exotic flowers only fit to be patronised by the very rich.' In the end she knew 'the real artist will always work for his own artistic expression and satisfaction whether he is recognised or not, Cézanne is an example of this, but we must remember Cézanne had private means.'

Mainie found much wrong with the teaching of art and with technical standards in painting.

> The art of architecture I imagine can not suffer as painting has done from some of the difficulties I have mentioned, the main reason being people will always want buildings to live in and those buildings must be so constructed that they will not fall down as soon as the tenant enters the door, a fact that would continually happen with the work of many well known painters if their pictures were houses!

Mainie told her audience of the sense of privilege she felt at addressing them because of their professionalism and sense of craft and art combined. 'All those who follow an artistic career with real sincerity count for a tremendous force, though they may be considered useless by the upholders of mechanical materialism it is in them the creative spark is engendered which, with religious emotion, is the fountainhead of inspiration for struggling humanity.'

To a small extent some of the clear encouragement in her lecture about the State's need to become involved and to give support to artists may not have fallen on deaf ears. Certainly, later in the 1930s, it was to Mainie Jellett that the government turned when the representation of Ireland at two world fairs, Glasgow and New York, became a live issue. And government ministers began to make appearances at exhibitions and to show a greater interest in the arts.

Mainie's notebook containing the outline for her broadcast talks and her lecture to the Architectural Association also has notes for another lecture, on the Church of Christ the King, in Cork.[7] She contrasted this ultra-modern building, designed by the American architect, Barry Byrne, and meeting at least some of her requirements about new architecture 'making itself felt in Ireland', with Honan's Chapel, the designs and decorations for which were done when she was at the Metropolitan School of Art, and 'with which I was profoundly disappointed.'[8] Honan's Chapel failed, she felt, because it

195. *Carpet Design*, c.1933. Gouache on paper mounted on card, 15.4 × 15.4. Dublin, private collection.

196. *Carpet Design*, c.1933. Gouache on paper mounted on card, 17.8 × 15.2. Dublin, private collection. Inscribed and dated on reverse 'Carpet Design 1933'.

197. *Carpet Design*, 1933. Gouache on paper mounted on card, 15.5 × 15.3. Dublin, private collection. Inscribed and dated on reverse 'Carpet Design 1933'.

was neither an exact reproduction of its medieval inspiration – Cormac's Chapel – nor an evolution from the old architecture into new and challenging forms. It was, as she judged it, characterless, whereas the Church of Christ the King developed ancient Irish architectural idioms in a satisfyingly modern way.

Mainie also debated at this time, mainly in a correspondence with a friend in Devon called Charles John Skrine, on the merit of cinema as an art form. But a more important debate, which was to have a lasting public impact, took place on radio on 1 October 1935, when she and Dermod O'Brien, President of the Royal Hibernian Academy, held a discussion on 'The Academic Tradition and the Modern Movement in Painting'. At that time in broadcasting, certainly in Ireland, there was none of the spontaneity to which we have become accustomed at the end of the twentieth century. Each of the two participants provided the other with an outline of their intended remarks, with cue lines to be picked by each respondent in turn. By one of those rare accidents so valuable to the biographer, not only have Mainie's working notes survived, showing that she prepared her script for the debate against strict word counts; we also have, from Dermod O'Brien's side, a transcription of the whole debate, apparently verbatim as broadcast.

They were a well-matched pair for such a debate despite the disparity in their ages. O'Brien, born in 1865, was more than thirty years Mainie's senior, and had become president of the Royal Hibernian Academy in 1910 when Mainie was only thirteen years old and had not even started her studies at the College of Art in Dublin. Far from becoming the crusty old academician one might have expected O'Brien had in fact moved very much with the times, was well aware of modern trends, and was friendly and encouraging towards those of modernist persuasion. He owned more than one work by Mainie, and bought from other artists who challenged the academic stranglehold on art as they saw it. He was, then, well qualified to enter the debate in a relatively unprejudiced way. Recognising this, Mainie adopted a temperate approach. Even so, they were both doughty adversaries, and soon got down to real, confrontational argument.

Dermod O'Brien's theme was that academics were mainly criticised for not recognising 'young talent and new movements in art', and that 'this is meant by this parrot cry of "too academic".' 'I rather resent you labelling our criticism "parrot cry",' Mainie replied. 'Present day painters, who are in opposition to academic standards, oppose and criticise those standards for the following reasons. The most important is that Academies lack vitality, become bound up in what they consider their tradition, and refuse to open their doors to new blood.' Young painters, she felt, working in a modern way, could not be bothered to submit to academy juries because they knew in advance they would be rejected for not being academic enough. But this was peripheral reasoning; more centrally she then stated: 'The modern painter reacts strongly against what he considers the story-telling element or problem picture, when the literary and realistic quality is the most important factor, or in particular, the "speaking likeness". The war cry of the modern movement is "Design and Composition" first in importance, "Subject" second.'

O'Brien, a competent portrait painter, challenged the modernist 'war cry' in the realm of portraiture: surely likeness was a portrait's *raison d'etre*? He stressed composition, and that 'intensity and selection' which differentiated it from photography. Mainie countered that the academic tradition was dead. This led to exchanges about that 'tradition', O'Brien's view being that it was fixed in many of its technical essentials: 'We believe that no really important work can be carried through without a sound knowledge of composition, drawing, construction and the application of pigment or the use of the chisel.' Mainie saw it quite differently, as a view on the content and inspiration of art which the moderns believed was not fixed according to set principles and was not about technique at all, since *all* paintings had to conquer a technical competence barrier, something she had achieved early in her training as an artist.

198. *Rug Design*, *c*.1933. Gouache on card, 20.4 × 12.8. Dublin, private collection.

199. *Rug Design*, *c*.1933. Pen and ink on paper, 14 × 8.5. Dublin, private collection.

'Tradition is the expression of fundamental truth in art, but . . . reinterpreted afresh according to the spirit of the age' by each generation. O'Brien favoured fixed principles, and emphasised technique, going so far as to claim that 'the standard of craftsmanship is consistently high' in Royal Hibernian Academy exhibitions, though 'the expression of emotions' he thought less important. He also pointed out, accurately enough, that the outsiders or rebels of one era became the academicians of the next, a view with which Mainie could not easily argue. The debate was inconclusive. In any sense in which such encounters are won or lost, Dermod O'Brien came out the better of the two. If there was a simple lesson it was that the moderns needed their own academy.

Now fully mature in her art and confident as a teacher, Mainie was almost apostolic in her dedication to the spread of modernism should be spread among artists and art lovers in Ireland. She was, however, swept off her feet by a new passion in the winter of 1935–6 when she visited the great exhibition in the Royal Academy of Arts in London, of Chinese Art.[8] Jointly sponsored by the British Monarchy and the President of the Chinese Republic, there were more than 3,800 exhibits drawn from collections throughout the world with no major owners of works refusing to lend. It covered a period of thirty-five centuries. Mainie said that she went to it with the 'express purpose' of study. 'This made a profound impression upon me and helped to form an approach to landscape painting, which I have used in varied forms ever since.' By this stage in her painting her work had evolved in several directions. There was the severely non-representational painting derived from the principles of translation and rotation as they had been further developed by Gleizes in the 1930s. Then there were the works which derived from Christian religious subject matter which she treated 'symbolically without realism'. She actually called them 'non-representational' as well, but this is not strictly accurate. There was her work in landscape. There were her numerous essays in design, notably for rugs, carpets and linoleum (Pls. 194–9). There were paintings of the nude, and of the human figure, executed along Cubist lines. There was some commercial work, including plant paintings and catalogue design, for which she won a prize at a Royal Horticultural Society of Ireland show in 1934.[9] And there was her work for theatre, and later for ballet.

The stylised human figure, in paintings based on such emblematic events as the Nativity, the Crucifixion, the *Pietà* and the simple pose of Mother and Child, formed an increasingly large segment of her output in the 1930s (Pl. 200). One grouping of work – realistic landscapes and genre scenes treated in a Cubist manner, but inspired by Chinese Art – was new. To it belongs a substantial number of paintings, in oil, watercolour and gouache, stretching from 1936 to the end of her life, and deriving from the impact of Chinese Art. Indeed, the last work she completed, *A Western Procession*, was in this category. She had, of course, throughout the very experimental period during the 1920s, kept up landscape painting as a discipline, an exercise, possibly also as a relaxation. But this work was mainly in gouache, and was rightly seen as an adjunct to the major works in oil, principally abstract paintings and symbolic religious works. Now, with paintings of west of Ireland scenes first, she moved landscape into a more central position in her work, and one which was to be sustained until she died.

The Chinese exhibition presented so many echoes to Mainie of art as she had come to conceive it. Here was landscape painting which transcended landscape with a combination of fantasy and simplicity. The rocks and crags, the delicately poised trees in spring blossom, the hint of water, had an ethereal quality which made them contemporary and even abstract in her mind. Yet the finest work of all from the beginning of the Sung era in the tenth and eleventh centuries, struck with her an immediate comparison with Celtic art, and the capacity of the Irish monks to decorate a given space so that realism and pictorial construction become inextricably woven. There was another close comparison: the Celts and the Chinese shared a common and profound respect for calligraphy. To the connoisseur of Chinese art painting is a branch of writing,

200. *Christ Carrying the Cross*, c. 1933. Gouache on card, 66.5 × 35.5. Dublin, private collection.

an extension of the magical properties of the brush, and as deft and irreversible in its demand on the practitioner. There is no hesitation, no fumbling; the labour cannot be corrected. The artist must have in his mind the exact purpose and design of the whole concept. Meaning and form are one. The mental concentration is clearly evident in the purity and the irreversible nature of the technique. There is in Chinese painting, a literary, a scholarly, even a poetic content. It is not there in any crude sense of representing a narrative or poetic idea, or even a fairy story or legend – though the ubiquitous Willow Pattern plate might have suggested to generations of the Western mind that this is what should be sought out – but in the more profound sense of atmosphere and space creating a poetic mood in which there is a palpable sense of harmony, repose, even happiness.

The other great appeal of Chinese art for Mainie was its capacity to transcend the various media. Visitors to this huge collection could see great imperial creations together with the begging bowls, incense burners, flasks, plates, bottles and vases which were there in such profusion. To Mainie this represented the artist and the craftsman working hand in hand with a common purpose; indeed, more often than not the craftsman and the artist were one, as they had been in the greater Celtic period, as they had generally ceased to be in Western society, as Mainie believed they should once again become. Laurence Binyon, who wrote the introduction to the catalogue of that exhibition, came close to expressing precisely Mainie's attitude of mind, when he concluded:

Just as the painter seems to have entered into the life of bird or flower or tree so that they paint it, so to speak, from the inside, the potters enter into and assimilate the genius of their material; and the shapes that grow up under their hands – at least, in the great periods – appear to have acquired a destined form like fruit that swells to ripeness from within.

Mainie absorbed these feelings, but then set them in quite a different context. Returning from London, after seeing the exhibition, she went to Achill. She wrote to Gleizes in May 1936:

I was in the West of Ireland on Achill Island one of the most westerly parts of the coast, the huge expanse of the Atlantic and the nearest land America – the colouring and atmosphere are wonderful and the strength of the rocks and huge cliffs, one feels they are the ramparts of Europe. I was staying with a friend on the rocks near the sea, the peace and the aloofness from the confusion and scrambling of the world of the moment was wonderful – one had the same feeling in the Chinese Exhibition in London directly you got into the exhibition out of the crowded streets, there was a natural rhythm running through the works as a whole, which caught you up and led you quickly on, and prevented you from being tired, as is usually the case – I wish you had seen it.

The impact of the Chinese exhibition, however, took Mainie in a direction that further separated her from Gleizes. For Gleizes, the representational image is always an integral part of the overall rhythmic movement of the painting. His masterpiece of 1938, *Seven Elements*, is entirely abstract. As we have seen, he himself insists in his article on Mainie that her representational images 'arose accidentally in the interlacing of the melodic line', but in fact, from this time onwards, they begin to take a much more dominant position in her work than they do in his, and her use of colour in such paintings as *I Have Trodden the Wine Press Alone* (see Pl. 244) and *The Crucifixion* becomes much more dramatic and expressionist.[10] The rhythm of the painting coincides with the form of the representational image in a way that it never does in Gleizes' painting, so that the 'figure' – as Gleizes would have called it – begins to detach itself from a non-representational background. Increasingly she uses the image as a starting point – a fully representational, and even sometimes quite sensuous drawing is reduced to a more abstract composition, without, however, losing its own integrity. Mainie could easily have found a justification for this practice in Chinese art which remains essentially representational however much the representation is 'spiritualised'. The impact of the Far Eastern invasions on the non-representational painting of Islam had a similar effect to the impact of the Chinese exhibition on Mainie's art.

A tension between the forms of the natural world and the demands of the picture plane begins to reappear in her work which could be said to bring her back to Lhote, who appears to have been much in her mind at this time. She lectured on him and was closely involved with a group of young Irish painters who had studied with him in the early thirties. Lhote's own painting of the thirties had become more 'rhythmic' in Gleizes' sense of the word, though in a correspondence between Gleizes and Lhote at the end of the decade Gleizes says that he regards Lhote as being at the opposite extreme in the development of Cubism to himself.[11] But Mainie was moving on. Her independence of thought and the individuality of her art, firmly established in earlier years through the unusual collaborative relationship on which her Cubist work was founded, had developed into a style which was detached, and which moved during the 1930s much more towards religious subject-matter, bringing drama and heightened feeling. This reflected in part her own spirituality, drew on the deep and abiding sense she had of the best of Celtic and Romanesque art, and derived a good deal of its strength and renewal, in the second half of the decade, from the huge impact of the exhibition of Chinese art.

CHAPTER TWENTY

Mainie as teacher

WILLIAM JELLETT WAS taken ill in the High Court in Dublin, on 26 October 1936. He stopped in mid-sentence and asked the judge if he might sit down. He protested that he would continue, but instead was taken home, having suffered a serious heart attack. Mainie came to put away his court clothes. Leave them, he said, he would want them in the morning. He died in the early hours of the following day. He was seventy-eight, the highly respected and much-loved Father of the Irish Bar (Pl. 201).

He was deeply missed by his family, perhaps by Mainie most of all. He had looked upon her with great respect, not untinged at times by bewilderment.[1] Her work and her public stance had made her more widely known than her father, and he deferred somewhat to this. The immediate practical result of his death was to leave the family with more limited financial resources. Mainie and Bay were now the breadwinners. 'We'll try and stay on [in the house],' Mainie wrote to Gleizes, 'let some of it, it is too big for us but to move out of it would be a great expense – and I must have a studio, which I have here.' She expressed relief that her father died 'as he did without any real suffering, and working up to the last,' and also admiration for her mother's courage in the face of the 'terrible blank' which was there after his death.

It would have been unthinkable to move from Fitzwilliam Square. The house was a centre for artistic endeavour embracing theatre and music as well as painting. The afternoon recitals and musical *soirées* over which Mrs Jellett had presided since the beginning of the century had evolved and changed but had in no sense lessened that flood of enthusiastic playing which increasingly became associated with Bay Jellett. By far the liveliest part of her busy and diverse musical career derived from her position as musical director of the Gate Theatre.

This theatre, founded in 1928, was to play an increasingly important role in Dublin artistic life, and to be an important element of the Jellett household during the remaining years of Mainie's life. The permanent company there was led by Micheal MacLiammoir,[2] a handsome and dashing actor who, together with his partner, Hilton Edwards,[3] dominated the company. With financial backing and literary skills from Lord Longford[4] (Pl. 202) and his wife, Christine Longford,[5] the company presented a permanent repertory of modern classics, Shakespeare, continental theatre, often translated with an Irish idiom or setting, American drama, and a wide range of comedy from the Restoration to Wilde and Shaw. *Peer Gynt* was its first ambitious production.

The partnership of Hilton Edwards and Micheal MacLiammoir was to Dublin theatre what the partnership of Mainie Jellett and Evie Hone had been to painting: it irreversibly changed Irish theatre's character, style and direction by bringing in a flood of international ideas and performances and by throwing aside all the ponderous shibboleths of the past. Denis Johnston,[6] whose plays were performed by the Gate Theatre Company, wrote:

The theatre was full on the first night. There were no speeches, manifestos or announcements to mark the occasion . . . One newspaper said of *Peer Gynt* 'the number of persons who admire that sort of thing to the extent of paying an admission

201. Family photograph, with William Jellett, shortly before his death, and probably in the spring of 1936. From left: Sean Purser, who was married to Mainie's sister, Betty, Miss Skerrett, nanny to Betty and her sister, Babbin, Mainie Jellett, with her poodle, Mishki, and Bay's Cairns terrier, William Jellett, Geraldine Purser (Mainie's neice), and her sister, Bay.

202. Lord Longford introducing Jellett lecture.

fee is not large enough to fill the theatre for sixteen nights'. Time has shown the wisdom or otherwise of much of the newspaper criticism that was levelled at the Gate and its productions in those early days, and there is now nothing more than some mild amusement to be gained in turning over the dusty files of the theatre scrap books, and reading the ponderous comments and ill-digested advice and observations by many of the theatre's early critics, whose words are now perished and forgotten like the May-fly, while the plays that they attacked have triumphantly lived on.

How closely this inauspicious birth of a powerful new presence and inspiration for the arts in Dublin parallels the equally dismal reception given five years earlier to Mainie's first showing of abstract art! MacLiammoir, no less than Mainie, combined in equal measure a fierce sense of national pride with an openness towards international and modern ideas. Hilton Edwards, by contrast, had happily abandoned any nationalism which might have drawn him back to his native country; he would have been content to work anywhere.

Bay Jellett's involvement had not been immediate. There was no orchestra for early productions, only a piano, but when the lease was taken out on the portion of the Rotunda building which is still the home of the Gate Theatre today, the Dublin architect, Michael Scott, incorporated the orchestra 'pit' in the box to the left of the stage, and it was from here, in the 1930s, after the remodelling of the theatre, that Bay Jellett became musical director. In addition to Denis Johnston, playwrights working directly for the company included, Edward and Christine Longford, Austin Clarke,[7] Padraic Colum,[8] Mary Manning,[9] and of course MacLiammoir himself. Indeed this prodigiously talented director of the Gate's affairs in its early days was responsible for set and costume designs, choreography and stage direction, and the writing of plays, as well as generally playing the lead in comedy, tragedy, farce, melodrama and pageant.

The siting of the orchestra pit provoked a correspondence in *The Irish Times* in which Mainie became involved. She wrote a long letter, examining sympathetically the problems of where to put the orchestra in a small theatre where priority had to be given to seating. In those days, before any electronic sound was available, the live music element was important. Bay herself recalls using adaptations of Beethoven's 'Moonlight Sonata' to introduce the love scene in Romeo and Juliet. She gives a brief history of the evolution of music at the Gate Theatre. Initially it was played on piano and violin, in the wings; this was an adequate solution for the muted sound during plays, with the curtains drawn back, but totally wrong during the interval, with the curtains closed. From this evolved the separate small stage to the left, since no orchestra pit could be cut in the eighteenth-century building. She argued for this, even suggesting a mechanism for raising the orchestra pit, 'like the organ at the Savoy' (a large Dublin cinema built in the 1930s).

The design and location of this small orchestra stage, or 'box', led to a far more dramatic event involving Mainie. The pianist was Kathleen Rogers, who fell in love with MacLiammoir in the summer of 1931. From her seat at the piano, not more than a yard or so from him at times, she could follow his every movement on stage with fervent adoration. This she did, quite mesmerised in her passion. Whether or not it affected her playing we do not know, but it certainly got on Micheal MacLiammoir's nerves. In a moment during the play when dramatic tension was directed elsewhere he approached the box and the besotted eyes of the pianist, hissing out with snake-like venom: 'Will you stop looking at me, you stupid, moon-faced bitch!' Poor Kathleen Rogers decamped that night, and Mainie was hastily summoned. 'I have had to play the piano', she wrote to Gleizes, in a somewhat more polite version, 'as the theatre pianist is suffering from a severe attack of "love-sickness" for one of the leading actors, he could not stand it any longer and she was sent away at very short notice so I was sent for till someone else could be got.'

MacLiammoir's work draws in a curious fashion on two artists: Mainie from whom he took an Art-Deco version of Cubism and Harry Clarke, whose stylish and vaguely grotesque figures suited the theatrical content of MacLiammoir's more imaginative works of art. MacLiammoir gave Clarke the sobriquet 'Master of the Heavily-Encrusted Detail', a description which fits at least some of the more exquisite drawings. Mainie got on well with Michael MacLiammoir,[10] who respected her courage and her talent, and was interested in the possible application of her forms of abstract cubism to theatre designs. She discussed it with him and she did some preliminary drawings which survive (Pl. 203). She may have been responsible for preliminary set designs for a production of Jean Giraudoux's play, La Guerre de Troye n'aura pas lieu.[11] But if any of her work was incorporated in designs for productions she was not credited.

The 1930s were grim years for Europe. In March 1936 Hitler's troops entered the Rhineland, and neither France nor Britain had seen fit to contest the act of aggression. Later in the same year the German dictator committed the 'Condor Legion' to fight in Spain on the side of Franco. The Abyssinian War had resulted in the defeat of Haile Selassie and the creation of an Italian 'Empire', effectively ruled by Mussolini, whose pact with Berlin was drafted just at the time when Franco was launching his offensive against Catalonia. The free nations of Europe – the democracies of Britain and France – were bent on appeasement. They had economic problems of their own, and had to face other crises, notably for the British the abdication of King Edward VIII in December. And even when they did look to the root causes of Fascism's rise to power in Spain, Italy and Germany, their response was ambivalent, since the 'enemy' in those countries was identified as international Bolshevism; the period had been punctuated by the dark shadow of Stalinist totalitarianism and by the brutal 'show trials' and executions which continued with added force and relentless brutality throughout the decade. Though we do not know Mainie's views on the international situation, she kept herself informed. She had in her papers newspaper cuttings about 'Hitler's Creed', and she clipped and kept various articles on international politics.

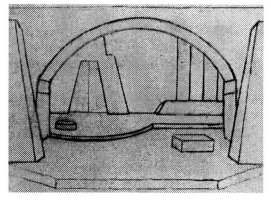

203. A Stage Set, c.1935. Pencil on paper, 38 × 50.5. Dublin, National Gallery of Ireland.

204. Robert Pouyaud, *Ecce lignum crucis in quo salus mundi pependit*, 1936. Oil on canvas, 95 × 116. Dublin, private collection.

The European situation did not prevent her from planning a visit to Gleizes in 1936. It was to be in September, and was, at least in part, for Evie's benefit, as she needed a rest.[12] 'I wish you could see her work,' Mainie wrote, 'it is very fine, and the colouring rich and alive.' Mainie herself was experimenting with *pointillisme* 'to help towards a more diffused effect of light, especially in the circular parts where the colours follow the law of the chromatic circle, some of the circles I have done in *pointillist* spots of colour others in the flat colours, it alters the speed of the rotation I think, and gives variety. But when you see what I have done you may think it quite wrong.' Though working in *pointilliste* style during 1936, her paintings at that year's Abstraction-Création exhibition were dominated by her use of Gleizean curves and have a rounded, fluid sense of line, coupled with intense and vivid colour.

As well as visiting Gleizes, it seems that Mainie at least went to see Robert Pouyaud, who was then living near Vézelay, at Asnières-sur-bois. It was a time of fruitful output for him, both in terms of his paintings, which included major canvases on religious and abstract themes (Pl. 204), and also with his writing. He published a pamphlet in 1936, *Considerations esthétiques sur le signe de la spirale*,[16] and sent an inscribed copy to Mainie that Christmas.

1936 was to be the last year of Abstraction-Création's existence. It had been formed to promote abstraction as an ideal in itself. It accepted only the work of painters and sculptors whose entire output was abstract. As we have seen, Gleizes and his associates never wished to make a fetish of abstraction, and Mainie herself was suspicious of and depressed by the endless succession of circles and squares. All the members of the Gleizes group were returning to figurative imagery – Mainie, and, in her very different way, Evie, most of all.

Abstraction-Création had become very large. The fourth issue of the magazine (1935) gives 416 'Members and Friends' from eighteen different countries. It was impossible to maintain the sense of coherence and mutual exchange of ideas which all the artists had undoubtedly hoped for when it was set up. The mere idea of abstraction alone was not enough, especially now that – largely through Abstraction-Création's own efforts – it had become respectable and widely accepted.

Non-representational painting was generally taking a direction very different from that of Gleizes and his associates, the differences only reaffirmed by the attempt at collaboration. It may be significant that in 1936 a group of non-representational painters signed a 'Dimensionist manifesto' arguing that each of the arts should acquire a new dimension.[13] Literature was to 'depart from the line and move in the plane'; painting 'to leave the plane and occupy space: painting in space, constructivism, spatial constructions, multimedia compositions'; and sculpture to abandon 'the three dimensional space of Euclid, in order to conquer for artistic expression the four dimensional space of Minkovsky'. There was an impressive array of signatories, including members of Abstraction-Création such as Ben Nicholson and Robert and Sonia Delaunay, but the names of Gleizes, Jellett and Hone, as well as those of the painters associated with Mondrian, are notably absent.

As well as sending work to Abstraction-Création, Mainie also sent in to the Royal Hibernian Academy and the Water Colour Society of Ireland. By this stage a number of Mainie's artistic colleagues and fellow members of the Society of Dublin Painters were exhibiting regularly with the Academy, among them Letitia Hamilton and Dorothy Blackham.[14] Her *Composition-Virgin Child*, was referred to in *The Irish Times* as 'engaging as an example of neocubism. There is in it the high-toned harmony of a time-mellowed, ancient stained glass.'[15] Mainie had several works in the annual Water Colour Society show, both Cubist compositions and landscapes.

At the end of 1936 she wrote to the director of Radio Eireann offering to give further radio talks, and she volunteered various subject-headings. But there is no record of the matter having gone any further. Those interested in art in Dublin at the time were much more obsessively concerned with other controversies, among which the question of the return of the Lane pictures was dominant once again. The matter, to Irish eyes and in terms at least of argument and debate, was reckoned to have already been brought to a comprehensive and final conclusion by Thomas Bodkin's book, *Hugh Lane and his Pictures*.[17] By the time the book appeared, in 1932, the government of Eamon de Valera had taken over, and it was on his instruction that it was distributed, with a personal note directing it 'to those who love justice and to those who love art'. Of course those who love justice have every reason to be mildly dismayed by the arguments put forward by Bodkin, who is at times in the book indefensibly biased, and bases his fundamental argument on two false premises: one, that the unwitnessed codicil to Lane's Will could somehow be given legal status, and two, that the City of Dublin, by opening the Municipal Gallery of Modern Art, in Charlemont House, had honoured its obligations to the dead benefactor. The best that could ever be obtained was a compromise, and this, in fact, was how the matter of Lane and his pictures was eventually settled. Wisely, Mainie did not become directly involved in this particular controversy, though the Jellett family were keenly interested in it.

What was new in the mid-1930s was the revelation by W.B. Yeats, who had been a member of the Senate, that King George V had played a role in the controversy. This, with other rows involving the statue of Robert Emmet that was on offer to Ireland (it was eventually erected more than half a century later) dominated interest at the expense of the kinds of subjects on which Mainie Jellett was prepared to talk.

Early in 1937 Mainie exhibited in the group show of the Society of Dublin Painters a work called *Rocks, Co. Mayo*. In letters to Gleizes in 1936 she had referred to work on this canvas, and it is clearly one of her earliest paintings directly inspired by Chinese Art. 'The artist has given a charmed atmosphere', wrote the *Irish Times* critic, 'to rugged forms of heaped boulders and strewn rocks in a foreground to far off bare hills.'[18] In addition she showed a *Pietà* in Cubist style.

One of Mainie's pupils at this time was the daughter of John A. Costello, who had been Attorney General under W.T. Cosgrave, and was himself to become leader of the two post-war, inter-party governments formed in 1948 and again in 1954. Costello had known Mainie's father. He and William Jellett had a mutual friend, John L. Burke, who collected Irish pictures and probably encouraged Costello to send his daughter, Eavan, for lessons. He persuaded him to buy paintings which he then gave to his children.

> What I got from her were some of the most peaceful and happy hours that I can remember from my childhood. Although many years have passed since I first went to her house in Fitzwilliam Square my memory of her is as bright as ever – I remember her as a quiet – rather than gentle – calm, pleasant person with whom, even as a child, I felt completely relaxed and at ease. She took her classes very seriously but she was certainly humorous.[19]

Mainie's paintings were propped up around the walls during these lessons. Initially, Eavan Sutton (as she is now) was disappointed to be having art lessons in Fitzwilliam Square – 'it did not fit in with my idea of where an artist should live and work' – but this prejudice was soon dispelled. Mainie's poodle, Mishki, and Bay's cairn, stayed in the studio during these lessons, and often enough Bay herself was in the front room next door, either practising with her chamber orchestra or giving music lessons. Mainie's teaching approach was unusual: she tried first to discover each pupil's principal interest and to let them pursue it, so that half-a-dozen children would all be doing different things; but then she imposed a quite serious, strict discipline. 'Everyone worked very hard and I don't ever remember anyone talking to each other!' The idea for a painting came from the child, its development was helped and encouraged by Mainie. 'She allowed me let my imagination fly around.' The most impressive teaching, still remembered vividly after more than half-a-century, was concerned with colour, and the endless fascination of trying out innumerable combinations. Each child had an individual colour chart as a constant reference.

Mainie did not hesitate to combine her classes for children with lessons she was giving to adults, and her adult students readily accepted this. One of them was Paul Egestorff,[20] 'an exquisite artist', who had lessons at the same time as Eavan Sutton. She said of the relationship between Mainie and Egerstorff: 'His painting took the same form as hers and she treated him with great respect.'

Paul Egerstorff was one of only two artists who studied abstract Cubist techniques with Mainie. The other was Hélène de Saint-Pierre. As has been noted, Mainie only taught Gleizes' principles to those who wished to learn them. People who came to her to learn 'how to draw' in a conventional manner were taught what they wanted to know. She expressed the principles in which she believed as clearly as possible in her lectures, articles and painting, but they were still too 'difficult' for a school to be formed in Ireland on the basis of them. And they were to remain a problem for those who bought and loved her work for a long time to come.

Mainie's expectations on behalf of her pupils was high. She entered them for competitions and expected them to win prizes; when they did, the tension and excitement were great. Eavan Sutton recalls: 'Once she told me somebody had wanted to buy one of my pictures. When indignantly I asked why she hadn't sold it she looked in mock horror at me and replied "I couldn't have done that – your parents would have been shocked". Gentle days!'

Two worlds, one of children enthusiastically pursuing their new and exciting experiments in art, the other of the professional artist involved on the frontiers of abstract painting, came close but did not really meet. Eavan Sutton recalls: 'One day I called in on a message and she was working alone. She asked me would I like to see her paintings and she showed them to me – I did not understand them well but I was given a brief glimpse into her world which was vibrant with colour and seemed very peaceful.'

205. Photograph of corner of Dublin Painters' Gallery 1937 Solo Exhibition.

facing page

207. *A Woman*, 1937. Oil on canvas, 111.7 × 45.5. Scotland, private collection.

208. *A Man*, 1937. Oil on canvas, 111.7 × 45.5. Scotland, private collection.

206. *Study for 'A Woman'*, 1937, Pencil on tracing paper, 21 × 8.3. Dublin, private collection.

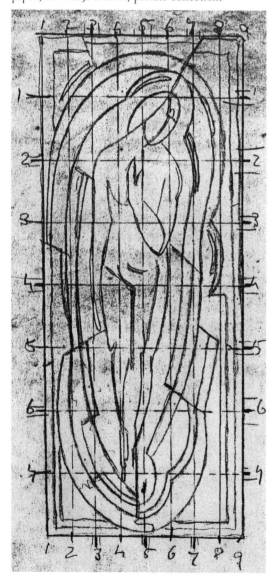

Mainie was delighted that her pupils, both adult and children, and several of her modernist colleagues were achieving recognition. In the 1937 announcement of prizes in art sponsored or administered by the Royal Dublin Society, Jack Hanlon[21] and Carmel Flynn[22] won prizes, as did Patricia Wallace[23] and several children who attended classes at 36 Fitzwilliam Square.

But it was her solo exhibition in the autumn of 1937 which gave her her greatest satisfaction. (Pls. 205–11).[24] Principally, though not exclusively of gouaches – twenty-seven out of a total of thirty-three, the remainder being oils – the show included many works which reflected the influence of Chinese Art and this was noted and admired in several reviews. Critics were now able to compare the three strands of her work, and admire and speculate upon religious Cubism, pure abstract, and the 'return' to realism which included Mayo and other Connaught landscapes, studies of rocks, surf, wind-swept trees, birch and bracken, and male and female figures. She had been commissioned by Gaisford St Lawrence, who lived at Howth Castle and ran a nursery there, to do flower illustrations for his catalogue, and these also were included.

It seems, on the surface, somewhat dismissive of the past to suggest some kind of 'return to realism' embracing works painted in the 1930s which depict landscape subjects and the human form, whether in portraiture or in the nude. Many of these works, like the religious paintings derived from great religious subjects of the past, are major statements by Mainie, and in no sense represent the 'falling back' implicit in the phrase 'return to realism'. As Gleizes emphasised, in writing about Mainie after her death, and as they had all stressed during the years of working together, there was no sacred dividing line between abstract and non-abstract art.[25] Much of the glory of her work in the 1930s lies in its rich flexibility of statement and the grandeur of the claims she made to represent elemental forces in life and art. Wind, earth, air, fire and water are summoned up in paintings, which are neither abstract nor realist; they are simply Mainie's expression of herself at a point of rich completion in her technical and spiritual journey of discovery.

160

209. *Abstract Composition*, 1936. Pen and ink on paper, 17.5 × 19. Dublin, private collection.

210. *Flower Form*, 1937. Oil on canvas, 45.5 × 61. Dublin, private collection.

211. *Meadows*, 1939. Gouache on card, 21 × 13. Dublin, Hugh Lane Municipal Gallery of Modern Art.

She advertised in her catalogue that she gave painting and drawing classes at her Fitzwilliam Square studio and that she taught children. The need to earn a living and support the household are evident. At this time Bay was still busy with the Gate Theatre Company, and it went on tour to Malta and Egypt, returning through London. As she had done in her diaries of holidays in 1919 and 1920, Bay wrote colourful accounts of the quite turbulent tour, which was led by Micheal MacLiammoir and Hilton Edwards.

Mainie was still exhibiting at the Salon des Surindépendents, and was noted by Maurice Raynal in October, in *L'Intransigeant*, as part of the Gleizes group, along with Evie Hone and Robert Pouyaud. Among exhibitors were Gleizes, Jean Lurçat, Paule Vézelay, the Japanese artist Okamoto, Herbin, Valmier, Power and Ozenfant.

The demise of Abstraction-Création by 1937 emphasised in another way the independence, if not the isolation of Mainie's position. She was not of course isolated either intellectually or materially from exhibitions in Paris and elsewhere or from frequent and detailed communication with Gleizes, even if visits had become less frequent. But her talent was now mature: the works which we can date to these years in the mid-1930s reveal extraordinary strength of purpose, sureness of touch in colour, form and composition, and great spiritual intensity.

CHAPTER TWENTY-ONE

'The best Miss Jellett has ever held '

NATIONALLY AND INTERNATIONALLY 1938 was an important year for Irish art and for Mainie Jellett, both as painter and in her capacity as leader of modernism. The group show of the Society of Dublin Painters was opened in early February by Sean T. O'Kelly.[1] In his speech he stressed the independence of the group of artists who made up the Dublin Painters and their determination to provide a forum for those who were out of sympathy with the academic tradition. He spoke also of the benefits of the artist to the community 'which enhanced the national culture and enriched the national life.' The presence of a senior member of the Fianna Fáil government on such an occasion represented a significant degree of acceptance of the modern movement in art in Ireland which was publicly endorsed shortly afterwards with the choice of Mainie Jellett as the artist responsible for the decorations of Ireland's pavilion at the Glasgow World Fair.

The artistic 'discovery' of the show was E. A. McGuire. Already well-known as a sportsman – he played polo and was a Davis Cup tennis player – he had taken up painting at the suggestion of Harriet Kirkwood, a leading member of the Dublin Painters, and this 'news story' aspect of his first venture as a painter was predictably seized on by the newspapers. This was not without subsequent justification, since McGuire became a leading figure in artistic circles, a Senator, a Governor and Guardian of the National Gallery, and father of the distinguished portrait painter, Edward McGuire.

The Dublin Painters had expanded their membership to eighteen, with Dolly Robinson (Lennox Robinson's wife), Margaret Clarke and Mabel Annesley the most recent recruits. Among Mainie's exhibits were *Study: Waterfall*, of which she did several versions, all based on the waterfall at Powerscourt, *Wood in August*, another naturalistic subject, and a large abstract painting in oil.

Rivalry between the two traditions still existed, though ameliorated by joint membership. Several of the Dublin Painters – Charles Lamb, Margaret Clarke, Letitia Hamilton – were also members of the Royal Hibernian Academy. Jack Hanlon painted a portrait of Maurice McGonigal and exhibited it in the February show, and McGonigal himself, who was in due course to succeed Sean Keating as President of the Royal Hibernian Academy, showed with the Dublin Painters. Keating himself was at the opening of the exhibition.

Behind the scenes there were still bruised feelings. Both Mainie and Evie Hone had work rejected by the Royal Hibernian Academy in 1938, as did Nano Reid and this echoed the much larger controversy provoked in Britain, in April 1938, when Wyndham Lewis's portrait of T.S. Eliot, now in Durban, South Africa, was rejected by the Royal Academy. Augustus John resigned in protest. Lewis himself described John's supportive action as 'a mortal blow to the Academy, if it is possible to use the expression, "mortal blow" with reference to a corpse'. Newspaper comments on the Irish controversy referred to the fact that both Mainie and Evie Hone had won gold and silver medals respectively from the Tailteann adjudicator.

On a different issue Mainie wrote to *The Irish Times* in response to, and in support of, a letter from Arnold Marsh on the difficult situation facing the artist in Ireland. She criticised the 'abysmal ignorance' about art, the lack of appreciation, the taxes on art

212. *Studies for Section of Mural Decoration*, 1938. Oil on canvas. Designs for the Irish Pavilion, Empire Exhibition, Glasgow, 1938.

materials, which, apart from linen, came from outside the country and were subject to high protective tariffs, and the further taxes on works taken out of the country for exhibition in Northern Ireland or further afield.

She also criticised the emphasis on British painting of the nineteenth and twentieth centuries which dominated the collection in the Municipal Gallery at the expense of Irish works. She singled out Jack Yeats, an artist of such standing that he 'would have whole rooms devoted to his work in Galleries in Germany and other continental countries; in the Municipal Gallery we have a few small examples of his early work. We have to go to the small gallery attached to the Cork Art School to find Jack Yeats and other contemporary Irish artists at all adequately represented.' Irish artists were forced to work abroad, and so serious were the customs difficulties in getting works sent in for exhibition, that painters had ceased sending their works home.

> Instead of keeping pictures out of this country (with perhaps the vague hope of thus encouraging the Irish nation to buy Irish work) we should do our best to encourage them in; both foreign and Irish work done abroad. It is the constant flow of artistic ideas which generates creative power, and not the stagnation of artistic ideas which is openly advocated here through the shutting of our doors to the outside world – we are not yet strong enough to stand alone artistically as we did in the great periods of Irish art of Pre-Christian and early Christian times, and even then we were not isolated in our work from the great art movements of the world.

The new figure in the Dublin Painters' exhibition, E.A. McGuire, was well off and influential, and he organised an exhibition for the group in April at the premises in Bedford Square in London, of the British Architectural Association. And this was followed by another exhibition at the Irish High Commission, in Piccadilly House, Regent Street, in June. The *Irish Press* reporter wrote: 'Miss Maimie [sic] Jellett has a number of works, ranging from Cubist design through objective transcription to ancient themes.'[2]

The Glasgow exhibition opened in May 1938. Mainie's two murals for the Irish pavilion, which depicted various aspects of Irish rural, industrial and cultural life, measured 10 feet by 80 feet each. The pavilion itself, which was built by a Greenock firm, was of modernist, Art Deco design, described in one report as 'the only one of its kind in the Exhibition', and it stood between the Canadian and Australian pavilions on what was called 'Dominion Avenue'. Mainie had already exhibited her small gouache studies for the murals at the summer exhibition of the Irish Water Colour Society, and sketches and squared-up drawings have survived, showing the extent of preparatory work for the final panels (Pl. 212).

Ireland's social and industrial development, its marketable produce, its history and tradition, its contribution through Shannon Airport to world travel, its theatrical, literary and horse-racing traditions, were all encompassed in the exhibition, a triumph of organisation and diversity. Even before it was over the decision was made by the Irish government that Mainie's murals would be shipped to New York and used for the Irish pavilion at the world fair planned for 1939.[3]

The Glasgow exhibition underlined Ireland's divided political state; there were in fact *two* Irish pavilions, the second one for the Six Counties, and this meant the separate assertion of things like butter coming from the Twenty-Six Counties, while linen came from the North. And Dublin Corporation responded negatively to the idea that the city should follow New York's example, and hold the third successive world fair in 1940.

Mainie met Gleizes for the last time at the beginning of 1939. The meeting seems to have been an accidental one, during a brief visit which she and Evie made to Paris. They attended a *soirée* at the studio of Robert Delaunay, and Gleizes was there. It was one of a series which Delaunay organised for young painters in which he explained the various phases he had passed through from his early Cubist days to his fully abstract paintings of the 1930s. Of all the original Cubist painters, Delaunay came closest to Gleizes. We have already seen the importance Gleizes attached to Delaunay's near abstract paintings – the *Windows* and *Suns, Moons, Discs*, done just before the First World War. Reflections on the circular movement of colours he achieved in these latter paintings had played an important part in his own radical development of 1934. In 1933, Gleizes had written a book on Delaunay he hoped would be published by Abstraction-Création. It remains unpublished. After the *Suns, Moons and Discs*, however, Delaunay had fallen back into an essentially representational style in which the great circular movements of colour are subordinated to the representational image. Gleizes was largely responsible for Delaunay's return to abstraction, and to serious pictorial research in the 1930s – his *rythmes sans fin* and *joie de vivre* paintings.[4]

Mainie's first cousin, Olivia Hughes, was in Paris at the same time, with her youngest sister, who was delicate and who became ill. Not knowing French at all well, Mrs Hughes went to the English church, thinking she might get help. She knew Mainie was in Paris:

> Of course I was not particularly devout as I was looking for Mainie. The hat of a very devout person seemed familiar. It was the sort of hat then called Liberties. She was with her friend Evie Hone, and at the end of the service I thought they would never leave off praying. Anyway they did eventually let up, and it was Mainie, and she was able to tell me what to do, and anyway my sister got better.[5]

Shortly after her return to Ireland, Mainie wrote to Gleizes. Her letter gives a lively account of Delaunay's strengths as a painter, but also of his weaknesses, and the limitations of his method of dealing with young painters. We see the importance that Mainie attaches to disciplined study, not as a means of arriving at a 'mechanical' conception of painting, but, by contrast, as the only possible means of avoiding it. Her remarks on Turner are also interesting. Gleizes never expressed any interest in Turner but it is arguable that Turner's late work is at the beginning of the great revolution in painting of which Gleizes was a part.

War in Europe was now a brooding reality, as a result of the agreement signed with Hitler over the Sudetenland. German occupation of this territory was followed in the spring of 1939 by the complete annexation of Czechoslovakia. The civil war in Spain ended, with Franco victorious. It is interesting that during the previous three years many of the workers on Gleizes' estate on the outskirts of St Remy had been refugees from Spain. A 'Pact of Steel' was signed between Mussolini and Hitler, and this agreement was followed, in August, by the Non-Aggression Pact between Hitler and Stalin. A week later Russian and German troops entered Poland. War was declared by Britain and France on 3 September.

Ireland's official position was neutrality. This was in keeping with the traditional policy of small European nations, yet somewhat pretentious in that Ireland could not back up its neutrality and had arrived at it in confused circumstances. The unofficial position – 'the Irish solution' which always seems to emerge to resolve difficult national questions – was that Ireland's neutrality was essentially pro-British, becoming more so as the war progressed. Neutrality was an impressive, statesmanlike stance to adopt in 1939, and twenty nations, including the United States, did so. Only five preserved it for the duration, and in the short space of six months from April 1940 the Axis Powers swept into eight 'neutral' countries, taking them over. Mild consideration was given to treating Ireland in the same way, but abandoned. All German agents were captured and interrogated, and their information passed on to British Intelligence interests. All German pilots and other military personnel arrested or captured in Ireland were interned; their British, American, or other allied opposite numbers were generally repatriated.

The Irish economy during the 1930s had survived in ways markedly in contrast with

213. *Let There Be Light*, 1939. Oil on canvas, 120 × 68. Dublin, private collection.

214. *Descent from the Cross*, 1939. Oil on canvas, 121 × 69. Dublin, Hugh Lane Municipal Gallery of Art.

the baleful fate of many European societies, whose miseries had strongly contributed to the rise of Fascism and the holocaust which followed. Eamon de Valera had successfully negotiated an end to the Economic War in 1938, the return of the Ports, and a one-off payment settling all long-standing debts to the British. It was a triumph, cementing him in position politically.

Mainie flourished throughout this period. During the 1930s we have seen a consistent growth in her output, the confidence of her work and her views, and the stature of her influence on others. She was restricted somewhat in financial terms, by the added responsibilities which had descended on herself and Bay with their father's death. Foreign travel, which, as we have noted, had been made more difficult by the devaluation of the pound, had lessened but in no sense stopped entirely, and the decade had been punctuated by visits to Lithuania, Amsterdam and, of course, France. What the outbreak

215. *The Assumption*, 1937. Oil on canvas, 91.5 × 61. London, private collection.

216. *Achill Horses*, 1939. Oil on canvas, 61 × 92. Dublin, National Gallery of Ireland.

of war and Ireland's declaration of neutrality also brought was an influx of foreigners and a heightened interest in the life of the country among diplomats stationed in Dublin. Among those who came were a number of artists, known as the 'Blitz Gaels', including Basil Rákóczí and Kenneth Hall, two young painters who were to have a considerable influence on Irish art in the 1940s, and to provide Mainie with new allies and a new platform for her work and ideas.

It was not, then, a black period into which the artistic community entered, with the coming of 'the Emergency'. It was, on the contrary, an exciting, controversial phase for the arts generally, with even the phenomenon of buyers for works of art. Though Mainie regrettably kept no consistent records of the sales and ownership of her own works, her rough notes for her 1939 solo exhibition show an impressive number of works sold. Her fellow artists, Ralph Cusack and Jack Hanlon,[6] both bought from her show. So did the head of the German Mission in Dublin.[7] The main paintings in the 1939 solo exhibitions included *Let There be Light* (Pl. 213), *Descent from the Cross* (Pl. 214), a *Madonna* and *Madonna of the Spring* (Pl. 224) two abstract compositions and *Achill Horses II* (Pl. 216). Further studies for the Glasgow murals, and her gouaches of the *Elements* were included.

One reviewer claimed: 'This artist has won her struggle to educate her public in the most modern methods and her Cubist work is now familiar . . . The exhibition brought many visitors during the month, and was regarded as the best Miss Jellett has ever held.'[8] *The Irish Times* described the exhibition as the most interesting she had ever given.[9] It would be a fruitless exercise to demonstrate the continued fumblings of the art critics of the time, as they search their minds for 'meaning', still blissfully unaware of the basic principles of Cubist abstraction, were it not important from Mainie's own point of view. She had clearly triumphed in terms of her acceptance at every level, including the most difficult, technical one, of having pupils, followers and collectors of her work who understood, in part, what she was doing. But she still had not *educated* her own critics. They all seem to be *frightened* of her. At the end of the 1930s perhaps the two most determined and self-confident voices in art criticism were Stephen Rynne[10] and John Dowling.[11] Rynne wrote of her work: 'But she does *not* paint in the style which she is most frequently said to, the Cubist.' This comment may indicate that by the time Rynne was writing, the view that the term 'Cubism' could only be applied to the early work of Picasso and Braque was already prevalent.

Criticism of her work had by this stage fallen into two definite groupings. The regular

217. *Head of a Man*, c.1939. Pen and ink on tracing paper, 15.5 × 12. Dublin, private collection. An old negative of the oil painting (present whereabouts unknown) is in the Ulster Museum collection.

newspaper critics indulged in little more than generally respectful descriptive reporting. The more serious criticism – confined to weeklies and monthlies – endeavoured to argue and confront her intentions.

At a more practical level, as Mainie's mother told to her daughter, Betty, in Glasgow, 'Unfortunately Paul Henry and another popular Belfast painter [this was William Conor] have just had shows and sold a lot.' But her fears that Mainie would not sell were groundless; in fact Mainie sold quite well at her exhibition. Mainie was always helped in hanging her shows by Maude Ball, whose faithful support since the first great abstract art controversy in Dublin in 1923 had been so valuable. But for the 1939 exhibition 'Maw Baw', as she was known in the Jellett family, 'was so submerged in new pipes in her house and a new maid' that she could not assist. The exhibition included more flower paintings arranged on tables, on white paper under sheets of glass, and in Bay's opinion 'the little exhibition looks lovely!' Janet Jellett, who seems never to have greatly understood or sympathised with the pure abstract work preferring paintings and watercolours from the Sickert and pre-Sickert period, wrote: 'She certainly has far more interesting and varied work this time.'

Towards the end of 1939 a new figure emerged in Irish art who was to have a significant if eventually rather brief impact. This was Jack Longford[12] who came to public attention when he organised an exhibition in South Leinster Street in October, described as 'A Loan and Cross-Section Exhibition of Contemporary Paintings'. The opening ceremony was performed by Dermod O'Brien who stressed the importance of 'carrying on work in the arts' in spite of the international crisis. The modern commercial gallery where the show was held had been opened in 1938 by Deirdre McDonogh.[13] The approach was not exclusively modernist. Maurice MacGonigal, Sean Keating and Harry Kernoff, all full members of the Royal Hibernian Academy, were included, as was Jack Yeats. Duncan Grant was one of several English painters. Others who exhibited works then and later included Graham and Vanessa Bell, William Coldstream, John Piper and Edward Ardizzone, introduced to Ireland by Jack Longford. Mainie was also an exhibitor, and gave one of the four lectures on French Painting which were part of the October programme for the gallery.[14]

For its time the loan side of the exhibition was very distinguished. Bonnard, Braque, Picasso, Vlaminck, Kisling, Marquet, Derain, Dufy, de Chirico, Gris and Gleizes were all represented by significant works, several of which are now in the National Gallery of Ireland. English painters, in addition to those already mentioned, included Orpen, Tonks, Sickert, Steer, Christopher Richard Wynne Nevinson and Mark Gertler, with his painting *S.S. Koteliansky*. Many members of the Society of Dublin Painters had pictures for sale.

Mainie's lecture began with advice on how to look at pictures and employed the witty and elegant quotation from Schopenhauer: 'A work of art should be treated like a prince – It must speak to you first.' She developed this idea that one might have to wait in silence for some time, also that the 'words' may be quite unfamiliar and convey nothing. The fault, she went on, could be in the beholder.

> Remember that the artist if he is worthy of the name is someone whose business it is to have a wider vision in several senses of the word, than his fellows. It is nothing for the artist to boast about, it should be simply a result of his work which is contemplative and directed towards universal truths, which others can not give time from their more material occupations to consider. Therefore the creative artist's vision is often ahead of his time and on that account the onlooker must realise that the artist is very often a forerunner of new ideas, not yet sensed in the material world, and again not condemn without a few moments thought as to what the new idea may be.

Though the basic argument of her lecture is the relatively familiar one, in which she

168

takes up the distinctions between academic and materialist painting on the one hand, and on the other, the modern adventure of research and analysis represented particularly by Post-Impressionism and by the Cubists, there are still new elements in what she has to say. She develops, for example, the argument, central to her own work, of the divisions within Cubist and Post-Cubist art which led to the emergence of pure abstraction and what was then referred to, with a combination of ambiguity and common-sense, as 'semi-abstract'. 'By degrees,' she told her audience,

> the Cubist abstract movement divided itself into two main groups – those who created with natural forms as a basis for their researches, of whom Lhote was one, and those who created on geometric principles and rhythmic harmonies evolved from the particular shape of the two-dimensional surfaces they were filling. Of the first group Braque I would consider the finest example – And of the second Albert Gleizes from the theoretical standpoint is the purest example.

She then turns to the vexed question of Picasso, 'a brilliant genius', but one who fluctuates between the two extremes 'always pushing out at a tangent, restless, a product of the times'. She admired his Spanish Civil War painting, *Guernica*, 'that great human document in art', but is otherwise unable to place him clearly in a position that related to herself or to what she believed modernism had achieved. Among a number of quotations culled from the artists she admired she included this from Picasso himself: 'They speak of naturalism in opposition to Modern Painting. I would like to know if anyone has ever seen a natural work of art. Nature and art, being too [sic] different things, cannot be the same thing. Through art we express our conception of what nature is not.'

She also quoted from Braque[15] and Gris[16] and the following from Gleizes:

> In the reality of the outside world it is the physical aspect at first which strikes the senses exclusively – the spirit is hidden, mysterious and it takes an effort to reveal it. In the truth of a work of art it is the spirit which first demands exclusive attention. Painting is therefore not an imitation of objects. The reality of the exterior world serves as a departure, but that reality is purified so as to attain the spirit. Painting starting from the temporal tends towards the eternal.[17]

Mainie also argued, as she had done before, that Matisse was 'perhaps France's greatest colourist' and she linked this to a discussions about the Fauves and about the working relationship between Vlaminck and Derain, as well as an expression of her great admiration for Bonnard and Vuillard. She ended unequivocally:

> An artist who has the creative instinct and advances beyond the picture postcard type of painting must face these facts – they are born of his time, he <u>can not</u> escape them and they are not only a product of France – they resolve themselves into a very simple question – do you stand for the creative universal spiritual qualities in art, or do you stand for the materialistic photographic picture postcard standard of so called art – The creative spirit in opposition to the machine.

That simple conflict, redolent of the campaigning years through which she had struggled and suffered, may seem simplistic now. The divisions have been overtaken and changed. Those battles and the territory over which they were fought lie mostly in the past. Yet if the 'photographic picture postcard standard' no longer prevails in modern art, the photograph itself, as opposed to 'the creative universal spiritual qualities in art', is prevalent everywhere. The clarity and determination of spirit with which she addressed the main issue was characterised by the flash and surge of her courage. She was a solitary figure, at least in the campaigning sense, still the only person in Ireland speaking out unequivocally in defence of abstract Cubism.

With the outbreak of war, Mainie's sister, Babbin Phillips, had returned to Ireland and was living with her children at Howth, in the house of her uncle, Noel Guinness.

Will, her husband, had been posted to the Brewers' Society in London to take charge of beer for all the troops in the British Army, a significant war duty! Her nephew, Michael Purser, at the age of four, wrote from Glasgow: 'My dear Aunt Mainie, I've got a few soldiers and some farm things. I've got two trains. There were pretty balls on the Christmas tree and lovely tinsel. We went to tea and were in candlelight in the air raid shelter. Dear love from Michael to Aunt Mainie.'

Bay was busy with her music, giving recitals in various parts of Ireland. She had parted company with the Gate Theatre, and was about to take over as director of music for the Gaiety Theatre. Mainie sent one of her Achill watercolours to an exhibition to raise money for Jewish refugee children. It sold for £4 and the exhibition raised £200 altogether.

She socialised a good deal at the time, often going to Marlay to see Evie, and also to tea with May Guinness, at Tibradden in the Dublin Mountains above Rathfarnham. Mrs Jellett reported an odd occurrence on the death of 'nice old Colonel Guinness', who was May Guinness's brother: 'He was, so to speak, laid in State in the little church nearby – and the coffin left open for anyone who wished to look at him – Poor Miss G. was horrified – and won't have anything to say to them – I think it was the Nephew's wife who wished it to be done – I've met her, and thought her most unattractive cold – and I'm sure English.'

There was more dramatic news. The painter, Louis le Brocquy, had run away to London and married Jean Storey. 'Italia', Mrs Jellett wrote to Bay, ' and the mother of the boy who eloped with the Moore girl the other day are coming to tea.' A tantalising report followed: 'Mainie had Mrs le Broquet [sic] the mother of the eloped son – to tea, she was very interesting, and told us of an extraordinary ghost story which happened to her about Miss Fitzpatrick who lived in Roundwood Park – When you come home we'll tell you.' There was also gossip about other painters: 'Will you send me back Miss Yeats's letter – I think it is a beautiful one – Mrs Jack Yeats had a heart to heart talk with Mainie last night about the family, and is very anxious about them.'

Evie was a frequent caller at the house. She had not been well, and her sister, Mrs Connell, who was dedicated to horses, had suffered one of many accidents while out riding. Evie entered the Catholic Church in 1939, though with what seems to have been further spiritual indecision. In a letter Mainie wrote to the painter Margaret Clarke, who had been William Orpen's pupil, she said, 'I am very distressed over Evie. She has changed her plans so often that I will be away now when she makes the final step. I do wish she could find the peace of Christianity and trust she will find it in your Church and I wish she had made the move sooner.' Evie, among that immediate pre-war generation of artists, was something of a pioneer in this move. Gleizes entered the Catholic Church in 1942, to be followed some time after by both Robert Pouyaud and Anne Dangar.

CHAPTER TWENTY-TWO

Irish art and 'the Emergency'

PUBLIC ATTITUDES TO art in Ireland changed in the late 1930s. They became more positive both at national and municipal levels, and the enlightened enthusiasm which had sustained private groups and individuals like the Society of Dublin Painters and owners of commercial galleries such as Jack Longford, was echoed by government ministers and local councillors. The Metropolitan School of Art became the National College of Art and took on 'design' as a responsibility.[1]

A second development was the setting up of an art gallery for Limerick City, the third-largest city in the Republic. As with Dublin and Cork in the earlier part of the twentieth century, and as was also the case with later developments, the problem was not one of paintings, or indeed whole collections, but one of buildings and the staff to manage them. Limerick quickly had paintings offered by many artists and collectors, but it had to wait for premises. Mainie was among those who gave work, and by the summer of 1938 the process had been so successful that a *second* complete exhibition of donated works of art became possible and a buying programme was initiated.[2]

In 1939 it looked as though Waterford City would follow Limerick's example. Again, paintings were forthcoming, but no city-funded building was available. In other parts of the country similar efforts were made – and went on being made for many years – to establish civic art galleries, though with very limited success. Half a century later only Dublin, Cork and Limerick have separately funded art galleries in their own buildings and with respectable collections of Irish art which have grown and developed beyond the *ad hoc* accidents of generous benefaction.

As we have seen, Mainie had for some years been giving classes in art to children. In some cases, notably with the Irish painter and woodcut artist, Margaret Stokes,[3] the lessons with Mainie Jellett, who was incidentally her cousin and a neighbour in Fitzwilliam Square, went on when childhood enthusiasm gave way to formal art school studies. Both Paul Egestorff, another pupil of Mainie's at this time, and Margaret Stokes, painted the same still-life subject under Mainie's direction.

In addition to teaching at her studio Mainie became teacher at Park House school in 1940, and late in the year she gave a lecture, 'Art for Children', in which she formulated ideas which, in practical terms, had already operated well for a number of years in the studio. Her primary purpose was to realise the creative faculty in the child, stimulating it 'to the utmost degree'. There should be no attempt to make children *see* like adults; she expressed in her lecture notes the familiar fears of 'photographic' repetition in art. The balance she sought was between the development of the imagination and the training of powers of observation and memory. She believed that, from the very start, the idea should predominate that the child is not drawing something, reproducing something, copying something, but is engaged in the creative practice of art 'and that his picture no matter how simple is first to fill its space harmoniously *apart from the subject matter*'. Vital to this was the creative use of colour combined with a mastery of the laws of colour and the properties of the spectrum. Children, she felt, should begin with primary colours and the colours of the spectrum. She preferred that children work in gouache rather than watercolour; it gave them more control through greater simplicity.

She had strong reservations about the teaching of art in Ireland. It had a negligible position in the curriculum, counted for nothing in examinations, and was not included in teacher-training programmes. The reality was that art had become a casualty, relatively early in the life of the State, of the insistence to include the Irish language throughout school courses, and give a predominance to it quite out of proportion to any practical need. This was a political requirement, related to a particular interpretation of nationalism; it was not primarily educational. It prevailed into the 1970s and was accompanied by the even more distorted *canard*, that the Irish people were *verbal* in their artistic expression rather than *visual*, a view which carried serious weight over a period of many years. Mainie's emphasis was on the development of personality. She did not rule out art as a vocation – emphasis on it, perhaps unusually in a lecture concerned with art for children, was her concluding point – but she stressed its value as a means of broadening the mind, of offering a positive means of self-expression, and extending the powers of observation.

This interest in art education led to other involvements in art in schools. At the time the painter and musician Brian Boydell taught art at St Columba's College in Rathfarnham. He drew Mainie Jellett into the life of the school. She visited the art department, which had a high reputation, with the emphasis on modernist principles; the school's brochure asserted: 'Instruction in perspective is, for example, only given if requested by the pupil, or in exceptional cases, and the art master never on any account imposes his own work on that of a student'.[4] This was at a time when the teaching of art at all was rare in secondary schools in the country. Brian Boydell was a regular visitor to the Jellett house. He attended a small private show of works there in July of 1941, and brought boys from the school to see it and to meet her. Later, when she held her solo exhibition groups of boys visited it on several occasions. Mainie judged the summer art exhibition at the school, which was opened by Françoise Henry, the art historian.

An exhibition of the work of 'Six Irish Artists who have studied at L'Academie Lhote' opened at the Contemporary Pictures Gallery, at 133 Lower Baggot Street, Dublin. Notwithstanding the presence in the group of two men, Father Jack Hanlon and Eugene Judge, the group of six became known as 'Lhote's Wives'. Mainie Jellett and Evie Hone were of course among the number, the other two being Norah McGuinness and Harriet Kirkwood.

Mainie exhibited two major oils of 1940, her *Nativity* (Pl. 218) and *The Land, Eire*. But unusually she also included dated works from almost twenty years earlier, *Abstract Composition* of 1923, the study for it in watercolour, and a *Nude Study* of 1922. Father Jack Hanlon, with twenty works in the show, had by far the largest number. Harriet Kirkwood had only three, while Evie Hone included three paintings, five pieces of stained glass, and two banners.

These last two works, banners of St Joseph and St Dominic, were executed for Evie by Hélène de St Pierre,[5] who had arrived in Ireland shortly after the outbreak of the war and had been drawn into the circle of modern painters by Mainie. She met Mainie on the day after the fall of France, when she was in a state of shock and distress. Mainie had offered her the use of her Fitzwilliam Square studio and had introduced her to friends, among them the pianist, Charles Lynch.[6]

Hélène de St Pierre, much younger than the artist, saw a different side of Mainie's complex personality. Less intimidated by her achievements, she was more drawn to her in human terms. Mainie's commitments as an artist had plunged her repeatedly into controversy from which she found profound relief in her art. Yet in both sides of her activity – the creative and the proselytising – she was essentially alone. Also, as the leader of a movement, she carried considerable responsibilities which led to a perception of her as someone who was austere and somewhat distant. She communicated through the mind and spirit, and at times appeared to lack the common touch. Of course she also met and developed friendships with a wide circle of people in the arts generally,

218. *The Nativity*, 1940. Oil on canvas, 89 × 89, London, Pyms Gallery.

219.   Photograph of picnic; Mainie with her sister's children.

and she had a reputation for great kindness and encouragement to other artists. But the general view was of a certain emotional and human awkwardness. By contrast, Hélène de St Pierre remembers her as radiant, vibrant, filled with enthusiasm, particularly towards other artists, and often prepared to enjoy herself with her friends. With Charles Lynch at the piano and others to sing, 'Nanny' would be summoned to join in the performances of rebel songs and other entertainments. She was perpetually full of encouragement, and offered help always with a total clarity of mind. There was also a great love of nature; 'She loved relaxing, picking wild flowers and plants. She once said ''One can't live without love''. It was at a Jack Yeats exhibition. Mainie liked Jack Yeats's paintings because she liked his sense of humour.' Hélène de St Pierre was one of the younger artists to benefit from reduced charges for lessons. Because she was a refugee, Mainie charged her only sixpence for her lessons. Two other pupils at the time – a Jewish refugee from Germany and a young man suffering from spinal paralysis – also benefited. Yet, despite the importance she placed on love, there were no love affairs in Mainie's life. Emotion, passion, the idea of her heart being consumed, can be understood only in the context of her work as a painter. Side by side with her friendships there was, of course, her strong sense of family, reflected, for instance, in the time she found to relax with her nephews and neices (Pl. 219).

The lecture provoked by the exhibition of work by André Lhote's pupils in 1940 presents a detailed outline of his teaching methods, of his style – and his limitations – as a painter, and of his contribution to art in what he wrote. When she had studied under André Lhote, in 1921 and for a short period during 1922, his academy was the best and the most advanced of the public academies. In addition to Evie and Mainie, May Guinness was also at the Lhote Academy (though her work was not included in the 1940 Dublin exhibition), and she later acquired two watercolours and an oil by Lhote. An Irish judge called Meredith also acquired a Lhote watercolour, but in 1940 this probably constituted the full extent of his works in Irish collections.

Mainie looked back on the impact of his teaching over a span of twenty years, from a standpoint of abstract painting quite different from what Lhote had taught her. She nevertheless expresses the greatest admiration for him both as a teacher and from her own point of view. She would never have gone on to the study of abstract Cubist painting without his 'teaching as a preparation'. She sets great store in her lecture by his respect

174

for the Old Masters; they were part of a living tradition from which each new cycle, movement or generation of artists could draw and 're-experience'.

The middle section of her lecture was more restrained; she dealt with Lhote as a practitioner, and found him somewhat limited: a fine draughtsman, but with a colour sense 'not nearly as pronounced as his sense of form'. She admired greatly his painting of the nude, and his intellectual grasp of landscape painting 'in the manner of a modern Poussin'. By the time Mainie came to give her lecture Lhote's own fame, not just in France but in Europe generally and in America, had spread – though 'not so well in England' and by inference not so well in Ireland either. In 1937 he had been among the many artists who had worked on the decorations for the Paris Exhibition.

Like Gleizes, Lhote was a writer of distinction and produced two works which were of lasting value, *Parlons peinture* and *Traité du paysage*.[7] Mainie endeavoured to explain the modern phenomenon of artists writing and publishing their works because of the obvious need to explain and justify their art at a time when it was under attack, particularly if they belonged to the modernist persuasion. Mainie considered writings by the artists themselves were of enormous value. This was particularly so with Lhote because of the lucidity and strength of his style. He offered solutions in painting to younger artists. At the end of her lecture she offered a series of these in translations she had made from his books, and which she read out to her audience.

Her focus on Lhote was in one sense climactic: it represented the acceptance by her of one school of modernism, with adherents who were at different stages in their development. But they were only one group, and the reality in Dublin at the time was of a proliferation of talent and a considerable increase in interest in art and in the holding of exhibitions. Earnán O'Malley, writing about Louis le Brocquy in *Horizon*,[8] referred to Ireland during the war as cut off from outside activity and 'driven' back to her sea boundaries. 'Economically the country had to become self-supporting and in this attempt a new strength and assurance were created, reflected by an added interest in painting and in music . . . people and painters here will remain isolated from first-class minds expressing contemporary ideas in terms of paint.' But one result of this withdrawal was that artists had more time to assess themselves and to develop their own personal contribution. Margaret Moffett, who also wrote on the subject of wartime art in Ireland for the same magazine, described Ireland as having 'locked up her artists', but also as having imported something of real artistic wealth: refugees. 'Those who have been refugees in the most profound sense are the artists – poets, painters, sculptors, architects. There will be, no doubt, a general dispersal during the aftermath, but the work of these artists has certainly radiated a strong and, I am convinced, a lasting influence.'[9]

Margaret Moffett's lyrical view captures something of the mild hysteria which everyone felt in Ireland, but particularly in Dublin. She even constructed a quaint formula: 'Add to a low standard of living a *laissez-faire* spirit, and divide by no effective control of the cost of everyday household commodities, and what have you?' Wisely, perhaps, she does not endeavour to answer her own question, but she does claim it to have been a rare experience to have lived in the company of artists during those war years in Dublin, despite the apparent and dominant conflict between two outworn 'authoritarian cultures' – the Anglo-Irish and the Catholic Church.

> During the first two or three years of the war it was possible to sense hysteria. The nation was thrown in on itself. There was no escape from this intensification of insularity: water on one side, blood on the other . . . To me the most interesting thing about the modern movement in the plastic arts in Eire is the fact that it reflects current trends in European art which, if known, were not absorbed by even the intellectual minority in Dublin.

Hélène de St Pierre confirms this sense of excitement which prevailed during the early war years in particular: 'The explosion of art in Ireland during the war was partly due to a reaction, that here we were not in it, and could meet friends and enemies of my country and others at war without thinking of the war; in other words not on destruction but on creation, the reverse of war.'[10]

Undoubtedly the leading figure among these 'refugees' was Basil Rákóczí. Basil Ivan Rákóczí was the son of a Hungarian gipsy and a girl from Cork, who had become an artists' model in London, where he was born in 1908.[11] He arrived in Ireland in 1939, and it was generally thought that he was part of the 'refugee' population whose main motive was to avoid the war. But unlike the many other artists who came to live and work in Dublin, Rákóczí could claim to be, in a rather eccentric way, an Irish artist. His name is inextricably linked with the White Stag Group,[12] which he seems to have re-formed as soon as he arrived. Certainly, by the spring of 1940 it was firmly enough established not just to hold its first exhibition but to include works by Mainie Jellett. Her endorsement was important, and remained consistent until her death in 1944. The only members of the White Stag Group were Basil Rákóczí and his friend the painter Kenneth Hall,[13] though they did have a number of associates.

The group held a second show in October 1940, this time at 30 Upper Mount Street. The exhibition was opened by Mainie. There were several new artists showing with the group: Dorothy Blackham, Jocelyn Chewett[14] and her husband, Stephen Gilbert,[15] Bobby Dawson,[16] Paul Egestorff and Eugene Judge. Judge was one of the six painters who took part in the exhibition of those who had studied in Paris under André Lhote. In her address Mainie Jellett spoke of the intention of those exhibiting 'to interpret the times in which they live' without being 'hidebound to any particular school or cramped by academic conventionality'.

In November 1940 Basil Rákóczí held his first one-man show in Dublin, again at the Mount Street address. It was opened in the afternoon of 21 November by Lennox Robinson, whose wife was a painter, and that evening Mainie gave a lecture at the gallery, almost certainly on an aspect of the modern movement, though details of its contents have not survived. Yet another White Stag Group show was held in December, and on 20 December Henri Silvy of the French Legation gave a lecture entitled 'The Legacy of Cubism'.

Diplomats in Dublin took considerable interest in artistic events generally. Though at first this might be seen as evidence of the limited scope offered by their employment in a small neutral country effectively cut off from the rest of Europe, there was a hidden motive: among the many refugees who were associated with different aspects of the arts there might be found foreign agents. This was particularly so with the White Stag Group whose members attracted additional interest because of their bohemian style of life, eccentric behaviour, and the fact that one or two of them were known to be homosexual. The group's principal address, in Lower Baggot Street, was watched regularly by members of the Irish Special Branch (the security section in the country's police force, roughly equivalent to MI6); this attention did not go unnoticed. It became a subject of speculation and much humour.[17] The main energies of the Special Branch, and of the government, were directed against the Irish Republican Army (IRA). This organisation, still working for a revolutionary 'solution' to Ireland's problem (which meant, in essence, the removal of British rule from the six northern counties), had adopted the ancient principle that Britain's difficulties were Ireland's opportunity, and had launched a sabotage campaign on mainland Britain and in Belfast aimed specifically against the war effort. Within the Republic the IRA provided a Fifth Column in support of German intelligence officers, who were sent into Ireland in various ways, including parachuting. There were 'safe houses' offered to the relatively inexperienced agents, as well as other protective facilities. It amounted to a distinctly futile episode, both for the IRA and for German intelligence.[18]

Painters and writers at the time were unaware of the more serious side of intelligence and counter-intelligence. There was a shrewd decision on the part of the Special Branch to ensure some public knowledge of the fact that possible British spies were under surveillance, if for no other reason than to present a balanced picture of how a neutral country dealt evenly with both Allied and Axis powers. Well before the war, as a result of the IRA decision to carry out a bombing campaign in Britain, draconian measures had been taken by de Valera against his former revolutionary companions-in-arms. In June 1939 the IRA had been proscribed. Worse was to follow, including the executions of IRA members.

Through all of this the public perception remained superficial, with the majority accepting the objectivity of de Valera's interpretation of neutrality. This was in part as a result of press censorship, in part due to press inertia – Joseph Lee refers to 'this thirst for ignorance' extending into journalistic circles,[19] and cites *The Irish Press*, which refused to publish atrocity stories because of their unreliability, and claimed that 'no kind of oppression' in Europe was worse than what the 'Six County nationalists' endured!

Thus, 1940 was an astonishingly rich year for Irish art, its calendar filled with exhibitions, with the emergence of new groups and new galleries, with public enterprises being undertaken which brought art to the public, and with the general sense of isolation and distance from the war in Europe being turned to psychological advantage by a population whose leaders were determined to keep them ignorant, detached or divorced from involvements of any kind.

Just before Christmas, in a letter to her sister Betty, Mainie sent a cheque, 'from Nannie and me – 15/- from me 10/- for you and Sean and 5/- to be divided between G. and M. I suggest if you have not already got it you get the Studio publication ''Art for Children'' by Anne M. Berry. 5/- – You and Sean go to a concert or anything you like with the rest.' As we have seen, art for children was much on Mainie's mind, immersed as she was in teaching them. The Parents' National Education Union, an organisation committed to the idea of the education of children at home, held a meeting that December at the O'Briens, across the square from the Jelletts. Mainie gave a talk on children's art at which she showed paintings by her eldest niece, Geraldine Purser. Sarah Purser, the great-aunt of Betty's husband, Sean, in her nineties at this stage, was still a visitor at the Jelletts' house and 'looking very well and in good spirits' when she visited them for lunch. Mainie was attending Royal Dublin Society concerts, including a piano recital by Charles Lynch. She also wrote about visiting the Abbey Theatre 'to see the new Francis Stuart play. Evie wants to see it. I hope it is better than his books.' Geraldine had expressed a dislike for Walt Disney. Mainie approved; she wrote 'I hate those drawing films.'

Francis Stuart,[20] known better as a novelist than a playwright, was married to Yseult Gonne, daughter of Maud Gonne, the inspiration behind many of W.B. Yeats's poems. Yseult Gonne was well known for her anti-British and pro-Nazi sympathies, and Stuart had gone to Berlin just before the beginning of the war, where he was engaged in broadcasting activities for the Germans. Some of his material was used by William Joyce, better known as 'Lord Haw Haw', the propagandist broadcaster for Hitler's Third Reich.

That winter twelve artists were invited by Sean O'Faolain to describe, for *The Bell*, 'the most lovely thing they had seen in Ireland'.[21] Norah McGuinness said it was the colour of Ireland. Sean Keating – 'a cattle fair in Aran on a day in June'. Jack Yeats: 'I couldn't possibly tell you. But I can tell you it has nothing at all to do with arithmetic. It reflects only one light, from far more than twenty facets.' George Atkinson said it was a four-master in full rig, approaching the harbour at Cobh on a summer's evening.[22] Mainie expressed her own interpretation of loveliness in the context of work which she had been increasingly involved in, her landscapes in the west of Ireland (Pl. 220). She wrote:

220. *Study: Seashore*, c.1938. Pencil on paper,
40.5 × 49. Dublin, private collection.

In County Mayo I was on the seashore. I crossed a great expanse of gold-coloured sand. I climbed over rocks to a long promontory with sand-banks. As I got to the end of the promontory there was a stretch of fine, deep, green grass. On it, were a series of rough stones covering small mounds. The mounds were the graves of unbaptised infants. There was a bigger mound which may have been the grave of a ship-wrecked sailor. The scene gave an intense feeling of peace, dignity, and the uttermost simplicity. The sun was brilliant and the sea ultramarine blue and white. One felt the everlasting beauty of life and death.

CHAPTER TWENTY-THREE

Art as a spritual force

SO, DUBLIN WAS one of the very few European capitals unaffected by the conflict of the Second World War and free to pursue life as normally as the economic constraints allowed. This made the arts freer than most other activities, and produced in Mainie an expansion of her talents and thinking. In one year alone, 1941, she became involved in theatre design, book illustration, photography and dance. She also held what was to be her last solo exhibition, at the end of the year.

She became involved in the ballet, *Puck Fair*, at the Gaiety Theatre in February as part of a larger programme organised by Cepta Cullen.[1] *Puck Fair* was her most ambitious project. The script was by the poet, F.R. Higgins;[2] Elizabeth Maconchy composed the music;[3] Cepta Cullen was responsible for the choreography while Mainie designed the sets and the decor generally, as well as costumes and the elegant centre-piece of the goat (Pls. 221–3). Vivid colours and sharp angles created a strongly Cubist, somewhat surrealist stage atmosphere. Into this Cepta Cullen plunged the brief and passionate encounter between Pat McLean, dancing the part of the 'lovable girl', and Nigel Burke as the 'Fiery Tinker'. The ballet had such characters as 'the Black-coated Gentleman', who stood for bureaucracy and the Church combined, and 'The Civic Guard'. 'Here was a ballet,' wrote the *Irish Times* critic, 'conceived by a poet, and essentially Irish in its conceptions, that had been translated from the poetry of words into the poetry of motion and music . . . It is new, it is exciting, it is a triumph for the Irish Ballet Club, and a monument to Fred Higgins, to whom Donough McDonagh[4] paid a graceful tribute at the conclusion of the performance.'[5]

Mainie's interest in theatre design dated back to the early 1930s with the Gate Theatre. Michael MacLiammoir was too much of an artistic polymath, and too restricted in his funding, to allow her much involvement in design for plays, so that *Puck Fair* became the only considered and comprehensive work of theatre design in her career.

Dance was very popular in Ireland at the time. Ninette de Valois,[6] had been choreographic director of the Abbey Theatre from 1926–30, and returned to Ireland during the Second World War for certain performances; this had a positive effect on dance in Dublin. Her accompanist in the recital of works in 1941 was Jacqueline Robinson,[7] who went on to become a leading practitioner of dance in France. She was a friend of Mainie's and an early collector of her paintings.

The vitality of artistic life in the early years of the war, and the smallness of the city, together with Mainie's own range of accomplishments, created a vortex around her reflected in her letters to her sister, Betty, in Glasgow. In addition to the exhibitions of the White Stag Group, which were held monthly through most of the year, there was the Water Colour Society, the Academy, and Contemporary Pictures Gallery. The loan exhibition for the new gallery in Limerick was held in 1941. As a result of an outbreak of foot-and-mouth disease, the 1941 Royal Dublin Society Spring Show, the country's main agricultural show, was cancelled, apart from a horse-jumping competition. In its place Victor Waddington organised an exhibition of Irish art in the members' hall at the society's request,[8] and Mainie sent in four works. In February Gerard Dillon held his first solo exhibition, and invited Mainie to open it (Pl. 234). She spoke of his courage,

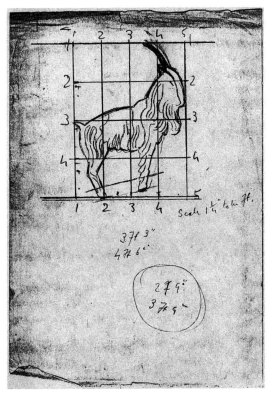

221. *Study for the Goat, Puck Fair*, 1941. Pencil on paper, 11.5 × 8.3. Dublin, private collection.

222. *Puck*, 1941. Gouache on paper, 32.5 × 16.5. Dublin, private collection.

223. Stage set for *Puck Fair* designed by Mainie Jellett.

launching out at a time like this, with the 'forces of destruction rampant', and expressed her familiar belief in the importance to the artist of 'the open mind'. In March a Picture Hire Club was founded to encourage people to borrow, and eventually buy paintings.

Just before the war, Cecil French Salkeld had founded the Gayfield Press, a small printing and publishing business which produced two or three titles each year, mainly poetry in very small editions. The series' general title was *Dublin Poets and Artists*, and *The Straying Student*, by Austin Clarke,[9] was published in August. Mainie did the illustration, *The Assumption* (see Pl. 215).[10]

Mainie's interest in photography was stimulated by her friendship with Joan Cavers,[11] and she prepared notes for a lecture. Her argument was *against* photography as an art form, except where it was allied with drama in the making of films. There, though the overall work is composed of a series of 'instantaneous fragments', they 'are bound into a whole by the art of the author producer actors and photographer and musician and because of this collaboration of the other arts it then becomes an art.' She saw immense value in photography as an aid to study and research, particularly for artists themselves; and she accepted that a sense of composition, which she valued highly in painting, was its central quality. The photograph was an instantaneous impression, produced by machine, and remained 'the registration of a fleeting moment'. She contrasted this with the painter:

> He creates all through from the moment his pencil touches the paper to the moment his brush puts on the last touch of paint on the completed work of art – He is working in the order of natural creation, he is in complete control of the making of the picture till it evolves as an organism complete in itself, ordered as a natural creation. A photo is a fragment a work of art is a whole.

Though the relationship between Celtic art and abstract Cubism had often been referred to by Mainie in lectures and correspondence, it was not until 1941 that she formulated her ideas into a lecture. She first gave it in October, to the White Stag Group, during Kenneth Hall's one-man show there; then again, the following year, to the Munster Fine Arts Club in Cork.[12]

The theme explored the very root of her understanding and practice of art in Ireland. She confronted her audience with a paradox: how was it possible for Ireland to produce, between the fifth and twelfth centuries so consistently powerful an expression of Celtic art, possibly the greatest throughout Europe, and then fail to repeat the phenomenon? Unlike so many of her compatriots, Mainie could not lay it at the door of oppression. 'Other countries have had a troubled history, but their artistic life has gone on, ours has had manifestations in the art of literature fairly continuously, but in painting and sculpture there has since the close of the 12th Century, been no attempt at anything approaching a school of Irish painting and sculpture flourishing in Ireland.' Instead, Irish art has simply become an extension of various English schools of painters, when it existed at all. What it had failed to do was to take that neighbouring tradition and remould it. 'Ideas can not be trammelled by exaggerated nationalism but if the particular country which adopts or absorbs them has any creative capacity worthy of the name, they can be re-born and bear the stamp of the country and nation of their rebirth.'

The second, more fundamental point concerned the close relationship between the form of abstract Cubism she had practised and the art of Celtic Ireland she so admired.

> The sense of filling and decorating a given space rhythmically and harmoniously, one of the first principles of Cubist painting and subsequent non-realistic schools, is clearly shown in Celtic work. The forms are all enclosed and held within the limits of their outside shape, there is a wonderful play of interlaced rhythmically organised movement running through all. The realism, if any, is secondary to the element of form considered in pure relation of one shape to another. The richness and variety is

224. *Madonna of Spring*, 1939. Oil on canvas, 210 × 68. Ireland, private collection.

amazing and the consummate skill of the painters on parchment more so. Much of the work is so minute that it can stand close study under a magnifying glass. At the same time it is held together by a strong rhythmic swing and movement which prevents any sense of fussiness and over-elaboration. The position of the realistic form is entirely controlled by the rhythm and design. The hair the beard the toes and fingers in the stylised figures, the curves of the draperies all flow into an interturning rhythm, so that at one and the same moment they are material and spiritual, body and soul. The twin elements of life in the highest natural creation, man . . . It is the fight to balance these elements and through their fusion in harmonious proportion create a living whole, which is the struggle behind the Cubist and subsequent movements in modern painting.

She examined in some detail the broader argument of materialistic and non-materialistic inspiration in art from Botticelli, Fra Angelico and Titian onward, comparing concepts of form, movement and colour, and creating the essential tensions upon which succeeding generations of painters had fed. But then, at the very close of the nineteenth century and in the early years of the twentieth, came the revolt, and a return to the principles 'embodied in art forms such as Celtic'. Modern art, she explained, was still evolving; it

was a strange chaotic struggling organism stretching out feelers in all directions searching for truth, but only strong enough to attack aspects of it singly, not capable of making synthesis. Hence all the different isms, attacking separate aspects of the problem, prospecting the land for a future renaissance. Those explorers who stressed formal research to its uttermost, the Cubists, were most naturally drawn towards historic periods in art where the principles they were studying were clearly shown.

Mainie consciously added to Negro art, another of the great primitive forces upon which modernism had fed in the early years of the twentieth century, both Romanesque and Celtic inspiration. 'If a Celtic artist of the 8th or 9th century were to meet a present day Cubist or non-representational painter, they would understand one another.' The pity was that present-day Irish artists had misunderstood or overlooked this relationship which they, above all painters in Europe, should have recognised. Instead, Ireland 'has been content to sleep artistically in the arms of a worn-out English tradition.'

The isolation of Ireland in 1941 emphasised for Mainie the glorious contribution once made by Irish artist-monks to the creative, cultural life of Europe, and the legitimacy of now taking back from Europe the modernist inspirations it had to offer. Being cut off by war was not the problem.

It is not a question of our geographical position or of difficulties of transport, ideas are felt and are like wireless waves to be picked up by sensitive receivers, it is not always necessary to have to move in space to find them, it is a state of mind. If our minds are alive and active, craving for ideas, not content with the bare fringe of knowledge and attainment, we will even in these days of difficulty be able to feel the great inner rhythms of the universe, to be part of a whole and to draw into and be made part of the new civilisation which is in painful process of birth.

In a note appended to an early draft of her lecture, and written in the form of an *aide-memoire*, she concluded:

I will try to point out the similarity of ideals between the art of the modern movement (headquarters Paris) and the ideals inspiring Celtic art, and try and show that if we could only open our eyes to the truth behind Celtic art and the treasure house we have in this country in what it has left us, we might then become conscious of a reality that would give our art a national character.

181

227. (*facing page*) *The Ninth Hour*, 1941. Oil on canvas, 86 × 64. Dublin, Hugh Lane Municipal Gallery of Modern Art.

225. *Seated Nude*, 1940. Oil on canvas, 66 × 47.5. Dublin, private collection.

226. *Study for Seated Nude*, 1940. Pencil on paper, 35.5 × 25.5. Dublin, private collection. One of three studies for the oil.

Mainie had progressed a long way. Everything about her was exclusive; her Protestantism, her Unionism, her class, the family background on both her mother's and her father's side, her intellect with its strong dependence on European cultures, these were all handicaps in the new Irish State. During the two decades of her adult working life the scope for alienation had been enlarged by a number of political developments, with the ascendancy of Eamon de Valera and the party of extreme republicanism. In framing the 1937 Constitution, de Valera had laid the foundation stones for a Catholic, rather than a pluralist, state and no opportunity was missed by the Catholic Church to ensure that this predisposition was spread to its own advantage. Many of the aspects of Irish life which Mainie attacked derived directly from this parallel hold on power which the largest political party and the dominant Church seemed to exercise. Health, education, welfare, the censorship of thought and ideas, the control over marriage and sexuality, were all managed in ways not to Mainie's liking. Yet she had not just come to terms with what had happened, but had turned it to her own advantage. Far from being, or feeling alien, she enjoyed a consciousness of being at the very heart of cultural life in its broadest sense. She spoke out about the nature of Irishness in most of her lectures. Whether it was specific, as in her views on Celtic art and its value in modern times, or more generally addressed to broad concepts of cultural identity, her assurance and determination demonstrate the degree to which she saw herself as a leader, and identified herself with the needs of the country as a whole. There was a passionate intensity in this, and a blunt directness in the ways in which she expressed it. 'There was something about her that would discountenance ''sought'' phrases and carefully chosen words', was how Elizabeth Bowen expressed it.[13] And this bluntness of hers, designed to make plain concepts which are often difficult, has also a dogged, relentless fervour which is evident in any reading of the texts of her lectures. She wrote out the whole statement of her intent. She delivered it with modest additions and comments. But the essential purpose and argument is a logical and fully resolved treatise, and the dynamic flow has a force to it which is breathtaking.

In May 1941 she gave a lecture to the White Stag Group entitled 'Art as a Spiritual Force'.[14] She attempted in her lecture to define that 'power [which] draws the onlooker or listener out of himself and away into a new world, a world which he returns from rejuvenated exalted or in the old Greek interpretation of this state purged'. She explained it first with the classic analogies from theatre, of tragedy and comedy, merely adding a marginal note to herself: 'demonstrate this in a painting'. And she goes on to draw the distinction between the originality of the artistic creative act compared with the desire to copy. 'The only way the artist can copy nature is by creating on a lesser plane but with the same order of principles as natural creations.' In order to demonstrate the contemplative and irreversible nature of this artistic process of absorbing and expressing the spiritual force, she offers the example of the Chinese artist painting on silk who

> when he wishes to paint a landscape spends days in contemplation of his subject till he has completely absorbed it into himself and probed the inner depths of its rhythmic order and construction and clarified the emotional reaction he has experienced from the subject in the first instance, into a complete form of expression . . . Chinese pictures to me are cosmic, they are charged with the inner rhythms of the universe and are in my opinion amongst the most perfect works of art man has produced.

She distinguished clearly between this spiritual force and any moral qualities or defects in the artist.

> You may have magnificent artistic effort and results from an artist or composer whose personality is disagreeable selfish and without moral standards, but this individual when his artistic capabilities come into action is full of integrity and would never

228. *The Children of Lir*, 1941. Gouache on paper,
30.5 × 40.5. Dublin, private collection.

contemplate committing an artistic sin or behave in his capacity as an artist in the same way as he would behave in his capacity as a man.

Mainie preferred to think that the combination of consummate artistic ability with 'a beautiful personality' would produce the finest art of all, and she cited Fra Angelico, Beethoven and Botticelli as examples. But then she felt she had to confront what she saw as the 'problem' of Turner, a sublime and powerful painter, but 'a misshapen, heavy slovenly dressed creature, miserly, mean, an astute man of business, proprietor of a public house, moral character rather shady'!

She concluded her lecture with an attempt to define the difference between the artist and other men and women. Artists had an ability 'to delve deeply into the consciousness of things, to feel the inner rhythms of this universe and its eternal laws of harmony and balance beating through their very being, and because of this power they are able to infuse life into their works.' To be an artist was no easy vocation; 'it means work work and more work a never ending struggle towards an ideal which as the powers of the artist increase recedes ever further as his standard becomes higher and he asks more and more of himself till like Titian he says on his death bed he is only beginning.'

Mainie Jellett's solo exhibition at the end of 1941 had no pure abstract works in it at

229. *Circus Procession*, 1940. Gouache on paper, 40.5 × 49.5. Dublin, National Gallery of Ireland.

all. Only eight out of the thirty-five works catalogued were oils; the rest were gouaches, and included studies for the eight paintings together with her designs for *Puck Fair*. This 'return to realism' did not imply a departure from her earlier preoccupation as discussed earlier. Rather, it was a natural development of her visual ideas, an adaptation of the rigour and discipline with which colour and form had been made rhythmic and harmonic throughout her painting life. The composition of the *Pietà*, for example, referred back to a motif in one of her major pure abstract compositions of the 1920s. But it was in the service of a Christian spirituality covering the great moments of the Nativity and the Ninth Hour (Pl. 227), the first of these joyful in colour, light in tone, the second employing a marvellous palette of deep greens, blue and purple, and the reds of fire and anguish at the foot of the cross. Her 'sombre tone and dynamic composition' noted by the *Irish Times* critic, who contrasted it with the traditional, Old Master capacity of Perugino and Raphael in making Calvary 'a serene rather than a tragic place'. Mainie Jellett's work is 'the kind of art which shakes us out of our complacency'.[15] The *Irish Independent* carried a notice signed 'H.S.K.' which placed considerable emphasis on the impact of her religious works, and on their 'intense emotion'.[16]

She sold *Study for the Ninth Hour* and *Sea Horses* for ten guineas; she also sold *Circus Procession*, a gouache, for fourteen. No other oils were sold at the show itself, though

185

230. *Adam and Eve*, 1940. Gouache on paper mounted on card, 22 × 12. Dublin, private collection.

231. Mainie Jellett in 1940.

shortly afterwards *Achill Horses*, which subsequently went to the National Gallery of Ireland, was bought by Miss Kirkpatrick. Her *Seated Nude* (Pl. 225) was in the exhibition, and of it several studies have survived (Pl. 226) which emphasise the linear building up of shape through elongated panels, so successful in *The Ninth Hour*, and also evident in *The Children of Lir* (Pl. 228). *Circus Procession* (Pl. 229) and *Adam and Eve* (Pl. 230) were also in the exhibition, as well as *Sligo Memory*, *Study for The Nativity*, and *Evening*, which were among works sold. Sales totalled £60. 18*s*. in all. £7. 13*s*. 6*d*. was taken in receipts at the door, while Mainie's expenses, which included advertising in all three morning newspapers as well as the *Evening Mail*, framing and taxis (presumably to bring her works to and from the Dublin Painters' Gallery), came to £18. 9*s*. 3*d*. (Pl. 231). After the opening Mainie wrote to her sister, Betty, in Glasgow: 'I had a most successful opening of my show on Thursday masses of people came and I sold six pictures. One to Hilda Griffith and one to David Webb one to Harriet Kirkwood one to Ernie O'Malley and two to the Gavan Duffys. Everyone seems very pleased and think it the best show I have had yet.'

CHAPTER TWENTY-FOUR

The Rouault row

ON 21 NOVEMBER 1942, Mainie wrote to her sister, Betty, then still living in Glasgow: 'We have had complete victory with the Rouault picture, it is now to go on loan to Maynooth! A picture that was refused hanging in a public gallery because it was supposed to be blasphemous irreverent ugly, not a work of art, is now to go to be a source of inspiration to the country's future clergy!!'[1] Yet again Mainie had thrown herself into a controversy about modern art, had fought with shrewdness and vigour, and had come out victorious. It was to be the last of such conflicts.

'The Rouault picture' was *Christ in His Passion*, by Georges Rouault (Pl. 232). It had been bought earlier that same year by the Friends of the National Collections of Ireland,[2] of which Mainie had been a member since the group was founded, in 1924. The painting had been part of a large exhibition of modern French art held in London in January 1942, at the Leicester Galleries. The Friends offered the painting to the Municipal Gallery of Modern Art in Dublin, in the summer of 1942. The offer was turned down by the gallery's Art Advisory Committee.[3]

The leading figure among those who had sought to have the painting accepted by the gallery was Dermod O'Brien, President of the Royal Hibernian Academy (Pl. 233). He made a statement to the press in which he challenged the idea that the painting was either irreverent or blasphemous. He could accept the view that Rouault's vision was 'grotesque', but saw in this no reason for rejecting him. He expressed an inability to understand the work of many modern French painters, but did not include Rouault in this category. The picture was 'suitable for the Municipal Gallery'. His main opponent was Mrs Kathleen Clarke, a former Lady Mayoress of Dublin.[4] Mrs Clarke proudly claimed that she had been 'the strongest objector to the acceptance of the picture'. The painting was, she said, 'offensive to Christian sentiment'. It could be taken as a travesty, and she was 'especially afraid of its effect on young people'. Any other work by Rouault would have her support, she said, not having seen any other works, and almost certainly not being aware of Rouault's capacity to horrify, with his vivid and cruel scenes of the lower depths of life; but this one, even if the Friends of the National Collections assured her that it was 'the greatest work of art in the world', would not change her attitude. 'This work, however, offended me as a Catholic and as a Christian.'

Lady Dunalley also entered the fray with a physical diagnosis of the seated Christ: 'It has got cancer. It has no hair on it. That meant leprosy. It has a great lump on its body. That means cancer. It is a foretaste of Hell. In Hell we will hear jazz music and the wailing of the damned.' 'Dirty and very dirty at that – in other words, decadent', was how Leo Whelan described it.

The Irish Times itself came down firmly on the side of Rouault, pointing out that the painting was the *only* work by the artist to have been shown at the London exhibition, where it had been much admired by the critics. One of these, Count Michael de la Bedoyère,[5] had been in Dublin only a short time before to give a lecture; he is quoted in a review of the London exhibition:

Rouault is generally acknowledged to be the most important, as he is certainly the

232. Georges Rouault, *Christ in His Passion*. Oil on canvas, 63.5 × 48.3. Dublin, Hugh Lane Municipal Gallery of Modern Art.

233. Irish artists at a varnishing day at the Royal Hibernian Academy Summer Show. From left: Dermod O'Brien, Mainie Jellett, Kitty Wilmer, Brigid Ganly, Maurice MacGonigal, Frank McKelvey, Charles Lamb and Arthur Power, with Howard Knee behind them. The partly concealed figure is not identified.

234. Mainie Jellett at the opening of Gerard Dillon's first solo exhibition, in February 1942.

most striking of contemporary painters of sacred subjects . . . Rouault belongs to no acknowledged school, except that he shares the general sense of the best artists of our time, that the old conventions are useless, and then he must find the most direct means of creating that which he feels to be in him to give.[6]

Another critic, whose own works were known to Dublin art enthusiasts through the exhibitions already held at the Contemporary Picture Galleries, was John Piper.[7] His review was also quoted: 'Rouault is a painter whose work is more significant now than ever. He is, among other things, the only painter alive who has found forms convincing enough and imposing enough to set beside medieval variations on Christian themes.'

The protagonists on either side entrenched themselves with energy and fortitude. Even before the news of the rejections of the painting had been made public, Mainie was organising what was to become the main protest meeting on the event. On 1 October she wrote to Thomas MacGreevy, telling him that the next meeting of the Friends of the National Collections would be in the form of a group of lectures on the art of Rouault, and would be held in November in the main hall of the College of Surgeons in St Stephen's Green ('it can be got for nothing'.) 'The three victims selected to speak are Evie Hone, you and myself. We would be expected to speak for about 20 minutes each — then other members in the audience might be called upon.' For Evie, always shy on account of her disabilities, this was a rare public appearance (Pl. 235). The idea was for MacGreevy to talk on Rouault's religious art and religious art in general, while Mainie and Evie would discuss his life and his painting, with Evie adding something about his work as a designer of stained glass . 'I do hope you will do this — it would be a great help to have you with us on the scaffold!' The emphasis, she said, was not to be on the controversy — 'the nonsense that has gone on over the Rouault picture' — but on placing Rouault in his proper context in twentieth-century art, and explaining his importance.

Mainie, of course, as well as being a member of the Friends and actively involved in its organising committee, was also on the Arts Advisory Committee, and had seen the progress of the debate there during the summer. The curator of the Municipal Gallery,

235. Evie Hone at work in her studio, after Mainie's death. The cartoons on which she is working are for the Eton College Window, which she began in 1949. It was erected in 1952.

John F. Kelly,[8] was on the council of the Friends as well, and its annual receptions were held in the gallery. Sean Keating, also on the Art Advisory Committee, entered the controversy at an early stage after the rejection had been announced, giving it as his opinion that the painting was 'naive, childish and unintelligible'. C.P. Curran seized on this in a long and detailed letter to *The Irish Times*, published on 8 October, and giving a full account of Rouault's career and training.[9] 'He is, it is true, only a workman's son – but Mr. Keating will not hold this against him – born in 1871 in a Paris cellar when the guns were bombarding the city, and he lived many years in poverty, an obstinate recluse, perfecting what he thought was his art, and disdaining official recognition.' Curran shrewdly invoked the names of great Catholic thinkers, like Maritain, respected Catholics nearer home, including Father D'Arcy of Campion College in Oxford, and a list of international art critics, museum directors, and politicians.

Other correspondents were less serious. 'We live on our wits, and like myself, they are mostly ploughmen,' wrote Niall Montgomery.[10] 'It interests me, as a well-known alienist, to listen to loose-mouthed, wet-eyed, eloquent peasants condemning Parisian art for its lack of sophistication. There's one thing about the old crowd – no one can say there's very few of them left.' And he referred to 'the saint-and-scholar act, with its subsidiary poet-and-peasant turns' as being the Irish speciality.

Louis le Brocquy, who had returned from Europe and was then living or working at 13 Merrion Row, appealed for the painting to be made available in the gallery, and the decision to be reversed. And he addressed to Sean Keating a rebuke for insulting the name of Rouault. Myles Na gCopaleen (Flann O'Brien), naturally enough, had made fun of the whole row in his 'Cruiskeen Lawn' column in *The Irish Times*.[11]

It was six weeks before the meeting of the Friends in the College of Surgeons took place, on 8 November. By then a new champion had aligned himself beside Mainie, Evie and Thomas MacGreevy. This was Father Edward Leen.[12] He was to become a close friend of Mainie's.

Edward Leen was a distinguished prelate, and President of Blackrock College. He returned to the College from North America as a teacher of senior pupils destined for the priesthood. Earlier, in 1938, he had been responsible for a number of retreats, several of which were based on a somewhat daring idea for Dublin at the time: the conversion of Protestants. The Legion of Mary organised the event, each Catholic bringing a Protestant friend. It was the first venture of its kind in Ireland since the Reformation.[13] It is highly likely that Evie Hone attended – she was by then a good friend of Dr McQuaid. And it is possible that Mainie was there.

Father Leen emerged as the leading speaker in the College of Surgeons.[14] He addressed the key controversial issues – whether the painting was irreverent, whether the painting was blasphemous – in unequivocal terms.

> There can be no irreverence where there is such profound understanding. The truth cannot be blasphemous even when it lays bare, relentlessly, even cruelly, the inner sense of a reality which crashes through our miserable conventionality. There are words which that conventionality would deem blasphemous were they not uttered by a divinely inspired prophet of old: ''He hath no form, nor comeliness; and when we see him there is no beauty that we should desire him . . .'' Here we have in words of haunting sadness a truth that Rouault gives us in light and shade and bold design.

Both Evie and Mainie spoke of Rouault as painter and designer, while Thomas MacGreevy's address was directed at the Irish people, and the progress they were making towards a better understanding of art. Dermod O'Brien should have chaired the meeting, but was replaced by C.P. Curran.

In a later article, Mainie echoed something of what Thomas MacGreevy had said, but went further in an explanation of the importance of a public gallery showing the Rouault canvas. She saw it as an extension of what her whole career had sought to achieve: 'We in this country, unless we have travelled, are in no position whatever to judge the great modern art movements of Europe; they have not touched us except through a few of our artists who have ventured abroad (as the Irish monks of the early centuries) to glean European culture and ideas, and bring them back again to Ireland, where they are usually rejected.'[15] Her words had greatly added force in November 1942, with the battles of El Alamein and Stalingrad at their height, and news coming in of the total annihilation of the Warsaw Ghetto, with the deaths of 50,000 people. She invoked also the sad story of Hugh Lane: 'Sir Hugh Lane's wishes have not been carried out; if they had, a situation like the present one could not have arisen.'

She reserved her more complete analysis of Rouault's place among his peers, and the special quality in his work, until December, when she gave a lecture to the White Stag Group entitled 'Rouault and Tradition':

> The tone organisation of colour is closely akin to the organisation of sound in music. The colour scheme of a picture is similar to the key in which a piece of music is written. The picture can live as a harmony of well-organised and perfectly balanced colour rightly fitted to the forms it is filling, quite apart from whether the forms of the picture are realistic or non-realistic. I feel this harmonic quality of colour is particularly strong in Rouault, and linked to this musical sense is the dramatic sense. Colour used to stress the drama in the subject matter. Velvety black lines used to emphasise the rhythm of the form, luminous blues and wine reds accentuating the mystic quality.[16]

She saw in Rouault and tradition a link between his art and Romanesque art. He pointed back across the materialist centuries to a purity of conception found in Byzantine and Sienese painting: 'Also a close link with primitive Christian art and Celtic Christian art can be felt.'

In her stained-glass work, Evie could be said to have passed from Gleizes to the rugged, emotional, representational style of Rouault's painting. In France, Rouault had been taken up by the French Roman Catholic philosopher, Jacques Maritain, who constructed a philosophy of art derived from his understanding of St Thomas Aquinas. Maritain was greatly appreciated by the Irish Catholic intelligentsia, and his influence probably accounts for the decision by Maynooth to accept the painting. Gleizes liked to quote St Thomas's dictum that 'Art must imitate nature, not in its external appearance, but in its way of working (*operatione*).' (Mainie preferred to translate this as 'internal organisation'.) But on the whole he regarded St Thomas, who belonged to the thirteenth century, as marking the end of the great spiritual epoch of European Catholicism – the transition from Romanesque to Gothic, from an internal spiritual life to an interest in external appearances. He had little sympathy for Rouault's emotionalism. After the Second World War, the Roman Catholic Church in France, influenced by Maritain, did much to promote modern art in its church building, using non-Catholic artists such as Picasso, Léger and Matisse. The Catholic, Gleizes, was regarded with distrust, and this may partly be accounted for by his opposition to Thomism.

The Rouault controversy brought out the best and the worst of Dublin parochialism. Everyone dived in and took part. It polarised attitudes and invoked questions about moral purity, Christian values, human decadence and the purpose of art. Mainie's contribution sought to transcend the row, and find in it the necessary material for educating the public in the widest sense. But it also had a more personal significance; Rouault had achieved in his art that integration of pre-Renaissance spiritual directness and simplicity with modernism, which she herself was increasingly concerned to resolve in her later paintings, a growing number of which had been on religious themes, and all of which were concerned with visual re-interpretation, as were those of Rouault. The essential events of the life of Christ, painted by artists throughout history, neglected more in the twentieth century than in any other, had become an important part of Mainie's output as a painter.

CHAPTER TWENTY-FIVE

Her most cherished ambition fulfilled

THERE WERE MANY efforts in the middle years of the Second World War to define the 'Irishness' of Irish art. The flood of activity which had engulfed theatre, painting, literature, music, sculpture, and all the crafts, resulted also in certain exercises of self-examination. One of these was the *Irish Art Handbook*, edited by Basil Clancy, and published in 1943. The following year *Irish Art* appeared, also under his editorship.[1]

Mainie completed her contribution to the first of these in September 1942, an essay she called 'Definition of My Art' but which was published under the title 'An Approach to Painting'.[2] She gives a rounded portrait of herself as a mature painter, defining her work in three distinct categories. The first of these she defines as 'non-representational painting based on some emotional contact received from nature or experience, but first born in the mind.' The second, which embraces work essentially from the mid-1930s on, with the exception of *Homage to Fra Angelico* (painted 1928), is of 'non-representational work based on Christian religious subjects treated symbolically without realism'. The third was 'realistic landscape treated in a manner inspired by Chinese Art, and direct realistic studies for exercises and reference'. To this last she might have added nudes, since she painted and exhibited late nudes in her 1939 and 1941 solo exhibitions, and taught life drawing extensively in 1940 and 1941, producing a substantial body of work (Pls. 236–40).

Inevitably, because she was writing for a general publication on the arts inspired by the fervent atmosphere of concern and interest in Ireland, her thoughts about her own art were inextricably linked with her thoughts about art in Ireland: 'The art of a nation is one of the ultimate facts by which its spiritual health is judged and appraised by posterity.' And she extended her views on her own work, both content and 'modernist' approach, to views on art generally, particularly stressing the need for a highly developed sense of craftsmanship. She refers to the guild system to emphasise her views about the artist as a socially involved 'worker':

> The idea of an artist being a special person, an exotic flower set apart from other people, is one of the errors resulting from the industrial revolution, and the cause of artists being pushed out of their lawful position in the life and society of the present day . . . Their present enforced isolation from the majority is to be deplored and, I believe, is one of the many causes which has resulted in the present chaos we live in.

She expressed again some of her beliefs about modern art and 'the Modernist Movement' – the inverted commas are used in her essay – and claimed that the movement had purified and revitalised art in the twentieth century.

> It has shaken the materialism of the so-called academic tradition and has shown those who were alive enough to see, where the true traditions lie. It has shown the futility of merely copying the great works of the past and, by so doing, fondly imagining a tradition was being carried on. It has demonstrated with clarity and success that the only way to carry on a live tradition is to understand and venerate the great works of the past and to realise the unchanging artistic laws which must be reinterpreted by each period in turn so as to express its needs and character.

Mainie had fulfilled a remarkable cycle of creative self-examination and self-

236.   *Seated Woman*, 1941. Pencil on paper, 54 × 34. Dublin, private collection.

237. *Seated Woman*, 1941. Pencil on paper, 54 × 34. Dublin, private collection.

238. *Woman Standing – Back View*, 1941. Pencil on paper, 54 × 34. Dublin, private collection.

discovery. Those around her had done the same, particularly Jack Yeats, who by the end of the 1930s had embarked on the last great phase of his painting. From his regular appearance in the Royal Hibernian Academy it could be assumed that he maintained a steady pace in his work; yet in reality his output fluctuated, and the 1930s had seen considerable emphasis on writing. His impact as a painter was heightened by his showing in the Cross Section and Loan Exhibition, by his two solo shows in the Contemporary Painting Gallery in 1939 and 1940, by his exhibition in the London National Gallery exhibition 'After Whistler' and by Victor Waddington's start as a dealer in Dublin, in 1941, when he took on Yeats in an association which then lasted until the end of the painter's life, in 1957. Much else was going on around her in these late years of the 1930s and into the early years of the war, sufficient to rate the period as extremely important in the overall context of twentieth-century Irish art, much of the research for which, after half a century, still lies ahead.

Basil Clancy reflected this in his two publications. Neither the *Irish Art Handbook* nor *Irish Art* was partisan in favour of modernism. Indeed Clancy, in his contribution to the second, 'A Note on Art and Reality', takes a very conservative, if not reactionary, line and gives expression to a deeply Christian view of art, equating realism with God, and suggesting that from a current rebellion against God's will 'every evil has ever flowed, as blood from a wound, until today all humanity bleeds on the field of war'. Yet despite the horrifying tide of death which by 1943 had extended world-wide, he claimed that

> Nothing is more significant of the times in which we live, no, not even the war, than the fact that the art which is designated 'modern' is not concerned with what is common to all mankind but attempts to present things which have never been a reality in the experience of anyone. It is an attempt to escape from life and its implications, of man's relation to his Creator, his sinful nature, his fallen state, redemption, supernatural life, and last end.

Father Edward Leen, who had by this stage become a friend of Mainie's, and a help to her spiritually, contributed an essay entitled 'The Relations of Art and Philosophy' and not unlike Basil Clancy places the Church in a central role in respect of art. Basil Rákóczi paid tribute to the modernists in his essay 'The Artist and Society' which named Yeats, Jellett, Hone and Norah McGuinness, as well as his closer White Stag Group associates, Nick Nicholls, Jocelyn Chewett, Kenneth Hall and Pat Scott.

Even so, the great annual exhibition of Irish art remained that of the Royal Hibernian Academy. There was no comparable modernist show. When the 1942 annual exhibition opened the editor of *Commentary* asked Mainie to go and see it and write her impressions.[3]

> I very reluctantly consented to write this article – But having consented, I now give my honest opinion for what it is worth, and in no way resent the honest opinion of my fellow artists of different points of view, when it is levelled against my own work, provided it is an honest opinion. Every year I go to the R.H.A. Ex. I go in a spirit of hopefulness expecting there may be some new young head pushing itself up through the miasma of vulgarity and self-satisfaction, which is the general impression I unfortunately register every year.

1942 proved to be no exception. She set aside Jack Yeats, whose painting she considered had fulfilled the essential set of requirements – to be technically and artistically excellent as well as having that 'quality of nationality' which should be present in the works shown in a country's academy shows. She also picked out three other painters: Grace Henry, James Sleator[4] and Margaret Clarke,[5] the two last academicians 'in the true sense of the word' who were exhibiting after a long absence and whose paintings revealed 'dignity and distinction'. In other respects,

this year's Academy seems to suffer even more from the faults I have mentioned than

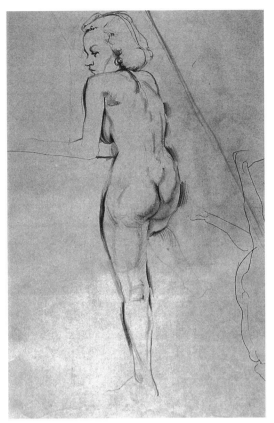

239. *Standing Female Nude*, 1941. Pencil on paper, 49.3 × 32. Dublin, private collection.

240. *Standing Female Nude*, 1941. Pencil on paper, 32.5 × 28.5. Dublin, private collection.

last year . . . The R.H.A. must not shut its doors to life, otherwise it will of necessity die of senile decay. This present exhibition is with very few exceptions an all Irish exhibition, therefore we are in a position to take stock of what academic art is and what it stands for in this country – let us open our eyes and our minds and form our own honest opinions and ask ourselves, is this what we want as Irish art, if it is then there is no more to be said.

The other point emphasised by Mainie in the article concerned the influence of the Academy's standards on young painters (when published the article was given the title, 'The R.H.A. and Youth'). 'I had sometimes come away so mortified by what I had seen, not minding for myself and older artists who are more or less formed and their feet set on the broad or narrow path – but what worried me was the younger generation.' She was making to the Royal Hibernian Society the same plea that Walter Sickert had made to the Royal Academy, 'if it can do nothing else, at least to give us good academic work'. She felt that the Royal Academy did have 'a certain standard of craftsmanship much higher than the unspeakable Paris Salon des Artistes Francais and its slightly better companion Salon des Beaux Arts; but our R.H.A. has no standard of any kind, excepting perhaps the standard of the chocolate box cover'. In her references to the bad influence on young painters she had in mind particularly the fact that the Royal Hibernian Academy had rejected in 1942 two of Louis le Brocquy's paintings, his *Image of Chaos* and *The Spanish Shawl*.[6]

Sybil le Brocquy is credited with having conceived of the idea for an alternative to the Royal Hibernian Academy, and its name: 'The Irish Exhibition of Living Art'. Everything about the title suggests, in fact, the inspiration of Mainie Jellett. Her article stresses the need for an Irish identity, and repeats again that word which recurs so often in her lectures, 'living' associated with 'art'. The initial meetings took place at the time of Mainie's visit to the Royal Hibernian Academy for her article, and on 12 May 1943, she was elected chairman.

The foundations for its 'national' character were carefully laid. The Provost of Trinity College, E.H. Alton; the President of University College, Arthur Conway; the Director of the National Gallery of Ireland, George Furlong and the President of the Royal Hibernian Academy itself, Dermod O'Brien, all agreed to be patrons. The organising committee, under Mainie's chairmanship, consisted of Evie Hone, Margaret Clarke, Laurence Campbell,[7] Louis le Brocquy, Norah McGuinness, Ralph Cusack, Father Jack Hanlon, and Elizabeth Curran, who was secretary.

The exhibition, which opened to the public on 16 September 1943, contained 154 paintings and 14 works of sculpture. In addition, there was a memorial loan exhibition of works of sculpture by Jerome Connor,[8] who had died in Dublin earlier that year. The memorial show established a tradition which was followed in later years, of showing small groups of works of art of recently dead painters and sculptors.

Dermod O'Brien, exhibited *Sulphur Carnations* and *Tanrago Corn*. It must be remembered that he was then seventy-eight, and had been president of the Academy since 1910. His support for the new, rival, art forum was characteristic of his profoundly generous and catholic attitude to painting and painters, and was an endorsement of change. Sean Keating was another academician who participated, his work, lent by the Electricity Supply Board (presumably with his permission), being one of his series on the development of Ireland's electrical power system, *Tip Wagons at Poulaphouca*. The other academicians to show were predisposed in favour of the Living Art concept, and included Laurence Campbell, the sculptor, who taught at the National College of Art and whose brother, Christopher, also showed in the exhibition; Margaret Clarke; Beatrice Glenavy;[9] and of course Jack Yeats, whose three works in the show were *Farewell*, *The Velvet Strand* and *A Homage to Bret Harte*. Though they represented a very small part of the overall exhibition, and were by no means all traditional academicians,

241. *Western Procession*, 1943. Oil on canvas, 43 × 86.5. Dublin, private collection.

they gave authority and a sense of continuity to the exhibition. Mainie's involvement attracted many of her followers.[10]

Because of the emphasis on *Irish* art, neither Basil Rákóczí nor Kenneth Hall took part. Basil Rákóczí, whose mother came from Cork, was legally entitled to call himself Irish, and could have acquired an Irish passport at the time, had he so wanted. But he did not view himself in this light. However, as a result of criticism of the exhibition entry restriction to Irish nationals, access to Living Art was extended from 1944, and Rákóczí and others appeared in later annual exhibitions.

The writer and artist, Edith Somerville,[11] was a cousin of Mainie's. She had been an art student in Paris in the 1880s, and had continued to paint; she had two landscapes in the show, one of Normandy and one near Baltimore, County Cork. There were several designs for stained glass. And among the sculpture there were three works by Louis le Brocquy's younger sister, Melanie,[12] who was embarking on a career as a sculptor.

The exhibition was well-received; the *Irish Times* critic reminded readers of how the Impressionists had been given an alternative gallery in Paris by the Emperor Napoleon III to show the work of the *refusés*. 'Today, in Dublin, the Minister for Education comes, in a somewhat similar way, to the help of those Irish artists whose work is seldom seen at the Royal Hibernian Academy exhibitions, but who have nevertheless achieved fame or fortune, though mostly the former, on their own merits.'[13] The paper was quick to point out that the spirit was not of rivalry nor inspired altogether by frustration; evidence of a certain harmony between the 'moderns' and the academic tradition was there in Dermod O'Brien's participation. 'The result of it all is the most vital and distinguished exhibition of work by Irish artists that has ever been held; and, as is to be expected at an exhibition in the organisation of which women artists have had as much say as men, there is everywhere evidence of that elusive quality – good taste.' It was not a substitute for technical accomplishment, the writer maintained, and went on to list the vitality and power in works by Jack Yeats, Grace Henry, Mary Swanzy, Evie Hone and May Guinness, who are dealt with in slightly more extended detail than the rest, in a notice

242. *Western Procession*, 1943. Gouache on paper mounted on card, 28 × 47.5. London, private collection.

which suffers in its liberality from wartime shortage of newsprint, rather than from any failure to recognise the importance of the occasion and the remarkable quality of the very extensive body of work. It seems strange now to see painters such as Louis le Brocquy, Nano Reid, Norah McGuinness, Jack Hanlon, Gerard Dillon and Margaret Clarke, reduced to being 'noted'. Mainie shared pride of place with Jack Yeats, and her works 'stand up nobly to the exacting test'. The same tone of warm approbation and a recognition of the liberal and generous range of work, as well as its vitality, pervaded the reviews in the *Evening Mail* and *Irish Independent*. Mainie Jellett, 'this fine artist', was seen at her best in *The Ninth Hour* (see Pl. 227) claimed the *Independent* critic. The critic in the *Mail* suggested that the organisers had 'given a fair deal to modern Irish art'.[14]

Dr A. J. Leventhal, who taught at Trinity and was a friend of Samuel Beckett, wrote a long essay about the exhibition which appeared in *Irish Art* and which gave some attention to guiding principles. He hinted that perhaps the organisers had compromised, locating themselves midway between academic and modernist poles. The parallel he chose was the Salon d'Automne, 'midway between the Academy and the Indépendents, but in practice the Salon half-heartedly rejected Academism and lacked the courage to ally itself with the prevailing modern tendencies.' Mainie, as a regular exhibitor with the Indépendents in Paris from the early 1920s, would have appreciated this judgment, while at the same time knowing that for Irish Living Art to succeed it was necessary to avoid being opposed to the academic tradition. But Leventhal was speaking from the standpoint of the avant-garde, and devoted much of his essay to a consideration of the work of the younger and more adventurous painters. He singles out Nick Nicholls, Ralph Cusack, Doreen Vanston, Thurloe Conolly, Mainie herself and Louis le Brocquy for early and comparatively detailed attention. And it is clear that he has more interest in a European Surrealist influence – he names Picasso, Miro, Chirico, Dali and Yves Tanguy – than in a Cubist one. He writes that Mainie's 'cubist technique may be excused, for it is now a little outmoded, on account of its unusual representational quality and altogether pleasing sense of symbolical motion,' but goes on to admire *Western Procession* (Pl. 241), one of Mainie's four works in the show. 'European influence', he concluded, 'was the dominant note.'[15]

Mainie did not attend the opening. As the *Irish Times* critic wrote:

Where the pervading (if, unfortunately, not presiding) genius is that most analytical of modern Irish artists, Miss Mainie Jellett, good taste without ardent study would get short shrift. Those who have followed Miss Jellett's long and valiantly fought battle for 'modern' art in Ireland will be sorry to hear that she is ill, and has not been able to assist at the preparation of an exhibition which is in many ways the fulfilment of her most cherished ambition.

243. *Donkey in a Bog, Achill*, 1943. Oil on canvas, 49.5 × 65. Dublin, private collection.

CHAPTER TWENTY-SIX

'A wonderful picture in my mind'

SHE WAS NOT just ill; she was dying. With all the preparations completed for the opening of the Irish Exhibition of Living Art, Mainie had gone to Cork, for a brief holiday with her friend, Sylvia Cooke-Collis. When she returned it was thought she had pleurisy and suspected TB. The suspicion about her having TB was ill-founded; it derived from the fact that Mainie and Evie had both been visiting a young man who was seriously ill with the disease, and it was felt that they might both have been at risk. They were warned, for example, not to take tea with him, which they did. And in the first diagnosis of her own illness, at a time when TB was widespread in Ireland, and the cause of many fatalities, this was the line of the medical investigation.

Mainie's mother, who was seventy-five, and none too well herself, was unable to nurse her eldest daughter, and so Mainie went into a nursing home at 96 Lower Leeson Street run by the Irish Sisters of Charity.

She gave her last painting lesson on 5 August, before going in for treatment. On 7 August Sarah Purser died and was buried on 10 August. Only three months earlier, writing to her sister in Glasgow, Mainie had reported that 'Miss Purser is delighted over Geraldine's school successes', so that the grand old lady of Irish art, who was ninety-five at the time of her death, was still fully aware and concerned about her great-great-grand-niece.

Her mother wrote to tell her daughter that a very large number of people went to the funeral; 'Miss Purser will leave a great gap behind her'. Sean Purser, married to Betty, was of course over from Glasgow and 'with us a good deal'. Her letter, scrawled in quite clumsy writing on 'greasy' note paper which drove her mad and made her think Mainie would be unable to read it, is full of everyday events; the dogs flourish, Babbin buys a pretty jersey for herself and one for her daughter, Rosamund, who is off to Knocknaheen (a Purser family house in Wicklow) for a holiday. Bay is setting off with a friend, to see the latest Jimmy O'Dea play, and those left in the house 'are listening to the war news'. Janet Jellett confesses to feeling 'very stupid, so many people coming in and out . . . we miss you all the time'.

The 'war news', though still grim enough, had shown a steady tide in events which favoured the Allied cause. From the German surrender at Stalingrad in January 1944, through to the landing of the American Seventh Army in Sicily in July, the steady march on Berlin had already begun. It was to cost many more lives; the horrors that spring perpetrated on the total Jewish population in Warsaw represented only the tiniest hint of the holocaust which was eventually to be revealed. And the struggle in the Far East was at that stage only showing modest signs of success. The tide had also turned in the Atlantic war: it had changed from being a question of if, to being one of when.

From her nursing home bed Mainie monitored as ever the events closest to her own life. She had exhibited works in other shows that year, and had been responsible for the selections of the Living Art Exhibition which she was now unable to see. One of the exhibitions had been a summer show of watercolours and stained glass at the Contemporary Picture Galleries and she read in her room at the nursing home Theodore Goodman's review in *Commentary*,[1] which yet again displayed hints and echoes of past prejudices about the very gulf which she had worked to bridge in everything, including her latest Living Art endeavours. He wrote of 'the good, honest Irish stew' section of the show, and of 'the different varieties of "caviare to the general", the followers of cubism, sur-realism and abstraction who have with such determination plagued the Dublin "man in the gallery" for so long'. He includes Mainie in the caviare, along with Evie Hone, Nano Reid, and goes on: 'It is interesting however to observe in Miss Jellett's latest work signs of a greater freedom and fluency than in so much of her recent painting, and I am curious to see if her next one-man exhibition shows her to have broken away from traditional cubism.' Mainie's next solo show was due later that year, and she was already planning it. But work on Living Art had taken up a great deal of her time and she did not at that stage have enough new work to constitute a show. She wrote from the nursing home to Eileen McCarvill who had bought *Western Procession* from the Exhibition of Living Art, thanking her for the cheque, and saying how pleased she was that the picture 'has found a home with you . . . I am very much better and get up every afternoon now, but I have to go slow – I am wonderfully well looked after here. Again so very many thanks.' She sent 'best love' to the four McCarvill children, Eilis, Diarmod, Niall, Evon, all of whom were pupils. The writing is somewhat scrawled, as though written either in bed or in a chair; the salutation is formal – 'Yours very sincerely Mainie H. Jellett'.

Eileen McCarvill herself had taken lessons with Mainie, and it is from Mainie's detailed accounts with the family for the whole of 1943 that we know that her last lesson was given on 5 August, to three of her children. The payments seem pathetically small; irrespective of the numbers attending, she charged 3s. 6d. (less than 20p) an hour. For May, June and July, a total of thirty-four hours, Mainie received £5. 17s. 6d. And for the first few months of 1943, teaching without any break from mid-January until 20 April, she received £12. 2s. 6d.

Mainie did not get better, nor did she return home. There is some question as to exactly when the early diagnosis of her illness was recognised as wrong, and alternative treatment contemplated, though even so there was little likelihood of this making any great difference. She was suffering from cancer of the pancreas, with the prospects of any kind of cure remote.

In October 1943, the novelist Elizabeth Bowen visited her in the Leeson Street nursing home. She had been entirely unaware that Mainie was ill until, travelling over to Ireland on the boat train to visit her home, she met Babbin, who gave her details of the seriousness of her sister's illness, and encouraged an early visit. The two women had been friends since early childhood, when Elizabeth Bowen and her parents had wintered in Dublin, where they had a house in Herbert Place.

Mainie's bed in the back room of the late eighteenth-century house was pulled out under the window. The October sunlight reflected off the nearby redbrick buildings filled the room with brightness. Notwithstanding the brave words in her letter earlier that month to Eileen MacCarvill, Mainie was weak and in some pain. 'The eager generous little girl of my first memories was now a thin woman, in whom the fatigue of illness, mingling with that unlost generosity and eagerness, translated itself into a beauty I cannot forget.'[2] Bowen was conscious of lost opportunities. Their lives had diverged; in art they had pursued separate paths, worked in different places, and met, as far as the writer was concerned, too seldom. 'But I have never lost the proud sense of being at least a contemporary of Mainie's, and a friend in the sense that distance and separation do not damage. To have worked with her must surely have been a great thing.'

They talked on that occasion about writing. Mainie was reading *Pilgrimage* by Dorothy Richardson, a work of experimental fiction which sought to express a 'contemplated reality' unrestrained by the conventions of the normal novel form, the finalities of which were unacceptable to her. 'No drama, no situation, no set scene . . . just life going on and on' in the more èxperimental mode pursued by Virginia Woolf. Neither Mainie nor Bowen knew her personally, but Bowen, writing much later, refers to the fact that her 'strain of genius has not yet been enough recognised by the world,' though she claimed that Mainie had recognised it. 'She talked to me about writing with a pure comprehension of which, I think, few actual writers are capable.'

The meeting between these two women was overshadowed by thoughts of the war, and though Mainie was gravely ill, and Bowen's recollections were to be coloured by the fact that the essay she was to write became a posthumous tribute, there was at the time no sense of it being their last encounter. The 'death throes and birth pangs' of the world itself, phrases which Mainie had used in lectures which recognised the challenges to art of countries and indeed continents in conflict, came to the surface on that October afternoon as those two proud and independent Irish women artists, whose creativity in both cases had an austere singularity of purpose, exchanged sad and sober reminiscences.

Mainie's mother was not well enough to visit her daughter, and was discouraged from even considering it, since the family felt that the seriousness of her daughter's illness would prove too much of a shock; Mainie's steady decline was kept secret from her. Bay was a constant visitor. In addition, Mainie's artist friend, Hélène de St Pierre, spent a great deal of time at the nursing home.

Mainie accepted, some time late in 1943 that she was dying, and summoned her friend and fellow protagonist from the days of the Rouault controversy, Father Edward Leen. She asked him to help her prepare for death. He did so with great delicacy. He was conscious of the enormous diversity of faiths which seemed to surround that nursing home room. Mainie's mother came from an evangelical background. Bay, too, favoured a more downright form of Christianity than Mainie, who had worshipped for most of her adult life at St Bartholomew's Church in Clyde Road, a High Anglican discipline, unusual in the Church of Ireland. Mainie's father, like her grandfather, had been a straightforward Church of Ireland Protestant to whom the idea of an established church was probably still half-attractive, as was the concept of Ireland ruled by Britain, at least until the closing years of his life. Hélène de St Pierre was a devout Roman Catholic, and of course Father Leen was an experienced and perceptive theologian and philosopher. It did not end there. Evie Hone had been accepted into the Roman Catholic Church by her friend and mentor, John Charles McQuaid, who was Archbishop of Dublin. Too much emphasis on the Roman Catholic help and guidance should not obscure the fact that Mainie's own vicar, Canon Walter C. Simpson, visited her regularly, having catered to her spiritual welfare through the later years of her active life.

In reality Mainie took much greater comfort from the spiritual help and advice she got from Father Leen than she did from Canon Simpson. She told her sister that whenever he visited her it made her depressed, while Father Leen had an uplifting effect. 'She appeared younger whenever he had been to see her.' At one stage Father Leen stopped coming. This made Mainie so distressed that Babbin determined to find out what the problem was, and discovered that Father Leen had become frightened that he would be seen as proselytising. With the strong endorsement of Mainie's sisters, the visits resumed.

Early in 1944 Evie wrote to Gleizes that Mainie was sick with cancer and would not recover. She said that Mainie did not know the full extent of her illness and was not suffering greatly ('elle n'a pas beaucoup de souffrance'). It was thought that she would not live longer than a month. The suffering did increase, though when Evie visited her lifelong friend the night before she died she found her 'happy and serene'.

Despite her strong sympathies with Father Edward Leen, and the obvious spiritual comfort he offered, Mainie went through the formalities of her own church in anticipation of death. She was visited a few hours before her death by Canon Simpson. She joined with him in the Confession, the Lord's Prayer, the Creed, the *Anima Christi*, the *Sursum Corda*, 'and other acts of faith' and 'in perfect peace and happiness she passed on to her rest'.[3]

Mainie's death certificate recorded cardiac failure and carcinoma of the pancreas. She

244.   *I Have Trodden the Wine Press Alone*, 1943. Oil on canvas, 76 × 56. Dublin, National Gallery of Ireland.

200

245. *Study for 'The Virgin of Eire'*, 1943. Pencil and wash on paper, 40.4 × 49.6. Dublin, National Gallery of Ireland. Shows (from left to right) St Brigid, The Virgin and Child, and St Patrick.

was forty-seven. Pat Scott,[4] then only twenty-two, arrived at the nursing home on the morning of Mainie's death. He had made an arrangement of dried flowers to give to her, and was met on the steps by Sister Camisias who gave him the news. This Irish Sister of Charity, who had nursed Mainie, wrote also to Bay, saying what a trying time she had had and how brave she had been. 'I am sure Miss Jellett is praying for us – she was so good and patient – and had such a personal love for our dear Lord.' She was buried on the hillside at Howth, facing back towards the city of Dublin, to the intellectual and cultural life of which she had given so much. Her painting, *I Have Trodden the Wine Press Alone* (Pl. 244) might be considered, in its title and theme, a fitting epitaph for her life.

The obituary was combined with an appreciation by Thomas McGreevy, in the *Irish Times*, and was an unworthy tribute on the whole, emphasising Mainie as a theorist first, mentioning only two late religious works and giving no real picture of her life, her work and her contribution to Irish art.[5] An even briefer notice appeared in the *Irish Independent* above a review of the Dublin Painters' Group Exhibition, to which Mainie's own *Virgin of Eire* (Pl. 245) and *Madonna of Spring* (Pl. 224) had been sent. At its opening there had been a number of tributes to her, and it was decided to close it until lunch on the following day as a mark of respect.

The more serious tributes came later, as did the memorial exhibitions. Of these there were three, the first of which was at the Dublin Painters' Gallery, where her solo exhibitions had been held during her life. Victor Waddington also put on a show of gouache works in association with the Dublin Painters.[6] Later, the Irish Exhibition of Living Art, in its second year, was to include a small group of works as a tribute.

Many wrote about her. A common theme emerges of the lonely, austere, isolated woman who had a great capacity for friendship and affection, and who inspired such feelings in others. There is also a sense of deprivation in these tributes. Theodore Goodman, writing in the arts magazine, *Commentary*,[7] edited by Sean Dorman, to which Mainie had contributed, reflected sadly both the sense of personal and national loss. Those who had known her had enjoyed a privilege in her generous and distinguished personality:

It was sad to reflect that not only has Ireland lost a sincere and intelligent artist, but a teacher who is impossible to replace, a patron of every young artist who came to her for advice and assistance, and a cultured and sensitive woman who had genuine sympathy and interest not only in individual artists but with the general development of art.

Goodman referred to her 'tireless and thankless pioneer work' in making Cubism and modernism understood. Others felt and said the same.

'She was making an important contribution to the future of good painting in Ireland' Mairin Allen wrote in *The Standard*.[8] The Waddington memorial show recalled forcibly for this critic 'the principles for which this unusual Irish woman painter fought throughout her short but intensely creative life'. She had possessed the qualities of an ascetic and an idealist, had followed her own path, despite opposition and misunderstanding, and had reasserted many forgotten truths about painting. These had included 'the importance of mind over eye, or heart, or subconscious instinct, in the making of a picture.'

Some of her fellow-artists paid tribute to her in different ways. Paul Egestorff painted an abstract work, *To Mainie Jellett*. The same title was taken by Rákóczí for a poem:

> She was the body of the sacrifice.
> Her art, the vessel of an act of worship.
> Now –
> Softly folded are the skilled hands
> before the many forms of the Supreme.[9]

Some of the comment was more restrained, more cautious. Charles Sidney, writing in *The Bell*, voiced the view that Mainie Jellett's work was derivative.[10]

When the second Irish Exhibition of Living Art opened in mid-September Mainie Jellett's *Homage to Fra Angelico* was hung as a single memorial tribute – 'the centre of attraction' Stephen Rynne called it in *The Leader*[11] – and the committee announced a Mainie Jellett Memorial Scholarship which would allow young artists to travel. In pursuit of funding, three recitals were given in early October, in the National College of Art where the exhibition was hanging. Charles Lynch, a friend of Mainie's throughout her life, played, as did her sister, Bay, and a former pupil, Brian Boydell, whose own oboe quintet was one of the works performed.

In her article in *The Bell*, Elizabeth Bowen identified the intellectual emphasis which Mainie brought to painting as both a strength and a reason for the difficulties of misunderstanding which she faced.

> So it happened that Mainie Jellett brought back to her native city a dynamicism (sic) that at first, as she had expected, was found unfriendly, destructive, even repellent. She had gone so far as to go, it seemed, out of view. A mystique without the familiar softness, expressing itself in the ice of abstract terms, and the apparent subjugation of the soul to the intellect, took some accepting. A whole force of opinion clings strongly to the idea (or superstition) of art's *spontaneity*, and believes that in theory and discipline, past an accepted point, the artist can do himself nothing but injury. Such opinion she was very slowly and very quietly to confound. (Humanly she was of the type that obeys Christ's injunction to offend none of these little ones.) It became apparent that her spirit had only gained in fullness through its recognition of intellect. Her poetic spontaneity, her human apprehension of life round her, had been strong enough to 'take' the cold discipline.

On her deathbed, she told Babbin: 'You know, I have a wonderful picture in my mind, I wonder will I ever be able to paint it?' Perhaps in her mind she echoed the words she had used in a lecture, many years before, when she had invoked the thought of Titian, on his deathbed, suggesting, at the age of ninety-nine, that his work was just beginning. She had painted many wonderful pictures, yet the quest went on.

Mainie's impact on her time and generation was immense. Yet the scale of it, hard to measure when she was alive, is even more difficult to assess after her death. In international terms she is virtually unknown. Had she sought to pursue the life of a modernist painter in Paris from the time of her encounter with Gleizes for the rest of her life, she might have achieved a reputation there of some magnitude, though of course Gleizes' own views about such pursuits would have acted as a restraint. Instead, she returned to her own country, to challenge the conventional view of art which was essentially limited and cautious, and where the abstract paintings she produced were misunderstood and derided. Even then, her convictions were generalised, in favour of the modernist movement, rather than as a justification of her own work. This would speak for itself.

She created no Irish school of Cubist abstraction, and fostered no style in her pupils or followers. She had no desire to impose her thinking on others: powerfully convinced herself, she sought to make people think for themselves and thereby to liberate them. Education, for her, was a profound and subtle process of leading, encouraging, inspiring, provoking. Her paintings were her principal legacy. She had said, about the purpose of her work as an artist: 'The surface is my starting point. My aim is to make it live'. This was achieved, and her life will be judged by her works. She brought to paint and composition the pulse of an inner set of convictions, derived from the philosophic contemplation of fundamental artistic problems of meaning, form, colour, movement and rhythm. Her paintings sing with a joy in colour and form which is powerful and unique. Hers was a lonely profession, in which she bore an immense burden, strengthened by her faith, for which art was the supreme expression. She stands among the giant figures of Irish art in the twentieth century, as powerful in her impact as Jack Yeats or William Orpen, quite simply the greatest woman painter the country has ever produced.

CHAPTER ONE

1.   Family details come from surviving members of the Jellett family, or from the family archive of letters and documents. Unreferenced information and direct quotations throughout this book, either attributed to the artist, or about the artist, derive from this source. An account of the Jellett family, from its arrival in Ireland in the seventeenth century, may be found in *The Pooles of Mayfield And Other Irish Families*, by Rosemary ffolliott, Dublin, 1958, which gives two family trees, one from 1631 down to John Hewitt Jellett (1817–88), the other from 1855 to the present generation of the family. Details of the Stokes family may be found in *Burke's Irish Family Records*.

2.   Captain Henry Jellett was an officer in General Monck's army in Ireland who, with two colleagues, was given the task of demanding Monck's reasons for not signing the Solemn League and Covenant. His son, William, though born in England, married Katherine Morgan of Tullyard in County Down – the foundation of the Jellett family property. The Morgan name came down to Mainie's father.

3.   Morgan Jellett's first parish was Pallasgreen, in County Limerick, from where he moved to Tullycorbet in County Monaghan, in 1823.

4.   John Hewitt Jellett was born in 1817, was educated at Midleton College, County Cork, entered Trinity in 1833, was a scholar in 1836, and in 1840, at the age of twenty-three, was made a Fellow. He was Professor of Natural Philosophy and a noted mathematician, who published *An Elementary Treatise of the Calculus of Variations* (1850), and a book on the theory of friction. He took Orders in 1866, and on the death the following year of his fellow scientist, the astronomer the Earl of Rosse, who was also Chancellor of Dublin University, he preached on 'The Immortality of the Intellect'. Whether fortuitously or not, the sermon deals with ideas concerning the interrelationship of the religious and secular life which were to be of considerable importance to his grand-daughter.

5.   *Trinity College Dublin, 1592–1952 An Academic History*, by R.B. McDowell and D.A. Webb, Cambridge, 1952.

6.   R.B. McDowell, letter to the author, 1990.

7.   *William Stokes*, by Sir William Stokes, in the 'Masters of Medicine' Series, London, 1898.

8.   Ibid.

9.   Ibid.

10.   Ibid.

11.   Ibid.

CHAPTER TWO

1.   Hugh Lane (1875–1915) art dealer and Director of the National Gallery of Ireland. He was a friend of William Orpen, and nephew of Lady Gregory.

2.   Albert Power (1883–1945) Irish sculptor who modelled his work, in part, on the sculpture of Rodin. He worked in clay and stone, and did busts of several Jellett children, though not of Mainie herself.

3.   John Hughes (1865–1941) Irish sculptor and protégé of the painter, Sarah Purser.

4.   Yeats sisters: Susan Mary Yeats (1866–1949), known as 'Lily', and Elizabeth Corbet Yeats (1868–1940), known as 'Lolly', were the sisters of W.B. Yeats (1865–1939) and Jack Yeats (1871–1957). They ran the Dun Emer Press and the Cuala Press. E.C. Yeats wrote and illustrated *Brush Work* (London, 1896), *Brush Work Studies of Flowers, Fruit and Animals* (London, 1898) and a brushwork copy book.

5.   Elizabeth Bowen (1899–1973) novelist and short story writer. She spent her childhood in Dublin, and at her family house, Bowen's Court, in County Cork. She was a neighbour and friend of Mainie's.

6.   May Manning (d. 1930) Irish artist and teacher, who influenced a number of painters, including Mary Swanzy. She had a studio in Merrion Row, where Mainie took lessons.

7.   Douglas Hyde (1860–1949) writer and Gaelic scholar, he founded the Gaelic League, as a Gaelic language and culture organisation, but left it when it became political. He was the first President of Ireland.

CHAPTER THREE

1.   Elizabeth Bowen, *Seven Winters*, London, 1942. The Jellett governesses seem to have been made of sterner stuff than the Miss Wallis who ministered to Elizabeth Bowen's needs in Herbert Place, overacting 'the gravity of an adult', but boring Elizabeth Bowen as Elizabeth Bowen bored her.

2.   Mabel Länder studied with the legendary Theodore Leschetizky, pupil of Chopin. She taught all the Jellett children, and was active in Dublin until the end of the First World War. She moved to London, and later became piano teacher to the royal princesses, Elizabeth and Margaret.

3.   Norman Garstin (1842–1926) English painter, of the Newlyn School. He ran regular *plein air* schools for many years.

4.   William Orpen (1878–1931) Irish painter, born in Dublin, who became a fashionable and successful society portrait painter in London before the First World War. He was a war artist, much affected by what he saw in Flanders, and returned to a period of immense success in London before his death, in 1931, at the age of fifty-three. He was a great influence on art in Dublin from 1900 until the outbreak of war, and taught Mainie Jellett for a period of just over a year. See Bruce Arnold: *Orpen: Mirror to an Age*, London, 1981, for a fuller picture of Orpen's involvement in art education in Ireland.

5.   Sean Keating (1889–1978) Irish painter, born in Limerick, where he first studied art. He won a scholarship to the Metropolitan School of Art in Dublin, where he became one of Orpen's favoured pupils, and later his studio assistant in London. He returned to Ireland in 1916, became a teacher himself, and later President of the Royal Hibernian Academy (hereafter RHA).

6.   Leo Whelan (1892–1956) Irish painter, contemporary of Keating and Tuohy at the Metropolitan School of Art, and greatly influenced in his style by Orpen. He became a portrait painter in Dublin, with a studio in Baggot Street, exhibiting regularly with the RHA.

7.   Patrick Tuohy (1894–1930) Irish painter, born in Dublin, where he was a pupil of Patrick Pearse, who encouraged him to enrol at the Metropolitan School of Art. He became a favoured pupil of Orpen, who had a strong influence on his early painting, and a teacher at the school, but then moved to the United States. He took his own life in New York, at the early age of thirty-five.

CHAPTER FOUR

1.   Kathleen Fox (1880–1963) Irish artist, was a pupil and then assistant to William Orpen at the Metropolitan School of Art. She was a highly successful portrait painter, both in England and Ireland, but is best known for her flower studies.

2.   Harry Clarke (1889–1931) Irish stained-glass artist, and a student under Orpen at the Metropolitan School of Art. He was at the school for many years, both part-time and full-time, including the period when Mainie was a student there.

3.   Walter Osborne (1859–1903) Irish artist, and the son of the animal painter, William Osborne. He was an outstanding pupil at the RHA schools and then studied in Antwerp under Verlat. He became a significant influence on younger Irish artists, and was particularly noted for his studies of children.

4.   'Permit to Sketch: Permission is hereby granted to Miss M Jellett, 36 Fitzwilliam Square, W., Dublin, to Sketch within the prohibited area, but not within sight of Lough Swilly. 5.6.16' It was signed by the Lough Swilly Garrison Intelligence Officer.

5.   The General Post Office, in O'Connell Street, Dublin, was seized by the rebels and became their headquarters. Of the leaders of the 1916 Rising, both Padraig and Willie Pearse had been associated with the College, the latter applying unsuccessfully for a job there, and becoming a focus for strong nationalist feelings which were to prevail long after the tragic events of that week. Yet, broadly in line with the reaction of the country as a whole, students at the School of Art felt, in the words of Kathleen Fox, 'what an awful way the Irish have behaved'.

6.   Joseph Mary Plunkett (1887–1916) one of the signatories to the 1916 Declaration of Independence, and executed in that year. The day before his death, in Kilmainham Gaol, he married Grace Gifford.

7.   Grace Gifford (1888–1955) Irish artist and nationalist, best remembered for her stylish cartoons. She was a pupil at the Metropolitan School of Art, under Orpen, and was his model for *Young Ireland*.

8.   Orpen etching, *Abraham Sacrificing Isaac*, is illustrated in Arnold, *Orpen: Mirror to an Age*, p.52. The drawing for the etching is in the Victoria and Albert Museum, London.

9.   Walter Sickert (1860–1942) English painter, born in Munich of Danish and Anglo-Irish parentage, was a pupil of Whistler's. He worked with Edgar Degas in Paris.

10.   Henry Tonks (1862–1937) English painter and teacher at the Slade School of Art, in London. He stressed, virtually above all else, the importance of drawing.

11.   New English Art Club, an artists' society founded in London in 1886, in reaction against the conservative and complacent attitudes of the Royal Academy. Orpen exhibited with the NEAC, and George Moore, in his art criticism, was a supporter.

12.   Harold Gilman (1876–1919) English painter, founder of the Camden Town Group, and first president of the London Group. He belonged to Sickert's circle, and died in the influenza epidemic of 1919.

13.   John Nash (1893–1977) English painter and brother of Paul Nash, who painted landscapes and flower studies of exceptional beauty.

14.   Charles Ginner (1879–1952) English painter, born in Cannes, who studied in Paris and then settled in London in 1910. He is chiefly known for his urban scenes. He was one of Sickert's circle of friends and associates. He was a co-founder of the Camden Town Group.

15.   Paul Pissaro, French painter, son of Camille, brother of Lucien.

16.   William Rothenstein (1872–1945) English painter, writer and critic, who exhibited with the NEAC. He was a student at the Slade School of Art, and also at the Académie Julian. He was conservative in his views, and regarded pure abstraction as 'a cardinal heresy'.

17.   David Bomberg (1890–1957) English painter, born in Birmingham, studied at the Slade School of Art. He was associated with Wyndham Lewis's Vorticist Movement. He exhibited in the 'Cubist Room' at the Camden Town Group Exihibition in Brighton, in 1913–14. In 1914 he was a founding member of the London Group, with whom Mainie later exhibited. He is well known for his experiments in abstract painting, though he abandoned this.

18.   Percy Wyndham Lewis (1882–1957) English painter, novelist and critic. He studied at the Slade School of Art, and then worked in Munich. He was a founding member of the Camden Town Group, and of the London Group. He founded the Rebel Art Centre, from which the Vorticist Movement sprang. His experiments with abstraction were cut short by war service, which he served as a war artist.

19.   Roger Fry (1866–1934) English painter and critic, born in London, who became art critic of *The Athenaeum* from 1901, Director of the Metropolitan Museum of Art in New York, 1905–10, editor of *The Burlington Magazine*, and the organiser of the London Post-Impressionist Exhibitions in 1910 and 1912. He coined the term 'Post-Impressionism', in order to distinguish those he was most interested in, from the Neo-Impressionists, and in preference to the term 'Expressionism'.

20.   Camden Town Group, founded in 1911 by a group of Sickert's friends and followers. He suggested the name. Spencer Gore was the first president. Among the founder members was Walter Bayes, who taught Mainie at the Westminster School. See Chp. 5, n. 16.

21.   Omega Workshops, founded in 1913 by Roger Fry for the production of well-designed objects of daily use, instead of the pretentious and 'arty' artefacts which were then in fashion. Wyndham Lewis was also a member, but fell out with Fry, and left the group.

22.   *Blast*, the periodical of the Vorticist Movement. Its two numbers were published in June 1914, and July 1915. They were edited by Wyndham Lewis.

23.   Ursula Tyrrwhitt, English artist, student at the Slade School of Art, and model for both Orpen and John.

24.   Ida Nettleship, English artist, student at the Slade School of Art, and model for both Orpen and John.

CHAPTER FIVE

1.   'My Voyage of Discovery', from *Mainie Jellett: The Artist's Vision: Lectures and Essays on Art*, by Eileen MacCarvill, Dundalk, 1958 (hereafter MacCarvill, *Mainie Jellett*). The essay about her development as an artist was first published in *Irish Art Handbook*, Dublin, 1943, as 'An Approach to Painting'. The text used here is the manuscript version, which is entitled 'Definition of My Art'.

2.   Alphonse Legros (1837–1911) French artist who studied and worked in Paris, then came to England at Whistler's suggestion, in 1863, and settled. He was Slade Professor (1875–92).

3.   James Abbott McNeill Whistler (1834–1903) American painter, educated at West Point Military Academy, and then studied art in Paris, under Gleyre. He moved to London in 1859 and eventually settled in Chelsea. He was a major influence among English painters, and an inspiration to NEAC artists.

4.   Edgar Degas (1834–1917) French painter, born in Paris, and a major influence on Sickert.

5.   Spencer Frederick Gore (1878–1914) English painter, born in Epsom, and, like Orpen, a student of Fred Brown, Wilson Steer and Henry Tonks at the Slade School of Art. Friend and associate of Gilman and Sickert. Wyndham Lewis greatly admired his theatre paintings.

6.   Walter Bayes (1869–1956) English painter and much admired teacher, born in London, and both a student and teacher at the Westminister Art School, of which he became principal (1919–34). He was a member of the Camden Town Group. Mainie was his pupil at the Slade, and did a portrait of him (Pl. 35).

7.   Evie Hone (1894–1955) Irish painter and stained-glass artist. She was born on 22 April 1894, three years before Mainie. Her father was a maltster, banker and a successful businessman in Dublin who had served a term as Governor of the Bank of Ireland. Her mother died when she was born, and her father died in 1908, when she was fourteen. She contracted polio at this time. Like Mainie, she was one of four sisters, and by the time Mainie met her the other three sisters were married, all to British Army officers, and all to be widowed during the course of the First World War.

Since the eighteenth century Hones had been important figures in Irish painting. Among them was Nathaniel Hone the Elder, a founder member of the Royal Academy in London, and a great rival of Joshua Reynolds, whom he repeatedly assailed and lampooned, most notably in *The Conjuror* (National Gallery of Ireland), which created a scandal when it appeared in the RA exhibition in 1775, and was removed because of the offence to Reynolds and the supposedly indecent caricature of Angelica Kauffmann. Nathaniel's brother was a minor painter, and two of his sons, John Camillus and Horace, were fine miniaturists and portraitists. A dominant figure for their own generation, however, was Evie's distant cousin, Nathaniel Hone the Younger, born in 1831, who was still alive when Mainie and Evie met, and died only on 14 October 1917.

8.   The Byam Shaw School of Art, in Campden Street, Kensington, was started by the artist, Byam Shaw, before the First World War. It was then that Evie Hone went there and first met Winifred Nicholson, who was a pupil with her. Later, when Winifred Nicholson and her husband, Ben Nicholson, passed through Paris on their way to and from Lugano, they used to stay with Evie. She recalls Evie and Ben talking of 'squares and rectangles, and of this dawn of art which was discovering the potency of shapes, and their relationships in space when nothing but shape alone was contemplated'.

9.   Bernard Meninsky (1891–1950) English painter and draughtsman, who studied first at the Liverpool School of Art before moving to Paris. He was at the Slade School of Art in 1912, and later worked in Florence, teaching drawing and stage design. He taught in London, exhibiting with the London Group, and was then a war artist, before succeeding Sickert at the Westminster School.

10.   André Lhote (1885–1962) French painter and teacher, born in Bordeaux. His early interest in negro sculpture and the paintings of Gauguin directed him toward Cubism. He became a teacher and major influence on younger artists, forming his own atelier in 1922, though before then he ran a teaching studio at which both Mainie and Evie were students.

11.   Académie Julian, founded in 1868 by Rodolphe Julian. There was a strong emphasis on drawing. George Moore was a student in the 1870s. Many Irish artists attended (Sarah Purser, Henry Jones Thaddeus, John Lavery, Dermod O'Brien, Paul Henry, William John Leech).

12.   Edward Gordon Craig (1872–1966) English theatrical designer, and son of Ellen Terry. He is remembered as a pioneer of 'Luminism' and 'Kinetic Art'.

13.   The Central School of Arts and Crafts came under the London County Council. An early head of the school, William Richard Lethaby, had turned it into the first English art school based on craft training.

14.   Mervyn Lawrence (1868–?) Dublin-born painter and sculptor who taught at the Westminster School, and was a friend of Mainie's. He painted and modelled portraits, and did landscapes.

15.   Mia Cranwill (1880–1972) Irish craftworker in metal, she trained in Manchester and showed enamel-ware and jewellery in Dublin, becoming the most impressive of workers in the Arts and Crafts movement.

16.   London Group, an exhibiting association of English artists, which, between 1913–14 gathered under its wing most of the prominent small groups of younger artists outside the Royal Academy and the NEAC, but including the Camden Town Group. The London Group continued its exhibitions throughout the 1920–40 period, and it was at this stage that Mainie showed with the group.

17.   Fred Brown (1851–1941) English painter who studied in France and became a founding member of the NEAC in 1886. He was responsible for the rules of the club, and campaigned against the conservatism of the RA. He taught at the Westminster School (1877–92) and then became Professor at the Slade School of Art.

CHAPTER SIX

1.   The Taylor Art competitions and prizes were the most significant of their kind in Ireland. Captain George Archibald Taylor, who had died in 1860, had left an endowment for several money prizes and a scholarship. The Royal Dublin Society which administered the judging and the awards, nominated one of the judges, the other two being nominated by the RHA and the Governors and Guardians of the National Gallery of Ireland.

2.   Dermod O'Brien (1865–1945) Irish painter and, from 1910, President of the RHA. He studied in Paris, at the Académie Julian, and then returned to Dublin where he regularly exhibited work, mainly landscapes. He was a generous supporter of younger artists.

3.   Sarah Purser (1848–1943) Irish artist and a noted figure in the art world. She was responsible for the joint Nathaniel Hone-John Butler Yeats exhibition, in 1901, visited by Hugh Lane, who decided to shift his interest to modern art. She also founded An Túr Gloine (the Tower of Glass), the stained-glass studio in 1903, at the suggestion of

Edward Martyn, and the Friends of the National Collections of Ireland in 1924.

4. Eamon de Valera (1882–1975) one of the 1916 leaders, who, on account of his American citizenship, escaped execution. He led the Anti-Treaty side in the Civil War, but later entered the Dáil as leader of the Fianna Fáil Party, and became Taoiseach (prime minister) in a number of administrations between 1932 and 1959, when he became President of Ireland.

5. Lord Midleton (1856–1942) Unionist leader in the Republic, and an associate of William Morgan Jellett's during the period before the independence of the State.

6. Lloyd George (1863–1945) British Prime Minister during and immediately after the First World War.

7. This led to the introduction of the 'Black and Tans' and the Auxiliaries under General Sir Henry Tudor.

8. Ralph Cusack (1912–65) Irish artist and writer, he was related to Mainie, and became a follower and friend. He exhibited with the White Stag Group.

9. Jack Yeats (1871–1957) Irish artist and writer, son of the portrait painter, John Butler Yeats, and brother of the poet, and of the two sisters who ran the Cuala Press. Regular exhibitor with the RHA and with other groups, including the Irish Exhibition of Living Art.

10. Lilian Davidson (d. 1954) Irish artist, born in Wicklow, who studied at the Dublin Metropolitan School of Art, and exhibited at the RHA throughout her life. She was a friend of Mainie's and also of Pat Wallace, Stella Frost and Lily Williams. She painted portraits of J.J. Holloway and of Jack Yeats, whom she admired.

11. Advertised in *The Irish Times* on 12 October 1920, it ran from the 15th to the 23rd, at Mills's Hall, in Merrion Row, Dublin. It included some of the fruits of her studies at the Westminster School.

CHAPTER SEVEN

1. Roderic O'Conor (1860–1940) Irish painter, born in Roscommon but moved to Dublin where he studied at the Metropolitan School of Art, and the RHA schools. He studied also under Carolus-Duran in Paris. He worked at Pont-Aven with Gauguin, and exhibited regularly in Paris, his influence in Ireland becoming limited in later years.

2. Daniel Kahnweiler (1884–1976) a German-French art dealer and writer. In 1907 he opened a gallery in Paris, and dealt in works by the Fauves, particularly Derain and Vlaminck. He was chiefly known as the friend and promoter of the Cubists and though this refers almost exclusively to Braque and Picasso, he also supported Gris.

3. Albert Gleizes (1881–1953) French Cubist painter who became the founder of the Cubist-Abstract School, and a lifelong friend and associate of Mainie Jellett.

4. Though the subject of Cubism and its literature is vast, and publication on it extensive, remarkably little has been written about abstract Cubist painting, or the School of Albert Gleizes.

5. Lhote did not set up his own Academie Montparnasse until 1922, but was independently teaching art before that, his studio being referred to as 'Lhote's Academy' (by, among others, Evie Hone).

6. Mainie Jellett, lecture on André Lhote, November 1940. The lecture was given at the Contemporary Pictures Gallery, 133 Lower Baggot Street, during the exhibition, 'Six Irish Artists who have studied at L'Academie Lhote'.

CHAPTER EIGHT

1. Galerie de l'Effort Moderne, started by Léonce Rosenberg. The Purists joined it in 1921. Lhote had left, not liking the direction in which it was moving.

2. See: Albert Gleizes to Mme Gleizes, *Les Méjades*, undated; Gleizes MSS, Aubard, F/XYZ. The letter is a critique of the catalogue of the exhibition, *Le Cubisme, 1907–1914*, Musée Nationale d'Art Moderne, January to April, 1953 (Preface by Jean Cassou).

3 The term 'Epic Cubism' has been used by the American historian, Daniel Robbins.

4. *Du Cubisme*, by Albert Gleizes and Jean Metzinger, first published in 1912, went through at least seven editions in that year. A copy of the seventh edition was bought for Mainie on a visit to Paris by her mother, in March 1923. It was extensively read and annotated, falling to pieces in the process.

5. For a discussion of these New York paintings see Robert Rosenblum, *Cubism and Twentieth Century Art*, New York, 1976, p. 182.

6. *Du Cubisme et les moyens de le comprendre*, Paris, 1920.

7. Hélène de St Pierre, later Hélène O'Shaughnessy, French artist who settled in Dublin and became a pupil of Mainie's in 1940.

8. For Gleizes on Metzinger and Gris, see 'Spiritualité, rythme, forme' in Albert Gleizes, *Puissances du Cubisme*, Chambéry, 1969, p. 338.

9. For Gleizes' ideas on mass-produced paintings, and Léger's interest, see Christopher Green, *Léger and the avant garde*, New Haven and London, 1976, p. 245, and Christopher Green, *Cubism and Its Enemies*, New Haven and London, 1987, p. 147 (where Mme Gleizes is given as the source).

10. Gleizes, *Du Cubisme et les moyens de le comprendre*.

11. Ibid.

12. Ibid.

13. Léonce Rosenberg to Albert Gleizes, 15 October 1934 and 16 November 1934, Gleizes MSS, Aubard, F/ROS.

14. One simple theory, common among researchers in the period, is that André Lhote sent them both to Gleizes. Yet Gleizes' own account of Mainie and Evie coming to him (see MacCarvill, *Mainie Jellett*) would tend to discount this, since Gleizes feared that he would offend his own former friend by taking on his pupils. At the same time, according to Christopher Green, in *Cubism and Its Enemies*, Lhote, who had supported Gleizes in 1919, now, in 1921, saw him as the leader of a hostile tendency.

15. Anne Dangar (d. 1951) Australian artist who studied under André Lhote and then returned to France in 1930 to work at Moly-Sabata, with Gleizes. She became a potter, and the central figure in the community. See Chapter 14.

16. Moly-Sabata Archive, at Ampuis. She presumably refers to the *Book of Durrow*, and possibly also to the somewhat later *Book of Kells*. Mainie would have been directly familiar with both of these, as well as knowing them through the work of her great-aunt, the Celtic scholar Margaret Stokes.

17. Gleizes to André Lhote, 23 September 1943, Gleizes MSS, Aubard, F/LHO. Gleizes later marvelled at his own audacious showing of the works. 'I dared show, exhibit, the poor efforts which, for all that they were sincere, could neither attract sympathy, nor excite any intellectual interest in the world about me. I was made thoroughly aware of the fact. Only faith kept me going.'

CHAPTER NINE

1. MacCarvill, *Mainie Jellett*.

2. Ibid.

3. Ibid.

4. 'A Definition of My Art', by Mainie Jellett.

5. MacCarvill, *Mainie Jellett*.

6. Ibid.

7. Hélène de St Pierre, interview with the author, summer 1990.

8. Albert Gleizes, *Art et religion*, Chambéry, 1970, p. 15. *Art et religion* was originally a lecture, delivered as part of a series, in March 1931, in Paris, and in April 1932 in Dresden.

9. Albert Gleizes, *Kubismus*, Munich, 1928.

10. Robert Pouyaud (1900–79) French artist, joined Gleizes, Mainie and Evie in November 1924, and remained with these artists until the end of the 1930s. He was instructed in translation and rotation by Mainie. In 1927 he was the founding figure of Moly-Sabata. See Chp. 14.

11. Yanaga Posnansky, a pupil of Gleizes from 1922 or 1923. Though not mentioned by Mainie in any correspondence, Mme Gleizes claims, in her *Memoires*, 'including Jellett and Hone, and two other pupils of Gleizes, Yanaga Posnansky, who had been with them from the start, and Robert Pouyaud, who joined them in 1924 ...' In fact, Posnansky, a Polish banker living in Paris, who heard of Gleizes' acceptance of Mainie and Evie as pupils, asked if he could join the group.

12. MacCarvill, *Mainie Jellett*.

13. Ibid.

14. Ibid.

15. Robert Langton Douglas (1864–1951) Director of the National Gallery of Ireland from 1916–23. He was educated at New College, Oxford, and ordained into the Church of England. He left the Church in 1900. He published *A History of Siena*, London, 1902, and co-edited *A History of Italian Painting*. In 1902 he became an art dealer, and during his term of office bought some good pictures from himself. He fought with Thomas Bodkin, who sought at one stage to have him imprisoned.

16. Thomas Bodkin (1887–1961) had a distinguished career at Belvedere, Clongowes, and what was then the Royal University. He was called to the Bar in 1911 and practised as a barrister until 1916. The following year he had published his first book, *May it Please Your Lordships*, and was by way of becoming a poet, writer and critic on the fringes of the literary establishment. He was Director of the National Gallery of Ireland, and then (1935–52) of the Barber Institute of Fine Art in Birmingham.

17. See Nicola Gordon-Bowe, *The Life and Work of Harry Clarke*, Dublin, 1989, for an examination of the rivalry between the two stained glass establishments in Dublin.

18. MacCarvill, *Mainie Jellett*.

19. Jellett family papers.

20. Colette Allendy was the daughter of René Allende, a Scottish doctor practising homeopathic medicine in Paris, who became one of the first champions of Freudian psychoanalysis in France. He also wrote for *L'Esprit Nouveau* and *La Vie des lettres et des arts*. He was a defender of modern painting. He had been present on the memorable occasion when Mainie and Evie persuaded Gleizes to take them as pupils. They asked if he would take their daughter as a pupil. Colette Allendy later started an art gallery in Paris, the Colette Allendy Gallery, dealing in modern works.

21. Jellett family papers.

22. Ibid.

23. Ibid.

24. Eileen Gray came from the same Anglo-Irish background as the Jelletts and Hones. She was of William Orpen's generation and had been at the Slade School of Art shortly after him. She lived in London during that intensely rich period when the presence and influence of Orpen, Augustus John, Frederick Spencer Gore, William Rothenstein and many others who had been pupils of Henry Tonks and Philip Wilson Steer set a standard of excellence mixed with vitality, irreverence and intellectual excitement unparalleled in later years.

25. Kate Weatherby, who was English, and the daughter of a wealthy brewer, was always on the lookout for ways in which she could help her friend, Eileen Gray, whom she had known since 1907 when she had first come to Paris to study art. She was an independent and emancipated woman. She had come to Paris in the company of a young student of the Royal College of Music, the cellist Evelyn Wyld. Kate Weatherby was a great initiator of projects, 'a breath of fresh air' was how Eileen Gray described her. She had been responsible for several of the developments and departures in Eileen Gray's increasingly successful career as a designer.

26. Jellett family papers.

27. Ibid.

28. Ibid.

29. Ibid.

30. Ibid.

CHAPTER TEN

1. *Le Cubisme et la tradition*, Albert Gleizes, Paris, 1913.

2. Albert Gleizes and Jean Metzinger, *Du Cubisme*, Paris, Figuière, 1912.

3. Ibid.

4. Walter Firpo (b. 1900) American painter and follower of Albert Gleizes, who has spent his life in Paris painting abstract Cubism.

5. Frantisek Kupka (1871–1957) Czech painter. He was interested in spiritualism and the occult throughout his life. Became interested in folk art early in his life. Studied in Kunstegewerbeschule at Jaromer, under Alois Studnicka. A year later entered the Prague Academy. After settling in Paris in 1896, he became associated with the Cubists. His inspiration and motivation were different from theirs, and he always emphasised the difference. He was one of the earliest in Europe to investigate and exploit the spiritual symbolism inherent in abstract colour and shape. He joined Abstraction-Création in 1931.

6. Robert Delaunay (1885–1941) was born in Paris. About 1906 he became interested in Neo-Impressionism, and embarked upon the researches into the aesthetic applications of colour, which remained the central motif throughout his life. He associated with the Cubist movement, and exhibited with them at the Salons des Indépendants in 1911 and 1912. In 1910 he married Sonia Terk. In 1912–13 he produced his series of *Disques* and *Formes circulaires cosmiques*. These works gave rise to the movement of 'colour Cubism' which Apollinaire named 'Orphism'. Together with the work of Kupka, these were the earliest genuine colour abstracts in European art.

7. Sonia Delaunay (1885–1979) French artist, born in the Ukraine, studied drawing at Karlsruhe under Schmidt-Reutter. She moved to Paris in 1905, and studied at the Academie de la Palette. Associated with Delaunay in the founding of Orphism. Her fabrics were exhibited at the Art Deco Exhibition of 1925. In 1931 she became a member of Abstraction-Création.

8. *Der Weg Zum Kubismus*, Daniel Kahnweiler, Munich, 1920.

9. Albert Gleizes, *Puissances du Cubisme*, Paris, 1965.

10. Douglas Cooper, *The Essential Cubism*, London, 1983.

11. Albert Gleizes, 'L'Art moderne et la société nouvelle' (1923) in *Tradition et Cubisme*, Paris, 1927, p 149.

12. Ibid.

CHAPTER ELEVEN

1. Salon des Indépendants, founded by the Société des Artistes Indépendants in 1884, from which date it held regular exhibitions, with members free to show without a selection committee. This arrangement lasted until the First World War. Mainie exhibited from 1923.

2. Recorded discussions between Bay Jellett and Dr Michael Solomons, 1981.

3. The Society of Dublin Painters (1920–49) had been formed in 1920, principally by Paul and Grace Henry, as a more modern alternative for young artists who wanted a venue for exhibitions which was more adventurous than the Academy. They had a studio and exhibition room at 7 St Stephen's Green where Mary Swanzy seems to have been an active figure to begin with, showing her paintings in 1920, 1921 and 1922. Each member was entitled to a single-person exhibition each year, and of course to participation in group exhibitions. To begin with membership was limited to ten; it later increased to twenty, half of whom were women.

4. Letitia Hamilton (1878–1964) Irish artist and founder-member of the Society of Dublin Painters. She was a pupil at Alexandra College, and then at the Metropolitan School of Art, under William Orpen. She travelled on the continent, and was also a pupil of Frank Brangwyn.

5. Eva Hamilton (1876–1960) Irish artist, and elder sister of Letitia, with whom she studied at the Metropolitan School of Art, coming much under Orpen's influence. She was mainly a portrait painter.

6. Grace Henry (1868–1953) Irish artist, and one of the founder-members of the Society of Dublin Painters. She came from Scotland, and was one of ten children of a Church of Scotland minister, John Mitchell, whose wife was related to Byron. She was married to Paul Henry, from whom she subsequently separated.

7. Harriet Kirkwood (1880–1953) was a Jameson, and married a director of the Irish whisky distilling firm, a Major Thomas Kirkwood. She was president of the Society of Dublin Painters. She was much influenced by Mainie.

8. Paul Henry (1876–1958) Irish artist and founder of the Society of Dublin Painters. He was a landscape painter, much of whose work was done in the west of Ireland. He separated from his wife, Grace Henry, also a painter, and lived with Mabel Young, herself a painter.

9. Charles Lamb (1893–1965) Irish artist who painted in the west of Ireland, and eventually settled there. His work is mainly in genre scenes and landscapes. His early paintings, done in France, are among his finest works.

10. William Conor (1881–1968) Irish artist, who painted genre and urban scenes, principally in Belfast, his native city.

11. Edward O'Rourke Dickey (1894–1977) Irish artist, and member of the Society of Dublin Painters.

12. Mary Swanzy (1882–1978) Irish artist, who studied first at May Manning's studio, then went on to study modelling with John Hughes, before departing for Paris, around 1906. She was an admirer of William Orpen. She painted subsequently in Czechoslovakia and Samoa, and exhibited her work with the Society of Dublin Painters.

13. Jack Yeats (1871–1957) (see Chp. 6).

14. United Arts Club Post-Impressionist Show. The exhibition was organised by Mrs Ellen Duncan. Though there is no record of the association with Roger Fry's exhibitions in 1910 and 1911, Ellen Duncan did contribute to the Burlington Magazine, of which he was editor. The exhibition opened on 22 January 1911. W.B. Yeats was an enthusiastic visitor; George Russell an unenthusiastic one who felt that the lover of art would regard the painters represented, not as 'decadent, but merely decrepit . . . what no person should tolerate is the art which is lifeless, which is not even debauched, but is merely stupid; for so the greater part of these pictures appear to me.'

15. Dublin Arts Week, a cultural festival held in the city that year and not repeated again in the same form.

16. See n.15 above.

17. Review in *The Irish Times*, signed by the paper's art critic, 'A.D.', Saturday, 20 October 1923. The group exhibition had its private view the previous evening.

18. *The Irish Times*, 23 October 1923.

19. *Irish Statesman*, 27 October 1923. George Russell (1867–1935) Irish painter, writer and philosopher, was first editor of *Homestead*, which then became the *Irish Statesman*. He was better known as *Æ*, under which pseudonym much of his work was published, though for his art criticism he used the initials 'Y.O.'

20. Maude Ball was a family friend who always helped Mainic with the hanging of her exhibitions. She was responsible for organising the response to the attacks against Mainie's first abstract works.

21. *The Irish Times*, 24 October 1923.

22. Maude Ball also sent the review, her letter, and the photographs of the painting and the onion, with a draft of the *Irish Statesman* letter, to Dorothy Fitzgerald, for further consultation. She was an artist and a relation of Mainie's. 'She is delighted', Maude Ball reported to Mainie, 'I must keep her up in the progress of the fight. She has such a good thinking brain . . . she was reading Einstein some time ago, but I haven't heard what she made of him.'

23. *Irish Statesman*, 10 November 1923

24. Thomas MacGreevy later to become Director of the National Gallery.

25. *The Klaxon* was a short-lived Dublin quarterly. The issue dated from 1923.

26. Socrates, *Philebus*.

CHAPTER TWELVE

1. Cecil French Salkeld (d. 1969) Irish artist who was Mainie's and Evie's closest associate at the time, in terms of his style. Salkeld was then painting remarkably advanced work, much of it owing a debt to his close, if brief involvement with the German Neue Sachlichkeit movement, at the beginning of the 1920s.

2. *The Irish Times*, 10 February 1924.

3. *Irish Statesman*, 16 February 1924.

4. Eugene Delacroix (1798–1863), *Journal*.

5. Joshua Reynolds (1723–92). The quotations were taken from the XVIIIth Discourse: 'Painting is not only to be considered as an imitation, operating by deception, but it is, and ought to be, in many points of view, and, strictly speaking, no imitation at all of external nature.' 'Our elements are laid in gross common nature – an exact imitation of what is before us: but when we advance to the higher state, we consider this power of imitation, though first in the order of acquisition, as by no means the highest in the scale of perfection.' 'I think, therefore, the true test of all the arts is not solely whether the production is a true copy of nature, but whether it answers the end of art, which is, to produce a pleasing effect upon the mind.' (As quoted in catalogue.)

6. *Freeman's Journal*, 12 June 1924.

7. Ibid, 20 October 1923.

8. *The Dublin Magazine*, Vol. II, Number 1, August 1924, 'Notes of the Month'.

9. Ibid.

10. Ibid.

11. Now in the Hugh Lane Municipal Art Gallery, Dublin.

12. Now in the City Art Gallery, Manchester.

13. *Irish Statesman*, 16 August 1924.

14. The *Sunday Times*, 7 June 1925.

15. See Christopher Green, *Cubism and Its Enemies*, p. 92.

16. *Paris Midi*, 9 January 1925.

17. *The Paris Times*, January 1925.
18. Waldemar George, *Paris-Journal*, 16 January 1925.
19. *Irish Statesman*, 20 June 1925.
20. *Irish Independent*, 9 June 1925.
21. *The Irish Times*, 9 June 1925.
22. Letter from Mainie Jellett to Albert Gleizes, Gleizes Archives at the Pompidou Centre, Paris. A substantial body of correspondence between Mainie Jellett and Albert Gleizes, with other letters from Evie Hone to Gleizes, was bequeathed by Madame Gleizes to the French Nation on her death. Unless otherwise indicated, all references to letters from Mainie to Albert Gleizes are from this source, and will not be footnoted. She always addressed him in her letters as Monsieur Gleizes, signing herself 'Mainie'. He always wrote to her as 'Chère Mainie'.
23. It was the ninth exhibition of the 'Seven and Five' group, quite wide in its representation – George Clausen, Munnings, Philip Connard and Algernon Talmage were all involved – but with a section of Cubist work which expressed a major part of the inner strength of the group. Seven painters and five sculptors had been responsible for its foundation, some six years earlier, and by the time Mainie first showed it had a membership of twenty-one. The *Sunday Times* reviewer of 24 January, in praising Claude Flight as an exemplar of the society's experimental and Futurist endeavours, wrote of 'the tendency of the society as a body' being 'towards the abstract in art, its individual members having adopted the view that the interest in a picture is not to be centred in the representation of nature, but in the expression of the artist's mental conception.'
24. The Dublin Literary Society included among its members the poet Austin Clarke. Mainie later collaborated with him in the illustration of one of his poems published by the Gaisford Press.
25. Desmond FitzGerald (1888–1947) Irish Foreign Minister. He held office in the first, post-Treaty administration. He was a good friend of Sarah Purser. His son, Garret FitzGerald, became Irish Prime Minister in 1981.
26. Daniel Egan's Salon ran for a short time at 38 St Stephens Green, with a wide range of exhibitions. Mainie lectured there.
27. *Evening Mail*, 23 January 1926.
28. The lecture in full was subsequently published. The emphasis placed on this and other phrases is as Mainie indicated in that published text.
29. Ibid.
30. P. J. Konody in *The Observer*, 6 June 1926.
31. Clive Bell (1881–1964) English art critic.
32. Roger Fry, see n. 19, Chp. 4 above.
33. Gleizes proposed an *International Magazine for Abstract Art*. It would only have artists writing.
34. Frank Rutter, who had been *The Sunday Times* critic since 1903, was in no sense attuned to what Gleizes and Jellett were trying to do. But he was a powerful critical voice. He had published that year (1926) *Evolution in Modern Art: a Sudy of Modern Painting 1870–1925*, and Mainie undertook to get a copy for Gleizes.
35. *Vie et Mort de l'Occident Chrétien*, Sablons, Moly-Sabata, 1930. First published in 1928–29 in *Cahiers d'Étoile*.

CHAPTER THIRTEEN

1. Daniel Corkery, *The Hidden Ireland*, Dublin. Daniel Corkery was a writer and teacher from Cork.
2. *The Irish Times*, 8 January 1927.
3. *Irish Independent*, 8 January 1927.
4. *Irish Statesman*, 15 January 1927. It was signed 'Y.O.', Russell's usual pseudonym for art criticisms.
5. The lecture was given on 2 February, 1927, in the Mills Hall, in Merrion Row, before what *The Irish Times* described as 'quite a large audience'. It was titled 'Modern Painting and Some of Its Aspects', and was subsequently published (MacCarvill, *Mainie Jellett*, p. 77).
6. The letter, in the Jellett family archive, is dated 25 March.
7. *The Irish Times*, 3 February 1927.
8. See Albert Gleizes, 'Peinture et Perspective Descriptive', Sablons, Moly-Sabata, 1927; published in Gleizes, *Puissances du Cubisme*.
9. Letter to the author, 1990
10. This is the first record of Mainie travelling to visit Gleizes in his house at Serrières on the Rhone. Though Mme Gleizes came from Serrières, and there was a family home there, Mainie and Evie always worked in the early 1920s in the studio at Puteaux. As well as their home at Cavalaire, Gleizes and his wife also had property in Serrières, on the west bank of the Rhône, 60 kilometres south of Lyon, 'une maison ou nous passons l'automne'. In the 1930s they bought Les Méjades, a house with some land on the outskirts of the small market town of St Remy, in Provence with the idea of turning it into a community of kindred spirits. 'We bought a large property in Provence, thinking it would be easy to turn urban intellectuals into intelligent farmers. Alas! we were soon disenchanted when we were faced with the practical realities. It is certainly possible, but it can't be done all in one go. So we have to envisage a certain delay.' Gleizes did not actually live in Les Méjades until 1939.
11. The Fianna Fáil Party, known also as the Republican Party, opposed the Treaty, on the grounds that it did not go far enough. They fought and lost in the Civil War which followed, and remained outside constitutional politics during the first five years of the State's existence, part of their objection being the requirement on all public representatives to make a declaration of allegiance to the British Crown.
12. *Irish Statesman*, 25 June 1927.
13. Gleizes, *Tradition et Cubisme*. Gleizes' own selection of essays and articles published between 1912 and 1924.
14. The community at Moly-Sabata, a full account of which appears in Chp. 14, was the subject of considerable debate during 1927, and was eventually set up in the autumn by Robert Pouyaud.

CHAPTER FOURTEEN

1. See George Russell, *Irish Statesman*, 16 June 1928; see also *The Irish Times*, Tuesday 19 November 1929: 'Whatever may be thought of the cubist designs of the painting there can be no questioning the beautiful effect which has been achieved by the use of cubistic designs for carpets and rugs ... In this form of decorative art certainly there is a deal to be said for cubism.' The design and sale of rugs and carpets went on until the mid-1930s. They were sold in The Country Shop, in St Stephen's Green, run by Muriel Gahan, who was also one of the women who made up the rugs to Mainie's designs. She exhibited works by Mainie Jellett and other 'modernist' artists at this time.
2. The Cuala Press had extended its activities, and held regular 'at homes' at which craftware was displayed and sold. The Jellett family were regularly invited, and Mrs Jellett was a dedicated supporter.
3. It was an intense but short-lived experiment. The community, which consisted of Gleizes, several writers (Charles Vildrac, Georges Duhamel, René Arcos, Henri-Martin-Barzun), the musician Albert Doyen and the printer, Lucien Linard, hoped to pay for their communal venture by undertaking fine printing. Among the books they published was Jules Romains' highly influential *La Vie Unanime*, which is important for understanding the intellectual atmosphere in which Cubism was launched. Their patrons included Robert de Montesquieu, Charlus in Proust's *Remembrance of Things Past* (Mme Gleizes was a close friend of the Comtesse de Greffühle, Mme de Guermantes in Proust's novel, and thought that both she and Robert de Montesquieu were unfairly portrayed by Proust). First thoughts on it dated from a meeting in Vildrac's house in December 1905. The premises at Créteil were found on 1 November 1906. By February 1908 the project was abandoned. The participants called themselves *La Ligue des Arts Indépendants*, and wrote a manifesto: 'We want to remain individually masters of our own thoughts, and of their ideas, while enjoying the benefits of an effective solidarity. We will help each other in the realisation of our respective arts . . . and in this way we will enter on the great collective path which will stand against all attacks made on aesthetic values.' Owen Sheehy Skeffington (1909–70) Irish politician and academic, who became a lecturer in French at Dublin University, planned his doctoral thesis on l'Abbaye de Créteil at about this time (c.1930).
4. See Anne Dangar MSS, Moly-Sabata Archive at Ampuis, her notes for a course given at Moly in 1949; see also André Dubois, *Anne Dangar et Moly-Sabata, les sources chez Albert Gleizes*, unpublished MA thesis (Université de Lyon) 1971.
5. Robert Pouyaud, *Moly-Sabata*, Clamency, 1955. Pouyaud's essay, part of a collection which included memoires from César Geoffray, Lucie Deveyle, Anne Dangar, was published under the auspices of the Sociétés des Amis d'Albert Gleizes, Mainie Jellett, Anne Dangar and Evie Hone, who died in that year.
6. Ibid.
7. Ibid.
8. Dobo appears briefly in the Moly-Sabata story. He was a Rumanian poet who arrived at the same time as the floods, in the winter of 1927. Pouyaud described him as droll, and he became popular with the villagers in Sablon. Then he vanished, and was never heard of again. See Pouyaud, *Moly-Sabata*.
9. *Pochoirs* are stencils, usually cut in zinc plates. Each plate coresponds to a colour which is painted over it with a brush. The technique had traditionally been used for the manufacture of playing cards, and was doubtless what Gleizes had in mind when he envisaged the 'mass production' of pictures back in 1921. While slower and more demanding than more modern artistic means, such as *sériegraphe* or screen print techniques, it allows for a more precise and lively use of colour. Pouyaud's *pochoirs* were masterpieces of the genre. Many of the zinc plates used at Moly still survive, together with trial runs annotated by Gleizes which show how much attention was paid to getting the colour harmonies exactly right.
10. A series of popular artistic festivals which had been initiated by Albert Doyen, Gleizes' old colleague from the days of the Abbaye de Créteil.
11. The rules at Moly covered cooking, housework, gardening, caring for the livestock, collecting fuel, repairs to the buildings, and those activities which were designed to earn income, such as the making of *pochoirs*. Duties were divided between men and women along conventional lines, and there was a careful outline of the regulation of expenditure and the earning both of community and personal income. Free-time private enterprise, through painting or writing or other activity, was in no sense frowned upon. There were special regulations for children, new members and guests.
12. I am indebted to Peter Brooke for these details about

how Anne Dangar came to Moly-Sabata.

13.   César Geoffray and his wife Mido were pioneers of popular choral singing, creating a tradition of it throughout France which still survives under the name Geoffray gave it, *A Cœur Joie*. In 1990, their daughter, Gilka, was living at Moly, painting and in the process of restoring a measure of 'community' life. She reflected the same joyous attitude to the arts as her parents.

14.   Many other artists and craftsmen lived in or passed through Moly-Sabata, sometimes to the despair of Anne Dangar since they did not all share her devotion to a very difficult ideal. They included the painters Michel Seuphor and Serge Charchoune, and, occasionally, Walter Firpo!

15.   James Shirley (1596–1666) dramatist and poet, was a graduate of Davidson's college, St Catherine's. The society held regular meetings and debates, and invited writers, poets and painters to address the members. Among other guest speakers, during that period, were Richard Hughes, A.E. Coppard and Walter de la Mare. Mainie Jellett was the first woman ever to address the society.

16.   T.R. Henn (1901–80) Irish writer and president of St Catherine's College, Cambridge (1926–1969). His study of the poetry of W.B. Yeats, *The Lonely Tower*, London, 1950, remains a standard work.

17.   It has been known by the title *Death of Procris*, formerly the title of the painting in the National Gallery, which may indeed be concerned with the Cephalus and Procris story.

18.   Dermod O'Brien was in fact a kindly and generous leader of the academic painters of his day, supportive towards younger artists and more than ready to demonstrate this in a personal way by acquiring their works.

19.   'Exposition d'Art Irlandais', Musée Royaux des Beaux-Arts de Belgique, Brussels, 10 May–8 June 1930. Mainie exhibited two oil paintings and a gouache (all unidentified).

20.   Bodkin's foreword to the catalogue.

CHAPTER FIFTEEN

1.   The Pouyauds had a family and eventually settled in Asnières-sur-Bois, a few kilometres from Vézalay. Pouyaud worked as a monumental sculptor, as well as continuing his Cubist painting. He died in 1970. His widow gave valuable details of life at Moly-Sabata to the author in an interview in the summer of 1990.

2.   Letter to Mainie and Evie, written from Serrières on 9 October 1928. 'Stic B' was essentially a commercial paint, for builders, decorators and architects, designed for use on cement, concrete, brick and plaster. It was quite heavily textured, and thick, not unlike the weather-proofed exterior paints used for house decoration today, and its colour chart included *revêtement de pierre* and *revêtement imitation brique*. The colour range, given the type of paint, was also immense; more than fifty shades were available, nine blues, nine greens, among the latter vert *irlandais*! And the colour sheet carried this impressive message: 'Paints for building and decoration. Can be applied to anything, used anywhere, stands up against everything. "Stic B" for radiators, tennis courts, motor car tyres, etc . . . "Stic B" is a coating which is a material in its own right.' Developed in the late 1920s, it caught on as a paint, and the company opened a London office.

3.   Alfred Janneau, *L'Art Cubiste*, Paris, 1929

4.   The firm of Bernheim Brothers were major Paris dealers in modern art. They had been part of the syndicate which secretly bought up the Degas Collection from the painter's heirs. Georges Bernheim, in association with the partnership, acted for Renoir, and was Henri Matisse's dealer. The sharp exchanges between Gleizes and Janneau

were in *L'Intransigeant*, Gleizes writing on 4 November 1929; Janneau replying on 8 November.

5.   In his review for the *Irish Statesman*, Russell suggested, among other somewhat banal thoughts, that a room decorated by Mainie Jellett 'might be a very delightful room to live in', but went on to detect in her works 'realistic forms' – a 'remote reference to living winged figures' and so on – which could not have given the painter much pleasure or any grounds for believing that Russell's understanding had progressed anywhere at all.

6.   This long-established weekly had some standing but no national impact. The reviewer was Derek Verschoyle, who left Trinity College after his senior freshman year, and went on to become literary editor of *The Spectator* at the age of twenty-two.

7.   *Irish Statesman*, 16 June 1928.

8.   *The Irish Times*, 12 June 1928.

9.   C.P. Curran, 'Evie Hone: Stained Glass Artist', in Stella Frost, *A Tribute to Evie Hone and Mainie Jellett*, Dublin, 1957. C.P. Curran (1883–1962) was a student at University College, Dublin, with James Joyce, and remained a lifelong friend. He was pious, and his interest in Evie Hone's religious work was an extension of considerable research into, and knowledge of, Irish art of all periods. He became involved in the Rouault controversy; see Chp. 24.

10.   The succession of Jellett solo shows (1925, 1926, 1927) and group shows (1923, 1924, with Evie) and annually thereafter.

11.   'A Definition of My Art', MacCarvill.

12.   'Mainie Jellett', by Elizabeth Bowen in *A Tribute to Evie Hone and Mainie Jellett*, edited by Stella Frost, Dublin 1957 (originally published in *The Bell*, April 1944).

CHAPTER SIXTEEN

1.   Honor Purser was the neice of Sarah Purser. Her brother, Sean, later married Mainie's sister, Betty.

2.   Christine Duff was a family friend.

3.   *Palm Sunday, A.D. 33*, by William Orpen, painted in what he called 'marble medium' in 1930 and exhibited at the Royal Academy in 1931, the year of the artist's death. It is illustrated (p. 122) in *Sir William Orpen, Artist and Man*, by P.G. Konody and Sidney Dark, London 1932.

4.   *The Daily Express*, 19 October 1931.

5.   *The Irish Times*, 26 October 1931, p. 4. The review was unsigned.

6.   *The Daily Express*, 30 October 1931.

7.   The lecture is published in MacCarvill, *Mainie Jellet*, p. 83.

8.   Michael Scott (1905–88) Dublin architect, who was responsible for a number of public buildings in Dublin and elsewhere in Ireland, including the Abbey Theatre and the Opera House, Cork.

9.   This group of philosophers all published articles on the present state of the world, in *The Observer*. Mainie kept cuttings.

10.   Joseph Hone (1882–1959), a literary historian and a cousin of Evie's who was later to write the first biography of Yeats, as well as books on Henry Tonks and George Moore's family was then working on a life of Berkeley. In connection with this, and at Evie's suggestion, he was later to meet Gleizes in Paris.

11.   This was subsequently published as *Art et religion* and first given as a dissertation in Paris, in March 1931, followed by *Art et production* and *Art et science* in 1932.

CHAPTER SEVENTEEN

1.   Abstraction-Création was founded on 15 February 1931. The eight artists who formed the first executive

committee were: Arp, Gleizes, Hélion, Herbin, Kupka, Tutundjian, Valmier and Vantongerloo. It succeeded the group founded in 1930, Cercle et Carré. As the name implies, it was concerned with 'creative' abstraction; in other words, abstract works constructed from non-figurative elements. These ranged widely, from the geometric abstraction of Gabo, Pevsner and Lissitzky to the abstract Cubism of Gleizes, Mainie and Evie, all of whom participated through the crucial first five years, up to 1936.

2.   Auguste Herbin (1882–1960) Cubist and then pure abstract painter, living and working in Paris. His dealer was Léonce Rosenberg, and he was one of the first to exhibit at the dealer's new Galerie de l'Effort Moderne. He reverted to simplified Cubism in the early 1920s, then returned to pure abstraction from 1926 through the founding of Abstraction-Création, and on into the 1940s. He published *L'Art non-figuratif et non-objectif* in 1949.

3.   This definition of her art appears, with two illustrations of works, in the first issue of *Abstraction-Création-Art non-figuratif*, Paris, 1932.

4.   Edward Wadsworth (1889–1949) English painter who studied in Munich, at the Bradford Art School and the Slade, before joining the Omega Workshop, at Roger Fry's invitation, breaking from it with Wyndham Lewis. He was a pioneer among English abstract artists, and remained the most European and advanced of painters during the 1920s, leading to Mainie's admiration for his work, and perhaps to the fact that they exhibited together.

5.   Ben Nicholson (1894–1982) English painter, the son of two painters, William Nicholson and Mabel Pryde, and the husband of Winifred Nicholson. She brought him into contact with Evie Hone, whom they visited in Paris, probably also meeting Mainie, though there is no record of this. Later married Barbara Hepworth.

6.   Barbara Hepworth (1903–75) English sculptress and fellow-student of Henry Moore at the Leeds School of Art and then at the Royal College of Art. After her marriage to Ben Nicholson they travelled frequently to Paris, knew Gleizes, and took part in Abstraction-Création from 1933.

7.   Paule Vézelay was the daughter of a British doctor. She changed her name from Marjorie Watson-Williams in the 1920s when she settled in Paris and became the mistress of André Masson.

8.   John Power (fl. 1918–32) Australian surgeon-turned-artist who worked in Paris in the 1920s, studying Cubism, and was known to Gleizes through Abstraction-Création, and possibly earlier.

9.   Jean Hélion (1904–) French painter who knew and worked with Mondrian and Van Doesburg before joining Abstraction-Création in 1932. After its dissolution, in 1936, he went to America.

10.   Georges Vantongerloo (1886–1965) Belgian sculptor who joined with the De Stijl group, moving on to Abstraction-Création and becoming its vice-president in 1931. He exhibited in a small Abstraction-Création exhibition with Mainie Jellett in January 1934.

11.   Michel Seuphor (1901–) Belgian painter and critic who had edited *Cercle et Carré* and who later wrote a standard work on the main subject of their collective endeavour, *L'Art abstrait*. He also wrote a useful and influential *Dictionary of Abstract Painting* which, however, gives little space to Gleizes and none at all to Jellett or Hone.

12.   Reported in Mainie's letter to Gliezes, quoted here.

13.   Thomas Greenwood was an English philosopher and journalist. *The Philosopher* was 'A Quarterly of Practical Philosophy'. Mainie's article appeared in Vol. XIV, No. 1, in June, 1931.

14.   Adrian Stokes (1887–1927) Dublin University pro-

fessor of bacteriology and preventive medicine until 1922, when he moved to Guy's Hospital medical school. He was the much-loved uncle of the Jellett girls, and gave them their first motor car, which Bay drove.

15.   Royal Academy Exhibition of French Art, held in London, 1932.

16.   *The Irish Times*, 22 April 1932.

17.   Frantisek Kupka, see n. 5, Chp. 10. He settled in Paris in 1896, moving to Puteaux in 1904 where he came into contact with Villon, Duchamp and Gleizes. He returned to serve in the Czech army, and stayed on in Prague after the Great War. He joined Abstraction-Création in 1931.

18.   Emil Filla (1882–1953) Czech sculptor, trained in Prague, who became a Cubist, much influenced by Braque and Picasso.

CHAPTER EIGHTEEN

1.   The Academy of Christian Art was founded by George Noble, Count Plunkett, Minister of Fine Art in the First Dáil, and for a time Director of the National Museum. Membership of the Academy was open only to Roman Catholics, and its objective was to promote 'the intellectual commonplaces of Catholic life'. See Brian Kennedy, *Irish Art and Modernism*, Dublin, 1991.

2.   The Ben Nicholson canvas was acquired by the Tate Gallery in 1970. In *Ben Nicholson: The Years of Experiment 1919–1939*, Cambridge, 1983, Jeremy Lewison says of the work 'only the ghostly appearance of a table top prevents the painting from being completely non-referential'.

3.   The Mayor Gallery, in London, was among the first regularly to exhibit abstract works of art.

4.   Henry Moore (1898–1986) English sculptor who, after war service, studied first at the Leeds School of Art, with Barbara Hepworth, and then at the Royal College of Art. He received his first commission from London Transport, for the headquarters of the Underground. Exhibited with the 'Seven and Five' and many abstract exhibitions, though not with Abstraction-Création.

5.   Herbert Read (1893–1968) English art critic and leading exponent of 'Modernism', who published many books, including *Art and Society and the Philosophy of Modern Art*. He championed the work of Ben Nicholson and Henry Moore.

6.   Jean Chevalier, a contemporary of Walter Firpo among Gleizes' associates, and therefore later than Mainie, Evie and Robert Pouyaud. He is still involved, as is Firpo, in 'l'Association des Amis d'Albert Gleizes'.

7.   It was published in *Motley, the Gate Theatre Magazine*, October 1932. The magazine contained articles about the arts generally, though principally about theatre, and was founded and run by Michael Mac Liammoir and Hilton Edwards, founders of the Gate Theatre in Dublin.

8.   Gleizes letter to Anne Dangar, in the Moly-Sabata Archive at Ampuis. See Chp. 14 n. 4 above.

9.   Frost, 'Evie Hone', in *A Tribute to Evie Hone and Mainie Jellett*.

10.   MacCarvill, *Mainie Jellett*.

CHAPTER NINETEEN

1.   An Túr Gloine (The Tower of Glass) was the co-operative stained-glass studio workshop founded by Edward Martyn and Sarah Purser in 1903, in Upper Pembroke Street, Dublin.

2.   *Municipal Gallery of Modern Art, 17 Harcourt Street. Illustrated Catalogue with biographical and Critical Notes by S.C.H.* (Sarah Cecilia Harrison) Dublin, 1908.

3.   Charlemont House, the town house of the Earl of

Charlemont, in what was Rutland Square, and is now Parnell Square, was converted by the Corporation into a modern art gallery by the addition of substantial exhibition rooms at the back.

4.   *Irish Independent*, 9 June 1933; the 'Leaves from a Woman's Diary' described Holland as 'foremost among European countries in modern movements in painting and architecture'.

5.   Mainie's solo show in 1933, in the Dublin Painters' Gallery, was held from 8–21 June. The major works included *Sea Rhythm* and *Adam and Eve*.

6.   Roland Holst was a Dutch stained-glass artist, and an influence on Evie Hone.

7.   Church of Christ the King, Cork.

8.   Honan's Chapel, Cork; see Chp. 3.

9.   International Exhibition of Chinese Art, Royal Academy of Arts, London ,Thursday 28 November 1935 to Saturday 7 March 1936.

10.   She did fruit and flower paintings, in gouache, for this competition.

11.   MacCarvill, *Mainie Jellett*.

12.   Correspondence between Gleizes and Lhote at end of 1930s.

CHAPTER TWENTY

1.   The Jellett family never fully understood her abstract Cubism, and the paintings hanging in the house, long after Mainie's death, were mainly of the Sickert period, or later realist works, while the pure abstract paintings were stored away.

2.   Micheal MacLiammoir (1899–1977) Irish actor and brother-in-law to Anew MacMasters. He had acted since childhood, but had spent the early 1920s painting and writing, rejoining the company in 1927.

3.   Hilton Edwards (1903–82) English actor who accepted a season's engagement with Anew MacMaster's 'Intimate Shakespearean Company', and toured in England in the summer of 1927. He then came to Ireland, where the two men met, in Enniscorthy in County Wexford. They moved from there to Tipperary, where the decision was made to found a new theatre.

4.   Edward Pakenham, Sixth Earl of Longford (1902–61) provided the finance for the Gate Theatre and was involved in its direction for many years.

5.   Christine, Lady Longford (1900–78) shared in the direction of the Gate Theatre with her husband, wrote and translated plays, and produced other books of memoirs and criticism.

6.   Denis Johnston (1901–84) Irish playwright and author with the company, and also a director of its plays. He was an authority on the life and work of Jonathan Swift.

7.   Austin Clarke (1896–1974) distinguished Irish playwright and poet. Mainie collaborated with him in illustrating a joint-work published by the Gaisford Press.

8.   Padraic Colum (1881–1972) Irish poet and critic who befriended Joyce, organising financial help for him when he was working on *Ulysses*.

9.   Mary Manning (1905–) Irish Independent theatre critic who annoyed MacLiammoir so much that he offered her the job of editing *Motley* so long as she gave up reviewing theatre.

10.   MacLiammoir owned at least one of Mainie's gouaches, and after her death her palette went to him, probably given by her sister Bay. It was subsequently sold at the auction of the contents of his house in Earlsfort Terrace. It is now in a private collection in Dublin.

11.   Drawings for the Giraudoux set are in a private collection in Dublin.

12.   In May 1936 Evie had finished the window for Tara

Church, a two-light composition of the descent of the Holy Ghost. Her other big stained-glass commission that year had been the chapel window for the Dublin Bluecoat School, The King's Hospital, depicting the Resurrection. And she was at work on a further ambitious work, the heraldic window for the chapel entrance and three decorative windows for the chapel itself, at Blackrock College, completed in 1937.

13.   See Linda Dalrymple Henderson, *The Fourth Dimension and Non-Euclidian Geometry in Modern Art*, Princeton, 1983.

14.   Dorothy Blackham (1896–1975) Irish painter who was a pupil both at the RHA and the Metropolitan School of Art, before going to Goldsmith's College in London. She exhibited widely in Ireland during the 1930s and 1940s, becoming actively involved with the White Stag Group.

15.   *The Irish Times*, 22 April 1936.

16.   Robert Pouyaud, *Considérations esthétiques sur le signe de la Spirale*, Clamecy, 1936. (Extrait du Bulletin, 3e Série, No. 12 de la Société Scientifique et Artistique de Clamecy.)

17.   Thomas Bodkin, *Hugh Lane and his Pictures*, Pegasus Press, Paris, 1932. The first edition was published privately, in a de luxe edition, limited to 400 copies, and distributed by the Irish Free State, mainly through diplomatic channels, and as a quasi-diplomatic operation aimed at 'recovering' the paintings for Ireland. The second edition was published in Dublin in 1935. A subsequent edition appeared in 1956.

18.   *The Irish Times*, 18 November 1937.

19.   Letter from Mrs Sutton to the author, summer 1990.

20.   Paul Egestorff (1908–) Irish artist who came to Dublin after the First World War, and became a painter in the 1930s. He exhibited from then until the early 1950s. His work was a mixture of abstraction and realism.

21.   Jack Hanlon (1913–68) Irish artist and priest who studied with André Lhote. He was best in watercolour, in which medium he demonstrated excellent command of colour and composition.

22.   Carmel Flynn (1917–69) Irish artist who showed with a number of exhibitions and groups in the late 1930s and during the Second World War.

23.   Patricia Wallace (1913–72) Irish artist and member of the Society of Dublin Painters, which she joined in 1941. She married William Griffith, owner of the Unicorn Restaurant, which was a meeting place for the White Stag Group artists.

24.   Mainie Jellett's 1937 solo exhibition was held as usual in the Dublin Painters' Gallery,

25.   MacCarvill, *Mainie Jellett*.

CHAPTER TWENTY-ONE

1.   Sean T. O'Kelly (1882–1963) a leading member of the Fianna Fáil government, he was then Tánaiste (Deputy Prime Minister). He later became President of Ireland in succession to the eminent Gaelic scholar, Douglas Hyde.

2.   *Irish Press*, 10 June 1938.

3.   The painting, *Achill Horses*, was also requested for New York, by the Department of Industry and Commerce, who undertook responsibility for insurance and shipping in a letter dated 14 April. Mainie received an inscribed certificate from the Board of Directors of the New York World's Fair. It is now in the National Gallery of Ireland.

4.   See Gleizes' letters to Delaunay in the late twenties. Michel Seuphor, no friend of Gleizes, gives only a confined report of this in his *Dictionnaire de l'Art Abstrait*. Delaunay and Gleizes worked together closely on the great *Exposition Universelle* murals of 1937 and on the *Salle des Tuileries* in 1938. The talks given by Delaunay and published in *Du*

Cubisme à l'art abstrait are full of ideas that are clearly derived from Gleizes. Sonia Delaunay's autobiography *Nous irons jusqu'au soleil* gives a highly simplified version of Gleizes' whole historical perspective. These ideas, however, are attributed to herself and Robert, and Gleizes only appears in the book as a very marginal figure. The influence of Gleizes on Delaunay remains one of the best kept secrets of modern art history.

5. Letter from Olivia Hughes to the author, January 1986.

6. Buyers included J.J. Holloway, the diarist and veteran supporter of art in Dublin, who bought a gouache entitled *Meadows* (see Pl. 211).

7. Mainie's sister, Bay acquired for 10s a sketch of Croagh Patrick which had been listed in the catalogue at £2.10s. The names of other buyers included Boydell, Meredith, Gavan Duffy, Geoghegan, McCarron, Moore, Stevenson.

8. *Irish Independent* 30 November 1939.

9. *The Irish Times*, 30 November 1939.

10. Stephen Rynne, a Dublin journalist who wrote regularly for *The Leader*. In the issue of *The Leader* of 18 November he referred to Mainie's 'technique, medium, pigments, and the instruments of the painter's craft' as being 'accidents which lay far behind her intellectual invention. One gets the feeling that Mainie Jellett only paints a fraction of the pictorial images which form themselves in her mind ... Yet it is seldom her "metre" breaks down when she ventures to rhyme in paint as in her interpretation of Fire, Air, Earth, and Water.'

11. John Dowling, a Dublin journalist who wrote for *Ireland Today*.

12. Jack Longford (1911–44) partner in the Contemporary Picture Gallery. He had studied medicine at Trinity College and then in Edinburgh, but had given up these studies in favour of literature and art. He was one of the earliest champions of Jack Yeats, giving him one-man exhibitions, immediately after the Loan and Cross-Section Exhibition, in November 1939, and then again in 1940 and 1941. Many years later Stephen Rynne wrote of Yeats's relationship with Longford: 'The old man and young Longford were warm friends; there was something of a father and son affinity between them.'

13. Deirdre McDonogh (1897–1970) was a pseudonym. Her real name was Moira Pilkington. She had married Kathleen Tynan's son, a marriage which later failed. She was joined, a year after founding the gallery, by Jack Longford. The partnership had a distinct policy (represented in the 1939 Loan and Cross-Section Exhibition) of including works of art by international painters in a loan section, side by side with paintings for sale, mainly though not exclusively the work of Irish artists.

14. Mainie's lecture (in MacCarvill, *Mainie Jellett*) was entitled 'The Influence of Contemporary French Painting'. Louis MacNeice spoke on 'English Painting Today', the Director of the National Gallery of Ireland, Dr George Furlong, gave a lecture entitled 'Why Landscape?' and E. A. MacGuire spoke on 'Irish Painting Today'.

15. 'The aim is not a wish to reconstitute an anecdotal fact, but to constitute a pictorial fact.' 'To work from nature is to improvise.' 'The senses deform, the spirit forms.' 'Work towards the perfection of the spirit.' 'There is no certitude except in spiritual conceptions.' 'Nobility comes from controlled emotion.'

16. 'I work with the elements of the spirit, with imagination; I try to make concrete that which is abstract, I go from the general to the particular, which implies I go from an abstract to arrive at reality. My art is an art of synthesis and deduction.'

17. Gleizes, *Du Cubisme et les moyens de le comprendre*, pp. 22–3.

CHAPTER TWENTY-TWO

1. John Dowling, wrote in *Ireland Today* that 'the Professorship of Design was obviously intended to be the Keystone of the new edifice', and he related this to the country's industrial design needs and their development. What looked at first like a brave development soon took on, in the view of both Dowling and others, an appearance of threatening changes designed to bring in from abroad a new and powerful teacher – 'Herr von Something will be quietly introduced as the saviour of Irish Art' – and the immediate reaction of those who were already established in the school, now transformed into a college, was to block the appointment.

2. Works purchased included paintings by Dermod O'Brien, Crampton Walker, Humbert Craig and Sean O'Sullivan. The collection also included eighteenth and nineteenth century canvases of Irish interest, among them works by George Barret and James Arthur O'Connor.

3. Margaret Stokes, Irish painter and graphic artist who studied with Joan Hassell. She is a first cousin of Mainie Jellett.

4. Author's interview with Brian Boydell, summer 1990.

5. Hélène de St Pierre, interviews with the author, 1990–1. She arrived in Dublin in the early summer of 1940. Her encounter with Mainie Jellett was quite accidental. She was standing in front of the Shelbourne Hotel on the day after the fall of France, staring in disbelief at the display of newspapers, and at the front page of *The Irish Times* which carried a photograph of the Arc de Triomphe with the Swastika flying from it. The page itself was bordered in black. Suddenly someone tapped her on the shoulder. 'Vous êtes francaises, mademoiselle?' It was Mainie Jellett, offering help and consolation.

6. Charles Lynch (1906–85) pianist and close friend of Mainie's.

7. The first of these appeared in 1936 and the second in 1939. They are very different; *Parlons peinture* derives much more directly from André Lhote's essays for the *Nouvelle Revue Française* while the treatise is much more specifically a handbook, though an excellent one of its kind, distilling much of the brilliance with which Lhote had impressed many hundreds of younger painters.

8. Earnán O'Malley, 'Louis le Brocquy', *Horizon*, Vol. 14, No. 79, July, 1946. Cyril Connolly, who edited this magazine on literature and the arts, had an Irish background, and published a number of articles about Irish painters and writers.

9. Margot Moffet, 'Young Irish Painters', *Horizon*, Vol. 11, No. 64, April, 1945.

10. Interview with the author, see n. 5 above.

11. The relationship between his parents did not last, and his mother then married a Mr Beaumont, who was English. Basil Rákóczí took his mother's married name and the family settled in Brighton. His first paintings, which date from the 1930s, and which were all signed 'Basil Beaumont', include landscapes and seascapes of subjects in France and Italy, as well as England. He married early, having reverted to the name Rákóczí. This marriage was short-lived, though there was one child, Anthony Rákóczí who also became an artist.

12. The White Stag Group had existed in the 1930s in London, where both he and Kenneth Hall had painted, exhibiting their works with Lucy Wertheim. All the others were associates, or simply exhibited with the group. The group exhibited in various locations, always in Dublin, and mainly at 134 Baggot Street. This was where its first exhibition took place, in April 1940, and the other artists taking part were Nick Nichols, Georgette Rondel,

Patricia Wallace, Barbera Bayley, Anthony Reford, Elizabeth Ormsby, Endre Roszda and Tony Rakoczi.

13. Kenneth Hall (1913–46) artist of the White Stag Group, and friend of Basil Rákóczí. He exhibited in London with Lucy Wertheim, and came to Ireland in 1939. He committed suicide.

14. Jocelyn Chewitt (1906–79) was born in Canada, and was the only sculptress to exhibit with the White Stag Group. She was a student at the Slade, where she met her husband, Stephen Gilbert.

15. Stephen Gilbert (1910–) painter associated with the White Stag Group, and later a member of the Cobra Group.

16. Bobby Dawson (1923–) the youngest of the painters associated with the White Stag Group. He first exhibited in 1940.

17. Brian Boydell in interview for film, *To Make It Live: Mainie Jellett, 1897–1944*, summer of 1990. This filmed portrait of the artist was shown by Radio Telefis Eireann in 1991. He combined being an art master with an early career as a painter. (Later, he became one of Ireland's leading composers, and Professor of Music at Dublin University.)

18. Interview by the author with Dr Richard Hayes, former Director of the National Library of Ireland, who was responsible for much of the interrogation. Of the less than twenty German agents landed in Ireland between 1940 and 1944 almost all were arrested within their first week in the country (most within twenty-four hours) and were then interned on the Curragh. There was one exception: Herman Goertz. He was an experienced *Abwehr* officer, of the pre-Nazi school, an honourable man, and, in the end a tragic figure who committed suicide in distressing circumstances. With IRA help he remained at liberty for about two years before his capture and interrogation by Irish Intelligence.

19. Joseph Lee: *Ireland 1912–1985: Politics and Society*, Cambridge, 1989.

20. Francis Stuart (1902–) Irish novelist and poet, born in Australia.

21. *The Bell*, December 1940.

22. George Atkinson was headmaster of the Metropolitan School of Art.

CHAPTER TWENTY-THREE

1. Cepta Cullen ran what was called the Irish Ballet Club, which had its headquarters in Lower Abbey Street and which was trying to co-ordinate the various classical dance studios in the city, into a national ballet. The club's president was Brinsley McNamara, who was registrar of the National Gallery, drama critic of *The Irish Times*, and a writer who earned himself lifelong notoriety by publishing in 1918 a book about his native village, Delvin, in County Westmeath, called *The Valley of the Squinting Windows*.

2. F.R. Higgins, a noted poet, only forty-five years old and therefore almost an exact contemporary of Mainie's, had published verse since the early 1920s.

3. Elizabeth Maconchy (1907–) is an Irish-born composer, though by this stage established in England where works had been performed at Promenade concerts under Henry Wood at the Albert Hall since 1930. She was a student of Ralph Vaughan-Williams and was married to the author, William Richard Le Fanu.

4. Donagh MacDonough (1912–68) Irish poet and playwright.

5. *The Irish Times*, 24 March 1941.

6. Ninette de Valois (1898–1986) was a leading English ballerina. She was born Stannus, in Baltinglass, County Wicklow, and combined dancing with choreography by

the mid-1920s, when she worked in Ireland.

7.   Jacqueline Robinson (1928–) was a student of dance and music in Dublin, and was associated with the White Stag Group, in the wider sense of it being a movement affecting *all* the arts in Ireland. She became a close friend of Basil Rákóczí, and knew Charles Lynch and Brian Boydell, who was one of her pupils.

8.   Victor Waddington established a gallery in Dublin in the late 1930s and became a leading art dealer, representing many Irish painters whose works he then introduced to a London audience when he opened a second gallery there after the Second World War.

9.   Later that year Salkeld published Maurice Craig's first book, *Black Swans*, with a Sidney Smith lino-cut.

10.   *Madonna of Spring*, 1939. (See Pl. 224.)

11.   Joan Cavers was a professional photographer as well as being a painter. Indeed, Mainie attended an exhibition of her paintings which was held in November 1941.

12.   MacCarvill, *Mainie Jellett*, 'Modern Art and its Relation to the Past.' This published lecture only touches on the Celtic relationship. Two manuscript versions of the lecture survive, one of which, the Cork version, includes her notes about whom to thank. Seamus Murphy, the Cork sculptor, is among those members of the Munster Fine Arts Club listed.

13.   Bowen, *Mainie Jellett* in Frost, *A Tribute to Evie Hone and Mainie Jellett*.

14.   'Art as a Spiritual Force' in MacCarvill, *Mainie Jellett*, p. 68. The lecture was also published in *Commentary*, November 1941. Both versions are very much shortened. The full text remains unpublished.

15.   *The Irish Times*, 21 November 1941.

16.   *Irish Independent*, 21 November 1941.

CHAPTER TWENTY-FOUR

1.   St Patrick's College, Maynooth, was a Roman Catholic seminary fifteen miles west of Dublin (now a constituent college of the National University of Ireland) and the headquarters of the Roman Catholic Hierarchy.

2.   Friends of the National Collections of Ireland, founded in 1924, had bought and distributed to public collections a wide variety of works of art.

3.   Dublin's Municipal Gallery of Modern Art (now the Hugh Lane Municipal Gallery of Modern Art) was run then by a curator rather than a director, and had no board or governing body, coming directly under the city manager. The Corporation apppointed an Art Advisory Committee, which is still in existence, and still makes recommendations on purchases. This committee voted against accepting the painting, and the decision was published in *The Irish Times* on 6 October 1942.

4.   Mrs Kathleen Clarke was the widow of one of the 1916 leaders who had been executed, Tom Clarke, and sister to Edward Daly, another martyr of the 1916 Rising.

5.   Michael de la Bedoyère was editor of *The Catholic Herald*.

6.   *The Irish Times*, 6 October 1942.

7.   John Piper (1903–) English painter who studied at the Royal College of Art. He collaborated with Evie Hone on the windows for the Eton College Chapel. He reviewed the original exhibition in *The Spectator* of 16 January 1942.

8.   John F. Kelly, curator of the Municipal Gallery

9.   *The Irish Times*, 8 October 1942.

10.   Niall Montgomery (1915–87) Dublin architect, writer and noted wit.

11.   Myles Na gCopaleen (1911–66) Irish novelist, writer and civil servant, wrote journalism under the above name, and novels, including *At Swim Two Birds*, using the pseudonym, 'Flann O'Brien'. His real name was Brian

O'Noland, or O Nuallain.

12.   Father Edward Leen was a Holy Ghost Father who came originally from Limerick, where he was born in Abbeyfeale, and then educated at Rockwell College and at the Royal University, which, by the time he had passed his entry had become part of the National University. He went on to study in Rome, under the Jesuits, and after a period doing mission work returned to Blackrock College of which he became President in September, 1925.

13.   See Michael Carroll, *Father Edward Leen*, Dublin, 1952.

14.   Father Edward Leen delivered a carefully-reasoned address which was later published as *À propos of Rouault* in *The Irish Art Handbook*, Dublin, 1943.

15.   Published in the November 1942 issue of *Commentary*, a monthly critical magazine.

16.   MacCarvill, *Mainie Jellett*. 'Roualt and Tradition' was also published in *St Bartholomew's Magazine*, December 1942.

CHAPTER TWENTY-FIVE

1.   *Irish Art Handbook*, Dublin, 1943; *Irish Art*, Dublin, 1944. Though not acknowledged, Basil Clancy was the editor of both volumes. The following writers contributed to *Irish Art Handbook*: Arthur Power, A.E. Doolan, Mainie Jellett, Edward Leen, Sean Keating, Rupert Strong, James White, John Larchet, Joseph O'Neill, Michael Bowles, Aloys Fleischmann, C. Sauerzweig, John O'Gorman, Mairin Allen, John Dowling, Lord Longford, Micheál MacLiammóir, Gabriel Fallon, Seamus de Bhilmot, William Stanford, John Hennig and Austin Molloy. Additional commentators, writing a year later in *Irish Art*, included: Dáithi Hanly, Gerard Mac Nicholl, Margot and Noel Moffett, Raymond McGrath, Alan Hope, A.J. Leventhal, Basil Rákóczí and Basil Clancy, who wrote on 'Art and Reality'. Mainie did not live to see the second collection of essays.

2.   McCarvill, *Mainie Jellett*. MacCarvill changed its title to 'My Voyage of Discovery', but also added to it the Manifesto which Mainie had written for *Abstraction-Création* in the early 1930s. What Mainie wrote for the *Irish Art Handbook* was autobiographical, and included a brief chronological account of her career. It had been, she claimed, stormy and varied. It had included three major revolutions, at least, in her work, and she claimed – in the manuscript version – that she drew from all three of these different periods for 'the conclusions and ideas which I work on at the moment.' Inexplicably, this section was omitted from both published versions. There were also other less important changes, consistent with editorial tightening up of her copy.

3.   *Commentary*, May 1942.

4.   James Sleator (1885–1950) Irish painter who succeeded Dermod O'Brien as President of the Royal Hibernian Academy. He was a pupil of William Orpen, and then his studio assistant.

5.   Margaret Clarke (1888–1961) Irish painter who attended the Metropolitan School of Art when Orpen was teaching there. She also modelled for him. She was a member of the Society of Dublin Painters, and was on the committee of the Irish Exhibition of Living Art.

6.   Louis le Brocquy, was a self-taught painter who had travelled in Europe in the final years before the outbreak of the Second World War. Then he had moved to the south of France, living for a time in a tiny house owned by Ralph Cusack, where Louis le Brocquy's first child, Seyre, was born in 1939. By the end of 1940 he was back in Ireland, painting murals and theatre designs to sustain his independence as an artist, and being supported in this by his

mother, Sybil, a writer and formidable figure in Dublin literary circles.

7.   Laurence Campbell (1911–68) Irish sculptor, and teacher at the Metropolitan School of Art. His brother, Christopher, was a painter and stained-glass artist.

8.   Jerome Connor (1873–1943) Irish sculptor, born in Kerry, and educated in the United States, where he spent most of his life. Twenty-two of his works were shown at this exhibition.

9.   Beatrice Glenavy (1883–1968) Irish artist and pupil of William Orpen at the Metropolitan School of Art. She was gifted, and worked as a sculptress and in various forms of design as well as painting and exhibiting regularly at the RHA. The character of her work was faintly surrealist.

10.   Among those who took part were Jack Hanlon, Cecil Salkeld, Dorothy Blackham, Norah McGuinness, Nano Reid, May Guinness, Mary Swanzy, Lilian Davidson, Grace Henry, Letitia Hamilton (who was an associate of the RHA) and Harriet Kirkwood. Most of these artists were either members of the Society of Dublin Painters or had exhibited with group shows in the St Stephen's Green Gallery. An additional 'modernist' strand derived more directly from the younger artists and included Nick Nicholls, Paul Egestorff, Pat Scott, Doreen Vanston, Ralph Cusack, and Thurloe Conolly, who had all exhibited with the White Stag Group.

11.   Edith Somerville (1858–1949) Irish writer and painter, author, with Violet Martin, of a number of fictional works of comedy, the most famous of which was *Some Experiences of an Irish R.M.* She illustrated many of their joint books.

12.   Melanie le Brocquy (1919–) Irish sculptress and the younger sister of Louis le Brocquy.

13.   *The Irish Times*, 16 September 1943.

14.   *Evening Mail*, 16 September 1943.

15.   'The Living Art Exhibition, by A.J. Leventhal, in *Irish Art* ed. Clancy.

CHAPTER TWENTY-SIX

1.   Theodore Goodman, in *Commentary*, July 1944.

2.   Elizabeth Bowen, 'Mainie Jellett', *The Bell*, April 1944. Republished in Stella Frost, *A Tribute to Evie Hone and Mainie Jellett*, Dublin 1957.

3.   Obituary by Canon Simpson in *St Bartholomew's Parish Magazine*, March 1944. She was in reality fortified by both Churches, the spiritual care taken of her a harbinger of ecumenism, something which was to be long and difficult in its practical development in Ireland.

4.   Patrick Scott (b. 1921) Irish artist, mainly self-taught, but educated at St Columba's College and then at the School of Architecture, in University College, Dublin. He exhibited in 1940 with the White Stag Group, was in the first Irish Exhibition of Living Art, and had his first one-man exhibition in 1944.

5.   *The Irish Times*, 17 February 1944, 'Mainie Jellett, An Appreciation'.

5.   *Irish Independent*, 17 February 1944, 'Miss Mainie Jellett'.

6.   Memorial Exhibition, Victor Waddington Galleries, June 1944.

7.   Theodore Goodman, 'Mainie Jellett', *Commentary*, July 1944.

8.   Mairin Allen, 'The Achievement of Mainie Jellett', *The Standard*, 2 June 1944.

9.   *Commentary*, July 1944.

10.   Charles Sidney, 'Art Criticism in Dublin', *The Bell*, Vol. I, No. 9, 1944.

11.   Stephen Rynne, *The Leader*, 23 September 1944.

INDEX

Abbaye de Créteil, l', 105–6
Abbey Theatre, 177, 179
Abstraction-Création, 130–3, 139, 157, 162, 165
Abstraction-Création, 132
Académie Julian, 28
Academy of Christian Art, 137
'After Whistler' exhibition, 194
Allen, Mairin, 202
Allendy, Colette, 67, 69
Alton, E.H., 195
Anglo-French Exhibition (1908), 8
Apollinaire, Guillaume, 54, 73
Annesley, Mabel, 163
An Túr Gloinne, 144–5, 147
Aquinas, St Thomas, 191, 192
Architects' Society of Ireland, 149
Ardizzone, Edward, 168
Aristotle, 140
Arp, Jean Hans, 132
Art d'Aujourd'hui, l', 90–1, 92
Arts and Crafts Society of Ireland, 139
Ashton, Julia, 108
Asquith, 4
Atkinson, George, 177

Ball, Maude, 80, 83, 86, 168
Banting, John, 90, 95
Barbizon School, 135
Bauhaus, 105, 132
Baumeister, Willi, 132
Bayes, Walter, 28–9
Bazaine, Jean, 70
Beaux Art Galleries, 92
Beckett, Samuel, 197
Bedoyère, Count Michael de la, 187
Beethoven, Ludwig van, 156, 184
Belfast School of Art, 41
Bell, Clive, 95, 110
Bell, Graham, 168
Bell, The, 203
Bell, Vanessa, 78, 168
Bernheims, 119
Berry, Anne M., 177
Bevan, Robert, 78, 90
Binchy, Dr, 126
Binyon, Laurence, 152
Birkenhead, Lord, 14
Blackham, Dorothy, 158, 176
Blackrock College, Dublin, 144–5, 190
Blast, 22
Blauer Reiter group, 73
Blavatsky, Mme., 75
Bodkin, Thomas, 66, 82, 110, 158
Bomberg, David, 22
Bonnard, Pierre, 45, 168, 169
Botticelli, 181, 184
Boucher, François, 135
Bowen, Elizabeth, 10, 12, 124, 182, 199–200, 203
Boydell, Brian, 172, 203
Boyne, Battle of, 1
Brady, Evie Hone's nurse, 69
Brangwyn, Frank, 148
Braque, Georges, 45, 57, 58, 59, 63, 74, 95, 101, 129, 167, 168, 169
Brewers' Society, 170

British Architectural Association, 164
Brochelin, 148,
Brown, Fred, 31
Burke, John L., 159
Burke, Nigel, 179
Butterworth, Miss, 8, 12
Byam Shaw School of Art, 28
Byrne, Barry, 149

Cahn, Marcelle, 63
Calder, Alexander
Camden Town Group, 22, 31
Cameron, D.Y., 148
Camisias, Sister, 201
Campbell, Christopher, 195
Campbell, Laurence, 195
Carlyle, Thomas, 3
Cavers, Joan, 180
Central School of Arts and Crafts, 28
Cézanne, Paul, 23, 46, 92–3, 95, 100, 102, 149
Chardin, Jean-Baptiste-Siméon, 58, 135
Chenevix, Miss, 12
Chevalier, Jean, 138
Chewett, Jocelyn, 176, 194
Chopin, 19
Church of Christ the King, Cork, 149–50
Cimabue, 93, 139
Clancy, Basil, 193
Clarke, Austin, 155; Mainie illustrates *The Straying Student*, by, 180
Clarke, Harry, 17, 66, 78, 79, 80, 156
Clarke, Kathleen, 187
Clarke, Margaret, 163, 170, 194, 195, 197
Clausen, George
Clouet, 134
Cocteau, Jean, 119
Coldstream, William, 168
Colum, Padraic, 155
Commentary, 194, 198, 202
Connaught, Duke of, 8
Connell, Mrs, 170
Connor, Jerome, 195
Conolly, Thurloe, 197
Conor, William, 78, 103, 168
Constable, John, 8
Constitution of 1937, 182
Contemporary Pictures Gallery, 172, 179, 189, 194, 198
Conway, Arthur, 195
Cooke-Collis, Sylvia, 198
Cooper, Douglas, 74
Corbusier, Le, (See: Jeanneret)
Cork Art School, 164
Corkery, Daniel, 97
Cormac's Chapel, Cork, 150
Corneille de Lyons, 134
Cosgrave, W.T., 103, 146, 159
Cosimo, Piero di, 110
Costello, John A., 159
Courbet, Gustave, 45
Covenant, The Solemn, 14
Craig, Edward Gordon, 28
Cranwill, Mia, 30
Crookshank, Mary, 12–13
Crowley, Grace, 108
Cullen, Cepta, 179

Curran, C.P., 123, 190, 191
Curran, Elizabeth, 195
Cusack, Ralph, 43, 167, 195, 197

Daily Express, The, 128–9
Dalí, Salvador, 197
Dance, Charles (playwright), 3
Dangar, Anne, 59, 75, 106, 108, 132, 138, 139, 141, 144, 170
Daniel Egan's Salon, 92
d'Arcy, Father, 190
David, Jacques-Louis, 58, 135
Davidson, Lilian Lucy, 43
Davidson, Norris, 103, 110, 114
Dawson, Bobby, 176
De Chirico, 168, 197
Degas, Edgar, 25
Delacroix, Eugène, 86, 135
Delaunay, Robert, 57, 58, 73, 74, 90, 132, 137, 158, 164–5
Delaunay, Sonia, 73, 132, 158
Derain, André, 45, 168, 169
De Stijl, 56–7, 74
de Valera, Eamon, 41, 133, 136–7, 146, 147, 158, 166, 177, 182
Deveyle, Lucie, 108
Dickey, Edward O'Rourke, 78, 84
Dillon, Gerard, 179, 197
Dobo, 107
Dorman, Sean, 202
Douglas, Langton, 66
Dowling, John, 167
Dublin Arts Week, 78
Dublin Corporation, 147
Dublin Literary Society, 37, 92, 99–100
Dublin Magazine, The, 88
Dublin University (Trinity College), 2, 3, 59, 195, 197
Duccio, 93
Duchamp, Jacques, 57
Duchamp, Marcel, 57, 58, 65
Duchamp-Villon, Raymond, 57
Duff, Christine, 125–6
Duffy, Gavan, 186
Dufy, Raoul, 45, 168
Dunalley, Lady, 187
Dun Emer Guild, 128

Eddington, A.S., 130
Edward VII, 8
Edward VIII, 156
Edwards, Hilton, 154–5, 162
Egan, Daniel, 92
Egestorff, Paul, 159, 171, 176, 202
Elan, l', 82
Electricity Supply Board, 195
El Greco, 54, 93
Eliot, T.S., 163
Emmet, Robert, 158
'Epopée, l'', 139
Epstein, Jacob, 149
Estève, Maurice, 70
Eucharistic Congress, 134
Euclid, 157
Evening Mail, the, 128, 186, 197

Ferat, Serge, 58

Fianna Fáil, 103, 133, 136, 146, 163
Filla, Emil, 135
Firpo, Walter, 73, 78, 107, 138
FitzGerald, Desmond, 92
Fitzgerald, Dorothy, 110
Fitzgerald, Harry, 14
Fitzpatrick, Miss, 170
Flynn, Carmel, 160
Fouquet, 134
Fox, Kathleen, 17, 103
Fra Angelico, 93, *Coronation of the Virgin*, 121, 181, 184
Fragonard, Jean-Honoré, 135
Franco, 156, 165
Franks, Miss, 12
Freeman's Journal, The, 88
French, Lord, Viceroy, 41
Fresnaye, Roger de La, 58
Friends of the National Collections of Ireland, 187, 189, 190
Friezs, Othon, 82
Frith, William Powell, 28
Frost, Stella, 145
Fry, Roger, 22, 90, 95, 110, 138
Furlong, George, 195
Fuseli, Henry, 79

Gabo, Naum, 65, 132
Gaelic League, 10, 12
Gaiety Theatre, 170, 179
Gaisford St Lawrence, 160
Galerie de l'Effort Moderne, 56, 58, 59
Gandhi, Mahatma, 133
Garcin, 137
Garstin, Alethea, 13
Garstin, Norman, 12–13, 17, 29
Gate Theatre, The, 129, 147, 154–6, 162, 170, 179
Gauguin, Paul, 46, 102
Gayfield Press, 180
gCopaleen, Myles Na (See: O'Brien, Flann)
Geoffray, César, 108
George V, 8, 55, 158
George, Waldemar, 91
Gertler, Mark, 90, 168
Gifford, Grace, 19
Gilbert, Stephen, 176
Gill, Eric, 149
Gilman, Harold, 19, 78
Ginner, Charles, 19, 78
Giotto, 46, 67, 93
Giraudoux, Jean, 156
Gladstone, William Ewart, 1, 4
Glasgow World Fair, 163, 164
GLEIZES, Albert, 46, 47, 54, 55, Gleizes' place in modern art, and his involvement in Cubism, 56–9; Mainie's and Evie's reasons for going to Gleizes, 59, and early collaboration, 61–9; their first lessons, 61–9; the working out of theories on abstraction, 70–5; his work on *La Peinture et ses lois*, 70; his abstract theory, 70–5, 77–8; 84–6; and l'Art d'Aujourd'hui, 90–1, 92; 94; car accident, 96, 99; and early Christian art, 96; quoted by Mainie in lecture, 101–2; extensively quoted on Cézanne, 102; and

Moly-Sabata, 105–10, 114; visits by Mainie, and their collaboration, 117–18, 121; and Abstraction-Création, 131–3, 137–8, 157; Mainie's visits in the 1930s, 136; letter to Anne Dangar, 136–44; meeting with Delaunay and Mainie in Paris, 165, 168, 169, 192; told of Mainie's illness, 200, 203

Gleizes, Juliette, 96, 107
Glenavy, Beatrice, 195
Good, James Winder, 91, 103
Goodman, Theodore, 198, 202
Gonne, Maude, 177
Gonne, Yseult, 177
Gore, Frederick Spencer, 28, 78
Goulinat, 82
Grant, Duncan, 90, 168
Gray, Eileen, 67
Green Family, 14
Griffith, Hilda, 186
Gris, Juan, 56, 57, 59, 63, 99, 101, 168, 169
Guildhall Loan Exhibition of Irish Art, 12
Guinness, Col., 170
Guinness, May, 90, 92, 170, 174, 196
Guinness, Noel, 169

Hall, Kenneth, 167, 176, 180, 194, 196
Hamilton, Eva, 78, 110
Hamilton, Letitia, 78, 84, 110, 158, 163
Hanlon, Jack P., 160, 163, 167, 172, 195, 197
Hélion, Jean, 132
Henn, T.R., 110
Henry, Grace, 78, 84, 103, 110, 194, 196
Henry, Paul, 78, 92, 168
Hepworth, Barbara, 132, 138
Herbert, Gwenda, 19
Herbin, Auguste, 58, 59, 63, 101, 119, 131, 132, 137, 162
Hicks, James, 128
Higgins, F.R., 179
Hitler, Adolf, 133, 156, 165, 177
Holst, Roland, 148
Home Rule Bill, 5, 14, 18, 41
Honan's Chapel, Cork, 149–50
HONE, Evie, meeting with Mainie, 28, 44, 47, 54, 58–9; working with Gleizes, 61–3, 65–7, 69–73, 75, 83, 84; joint exhibition with Mainie, 86, 89–90; religious vocation, 92, 94–5, 97; doubts about vocation, decision to leave community, 103–4, 106, 107; progress during 1920s, 113–19, 123; 1929 solo exhibition, 123; and Abstraction-Création, 131; embarks on stained glass, 137, 138, 145, 154, 157, 162, 170, 174, 189, 194, 195, 196, 199; writes to Gleizes about Mainie's illness, 200
Hone, Joseph, 130, 132
Hone, Nathaniel, 17
Horizon, 175
Hughes, John, 8
Hughes, Olivia, 165
Huxley, Julian, 130
Hyde, Douglas, 10, 12
Hyde, Mrs., 12

Imperial War Museum, 28
Ingres, Jean-Dominique, 58, 135
Intransigeant, l', 119, 162
Irish Art, 193, 194, 197
Irish Art Handbook, 193, 194
Irish Ballet Club, 179
Irish Convention, 41
Irish Exhibition of Living Art, 195, 196, 197, 198–9, 202, 203
Irish High Commission, 164
Irish Independent, 91, 97, 148, 185, 197, 201
Irish Press, The, 164, 177
Irish Republican Army (IRA), 176–7
Irish Sisters of Charity, 201
Irish Special Branch, 176

Irish Statesman, 79, 82, 84, 91, 97–9, 103, 121–3
Irish Times, The, 42, 43, 78–80, 91, 92, 97, 122, 135, 155, 158, 163, 167, 179, 185, 187, 190, 197, 201
Irish Unionist Alliance, 42

James Shirley Society, 110
Janneau, Guillaume, 119
Jantzen, 148
Jaurès, Jean, 54
Jeanneret, Charles-Edouard (Le Corbusier), 56, 57, 58, 59
Jeans, Sir James, 130.
Jellett, Babbin (Rosamund), 8, 39, 103, 125, 128, 147, 169, 200, 203
Jellett, Bay (Dorothea Janet), 3, 7, 19, 39, 43, 147, 154, 155, 159, 162, 166, 168, 170, 201, 203,
Jellett, Betty (Elizabeth), 12, 139, 147, 168, 177, 179, 186, 187, 198
Jellett, Captain Henry, 1
Jellett, Janet (née Stokes), 1–6, 7–11, 30, 147, 168, 170, 198
Jellett, John, 1
Jellett, John Hewitt, 1–2, 6
JELLETT, MAINIE, family background, 1–6; growing up in Dublin, 1, 7–11, 12, 15; educated at home with governesses, 12; her early art education, 3, 7, 9–11; first works of art, 9; studies with May Manning, 10; visits to France, 12–14; studies with Norman Garstin, 13–14; attends Metropolitan School of Art, 14–15, 17–18; attends Westminster School of Art, London, 19–31; influence of Walter Sickert 25–6; describes it as the 'first revolution' in her art, 25; first meeting with Evie, 28; other teachers include Walter Bayes and Mervyn Lawrence, 28–9, 32–6; political uncertainty as background to this period, 18–19, 30, 32, 41–4; returns to Dublin for winter of 1919–20, 39; enters work for Taylor Prize, 39–41, 43–4; studies in Paris with André Lhote, 45–51; Lhote and Cubism, 45–6; his admiration for Cézanne, 46; his influence on Mainie, 47–8; Lhote's method of teaching, 51–3; her Lhote period sketchbooks, 53–4; Mainie's first encounter with Albert Gleizes, 55–6, 59–61; background on Gleizes and his involvement in Cubism, 56–9; Mainie's and Evie's reasons for going to Gleizes, 59; their first lessons, 61–9; the working out of theories on abstraction, 70–5; Mainie and Evie spend Christmas in Paris, 1922, 77; periods of study and collaboration with Gleizes, 61–5, 67–9, 86–7; enters paintings for Salon des Indépendants, 77; shows first abstract paintings in Dublin, 78–83; controversial critical reception, 80–3, 84–6, 88–9; joint show with Evie Hone, 86; returns to Dublin to teach, 84; Seamus O'Sullivan shows comprehension and sympathy, 88–9; Mainie exhibits in London, 90; involvement in l'Art d'Aujourd'hui, 90–1; first solo exhibition, 91–2; Evie decides to pursue religious vocation, 92; Mainie begins lecturing, 92; family holiday in Glandore, Co Cork, 97; 1927 solo exhibition, 97–9; criticism by Russell, 97–9; 1929 solo exhibitions, 97, 122–3; interest in crafts and decorative arts, 105–6; first meeting with Pouyaud, 106; Pouyaud and Moly-Sabata, 106–7; the arrival of Anne Dangar, 108; Manevy and César Geoffray, 108; Mainie's view of the Moly-Sabata experiment, 109; discussion with Gleizes on colour, 109–10; first 'Modernist' picture accepted by RHA; 110; lecture at Cambridge

University, 110; participates in 1930 Brussels exhibition of Irish art, 110–12; Mainie's view of Pouyaud's intense personality, 113; development of her style during 1920s, 113–16; the close collaboration of Gleizes, Mainie, Evie and Pouyaud, 114; experiments with 'Stic B', 117–89; Gleizes troubled by adverse reaction to abstract Cubism, 119; the painting of 'Homage to Fra Angelico', 121–3; Evie's progress, 123–4; Mainie's 1931 solo exhibition, 125, 128; travels to Lithuania, 125–8; dramatic press reporting on Mainie and 'Modernism', 128–9; Abstraction-Création, 130–2; and her statement of belief, 131; her later involvement (1932–5), 157–8; political developments in the early 1930s, 133–4, 136–7, 146; her views on de Valera, 133; the Eucharistic Congress, 134; changes in relationship with Gleizes, 137–9; changes in Gleizes' view of colour and composition, 139–41; expressed in letter to Anne Dangar, 141–5; two sisters marry and move away from Dublin, 147; first broadcast talk, 148; travels to Amsterdam, with Evie, 148; debate on radio with Dermod O'Brien, 150–1; religious motifs in her art, 151; influence of Chinese exhibition, 151–3; death of her father, 154; involvement with Gate Theatre, 154–6; political gloom in the 1930s, 156–7; 1936 visit to Gleizes and Pouyaud in France, 157–8; Mainie's teaching of adults and children 159–60, 162; 1937 solo exhibition, 160; growing interest in 'Modernism', 163; difficulties facing art in Ireland, 163–4; murals for Glasgow Fair, 164; last meeting with Gleizes, 165; the threat of war, 165–7; critical response to 1939 solo exhibition, 167–8; 'Loan and Cross-Section Exhibition', 168; the impact of the war, 170, 176–7; becomes teacher at Park House School, 171; interest in national education in art, 171; exhibits as one of six Lhote-educated artists, 1940, 172; the arrival of Basil Rákóczí and Kenneth Hall in Ireland, and the setting up of the White Stag Group, 176–7; vigour of war-time art in Ireland, 177; White Stag exhibitions, 176–7; 1941 solo exhibition, 184–6; the Rouault row, 187–92; works to set up Irish Exhibition of Living Art, 193–7; her last illness and death, 198–202; Pat Scott callls on morning of her death, 201; tributes to her, 202; Mainie Jellett Memorial Scholarship established, 203; a giant among Irish artists, 204.
Lectures and Articles: her first lecture, 'Cubism and Subsequent Movements in Painting', 92–4; responds to Russell's criticism by giving lecture, 99–103; on Cubism, entitled 'Modern Art and its Relation to the Past', 128–30; her creed as an artist, 131–2; lectures on French art, 134–5; Modern Art and the Dual Ideal of Form, 138; lectures on architecture of Amsterdam, 149; lectures on French art, 168; for children, 171; interest in art education, 172; lectures on André Lhote, 174–5; Cubism and Celtic Art, 180–1; Art as a Spiritual Force, 182–4; Rouault and Tradition, 191; lectures on the Modernist Movement, 193; her criticisms of RHA, 194–5; 'Definition of My Art' ('An Approach to Painting',) 193; The RHA and Youth (article) 195; on French painting, 168–9; on André Lhote, 174§; on 'Art as a Spiritual Force', 182–4; the Rouault controversy, 187–92; her last articles, 193–5; the

setting up of Irish Living Art, 195–7;
Individual Paintings: first works of art, 9; House in Brittany, 12; Peace, 32–41, 43–4; Family Portraits: 38, 39; Judith, 36, 43; Decoration, 80, 81; Abstract Crucifixion, 114–17; Homage to Fra Angelico, 121–3, 193, 203; The Nativity, 123, 172, 173, 185; Virgin and Child, 143, 144; A Western Procession, 151, 196, 197; I Have Trodden the Wine Press Alone, 152, 201; The Crucifixion, 152; Composition-Virgin and Child, 158; Rocks, Co Mayo, 158; Pietà, 158; Study: Waterfall, 163; Wood in August, 163; Let there be Light, 167; Descent from the Cross, 167; Madonna, 167, Madonna of the Spring, 166, 167; Achill Horses, 151, 185; Glasgow Murals, 164, 167; Four Elements, 167; Pietà, 185; The Ninth Hour, 183, 185, 186, 197; Sea Horses, 185; Circus Procession, 185, 186; Seated Nude, 182, 185; Children of Lir, 184, 186; Adam and Eve, 186; Evening, 186; Sligo Memory, 186; Madonna of Eire, 201, 202; Virgin of Spring, 201.
Jellett, Morgan, 1
Jellett, William Morgan, 1, 2–6, 7–11, 14, 30; wins seat in 1919 election, 32, 41–3; his view of the State, 146; his death, 154
John, Augustus, 163
Johnson, Denis, 154
Joyce, William ('Lord Haw-Haw'), 177
Judge, Eugene, 172, 176
Judith, 43

Kahnweiler, Daniel-Henri, 45, 74
Kaiser Friedrich Museum, 128
Kandinsky, Wassily, 73, 75, 101
Keating, Sean, 15, 18, 89, 163, 168, 177, 190, 195
Kelly, John F., 189
Kernoff, Harry, 168
King's Hospital, Dublin, 145
Kirkpatrick, Miss, 185
Kirkwood, Harriet, 78, 163, 172, 186
Klaxon, The, 82
Klee, Paul, 73
Konody, P.G., 95
Kupka, Frantisek, 73, 74, 75, 132, 135

Labour Party, 133
Lafayette (Photographers), 7
Lamb, Charles, 78, 110, 163
Lander, Miss, 12
Lane, Hugh, 8, 92, 147, 191
Lane Pictures, 158
Lawrence, Mervyn, 29, 32–6
Leader, The, 203
Le Brocquy, Louis, 170, 175, 190, 195, 196, 197
Le Brocquy, Melanie, 196
Le Brocquy, Sybil, 170, 195
Lee, Joseph, 177
Leen, Father Edward, 190, 191, 194, 200
Le Fauconnier, 57, 58, 74
Léger, Fernand, 56, 57, 58, 59, 63, 73, 74, 99, 101, 129, 132, 192
Legion of Mary, 191
Legros, Alphonse, 25
Leicester Galleries, 187
Leinster School of Music, 12
Le Nain brothers, 134
Lepage, Jules Bastien, 141
Leventhal, A.J., 197
Lewis, Wyndham, 22, 95, 163
Lhote, André, 28, 44, 46–7, 61, 65, 84, 85, 102, 108, 153, 169, 174, 175, 176,
Lloyd George, 42, 55
Loan and Cross Section Exhibition, 168, 194
London Group, 28, 31, 90, 95
Longford, Christine, 154–5
Longford, Jack, 168, 168, 171
Longford, Lord, 154–5

Louvre, 121, 139
Lurcat, Jean, 162
Lynch, Charles, 172, 174, 177, 203

Maconchy, Elizabeth, 179
McCarvill, Eileen, and family, 199
McDonagh, Deirdre, 168
McDonagh, Donagh, 179
McGonigal, Maurice, 163, 168
McGreevy, Thomas, 82, 86, 189, 190, 201
McGuinness, Nora, 172, 177, 194, 195, 197
McGuire, E.A., 163, 164
McGuire, Edward, 163
McLean, Pat, 179
MacLiammoir, Micheal, 154–5, 156, 162, 179
McQuaid, Archbishop John-Charles, 191, 200
Maeterlinck, Maurice, 54
Magdalen Asylum, 1
Magdalen Church, 1
Maillol, 78
Maitre de Moulin, 134
Malevich, Kasimir, 70, 74, 75
Manevy, Francis, 107–8
Manessier, Alfred, 70
Manning, Mary, 155
Manning, May, 10, 12, 14, 29
Marc, Franz, 73
Marchand, 78
Marcoussis, Louis, 58
Maritain, Jacques, 190, 191, 192
Marquet, Albert, 168
Marsh, Arnold, 163
Matisse, Henri, 45, 102, 145, 169, 192
Mayor Gallery, 138
Meninsky, Bernard, 28, 148
Meredith, Judge, 174
Metamorphosis of the Children of Lir, 43
Metropolitan School of Art, 14–15, 17, 41, 43, 87, 149; becomes National College of Art, 171
Metzinger, Jean, 56, 57, 58, 59, 63, 70, 74, 94, 101
Midleton, Lord, 42
Minkovsky, 158
Miro, Joan, 197
Modigliani, Amédéo, 78
Moffet, Margaret, 175
Moholy-Nagy, 132
Moisewitch, 19
Moly-Sabata, 105–13, 132, 136–7
Mondrian, Piet, 56, 70, 74, 75, 132, 137, 148, 158
Monet, Claude, 148
Montgomery, Niall, 190
Moore family, 30
Moore, Henry, 132, 138
Morgan, Katherine, 1
Morris, William, 10
Morrow, Larry, 88
Mozart, 82
Municipal Gallery of Modern Art, 8, 147, 158, 164, 187, 189
Munster Fine Arts Club, 180
Mussolini, Benito, 156, 165
Myrbor, 105

Napoleon III, 196
Nash, John, 19, 90
Nash, Paul, 78, 148
National College of Art, 171, 203
National Gallery, London, 110, 194
National Gallery of Ireland, 110, 125, 147, 163, 168, 185, 195
Nettleship, Ida, 23
Nevinson, C.R.W., 168
New English Art Club, 19
New Irish Salon, 84, 125

Newlyn and Penzance School, 12
New York World Fair, 164
Nicholas, 108
Nicholls, Nick, 194, 197
Nicholson, Ben, 107, 132, 138, 158
Notes from Ireland, 42

O'Brien, Dermod, 39, 110, 150–1, 168, 177, 187, 191, 195, 196
Observer, The, 95
O'Brien, Flann, 190
O'Connor, James Arthur, 3
O'Connor, Roderic, 45
O'Dea, Jimmy, 198
O'Faolain, Sean, 177
O'Higgins, Kevin, 146
Okamoto, 162
O'Kelly, Sean T., 163
Olympic Games (Paris, 1924), 89
O'Malley, Ernie, 175, 186
Omega Workshops, 22
Orpen, William Newenham Montague, 15, 17–19, 23, 29, 89, 128, 168, 170, 204
Osborne, Walter, 17
O'Sullivan, Seamus, 88–9
Ozenfant, Amédée, 56, 58, 59, 67, 82, 162

Painlevé, Paul, 130
Parents' National Education Union, 177
Paris Exhibition, 175
Paris Midi, 90
Paris Salon des Artistes Français, 195
Paris Times, 90–1
Park House School, 171
Palais des Beaux-Arts, Brussels, 110
Parnell, Charles Stewart, 4–5, 7
Peace, 32, 41, 43–4,
Peer Gynt, 154
Perugino, 54, 185
Petrie, George, 3
Pevnsner, Antoine, 132
Phillips, Willam, 125, 128, 170
Picabia, Francis, 57, 74
Picasso, Pablo, 46, 57, 58, 63, 74, 82, 94, 99, 101, 129, 139, 167, 168, 169, 192, 197
Picture Hire Club, 180
Piper, John, 168, 189
Pissarro, Camille, 45
Pissarro, Paul, 19
Planck, Ernst, 130
Plato, 82
Plunkett, Joseph Mary, 19
Prince de Broglie, 130
Poussin, Nicolas, 45, 54, 58, 93, 135, 175
Pouyaud, Cécile, 107
Pouyaud, Robert, 63, 75, 94; establishing Moly-Sabata, 106–10; departure from, 113–14; 121, 138, 157, 162, 170
Power, Albert, 8
Power, John, 132, 137, 162
Posnansky, Yanaga, 63, 90
Prikker, Thorn, 148
Protarchus, 82
Puck Fair, 179, 184
Purser, Geraldine, 177, 198
Purser, Honor, 125
Purser, Michael, 170
Purser, Sarah, 39, 65–6, 144, 147, 177; death of, 198
Purser, Sean, 147, 177, 198

Rachmaninov, 19
Radio Eireann, 148, 158
Rákóczi, Basil, 167, 176, 194, 196, 202–3
Rameau, 82
Raphael, 67, 121, 185
Rawdon, Sir Arthur, 1
Raynal, Maurice, 162

Read, Herbert, 138
Redmond, John, 5, 14, 18
Reid, Nano, 163, 197, 199
Rembrandt, 19, 148
Reth, 137
Reynolds, Sir Joshua, 86, 88
Richardson, Dorothy, 199
Ricketts, Charles, 148
Rising of 1916, 19
Roberts, William, 90, 95
Robinson, Dolly, 163
Robinson, Jacqueline, 179
Robinson, Lennox, 163, 176
Rodchenko, 74
Rogers, Kathleen, 156
Rosebery, Lord, 4
Rosenberg, Léonce, 56, 57, 59, 119
Rothenstein, William, 19, 148
Rouault, Georges, 187, 189, 190, 191, 192
'Rouge et le Noir, le', 139
Royal Academy, 13; exhibition of French art, 134–5; Chinese art exhibition, 151–3; 163, 195
Royal College of Surgeons, 189, 191
Royal Dublin Society, , 160, 177
Royal Hibernian Academy, 41, 110, 125, 150, 151, 158, 163, 168, 179, 187, 194, 195, 196
Royal Horticultural Society of Ireland, 151
Rubens, 46, 93
Ruisdael, 148
Russell, George ('AE'), 37, 79, 80, 82, 84–5, 95, 97–9, 119
Russian Constructivists, 105
Rutter, Frank, 90, 95
Rynne, Stephen, 167, 203

St Bartholomew's Church, 1, 125, 200
St Columba's College, 172
St Naithi's Church, Dundrum, 144
St Pierre, Hélène de, 57, 65, 159, 172, 174, 175, 200
Salkeld, Cecil French, 84, 85, 86, 180
Salon d'Automne, 197
Salon des Beaux Arts, 195
Salon des Indépendants, 77, 78, 84, 89–90, 197
Savoy Cinema, 156
Schmitt, Florent, 57
Schpoenhauer, 168
Schuster, Luise, 12
Schwitters, Kurt, 132
Scott, Michael, 129, 155
Scott, Patrick, 194, 201
Section d'Or Exhibition, 73
Selassie, Haile, 156
Seuphor, Michel, 132
Seurat, Georges, 45, 102
'Seven and Five', 92
Severini, Gino, 56, 59, 93, 119
Shaw, George Bernard, 154
Sickert, Walter, 19, 22, 25–31, 43, 78, 148, 168, 195
Sidney, Charles, 203
Signac, Paul, 45
Signorelli, 46, 54
Silvy, Henri, 176
Simms, Archbishop George Otto, 200
Simpson, Canon Walter C., 200
Sinn Féin, 18, 30, 41–2
Skrine, Charles John, 150
Slade School of Art, 28
Sleatro, James, 194
Society of Dublin Painters, 78, 86, 103, 110, 123–4, 125, 148, 158, 163, 164, 168, 171, 186, 201
Socrates, 82
Somerville, Edith, 196
Stalin, Joseph, 165
Stamp, Josiah, 130

Standard, The, 202
Stanford, Sir Charles, 82
Steer, Philip Wilson, 148, 168
Steiner, Rudolf, 75
Stokes, Adrian, 134
Stokes, Gabriel, 1, 3
Stokes, Grainne, 128
Stokes, Henry John, 2
Stokes, Margaret, 171
Stokes, Whitley, 3
Stokes, William, 2, 6
Storey, Jean, 170
Stravinsky, Igor, 57
Stuart, Francis, 177
Sunday Times, The, 95
Surindépendants, Salon des, 125, 162
Survage, Leopold, 58
Sutton, Eavan, 159
Swanzy, Mary, 78, 110, 196

T.C.D. A College Miscellany, 121
Tailteann Games, 89, 163
Tanguy, Yves, 197
Tate Gallery, 95
Tatlin, 74
Taylor Prize, 39, 43, 65
Titian, 181, 184, 203
Tone, Wolfe, 3
Tonks, Henry, 19, 168
Treaty, Anglo-Irish, 55, 133
Tuohy, Patrick, 15, 18, 30
Turner, J.M.W., 165, 184
Tyrrwhitt, Ursula, 23

Uffizi, 121
Ulster Volunteer Force, 14
United Arts Club, 78, 110
University College, Dublin, 195

Valois, Ninette de, 179
Valmier, Georges, 59, 63, 101, 137, 162
Van Doesburgh, 101, 148
Van Gogh, 95, 102, 148, 149
Vanston, Doreen, 197
Vantongerloo, Georges, 132–3
Vermeer, Jan van, 148
Vézelay, Paule, 132, 162
Victoria, Queen, 8, 18
Vinci, Leonardo da, 67
Vlaminck, 78, 168, 169
Vuillard, Edouard, 45, 169

Waddington, Victor, 179, 194, 202
Wadsworth, Edward, 132, 138
Wallace, Patricia, 160
Walsh, John E., 41–2
Walt Disney, 177
Water Colour Society of Ireland, 158, 164, 179
Watteau, Jean-Antoine, 135
Watts, George Frederick, 148
Weatherby, Kate, 67
Webb, David, 186
Weir, Judith, 32, 41, 43
Westminster School of Art, 19, 25–36
Whelan, Leo, 15, 187
Whistler, James Abbott McNeill, 25, 148
White Stag Group, 176, 179, 180, 182, 191
Wilde, Oscar, 3, 154
Woolf, Virginia, 199

Yeats, Cottie, 170
Yeats, Elizabeth Corbet, 9–10, 105, 170
Yeats, Jack, 43, 78, 79, 164, 168, 174, 177, 194, 196, 197, 204
Yeats, Susan Mary, 9–10, 105
Yeats, W.B., 158, 177

Zoubaloff Collection, 119